When This Evil War

WHEN THIS EVIL WAR IS OVER

The Correspondence of the Francis Family, 1860–1865

Edited by
JAMES P. PATE

THE UNIVERSITY OF ALABAMA PRESS
Tuscaloosa

Typeface: Granjon

∞

The paper on which this book is printed meets the minimum requirements of American National Standard for Information Sciences—Permanence of Paper for Printed Library Materials, ANSI Z39.48–1984.

Library of Congress Cataloging-in-Publication Data

When this evil war is over : the correspondence of the Francis family / edited by James P. Pate.

p. cm.

Includes bibliographical references and index.

ISBN-13: 978-0-8173-1517-7 (cloth : alk. paper)

ISBN-10: 0-8173-1517-9

1. United States—History—Civil War, 1861–1865—Personal narratives, Confederate. 2. Francis family—Correspondence. 3. Calhoun County (Ala.)—Biography. 4. Soldiers—Alabama—Calhoun County—Correspondence. 5. Alabama—History—Civil War, 1861–1865. 6. Alabama—Social conditions—19th century. 7. United States—History—Civil War, 1861–1865—Campaigns. I. Pate, James P.

E605.W57 2006

976.1′6305092—dc22

2006000854

For those who have crossed over
Delmus Victor Cantrell
Thomas Lawrence Connelly
Clara Jackson Martin
Frank Jackson Martin

Contents

Illustrations

Maps

Photographs

Acknowledgments

After delivering a lecture on the Creek Indian wars at Gadsden, Alabama, in 1977, I had the good fortune to meet the late Frank and Clara Jackson Martin. I learned that Mr. Martin was a descendant of the James Carrington Francis family of Jacksonville, Calhoun County, Alabama, and that their extensive nineteenth-century correspondence and documents had been collected and preserved by Mrs. Martin. Following Mr. Martin's death in 1992, Mrs. Martin asked me to consider editing the Francis family letters, particularly the letters of the six Francis brothers who served in the Confederate army.

The Francis family was quite literate, and their letters generally follow standard English usage, grammar, and spelling. However, as the reader will notice, there are occasional lapses, and I have chosen to transcribe the letters exactly as written with only a few exceptions and without using [*sic*] to mark departures from standard usage. Words or phrases accidentally omitted by the writer or missing because of illegible text or deterioration of the original letters have been added in brackets where practical or obvious. The random use of dashes and capitalization found in mid-nineteenth-century script has been replaced by standard usage and punctuation. In several letters, extremely long passages have been divided into paragraphs to assist the reader. Other letters have been edited to focus on the war.

The Francis brothers and other family members reference a number of individuals in their letters, some who are well known to students and scholars of the American Civil War and many who have been obscured or obliterated from the historical record. Unfortunately, a number of persons mentioned in the letters, often only by a last name, could not be identified by this writer. For those that could be identified, I have provided biographical information on the first reference to the individual and cited the source of this information in the notes.

I am indebted to many people who helped to make this project possible. My early research efforts were supported by Clara Jackson Martin and a 1998 Organized Research Grant from Southeastern Oklahoma State University. I was also assisted by the staff of the Alabama Department of Archives and History, Anniston-Calhoun County Public Library, Georgia Historical Society, Harold B. Simpson History Complex Research Center, Huntsville–Madison County Public Library, Linn-Henley Research Library of the Birmingham Public Library, Mobile Public Library, Tennessee State Library and Archives, The National Archives, and John Vaughan Library at Northeastern State University.

Several individuals helped shape and enhance the final product. I am grateful to Melissa Scrivner Holycross, a former staff assistant at the University of West Alabama, for her assistance in word processing the first draft of the manuscript. I am indebted to former colleagues at UWA who read early drafts of the manuscript, including Joe B. Wilkins and the late Winston E. Walker III. Several colleagues at Northeastern State University enhanced this work, especially Brad Agnew and Patrick Enright. My special gratitude goes to David M. Taylor, UWA, and Jeffrey Conine, Northeastern, who read and critiqued several iterations of the manuscript, improving its syntax, style, and structure. Tracy Ellen Smith, Fort Worth, Texas, is to be acknowledged for preparing the maps, and Don Fleming, Demopolis, Alabama, produced the photographs. Also, Mike Allen of Northeastern produced the Francis family tree chart. However, any shortcomings are the product of this writer.

The letters and other documents reproduced herein, except where noted, are housed in the Francis-Martin Family Papers at the Alabama Department of Archives and History. They are reproduced here along with several photographs from the collection by permission of the Alabama Department of Archives and History.

James P. Pate
University of Mississippi–Tupelo

When This Evil War Is Over

Introduction

By the late 1850s Alabamians and other Southerners sensed an imminent explosion threatening to mushroom from the sectional crisis between the proslave and free states. In North Alabama's Calhoun County, Dr. James Carrington Francis, a Jacksonville physician and town leader, with his extended family, was soon swept into the vortex of secession. The dangerous changes in the air caused him to step forward and commit his energies and resources to the protection of Alabama and southern rights. Like many fellow Alabamians, his personal journey from southern patriot to ardent secessionist was precipitous and unequivocal.

The 1859 reelection of Andrew Barry Moore, a Union Democrat turned secessionist, to his second term as governor of Alabama ignited a chain of events. William Lowndes Yancey, an active southern separatist, marshaled his followers to campaign for control of the state delegation to the Democratic National Convention at Charleston, South Carolina, in April 1860. He succeeded in establishing momentum and then garnering enough support for his Alabama Platform demanding federal protection of slavery in the territories. When the northern delegates rejected the proslavery platform, Yancey and the Alabama delegation withdrew from the convention. Eight other southern delegations also bolted, and the convention adjourned without selecting a national slate. Subsequent efforts to reach accord in Baltimore and Richmond left the Democratic Party divided over two national tickets.[1]

In January 1860, two months before the selection of the Alabama Democratic delegation, the state legislature enacted a statute calling for the organization of a volunteer military force of 8,000 men. John Brown's raid, among other events, had sparked a growing concern for public safety. The state's newspapers proclaimed this legislation, provoking an immediate statewide public response. In Calhoun County the Calhoun Light Infantry company was organized in early January 1860 at Jacksonville, the county seat, with a full complement of elected officers, including William M. Hames, a local attorney, as captain and Dr. Miller William Francis, a local physician, as surgeon. In reporting the company's organization, the *Jacksonville Republican* declared in its 19 January issue, "should soldiers be needed, no one will rally round the banner of our country with more alacrity than they." Seven days later, Richard G. Earle, a Mexican War veteran, writing in the same paper, predicted war and called for the recruitment of regular army forces over volunteer companies. He was convinced of the need for serious military preparedness in Alabama.[2]

Despite the inflammatory rhetoric calling for a standing army, most Calhoun County residents were more concerned about finishing the Alabama and Tennessee Rivers Railroad through their county.[3] This focused optimism was to alter, however, in a matter of weeks. By April, following the disruption of the National Democratic Convention at Charleston, the railroad debate quickly lost center stage to the spectre of sectional politics and disunion. Alabamians were faced with three choices in the 1860 presidential campaign: Stephen A. Douglas, candidate of the Northern Democrats; John C. Breckinridge, candidate of the Southern Democrats; and John Bell, a compromise candidate of the National Constitutional Union Party, composed of former Whigs and other estranged politicians. Abraham Lincoln, nominated by the Republican Party on a platform to prohibit slavery in the territories, would get no votes in Alabama.[4]

In Calhoun County, Dr. James Carrington Francis and his son Miller were even more involved in Democratic Party meetings. Miller was selected as one of thirty county delegates to the state Democratic convention at Montgomery on 4 July 1860. The *Jacksonville Republican,* managed by Francis family friend James Freeman Grant, endorsed the ticket of John C. Breckinridge and Joseph Lane in its issue of 26 July 1860. The *Republican* joined fifty other state papers that supported Breckinridge, compared with only nine backing Douglas and fifteen papers that endorsed Bell. Grant's paper mirrored the action taken by the Democratic Party of Calhoun County at Jacksonville on 23 July. After listening to John Tyler Morgan "for the space of about two hours," the local Democratic leaders ratified the Breckinridge and Lane ticket for president and vice president of the United States.[5]

Before Lincoln's election was confirmed by the presidential electors, Governor Moore issued a proclamation on 6 December 1860 calling for the election, on Monday, 24 December, of delegates to a special state convention. He also appointed sixteen commissioners to represent Alabama in the other southern states. In opposition to a sizeable segment of Alabamians who urged caution and cooperation to preserve the Union, Yancey and his supporters advocated immediate secession. In Calhoun County, secessionist candidates George C. Whatley, Daniel T. Ryan, and John M. Crook handily defeated the cooperationist slate of "McCauley, Ramsey and Taylor" by a three-to-one margin. Although the immediate secessionists statewide outnumbered the cooperationist delegates 54 to 46, Calhoun County stood alone as the only county in North Alabama to elect a secessionist slate. The tense atmosphere in Montgomery was ripe with disunion, and on 11 January the Alabama ordinance for secession was adopted by a vote of 61 to 39, without a direct vote of the people.[6]

Governor Moore's call for troops on 4 January 1861 was greeted with enthusiasm, which gained momentum following the adoption of Alabama's secession ordinance. On the same day, the governor ordered the seizure of the federal arsenal at Mount Vernon and Fort Gaines on Dauphin Island and Fort Morgan at the entrance to Mobile Bay. Volunteer militia companies from Mobile seized the Mount Vernon Arsenal on 4 January, and on the following day they occupied the two forts. Each installation came under state control without violence or injury.[7]

With secession hanging heavy in the air, Calhoun County responded enthusiastically to Moore's bold leadership. James Freeman Grant recorded in his paper, "The martial spirit is in ascendant in Jacksonville above business, pleasure, and all else that usually occupies the public mind." At a public meeting on Saturday, 26 January, Dr. James Carrington Francis joined with other community leaders to organize a Home Guard and adopt resolutions supporting the secession of Alabama as a free, sovereign state. His good friend Dr. Courtney James Clark wrote state senator Thomas A. Walker in Montgomery and committed the county to raising 1,000 men to defend Alabama. He reported that the county's young men were as eager for war "as for a camp hunt or a Christmas frolic."[8]

While the two physicians, Francis and Clark, helped shape Calhoun County's military preparedness, a new southern republic was formed in Montgomery in early February 1861. The Provisional Constitution of the Confederate States of America was unanimously adopted by the seven seceded states on 8 February. The next day the Provisional Congress selected Jefferson Davis of Mississippi and Alexander Stephens of Georgia as the Provisional president and vice president of the C.S.A. Ironically, Davis left his Brierfield plantation in Warren County, Mississippi, for Montgomery, at about the same time Lincoln departed his modest home in Springfield for his inauguration in Washington, D.C.[9]

From Mobile Bay to the Tennessee Valley, Alabamians eager to defend their state and fight for southern independence rushed to arms. In Calhoun

County, several hundred men formed volunteer companies. These included the Alexandria Rifles, Calhoun Beauregards, Calhoun Grays, Calhoun Guards, Calhoun Rangers, Calhoun Sharpshooters, Choccolocco Rifles, Pope Walker Guards, Ryan Guards, and White Plains Rangers. Even a juvenile company, the Jacksonville Cadets, composed of boys between the ages of twelve and eighteen, was organized in Jacksonville; its youth paraded on the public square in their "showy uniforms" on Saturday, 1 June 1861.[10] Other Calhoun County residents joined units in other counties or other states, and many older men joined local guards or county militias.

Through these trying months the Francis family of Jacksonville contributed its energy and resources, including six sons, to a war precipitated by the bombardment and surrender of Fort Sumter at Charleston, South Carolina, in April 1861. Dr. Francis, a highly respected physician, and his wife, Amy Ingram Francis, had lived in Jacksonville since 1837. Eight of their ten children were Alabama natives, including sons James Carrington, Jr., Hopkins Turney, John Clark, Joseph Hugh, and Charles Henry, and daughters Mary Emma, Willie Caroline, and Susan Hannah. Their six oldest sons served in Confederate units and posts from January 1861 through May 1865. They were joined by family servants and members of the Francises' extended family, including cousins, uncles, and brothers-in-law who enlisted in Alabama, Georgia, Tennessee, and Texas units.[11]

A native of Rhea County, Tennessee, Dr. Francis married Amy Ingram of Putnam County, Georgia, on 30 October 1832 in Winchester, Franklin County, Tennessee. He started his study of medicine in Knoxville at age eighteen and attended lectures at the medical college in Lexington, Kentucky. By 1834 he was practicing medicine in Jasper, Marion County, Tennessee. Their first three children, Miller William, Elizabeth Rebecca, and Thomas Woodson, were born in Tennessee. Following Elizabeth's death at eighteen months on 2 May 1837, he moved his young family to Jacksonville, where he practiced medicine for the next fifty years.[12] In 1860, he was forty-nine years old and owned real estate valued at $6,600 and a personal estate of $29,000. He also owned thirteen slaves, including seven females, one to forty-four years old, and six males, six to thirty-five years old.[13]

Besides being an avid secessionist Dr. Francis was an active Methodist, Mason, and Democrat, who served on the Jacksonville town council and supported local Democratic candidates for county and state offices. In the presidential election of 6 November 1860, Jacksonville and Calhoun County voted overwhelmingly in favor of Southern Democratic candidate John C. Breckinridge, who took Alabama's nine electoral votes.[14]

To all strong Breckinridge supporters, Abraham Lincoln's election was a

Francis Family Tree

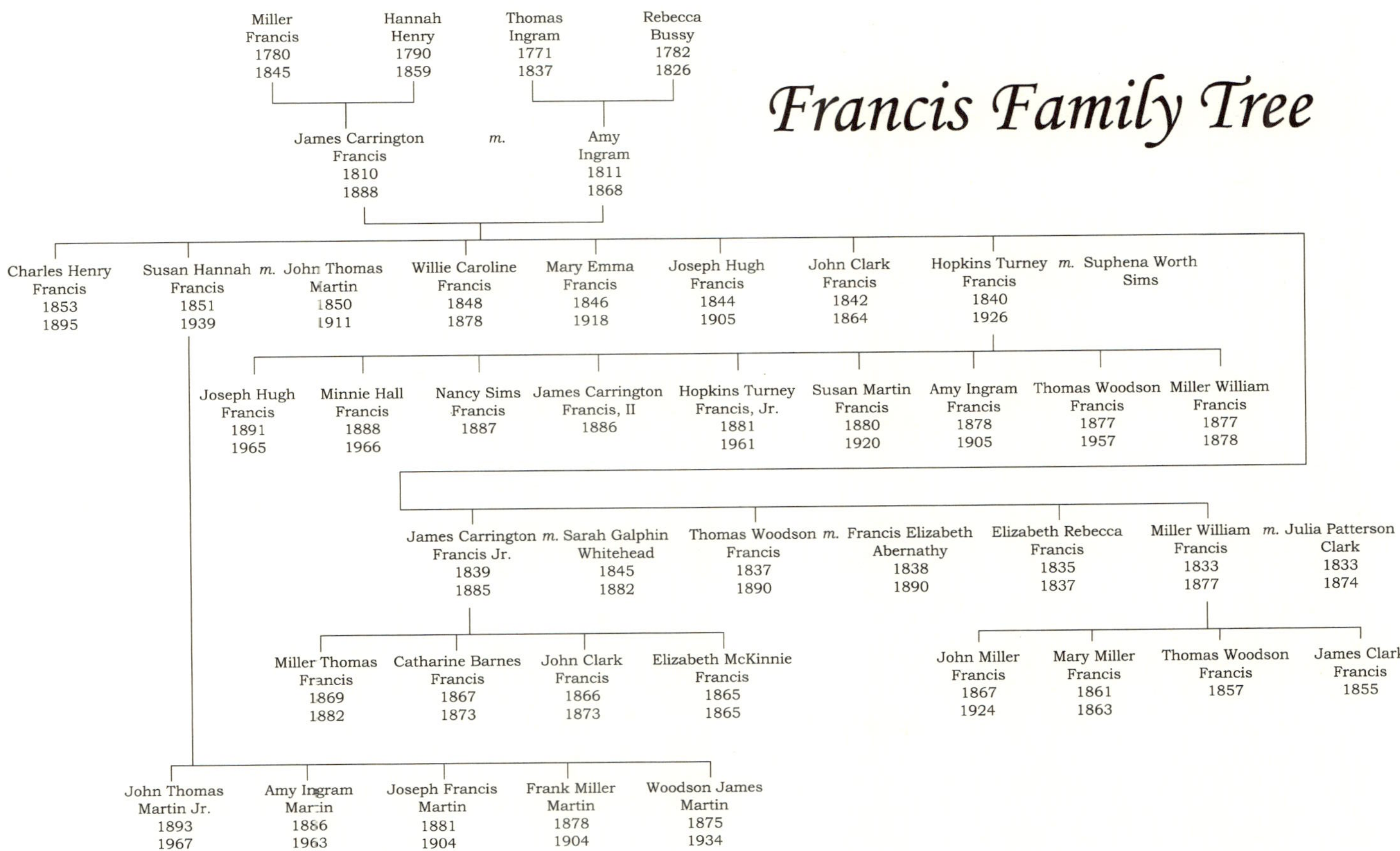

fire bell for secession, which placed Calhoun County at the forefront of the secessionist movement under Francis's leadership. The Jacksonville physician assumed this prominent leadership role at a Southern Rights meeting on 19 November 1860 at the courthouse in Jacksonville. In an impassioned address interrupted several times by applause, he declared his support for secession and the building of a new republic.[15] Francis joined other Southern Rights voters in Calhoun County to elect George C. Whatley, John M. Crook, and Daniel T. Ryan as delegates to the Constitutional Convention of 1861; all three voted for Alabama's secession ordinance.[16]

Following secession and mobilization for war, Dr. Francis also worked to secure commissions for his three oldest sons, Miller, Thomas, and James. James, known as Jim to the family, was the subject of two letter-writing campaigns in 1861 and 1862 by his father, supported by other prominent Alabamians. The letters requested that Jim receive a commission as an officer in the commissary department and touted his "education, intelligence & moral worth." Yet it was Miller who received the first commission as a surgeon and captain in the Sixth Alabama Volunteers from President Jefferson Davis on 17 May 1861. Later, Thomas, Tom to his family, was appointed captain and assistant commissary for subsistence for the Tenth Alabama Volunteers on 8 July 1861. Despite the support of influential Alabamians, including Governor Moore, Jim's commission resulted from Tom's promotion to major on 29 April 1862 and his reassignment to Brigadier General John H. Forney's staff at Mobile. Tom's transfer from his post at Chattanooga gave him the opportunity to recommend his brother Jim as his replacement to Brigadier General Danville Leadbetter. Leadbetter's telegram to the War Department in Richmond on 19 May produced a commission for Jim Francis as captain and appointment as post commissary at Chattanooga.[17]

Before mobilization, Miller Francis and his wife, Julia Patterson Clark, lived with their two young sons, James and Thomas, five and three, respectively, in Jacksonville. There he studied medicine with his father and Dr. Courtney James Clark, his brother-in-law. He joined his father's medical practice in his apothecary shop on the northwest corner of the public square in 1853 after completing medical and surgical studies in Louisville, Kentucky. Except for the war years, Miller continued his medical practice there until his death in 1877. By 4 March 1861, Julia was expecting their third child, Mary Miller Francis, who was born on 7 November.[18] Their household also included three slaves, two females, eleven and seventeen years old, and one fourteen-year-old male. The 1860 census records show Miller with a personal estate valued at $6,000 but listed no real estate except for a slave house.[19]

As the senior surgeon for the Sixth Alabama, Miller emerged during the first year of the war as a tough-minded, opinionated patriot. Secession rhetoric and the near bloodless surrender of Fort Sumter convinced him that the war would end quickly. Miller was not alone in those sentiments. During those early days many Southerners thought the conflict would be painless and would be successfully concluded by Christmas. At first Miller feared that the war might end too quickly and he would miss his opportunity to serve his country. In time, however, his graphic letters and medical reports betrayed a reversal of his original optimism. His descriptions of the diseases and deaths of his patients in northern Virginia soon provided him proof of the harsh realities of combat. During both of Miller's phases, initial idealism and subsequent reality, his courage and thirst for action remained constant. His fervor was tempered only by his commitment to duty and concern for his patients. His unfettered patriotism and optimism were double-edged as can be seen in the demonstrative personality reflected in his correspondence. Miller also shows his cynicism for officers and physicians who did not share his dedication and devotion to duty and southern independence. Even after he lost confidence in his commanders and President Davis, he declared in May 1862, "I don't want to leave until the fight is over here."[20]

Following his resignation from the Sixth Alabama in spring 1862, Miller joined the Fifty-first Alabama Mounted Infantry, a Partisan Rangers unit, commanded by Colonel John Tyler Morgan. He served as the senior surgeon and received a promotion to major. Unfortunately, his correspondence ends in 1863, though his service continued through Georgia and the Carolinas until early spring 1865.[21] Although letters from his younger brother Jo Francis provide details about Miller, they do not reveal his cynical, no-nonsense insights into the events that ended this bloody war.

The second oldest Francis brother, Tom Francis, also lived in Jacksonville with his wife, Frances "Fannie" Elizabeth Abernathy. He started his business career as an eighteen-year-old clerk in the Jacksonville mercantile business of Ryan, Tate & Rowland, where he remained until 1857 when he moved to Selma to take a position with Joseph Hardie & Company, wholesale grocers and cotton merchants. Following his marriage to Fannie in 1858, Tom started farming his land on Cane Creek in southwest Calhoun County and continued his association with Joseph Hardie.[22]

By 1860 twenty-three-year-old Tom Francis had amassed a significant investment in land, livestock, and slaves. With real estate valued at $5,000 and a personal estate valued at $10,000, he impatiently looked for opportunities to increase and expand his land and wealth. According to the 1860 slave schedule for Dallas County, Alabama, Tom owned eight slaves, four females two to twenty-two years old and four males eight to twenty-eight years old.

His slaves lived on property near Selma jointly owned with his father and perhaps his younger brother Jim Francis, who was working in Selma.[23] His military service and long absences from his land and investments were a constant source of frustration expressed in his wartime correspondence.

With Miller and Jim already in uniform, Tom and his younger brother John Clark Francis enlisted as privates in the Pope Walker Boys at Jacksonville on 4 June 1861. Their company, commanded by Captain William Henry Forney, a Jacksonville neighbor, was organized near Montgomery in late June as Company G in the Eighth Alabama Volunteers. When the regiment mustered into Confederate service at Richmond, Virginia, on 3 July, it became the Tenth Alabama. Five days later, Tom received his commission as captain and assistant commissary for subsistence in the Tenth Alabama.[24]

Tom buried himself in his commissary duties, and only a few of his letters from Virginia survived. Unfortunately, the extant correspondence, mostly directed to his father, related to his personal business interests, payment of taxes, cotton transactions, and pithy demands on his father. Despite his significant wartime assignments after Virginia, his letters yield little about the war. Always the consummate businessman and absentee landowner, he seldom discussed the war, choosing instead to concentrate on matters related to money, land, and slaves. On rare occasions, he does express his concern for his extended family in Jacksonville. Unfortunately for the reader, his focus was on surviving the war and building wealth for a postwar South that would prove different from his vision.[25]

Miller and Tom's younger brother Jim Francis was a twenty-one-year-old merchant before the war, living in Selma at Dr. James T. Gee's hotel, the St. James. When several of Selma's prominent young men responded to Governor Moore's call for troops, Jim enlisted in the Governor's Guard commanded by Captain Thomas J. Goldsby. On 12 January 1861 it left Selma with Captain James Kent's Selma Blues for Fort Morgan on Mobile Bay. Jim was listed on a company muster roll as a second sergeant and was assigned to a gun crew. The initial patriotic zeal that prompted Jim to join the Governor's Guard apparently stirred him to enlist for twelve months' further service when his company was reorganized as Company A, Fourth Alabama Volunteers, in April 1861. Although he regretted his decision and feared that his future was doomed, he honored his commitment and traveled to Virginia where the regiment was mustered into Confederate service on 7 May 1861. He emerged from his only scrape with death at the battle of First Manassas on 21 July 1861 with superficial wounds and with resolve to stay out of further bloodletting.[26]

After receiving a thirty-day furlough for lingering, unspecified illnesses,

Jim returned to Jacksonville and later to Selma in December 1861. He used his furlough to attend to his business enterprises in Selma and to develop a new partnership with William P. Becker. Operating as "Becker and Francis, General Commission Merchants," they traded in a variety of goods, including cotton, flour, leather, groceries, produce, and manufactured goods. Although the Jacksonville paper announced in December 1861 that Francis planned "to return to the army in a short time, should his health permit," his new business venture obviously delayed his return to active service. When Jim's letters resume in June 1862, he had received his commission as captain and assistant commissary for subsistence at Chattanooga.[27]

In contrast to his two older brothers who managed to keep themselves distant from the fray, and contra distinct from his outspoken oldest brother who seemed to spring up larger than life ready-made to war, John Clark Francis started on a different journey. In 1860 John was an eighteen-year-old college student at Florence Wesleyan University, now the University of North Alabama, in Florence. Before transferring to Florence Wesleyan as a senior for the fall quarter in 1860, he attended Carrick Academy in Winchester, Tennessee, where he lived with his Aunt Theresa Francis Turney and among his Tennessee cousins. John and his FWU classmates were prompted to join two university militia companies following Alabama's secession from the Union. After the firing on Fort Sumter on 12–14 April 1861, he and more than one hundred of his classmates, including thirty-two seniors, and four of their professors left the university in the spring quarter before graduation.[28]

As a private in the Pope Walker Guards, John's service in Virginia differed significantly from brothers Tom and Jim. He shared picket and camp duties with his comrades and mess mates in Company G, Calhoun County men who had known each other most of their lives. Writing to his family from Virginia during the first year of the war, the former college student expressed his commitment to become a good soldier. His letters focused on the daily lives of the men around him, especially those from Jacksonville and Calhoun County, and news of his brothers, while also sharing the latest military rumors.[29]

John's transition from uniformed soldier to warrior started with the battle of Dranesville on 19–20 December 1861. The Tenth Alabama and three other regiments, 150 cavalry, and four pieces of artillery marched out of their camps at Centreville, Virginia, on a foraging expedition under Brigadier General J. E. B. Stuart. They encountered a larger Union force commanded by Brigadier General Edward O. C. Ord near Dranesville. The Yankees quickly deployed and started shelling Stuart's forces and wagon train.[30]

The Tenth Alabama rushed into the melee under the leadership of Colonel John H. Forney and Lieutenant Colonel James B. Martin. The fighting was furious. The Tenth Alabama suffered several casualties, including Forney, who was shot through the right arm, and Martin, who was killed and left on the battlefield. Several members of the Pope Walker Guards were wounded, including John Francis, who was shot through the lower left arm.[31]

News of the battle of Dranesville shocked Jacksonville and the Francis family. The *Jacksonville Republican* on 2 January 1862 dedicated its second page to stories about the battle, its victims, and funeral services for fellow citizen James B. Martin. It also reported the return of John Francis on Monday, 30 December, on a thirty-day furlough to recover from the wound to his left forearm.[32]

Anxious to return to the war as a commissioned officer, John used his furlough home and an extension through 20 March 1862 to enlist the support of his father and other civic leaders to recruit a volunteer company. His efforts were timely, for Governor John Gill Shorter issued a call in January 1862 for twelve new Alabama regiments, and ex-Governor Moore arrived in Jacksonville on Tuesday, 25 February, to assist with the troop organizations. John's company, the Sallie Walker Boys, was mustered in as Company B, Thirtieth Alabama Volunteers, and he was elected captain.[33]

By May 1862 the Thirtieth Alabama was assigned to the Army of East Tennessee, and John's letters over the next two years gave his family remarkable access to the war. In his straightforward, unassuming style, John tried to elicit his family's interest with his reports of his experiences in the major campaigns in the Western Department. Judging by the tone and volume of his correspondence, John was feeling the devastating psychological effects of war. He was anxious to hear from his family and siblings and complained about the dearth of letters, continually prodding them to write often. He traveled the bloody roads from East Tennessee to Kentucky, Middle Tennessee to Vicksburg, and Lookout Mountain to North Georgia. He emerged as a savvy, modest twenty-two-year-old veteran infantry leader whose testament to character is revealed throughout his letters. Perhaps his self-effacing nature is best exemplified by his omitting any mention of his promotion to lieutenant colonel in his correspondence. Unlike his brothers, especially Tom and Jim, being in the midst of war never seemed to prompt John to consider any postwar future; he never discussed the war's impact on his postwar plans. His death almost seemed anticipated in letters devoid of speculation about the future. The warrior's quiet, unassuming voice was silenced in 1864, and his role in his nation's tragedy was concluded.[34]

With four brothers in the Confederate service by springtime 1862, twenty-year-old Hopkins Turney Francis and sixteen-year-old Joseph Hugh Francis remained at home with their younger siblings. Hopkins, called "Hop" by his family, was single and worked as a clerk in Jacksonville and as an overseer on his father's plantation near Ohatchee in western Calhoun County. Joseph, "Jo" as he was known to his family, worked at odd jobs for his father and brothers as the war stretched into its second year.[35]

Their younger siblings, sisters Mary Emma, Willie Caroline, and Susan Hannah and brother Charles Henry, were attending local schools. The teenagers Emma and Willie became important wartime correspondents, especially with John and later Jo. On occasion, their letters added levity, humor, and warm family insights to periods that were otherwise dull or filled only with news of death, losses, or tragedy. Susan and Charles, known as Charlie or "Bud" to his older siblings, joined their older sisters in writing to their absent soldier brothers. Their education, especially that of Emma and Willie, became the focus of several wartime letters from their older brothers.[36]

Although recruited by John for the Sallie Walker Boys, Hop Francis joined his older brother Tom at his commissary post at Chattanooga. He never joined a regular army unit, but he was active with the commissary bureau. His wartime service is validated by miscellaneous Confederate records, his letters, and those written by his brothers. He was listed as a "clerk" on a roll of noncommissioned officers and privates at Chattanooga during June 1862 and as a "storekeeper" on a third-quarter receipt roll for service between 1 July and 6 September 1862.[37] His wartime letters document his service with Tom and show his meager exposure to the harsh realities of combat.

In August 1862, Jo Francis joined his older brothers by enrolling as a volunteer in the Confederate service at Oxford, Alabama. It is hard to imagine Amy Ingram Francis approving the enlistment of her seventeen-year-old son as a private in Company A, Fifty-first Alabama Mounted Regiment. Despite his photograph in his new uniform clutching a cavalry saber, Jo's real war experiences with Morgan's Partisan Rangers were limited. He spent most of the conflict on detached service, on special detail to the commissary service or the medical department.[38] His brothers, especially Miller and Tom, used their positions to protect him and keep him out of active duty with his assigned cavalry unit.

Jo's youthful innocence, reflected in his commentary on his daily routine assignments, often out of harm's way, add a fresh voice to this collected correspondence, especially after John's death in 1864. Unencumbered by Tom and Jim's often myopic focus on business, Jo moved in the background of Braxton Bragg's Middle Tennessee campaign until he emerged during Joe Johnston's Georgia campaign. Whether reporting from a wagon camp in

North Georgia or from a horse recovery station at Fort Browder, Alabama, Jo's often poetic prose is entertaining and informative. His letters show an honest appraisal of events with little pretension or egoism. Even as the war wound to its grimy, bloody end, he cleverly contrasted his plight as a common soldier with the privileges enjoyed by his brother Miller, the senior surgeon, who was free to come and go as he pleased.[39]

From the first year of the war until his death in 1864, John Francis was the most prolific correspondent and became the primary voice of the war for his family. Although the brothers directed most of their correspondence to their father, few letters written by Dr. Francis survived. Besides the vicissitudes of war, it is reasonable to hypothesize that Dr. James Carrington Francis failed to write his sons regularly. As a result, Tom and Jim wrote their mother, Amy Francis, to solicit responses from their father.

After 1862, Amy Ingram Francis took on a great significance. The Francis matriarch became an important conduit, confidant, and mediator to her sons. Consequently, she is poignantly emblematic of a larger phenomenon of the war contained within this correspondence: war mother and female voice. Because of her husband's reluctance to write, her letters served many functions. They offered maternal comfort to her sons, constituted a conduit to the other members of the family, especially the females, and provided religious solace. The body of Amy's letters, and later those of the other Francis women, provide a commentary on war revealing parental and marital love, as well as female stoicism and optimism.[40]

Amy Francis had become an active correspondent by 1862 and continued through springtime 1865. Most of her surviving letters were directed to her daughters Emma and Willie, who became students at Centenary Institute at Summerfield, Dallas County, Alabama. A devout Methodist, she admonished her children to trust their God implicitly and routinely implored divine protection and intervention on their behalf. Besides her Bible, she subscribed to religious publications and tracts and declared her Christian faith at every opportunity. In her unpretentious, matter-of-fact style, she shared the latest news about her sons, other family members, Jacksonville, and Calhoun County.

In addition to Amy Francis and her daughters, two other significant female voices pervade these letters, those of her two daughters-in-law. These two strong voices, different from Mother Amy's and from each other, provide a broader perspective of civilian women caught up in war on the home front. The first voice is that of Miller's wife, Julia, who directed her letters to her father-in-law. Many were requests for Dr. Francis's help with mundane, domestic matters related to hearth and home. This routine correspondence takes a profound turn when she writes about the serious illness that eventually took her daughter's life. Dramatically different from Julia's letters and in dynamic contrast to Amy's were those written by Sarah "Sadie" Whitehead Francis, Jim's young wife. Sadie's fresh, passionate prose makes her come alive on the page. She emerges as an unflagging three-dimensional optimist, her sane womanhood a balm to the tragedy of war. Her obvious infatuation with her marriage and "Captain Francis" offers hope in the face of death and devastation.[41]

While the conflict escalated from skirmish to slaughter, so too did the intensity of the Francis family correspondence, as each family member became a wartime correspondent. But many of their letters never reached their destination because of the uncertainties of war and the Confederate postal service. Still more letters were lost in the decades following the war. In the first months of the conflict, letters written by the brothers from Virginia were filled with patriotic zeal and complete confidence in the war's outcome. They reveal no doubt of the Francis brothers' commitment to duty and honor or the rightness of their cause. The brothers were fighting for liberty and independence for Alabama and the South. To them, the war was not a fight for slavery but a means to securing freedom from the oppressive Northern regime under Abraham Lincoln. When the brothers found themselves huddled in camps at Christmas in 1861, their resolve and confidence were tempered by the harsh realities of war and the promise of more bloodshed. Yet they remained loyal southern patriots to the bitter end of the fighting.[42]

For the conflict's duration, the Francis brothers filled their letters with war news, reports about deaths and diseases, and gossip and rumors. Health issues were a major subject, and outbreaks of measles, mumps, and typhoid fever were routinely reported, as were the resulting deaths of their comrades. Miller Francis's letters and medical reports detailed the diseases and deaths of his patients. As an infantry officer, John Francis dealt with a wide range of health problems faced by his men. His letters report his efforts to find soldiers left behind to recover from diarrhea, dysentery, measles, mumps, typhoid fever, pneumonia, erysipelas, or physical exhaustion. John had been vaccinated for smallpox in Tennessee, but his company was hit by a devastating smallpox outbreak at Vicksburg between January and March 1863.[43]

While armies were often swept by epidemics, the traumatic effects of diseases were also felt on the home front. Several letters from Amy Francis, her daughters, and her daughters-in-law reported the impact of these diseases on the civilian population. Whooping cough, measles, mumps, typhoid fever, and erysipelas were contracted by adults and children alike. Amy Francis reported a case of erysipelas in Jacksonville that later took the life of fourteen-year-old Julia Scales on 9 May 1863. Despite the efforts of several physicians, Miller and Julia Francis lost their eighteen-month-old daughter, Minnie, to "brain fever" on 2 June 1863. Two weeks before her marriage to Jim Francis, Sadie Whitehead lost her seven-year-old niece to typhoid fever on 1 February 1864, and on the morning of their wedding, a second niece, five-year-old Clara Louise Wilde, died.[44]

While their letters shared news of battles, camps, and comrades, the Francis brothers also reported on the status of their personal servants, especially Gabe, Buck, Cy, Alfred, "Free Bill," and Fred. The Francises seldom used the word "slave" in their letters but referred to their slaves as servants or by their given names. Gabe, Buck, Cy, and Alfred spent the first months of the war in Virginia, and concerns for their health and welfare were often expressed in the letters. They joined thousands of black Southerners whose paramilitary contributions were vital to the Confederate war effort. "Free Bill" was a freeman hired by John Francis in 1862 in East Tennessee to help with camp chores. Gabe was mentioned prominently by Miller Francis from 1861 through 1863 and served as cook, medical assistant, and messenger. Equipped with passes, Gabe made several trips to Jacksonville from Virginia and Tennessee, and in 1863 he became one of the thousands of wartime runaways who sought their freedom. While there were few references to Fred, he assisted Tom Francis with his commissary duties and made at least one trip across Alabama in 1864, using passes and orders issued by Tom and other Confederate officials. Their domestic counterparts, especially Lark and Lon, also evoked comment from other family members.[45]

While the brothers directed most of their letters to family members, the correspondence among their mother, sisters, wives, and sister-in-laws exchanged the latest news about the brothers. Many of their letters were forwarded to other family members, including brothers serving in different theaters of the Confederacy. More than once a family member forwarded a brother's letter to another by writing a second message on the back pages of the original. Letters written in pencil were often recycled by a second correspondent using ink. This practice became more common in the last year of the war, especially by Hop and Jo Francis. Many Francis letters featured addenda or marginal notes written by other family members before the letter was sent. Although their letters were filled with all manner of stories and information, the paper and writing medium used by each correspondent also tells us about the war's impact on their lives.

The Francis letters show a remarkable family. They were a highly literate, upper-middle-class family, and every member of the immediate family, from Dr. Francis to seven-year-old Charles "Bud" Francis, became a wartime correspondent. Although the Francises penned their letters for a small audience, the collected correspondence provides a universal perspective of the war and its contradictions.

1 / *The Toxin of War*

The election of Abraham Lincoln on 6 November 1860 precipitated a chain of events that altered the lives of the Francis brothers forever. Their collective correspondence, written between November 1860 and late June 1861, documents the cataclysmic intrusion of these unfolding events. Jim Francis, a merchant/farmer living in Selma, Alabama, joined a volunteer company, the Governor's Guards, in early January 1861, and was dispatched to Fort Morgan on Mobile Bay. Brother Miller Francis received a commission and an appointment as surgeon in the Sixth Alabama Volunteers regiment in May 1861. In April, John Francis, a senior at Florence Wesleyan University, canceled his graduation plans. He and a hundred of his classmates, and four professors left FWU to enlist in local volunteer companies. John and brother Tom, John's FWU roommate, Lou Grant, Tom's eighteen-year-old brother-in-law, Macon Abernathy, and John's uncle, John W. Francis, enlisted in the Pope Walker Guards at Jacksonville in June 1861.[1]

Following his service at Fort Morgan, Jim Francis reenlisted as a private for twelve months after his company was reorganized as Company A, Fourth Alabama Volunteers, at Selma on 26 April 1861.[2] His regiment, commanded by Colonel Egbert J. Jones, included ten volunteer companies from Conecuh, Dallas, Jackson, Lauderdale, Macon, Madison, Marengo, and Perry counties. The Fourth Alabama was formally organized at Dalton, Georgia, on 2 May and traveled by rail to Lynchburg, Virginia, where the men were mustered into the Confederate service before proceeding to Harpers Ferry, Virginia. They retreated to Winchester in early July where they joined Brigadier Barnard E. Bee's Third Brigade.[3]

Before his enlistment in the Fourth Alabama, Jim applied for a commission as an officer. During early April 1861, his father lobbied in his son's behalf, supported by Jacksonville residents William M. Hames and Henry T. Snow. They wrote fellow Alabamian Leroy Pope Walker, Confederate secretary of war, to recommend Jim's appointment as a first lieutenant. Other voices included Selma lawyer/politician John Tyler Morgan, Jacksonville attorney Gideon C. Ellis, Selma physician Dr. James Kent, state senator and former chief justice Samuel F. Rice, and chief justice of the Alabama state supreme court Abram J. Walker. Collectively, they touted Jim Francis's character, intelligence, and other qualities required to make a good officer. Even Governor Moore himself sent a personal note to Secretary Walker declaring Jim Francis a brave and gallant young man who would serve well in any position.[4] This effort did not produce a commission, but Dr. Francis initiated a second lobbying campaign in 1862.

Back in Jacksonville on 6 June 1861, the *Republican* reported the call "War! War! War! Attention Pope Walker Guards." On Saturday, 1 June, at a courthouse rally in Jacksonville for the Pope Walker Guards and the Calhoun Rangers, William Henry Forney, a local attorney, and Judge James Benson Martin gave "glowing, eloquent and soul stirring" speeches. Their patriotic pleas spurred eighty men, including John and Tom Francis, to enlist, committing themselves to three years' service or the duration of the war.[5]

As Jim Francis journeyed to Virginia in May 1861, Miller Francis was on his way to Montgomery, Alabama, where the Sixth Alabama Volunteers regiment was being organized under Colonel John J. Seibels.[6] In East Tennessee, while traveling by train to Virginia, Miller encountered the first open hostility and opposition to the Confederacy and secession. There, as they rolled through, Miller and his fellow Alabama volunteers saw William G. "Parson" Brownlow, Unionist editor of the *Knoxville Whig,* and some fellow East Tennesseans defiantly flying the stars and stripes.[7] The regiment arrived without further incident on 16 June 1861 at Manassas Junction, Virginia, where it was assigned to the command of Brigadier General Richard Ewell.

As Miller Francis was traveling through East Tennessee, John and Tom were formally mustered into service with the Pope Walker Guards by Colonel John Horace Forney at Jacksonville on 10 June 1861. William H. Forney, Colonel Forney's older brother, was elected captain of the guards, and John W. Francis, Dr. James Carrington Francis's youngest brother, was elected third lieutenant. After being feted as heroes through tearful farewells, the Pope Walker Guards were transported on the Alabama & Tennessee Rivers Railroad to Selma on 20 June 1861. On the following day they clambered aboard a steamboat and shipped up the Alabama River to Montgomery. Once there, they were formally organized as Company G in the Eighth Alabama Volunteers regiment at Camp Moore.[8]

After traveling across Georgia and the Carolinas by rail, the Eighth Alabama arrived in Richmond on 3 July 1861, where it was formally mustered into the Confederate service as the Tenth Alabama Volunteer Infantry Regiment. The soldiers broke camp on 11 July for the Shenandoah Valley and traveled by rail to Strasburg, terminus of the Manassas Gap Railroad, in the Valley. From there, the Tenth Alabama marched by turnpike to Winchester, where the soldiers were brigaded with four other infantry regiments under the command of Brigadier General Edmund Kirby Smith.[9]

By July 1861, the four Francis brothers and four servants had settled into Confederate camps in northern Virginia. Miller set up his medical tent at Union Mills Ford on Bull Run Creek and became immersed in the daily routine of camp life. His Sixth Alabama regiment was located on the right wing of Brigadier General Pierre G. T. Beauregard's Army of the Potomac. Meanwhile, his brothers John, Tom, and Jim and many of their friends from Jacksonville were all stationed near Winchester in the upper Shenandoah Valley. Dr. Courtney James Clark, surgeon for the Tenth Alabama, in a letter published in the *Jacksonville Republican,* reported that "Tom Francis makes a splendid commissary. . . . Young John C. Francis makes a capital soldier."[10] As for their older Brother Miller, he and Dr. Clark faced a serious outbreak of measles and other camp illnesses.

The four Francis brothers and their Uncle John were accompanied by four body servants: Gabe, Buck, Cy, and Alfred. Based on family correspondence and census records, the four slaves were apparently all owned by Dr. James Carrington Francis.[11] The Francis servants were among several thousand Black Southerners who served with the Confederate armies in Virginia and elsewhere in the Confederate States. Although little personal information is known about them, their paramilitary service to the Francis brothers and the Confederacy continued, except for Gabe, from the campaigns in Virginia through the end of the war. Gabe's service to the Confederacy ended in July 1863, when he escaped to freedom.[12]

With four sons in uniform, Dr. James Carrington Francis became actively involved in the war effort on the home front. He joined several local leaders on 6 May 1861 at a meeting at the courthouse in Jacksonville to organize an association to aid the volunteer soldiers and their families. He was elected president of the Soldiers Aid Association, and his brother-in-law Edward L. Woodward was elected treasurer. In addition, community leaders were selected from the twenty-three beats in Calhoun County to solicit contributions and to report the soldiers and families needing assistance. The association and similar societies played an increasingly critical role in providing aid to indigent families and the soldiers in the field as the shadows of the war lengthened after 1862.[13]

John C. Francis to Mary Emma Francis
Florence Wesleyan University[14]
Florence, Ala. Nov. 2nd 1860

Dear Sister Emma,

I received yours of the 23rd a few days ago and have concluded to write to you tonight. As it is Friday night and there is nothing very pressing on me in the way of study for I have until Monday morning to study on. You all write too short letters. Write more and take time enough and write it right for you are almost a young lady now and you should try to improve every time you write not only in writing but in composing. I am not tell you this because it should benefit one a great deal but it will be for your own good. Think about this and in the right light. Take pains. That is all you need. You want to get through too quick.

I will tell you now about our school. We have about 115 scholars.[15] We have seven professors, viz Dr. Rivers (President),[16] Prof. Rice (Prof. of impure mathematics),[17] Briggs (Prof. of Chemistry),[18] Morgan (Prof. of pure mathematics),[19] Forbes (Prof. of Elocution),[20] Hurt (Prof. of the Ancient Languages),[21] Prouskoski (Prof. of Modern Languages),[22] and Prof. George, a Negro who cleans up the college. As for the *sweethearts* I have none. I am not acquainted with but few girls in Florence. We get good many chestnuts here. I have been in the woods once or twice for chestnuts. They are nearly all gone now. Give my love to all and write soon.

Your most affectionate bro,
John

John C. Francis to Susan H. Francis
F. W. U. Florence, Ala. Nov. 2nd 1860

Dear Sister Susan,

Why don't you write to me? You have not written me the first letter yet. I have been expecting one from you every mail but it don't get here some how or other. I believe I will write you a few lines. Florence is a very nice little town.[23] Tennessee River is within about a mile from us. There is a rail-road bridge across it.[24] It is about 300 yards across the river. As I was passing over it the other day on my way to Tuscumbia, I saw a little steamboat called the *Muscel.*[25] It is the first one I have seen on the river at F. This rail-road bridge has one underneath for wagons and horses to go through. It is called a toll-bridge because people have to pay to go through it. A man has to pay 10 cts., a man and horse 15 cts., a man, horse and buggy 25 cts., and a wagon 30 cts. When the train is coming from T. to this place, they take the engine loose from the passenger cars and come off and leave them the other side of the bridge and then the passengers come on by themselves. It is down grade and they come very well. Nothing more at present. Write soon.

Your Brother,
John

~

John C. Francis to Willie C. Francis
F. W. U. Florence, Ala. November 2nd 1860

Dear Sister Willie,

I received yours of the 28th a day or two ago and was glad to hear that you were all well. I am getting along very well at present. On last Tuesday evening the faculty gave us permission to go to Tuscumbia to the Fair. We all started about 9 o'clock on Wednesday morning on the cars for Tuscumbia. We arrived at T. about 9 1/4 and found all the cadets from Lagrange and also a great crowd from different parts of the county.[26] I found among the cadets S. Crawford and W. Wright and Hancock from Winchester.[27] Slater Crawford and W. W. were both in good health and are very well pleased with the school.[28] They will be at home Christmas so they told me. After a while we started for the fair ground and found a great many things of the best quality. There was some very nice ladies work on exhibition. There was some very fast trotting horses. There was one of them trotted 1 mile in 2′ 37″ and another in 2′ 40″. There was a good many people there. There was more women than as the saying is "you could shake a stick at." There was also a very nice brass-band present that produce very pretty music.[29]

I got a ginger cake for dinner as it was all that I could get. The tavern was too far off for us to go to. Nothing more at present except write soon.

Your Brother,
John

John C. Francis to James C. Francis
F. W. U. Florence, Ala. Nov. 23rd 1860

Dear Father,

As I have not written to you in some time I have concluded to write you a few lines. I am getting along very well at present. I am getting along very well with my studies though it requires a great deal to do what is required of us. I have five studies to carry on, four in the senior and one in the Junior class, that one is Analytical Geometry. I go to the college at 9 in the morning and stay until 12, at 2 in the evening and stay until 5.[30] We all paid for our board yesterday for the next month, i.e., until the 21st of December. After paying that I have $13.00 left. Lou is strapped and Tom has but little and if we don't get some money next month we will be in a bad fix.[31] I suppose Judge Foster will be here on the 10th of next month and I wish you would send some by him.[32] I don't spend any money only for what I am obliged to have. I don't think I will go to Tenn. Christmas as we will only have three days of that week

I have not been any where since I have been here except to Tuscumbia to the fair. There is no news of importance in Florence. They have formed a military company here since they have heard of the election of Lincoln.[33] There are more disunionists here now than there were before the election. I sent a magazine to Miller. Tell Emma to get and file it away. Nothing more at present.

Your Son,
John

James C. Francis to John C. Francis
Jacksonville, Ala.
Decr. 11th 1860

Dear John,

Enclosed I send the left hand half of a fifty dollar bill. The Commercial Bank of Ala. at Selma: Letter A. No. 2759. Mr. Grant sent the right hand half in a letter to Lou a few days ago. When you receive this put them together & git it changed and give Leonidas twenty five dollars.[34] You must be saving of your money & spend as little as the nature of the case will admit of. Times are harder than I ever saw them & money harder to git. I will send you money as you need it. You must let me know allways three or four weeks before you need it.

You must not take a private room off from your boarding house. I had rather pay a little more at a private boarding house than for you to room at one place & eat at another. Remain in some respectable boarding house if you have to pay more for it. Don't go to a public house either.[35] I would not go to Winchester in the vacation. Wait untill you git through & then come that way & you have more time to spend with your relations.

We have had several large meetings recently in this place on the subject of secession. I never saw as much unanimity in my life as there is in this county for secession in all the meetings that we have had here. There has not been a desenting voice though you have & can see the spirit of this county by examining the *Jacksonville Republican.*[36] Attend to your studys very closely, keep out of bad company & attend to your own business, treat every body kindly & c.

Your mothers health has not been good for sometime but is gitting good again. There is nothing of importance to write about. I suppose the little girls keep you posted as to what is going on hear. Judge Foster notified me a day or two before he started when he would start, but I failed to see him the evening before he started or I would have sent you some money by him. You must write on the reception of this. We are all well. You must be a good boy.

Yours affectionately & c
J. C. Francis

John C. Francis to Mary Emma Francis
F. W. U. Florence, Ala. Dec. 23rd 1860

Dear Sister Emma,

I received yours of the 7th with Father's and have forgotten whether or not I answered it. For fear that I did not I have concluded to answer it though you should not stop writing if I happen to neglect to answer yours. We received the box on last Wednesday and was very glad indeed to get as it came from home.[37] We have not eat yet though we expect to on tomorrow night. Our school was out Friday but will commence on next Thursday. The citizens were so rejoiced at the secession of South Carolina that part of them bought two or three barrels of tar (as they had no pine) and rolled them out on the square and set them on fire and then started a ringing of all the bells.[38] It scared a great many people. They thought that it was a house on fire.

I don't know of anything special to write. I stood two examinations last week. I got through on them both. What is Hop doing? I have not heard from him a single time since I have been here. I have written to him two or three times but have never heard a word from him. Tell him to write to me and also tell Willie and Sue and tell Bud he has quit too soon. Give my love to all and write soon. Excuse this scribbling as I have dim light and a bad pen.

Your affectionate Brother
"John"

John C. Francis to Mary Emma Francis
F. W. University Florence, Jan. 14th [18]61

Dear Sister Emma,

I received your letter yesterday morning. The first one that I have received from home in about three or four weeks. I have nothing of importance to write you at the present time. There is a great excitement here on account of the present funding crises. The military companies are drilling regularly and preparing themselves for action if they are needed. I think that I will join them so as to be prepared if I am needed.[39]

As Father can't see how I spend so much money as he thinks, I will give you a list of what I have spent since I received the twenty five dollars from him: one pr. of overshoes—1.50, letter-paper—.25, postage stamps—.25, powder & shot—.25, library fee—.50, one yard of blue ribbon—.25, apples—.30, half-soling boots—1.00, shaving—.10, oysters—.50, box per express—.65, going to a lecture—.25, a Dialectical badge[40]—2.50, one pk. handkerchief—.75, washing for two months—3.00, college party—1.00, board—14.50, mending coat—.75, trimming hair and shaving—.35, blacking boots pr. month—.25, one picture of the college—1.00, one lead pencil—.10, matches—.10, coal oil[41]—.50, postage stamps—.30, fine in the society—.25, mending pants—.25, one pk. knife—.60 = $ 32.00

I reckon that there is several things that I neglected to put down on my book. I have four or five dollars left. I have given an account which I believe is correct for I have kept an account of them on my book. These things that I have mentioned may some of them seem unnecessary, but I have to have all of them. Except the oysters and the apples those I got a while before Christmas. The powder and shot was during Christmas week.

I understand that you and Mary Grant received a letter from Mr. T. J. Walker of Florence. I wish you would send it to me in your next. I suppose Mary would have no objections.[42] Lou is getting along very well I believe at present. You write to me about [Hef's] returning to his home. I don't know anything about his home. I thought he was living at Jacksonville. He was living there when I left. As to his removal I have never heard a thing. Please let me know in your next where he has gone to live.

You must write oftener. For if you cease I will not hear from home at all. For I have heard from no one there except you in two or three months. Except once from Father. Give my love to all and write when you feel disposed.

Your Brother [John]

John C. Francis to James C. Francis
F. W. U., Florence, Ala. Jan. 27, [18]61

Dear Father,

I received yours of the 13th this morning, and was glad to get the money. I received the last twenty dollars you sent me through Miller's letter the other day. There is no news of importance about Florence. The military companies are ready for action.[43] I wrote to James today but don't know that he will get the letter.[44] I received a letter from Jo this morning he is getting along finely. I am getting along very well with my studies. I have to stand an examination on rhetoric tomorrow, and then we will take up mental philosophy.[45] Dr. Rivers will lecture us at his residence. He will not be able to go to the college. This session will be out on the 14th of next month, and will take up on the 15th. Our school is getting along very well at the present time. I am getting along very well at present and will try and spend no more money that I can help. Tom and Lou are getting along very well I believe. Give my love to all.

Your son,
John

Susan H. Francis to John C. Francis
Jacksonville, Ala.
Feb. 5, 1861

Dear Brother,

I thought I would write you a few lines as I have not written to you yet. We are all well at present. Mother got a letter from Joe and he is well & said he got a letter from Brother Jim and he said he is well. We are going to school now to Miss Cobb and I like her very well.[46] Pa hired brother Hop to oversee for him this year and Brother Tom and Sister Fanny live down there also. They have sowed over a 100 acres of wheat and as much more in corn. Pa sent Sis, Lark,[47] Gabe, Cy, and George down to the plantation. Ellen has a son and she calls it Henry Clay after her brother. Pa is going to send her and Aunt Sofa down to the plantation.[48] Brother Hop has not been up since Christmas and he spent Christmas week. You must write longer letters.

Sue F.

James C. Francis, Jr. to James C. Francis
In Camp Republic of Ala.
Fort Morgan, Feby. 19th /[18]61

Dear Father,

I have often thought of giving you something of a description of the above named place during my sojourn here, but lack of time has prevented until present, and even now my time is quite limited. I have just returned from "Dress-Parade", & in forty (40) minutes I must appear at the battery with my gun-squad to work the cannon.[49]

I arrived at this hereto-fore uncared for yet all important point to Alabama (Fort Morgan) Jan. in company with 120 of (Selma) Ala. offended sons.[50] We found this fort garrisoned by 400 souldiers. Sacrifice of life, of property & resistence to the last was depicted in every countenance. There could be seen the aged father as well as the strong arm of the youth; all partys (politicaly) are represented. They are now united in a common cause and same self interest.

Morgan is situated on the most southerly point of Ala. possessions; is the second piece of masonry as regards weight in the heretofore "U.S." It commands the entire entrance from the Gulf to Mobile Bay. Vessels are forced to come within ½ mile of the fort & immediately under the mouth of forty (40) 32 pds. It is a regular pentagon shape covering an area of about 12 acres.[51] Its bastions contain 52 mounted 32 pds. guns.[52] Its case-mates no. 50 & are thoroughaly ball & bomb proof; should we be driven from the batteries these are resorted to as means of safety.[53] Between the bastions & the case-mates are ditches about 50 ft. wide with perpendicular walls of brick and granate 30 to 40 ft. high; these ditches surround the case-mates & are defended or swept by 24 pd. howitzers; from these guns are thrown grape or canister.[54] Within the enclosure made by the case-mates is the citadel, within the citadel is about one (1) acre of unoccupyed ground; this is used for evening "Dress Parade"; besides this is the last means of defense; here the troops have comand of 500 port holes for the use of the rifle & side arms. There are mounted 92 guns 32 & 24 pds. in store over ten (10) ton of powder & other munition in proportion.

Should the North contemplate an attac upon "Fort Morgan" I think it would be judicious for them to consider the language of old "Gen. Scott" & wise for them to heed it.[55] It was "garrison Fort Morgan" with 500 well disciplined souldiers, give them a sufficiency of munitions of war & it would be almost invincible.

"Capt. Harry Maury" the noted "Nicaraguan" adventurer is chief of ordinance & is more than worthy of his position.[56]

To the N. & N.W., lies the Mobile Bay to the S. & S.E. is the "Gulf of Mexico." "Fort Gains" is situated on "Dauphan Island" 3 ¼ miles from Morgan.[57] It is in an unfinished condition but when complete will be a strong point for Ala. Altho in this incomplete condition the eye can feast on beauty of architecture & neatness of masonry for hours without being wearied. To the S. W. 3 miles from Morgan is "Sandy Island Light House."[58] It is 200 ft. high. Its chandalin was purchased in France at an expense of 13,000$, average consumption of oil per mo. is 8.5 gals., & has been seen on one occasion the distance of 32 miles. The call is beating I must hasten the close of this hurried sheet. We start for home tomorrow but still hold ourselves subject to the order of the governor. My love to all.

Your obdt. son,
Jim C. Francis, Jr.

P.S. When I reach home I will [see] to my merchandise, but should the toxin of war be sounded across our own dear south, I will willingly buckle on my napsack, which I expect ere long to set aside, & with confidence, & pride, stand face to face & measure bayonets with the black-harted agressors. J. C. F., Jr.

James C. Francis, Jr. to James C. Francis
Selma, Apl. 25th/[18]61

Dear Father & Mother,

Tonight I take up the line of march with my comrades in arms our destination I am not able to ascertain nor can we learn until we arrive at "Montgomery." We think however that we will be moved immediately to "Virginia."[59]

I would like to meet the family once more but time will not permit. I do not regret that I have to go (altho tis a death blow to my future). Yet when I think of the little ones at home, then *duty* prompts me to their protection. In the past few years that has been alloted to me I have been unfortunate, unlucky and vixt. with many things to blast my future but I am hapy to say that I have with some difficulty over leaped them all & should it be my fortune to pass the present move unharmed I think I can yet make myself independent. This letter is intended for you alone. Simply tell the family that I have gone & will write them soon. Give them my love. You have my wish as regards my little effects in black and white; as soon as a safe party passes up I will send my papers. Collect all you can. Good-bye in haste.

Your son,
Jim C. Francis, Jr.

Jabez L. M. Curry to James C. Francis[60]
Kelley's Springs, Ala.
May 12th [18]61

Dear Sir:

I noticed in the call in the last "Republican" requesting the use of my name as a candidate for congress.[61] I suspected that it probably originated from you, & therefore I address you this letter.

In the event that Sam Rice is not a candidate (and I do not think he will be, as Morgan is a candidate for the legislature,) and I can get anything like a fair field, I am willing to run.[62] If I am a candidate it shall be my endeavor so to conduct the canvass as to unite every States Rights Democrat and still secure the Southern Rights Whigs.[63] I think, it can be done.

I presume there will be a convention. The conflicting claims(?) of aspirants can not otherwise be reconciled. I should regret after having received such warm solicitations from Benton to see *all* the delegates from that county opposed to me.[64] *[Berburn] says* I ought to have some friends in Jacksonville who would not let my interest suffer.

Can't you help me some in Cherokee.[65] Who will the delegates from that county be for? Can't you go to the convention?

Say to my friend, Mr. Woodward (how does he stand on this other matter?) that I received his letter about the depot and made all the representations to my father, that I could.[66] He is very favorably disposed to Jacksonville, and is urging the board, to hold their next meeting in Jacksonville.[67] I hope they will, & will so write to Lapsley.[68]

I understand that a report has reached Jacksonville that the propositions for contracts have all been rejected by the Selma directors. Say to those interested that I am satisfied there is no foundation for the rumor.

I shall rely upon you Dr. to help me.

Yours truly,
J. L. M. Curry

Miller W. Francis to James C. Francis
Camp Seibels[69]
June 8, 1861

Dear Father,

Our last detachment leave for Richmond tomorrow. Col. Seibels & 6 cos. left yesterday. Lt. Col. Baker today with 3 cos. & Major Gordon leaves tomorrow with the other 3 cos. Our regiment consists of 12 companies that are full.[70] They can't be beat for morality & ability not one drunk man have I seen in our regiment yet, & they can buy as much as they want. My duties will be comparatively light when everything is arranged. No supplies sent here yet for use of the sick. Send to New Orleans & buy Dr. Nisbet a $25.00 amputating case.[71] I have left men behind sick with pneumonia all getting well. However one or two taken since my arrival. I am delighted with my position. Col. Seibels has expressed his satisfaction & c. at my concern with the sick. I will get along finely. Write to me at Richmond & tell Mr. Grant to send his paper there.

Yours in haste,
Miller

Miller W. Francis to James C. Francis
Bristol, Tenn. or Va.[72]
June 12th 1861

Dear Father,

I arrived here this morning at 7 o'clock, having left Corinth on Sunday at 11 o'clock.[73] We have had a bad time of it, one of our soldiers fell of the train on Sunday & I had to amputate 4 of his toes, & leave him at Chattanooga under the care of Dr. Kennedy, it was well done. Yesterday about two o'clock two of our cars were thrown off the track above Knoxville & were detained until 2 this morning no one severely injured, however. One detachment of 600 men left Corinth on last Friday with Col. Seibels, another of 300 left on Saturday with Lieut. Col. Baker. The detachment I was left was commanded by Major Gordon, who is a very clever gentleman & has treated me very kindly.[74] I am getting along finely.

We cut down a Union flag in the road today & tore it into shreds no resistance was offered. We started on Monday morning for Brownlow's house to get his flag but it was hauled down on the day before, by himself.[75] We would have taken it down, certain if it had been there. We passed by 1 Union flag which we left standing for this reason, the cars were in full speed & when our men ran to the breaks to stop them we found all the chains off them & could not use them. We then went to the engineer & told him to reverse steam & go back to it, & begged for his life to let him go on, as they would certainly kill him as he must back to Knoxville, as he would have only 4 or 5 men with him & we let him go on. The feeling is very strong for the union among some of the little towns in Tenn., but they don't dare to cheer around about it.[76] It was a continual run of handkerchiefs & hats from one end of our route to this place. I am getting along finely with every one in the regt. Major Gordon, has his wife with him and she is a very fine lady indeed. She says she will assist me with the sick & wounded at any time.[77]

I am in good health & c. We overtook our first detachment at this place.

They have left however, we go to Richmond & from there to Manassas Gap. I think we have 12 full companies in our rgt. & it is decided by competent judges to be the finest that they have seen. I will see Jim, I expect. If John wants to come & join our regt., I can get him in. I send you a piece of the flag we tore down today, my health is remarkably good. Gabe is fat & healthy.[78] We have a good many sick with measels & c., but none dangerous. Our worst cases of pneumonia are getting well.[79] Col. Seibels has complimented me several times for my attentions & c. I may need more money before long. When you write, address to Richmond care Col. Seibels 6th Rgt. Ala. Vols.

Your son,
M. W. F.

Miller W. Francis to James C. Francis
Camp near Manassas Junction
June 17th 1861

Dear Father,

We arrived here on Saturday last, had a hard time coming up, stayed one day at Lynchburg, were ordered here without a moments delay, in great haste, as a fight is expected here every day, any moment we may have a fight.[80] We are obliged to have a fight here before long & it will be a bloody one I can assure you. We have about 20,000 thousand troops here. Our regiment is between Alexandria & Manassas Junction.[81] We are in 30 miles of Washington City. Col. Gregg of S.C. is at Fairfax about 14 miles from us.[82] There is no doubt that we will have a hard fought battle beyond this place. This is only a place intended for us to fall back on in case we are driven back from our advanced posts. We I think will advance in a few days towards Alexandria.

We have a healthy climate here, in a wild and barren county, have a strong breeze every day & it is cool & comfortable. We have plenty to eat, I am well pleased & all are pleased with me so far as I know. I want you to send to New Orleans & buy Dr. Nisbet a case of amputating instruments as we have had none supplied us yet, & have received no supplies, only some that I obtained at Lynchburg. Tell Dr. Clark that every thing is going on as well as I could wish & that I will write to him before long.[83] I am about out of money. If you can send me that horse of Jim Farmer's & my saddle & bridle, have him shipped by express to Manassas Junction, care

Col. J. J. Seibels, Comd. Ala. Vols.[84] I want a horse badly. I am in excellent health & enjoy the life in camp finely, have plenty time to attend to every thing except when we move. Col. Seibels has complimented several times about my abilities to perform my duties & c.

All is going along smoothly & as well as I could want. I will try to get an order of transportation for that horse if you can get him. He is the finest horse in all this county & I could get 4 or 500 dollars for him if he was here, try & get him. The Confederate troops have abandoned Harpers Ferry & gone to Winchester about 80 miles from us.[85] We are very near to the enemy & are all anxious for a fight. Our scouts are all over the country & no one can get out except he has a pass from General Beauregard.[86] The Texas Rangers are some of them scouting here & kill one or two men every day, some days four or 5.

Yours in haste,
M. W. Francis

Miller W. Francis to James C. Francis
Fairfax Station, Va.
3 1/2 miles from Fairfax
[June 20, 1861]

Dear Father,

We arrived here from Manassas Junction today. We are in 4 or 5 miles of the federal troops, and at the end of the rail road to Alexandria as it is filled up, in a deep cut, in sight of our camp and there is no communication. For 9 miles from this place toward Alexandria, our scouts are continually picking of the federal troops. We will have a big fight before long as there has been a great deal of bringing troops from Manassas, in the last 24 hours. One battallion of our regiment of 4 companies are advanced in a very short distance of the enemy as they are scouting in all directions on both sides.[87] Our men are keen for a fight. They will tell a good tale when they have a chance. In Gregg's fight there is no telling how many were killed, as there was a regiment in the train & a 6 pounder was fired in at the end & went crashing through the whole line of cars. It was fired 3 times & evry ball struck the train. They were backing the train down or they could have captured all the rgt. They scampered like a flock of sheep.[88] The name of a southern man is dreaded here more than anything.

I am in good health. I heard from Jim yesterday he was at Winchester, Va. and in good health.[89] I left my watch with Major Gordon's wife at Manassas Junction to be sent to Julia if I did not come back.

We will have a severe fight before many days, write to Julia, where I am, as I have but little time to write.

Your son,
Miller

Miller W. Francis to James C. Francis
Fairfax Station
June 26th 1861

Dear Father,

I was over yesterday to see Col. Rhodes Rgt. of Ala. Vols.[90] I found the Talladega company & Hall Lewis, J. T. Morgan.[91] They are in 1¼ miles of us & are in our brigade commanded by Genl. Yuill.[92] I am in good health & c. Tom Renfro is at home & will come directly here[93] & I want you to send me Farmer's horse, if you can get him also my saddle & bridle. Camp Porter is here in good health I saw him yesterday.[94]

The health of our regt. is bad, have an epidemic of measles & the worst catarrh's I have ever seen. I has assumed the form of a violent epidemic.[95] I am in good health & fine spirits. Our scouts & pickets are in sight of the enemy every day. Our pickets brought in yesterday morning 13 prisoners, 9 men & 4 women, but they were discharged as they were coming from Alexandria out this way.

We will make another advance on the enemy in a day or two, as our surgeon of the post ordered me to send all our men back to Culpepper C. H., that would not be able to do duty in 5 days, & I am going to do so today.[96]

I am well pleased with my position & the officers & men treat me as well as if I had known them always, & seem to be perfectly satisfied with me. Allways some of them at my quarters, day & night. I have detailed 3 drs. to remain with the sick from Corinth to this point. There are about 40 drs. in the regt. but some hold office, some in ranks & a good many no earthly use to anyone.[97] I am out of money but expect to draw in a few days as our estimates have been made out for 2 months, & our quarter master has gone for the money.

I have dressed 1 bullet wound from a Yankee fight. Our brigadier general has come two mornings to me for having his wounds dressed. He was shot through his shoulder at Fairfax by a federal trooper in their charge on that place.[98] I must close as surgeon call is beating, send that horse.

M. W. Francis

P.S. Direct your letters to M. W. Francis, Surgeon, 6th Regt. Ala. Vols., Manassas Junction, Va. We are in 24 miles of the federal capital & I want to go to it, so do our men. I have a Colt navy pistol that can kill a Yankee 250 yds, & when ever I get a chance I am going to take a crack at them, between wound dressing times.[99] If there is any chance in the world, I will have one's gun certain.

Your son,
M. W. Francis

John C. Francis to James C. Francis
Camp Moore, Montgomery, Ala.[100]
June 29th 1861

Dear Father,

I don't know of anything of importance to write you but will tell you of our movements. We have been getting along finely since I arrived. Have been well ever since my arrival. There are three or four of our boys in the hospital. Mr. Glover shot himself in the thigh, it is not a dangerous wound.[101] Goodman the Dutchman has been sick ever since we arrived but is now up and going about.[102] All will be able to go to Richmond this evening with the company except Glover. Tom and Col. Forney went on to Richmond night before last.[103] Our company leaves tonight. I will stay until tomorrow night. I am having some printing done for the regiment and can't get off with the company. George Turnley went on a few days ago to see his relations in Tennessee.[104] We go by the way of Augusta. Tell Mr. Renfro that Mun is well and doing well.[105] I sleep in his tent, our tents are very comfortable. We have had several good rains here since our arrival. Crops look very good. You must excuse my writing with a pencil as it is so unhandy to write with a pen. All of our boys are well pleased and are anxious to get to Va. We have had no drills, except parade, since we came. Col. Forney said it was too hot. Jo came up with us and stayed until Wednesday. We sent our ambrotypes by him (Tom Walker, Macon &

I).[106] He will send them up the first chance. John Clark has joined our company and will go on with us.[107] Jo said he would be up to Jacksonville before long. I will write again when I get to Va. Give my love to all. Direct your letters in care of Capt. Forney.[108]

Your son,
John

2 / *Crowned Themselves with Glory*

In the summer of 1861, the inchoate war was brought to the Francis brothers by Union armies commanded by Major General Robert Patterson and Brigadier General Irvin McDowell. Patterson crossed the Potomac River into the Shenandoah Valley on 2 July 1861; there his army engaged Joe Johnston's forces, which included Jim, Tom, and John Francis. Patterson's subsequent march toward Martinsburg, Virginia, was contested at Falling Waters by a detachment of the Fifth Virginia Infantry Regiment. After a brief skirmish with Patterson, the Virginians under Colonel Thomas Jackson, soon to be known as "Stonewall," retreated and joined the main body of Joe Johnston's army near Winchester on 3 July. When Patterson failed to engage Johnston, he was mustered out of the Union army on 27 July.[1]

Johnston's Army of the Shenandoah numbered approximately 11,000 men divided into four brigades. The Tenth Alabama, including Tom and John Francis in the Pope Walker Guards, broke camp outside Richmond on 11 July 1861 for Winchester, where they joined the Fourth Brigade commanded by Brigadier General Edmund Kirby Smith. Brother Jim's Fourth Alabama was in camps nearby in Barnard E. Bee's Third Brigade.[2]

When a stalemate developed between Patterson and Johnston in the Shenandoah Valley, Brigadier General McDowell marched his army of 35,000 from Alexandria toward Centreville, north of Manassas Junction. Any hope of surprise to break the impasse was dashed, however, when Confederate forces encountered McDowell's Union reconnaissance force on 18 July at Mitchell's Ford on Bull Run Creek. This premature contact gave Beauregard enough warning to move the bulk of Johnston's forces out of the Valley to help break the Union advance. To counteract this effort, McDowell's artillery opened fire around 5:15 Sunday morning, 21 July. Then, at about 10:30 A.M., his army crossed Bull Run Creek, launching a frantic assault to turn Beauregard's left flank.[3]

Barnard Bee's brigade, including the Fourth Alabama, in which Jim Francis served, was located on the left flank of the ten-mile Confederate line. The brigade was caught in heavy fighting while holding a Union brigade of three regiments in check for nearly three hours at Henry House Hill. The cost was high. Bee's brigade lost 40 killed, including its commander, and 170 wounded.[4] Jim Francis received buckshot wounds to his left arm and a shrapnel wound to his left shoulder. He was treated by his brother Miller Francis and quickly recovered.[5]

Miller Francis's Sixth Alabama in Ewell's brigade was located near Union Mills on the Confederate right and was not itself actively engaged in the battle. Brothers John and Tom arrived at Manassas on Monday, 22 July 1861, with the last of Johnston's Valley forces.[6] In the meantime, the Confederate left flank was reinforced by the arrival of Jubal Early and Edmund Kirby Smith, whose combined forces halted the Union advance. McDowell's exhausted and dispirited Union army began to withdraw via the Sudley Springs' Ford and the Stone Bridge over Bull Run Creek.[7]

News of the Confederate victory at Manassas caused a swarm of visitors to view the carnage of the war's first major battle. Thousands trekked to the Virginia countryside to claim the remains of family members or to comfort survivors, a journey repeated throughout the war. Dr. James Carrington Francis was among many visitors from Calhoun County who made the trip from Alabama.[8] On the negative side, for several days after the battle, soldiers, servants, and civilians poured over the battlefield, robbing the dead, claiming horses and equipment, and collecting souvenirs. When Dr. James C. Francis left the camps of the Tenth Alabama near Bull Run Creek on 2 August 1861, the grisly battlefield scene of 21 July remained littered with the carcasses of dead men and horses.[9]

For several months following the battle of First Manassas, the Francis brothers saw no military action and settled into the routine of camp life. The respite, however, was not without its attendant tragedy. The poor health conditions of camp life soon took their toll. Widespread sickness and inadequate medicine and medical staffs compounded the suffering of thousands of Confederate soldiers who complained bitterly of their neglect and hardships. The usual mention of friends and servants and family and business in the brothers' letters during this period is interspersed with news of health conditions and issues and deaths that reflect the nature of camp life. Miller Francis's monthly medical reports from the Sixth Alabama document the numerous illnesses afflicting the soldiers in the Confederate camps. He records twenty-three deaths in the regiment, caused by complications from measles, pneumonia, typhoid fever, and other camp diseases. By mid-November 1861, fifty-two members of the Tenth Alabama were buried in a cemetery near their encampments at Bristoe, Virginia.[10]

One of the casualties of camp life was Tom Francis, who received a thirty-day furlough "in consequence of ill health" in mid-September 1862. He spent a few days in Richmond and returned to Jacksonville on Saturday, 21 September. His furlough was extended to two months, and he remained in Jacksonville until early November 1861. At the same time, his brother Jim was on sick leave in Richmond where he found accommodations in a private home while recovering from an unspecified illness. Owing to his continued poor health, Jim Francis was granted a thirty-day furlough in early December 1861.[11]

Throughout furloughs, sick leave, picket duty, and camp routine, the brothers stayed in touch with each other by visits and contacts with their kinsmen and friends in adjacent units and camps. A continual stream of visitors and the delivery of mail, packages, and warm clothing from home helped break the monotony of camp life. Politicians from Richmond came out to pay their respects to the troops and to get a firsthand look at the war. Despite rumors about the next great battle and a quick end of the war, the Francis brothers and their comrades eventually began settling into their winter camps with the realization that the war would not end by Christmas.[12]

The monotony changed dramatically on 20 December 1861 when the Tenth Alabama joined a foraging expedition under Brigadier General J. E. B. Stuart. With his wagon train spread out for several miles, Stuart's four regiments, artillery and cavalry, marched from Centreville for Dranesville, Virginia, where they encountered 5,000 Union troops under Brigadier General Edward O. C. Ord. When Ord's artillery began shelling the Confederates, Bailey George McClelen, Company D, Tenth Alabama, reported "the missiles of death flew thick and fast and had no respect for persons . . . which carnage was made on both sides."[13]

Seeing his own artillery partially disabled, Stuart ordered the Sixth South Carolina and Tenth Alabama to charge the center of the Union line anchored around a brick house. Charging across an open field, both regiments were exposed to withering fire and were forced to withdraw, suffering several casualties. Colonel John H. Forney was shot through the right arm, and his brother, Captain William H. Forney, was shot in the left leg. Lieutenant Colonel James B. Martin was killed while rushing forward "in a shower of bullets." The Tenth Alabama lost fifteen killed, forty-five wounded, and six missing. Although one of several wounded in the Pope Walker Guards, John

Francis escaped from this "first Federal victory south of the Potomac" with a shot through the lower left arm above the wrist but suffered no broken bones.[14]

On Monday, 30 December 1861, two heroes from the battle of Dranesville returned simultaneously to their respective homes: John Francis to Jacksonville on furlough to recover from his wound, and the body of Colonel James Benson Martin to Oxford, Alabama. With Dr. James Carrington Francis and Colonel John D. Hoke serving as marshals, Martin's funeral service was conducted the following day at the Jacksonville Presbyterian Church. His burial was accompanied by full military and Masonic honors and ceremonies as "old and young, white and black with saddened hearts, passed by and took a farewell look."[15]

~

John C. Francis to James C. Francis
Camp Alabama near
Richmond, Virginia
July 7th 1861

Dear Father,

We arrived here four days ago. All the boys stood the trip very well but few sick none of them much sick. I have not been sick since I left home. I went to town yesterday and it was telegraphed to President Davis that there was a fight at Martinsburg between Johnson and the federal forces, 3,000 Yankees killed, 1,000 southerners and 4,000 Yankee prisoners.[16] There is now in this place about fifty prisoners. I saw one of them yesterday through the window. No one is allowed to visit them.

Beauregard has been telegraphing here for some time for Forney to come immediately. He is not ready to go yet, we will start as soon as Col. F. says he is ready. We may start this evening or tomorrow morning, but we will be certain to leave in a few days for Martinsburg. There are about 10,000 troops stationed here at the present time. Our regiment has been changed from the 8th to the 10th.[17] The boys are anxious to get off. Our capt. ordered us last night to pack our clothing 6 o'clock this morning and have ever thing ready so as to start at any moment. We have the old musket with a percussion lock.[18] Write soon.

Your son,
John

John C. Francis to Willie C. Francis
Camp Alabama, Richmond, Va.
July 11th [1861]

Dear Sister,

I received your letter through Mr. Mitchell while on my way from Montgomery to this place. It is the only one I have received from home since I left. I have written several times to Father. We are in camp now about 3 miles from the city. I have only been to town once since I arrived. I heard from Miller a few days ago he wrote on the 7th. He says that he is in good health and getting along finely. He is stationed at Fairfax Station under Beaureguard.[19] There is no news of importance now. I wrote Father that I thought we would leave Tuesday evening. We could not get off at that time. We have orders to leave this evening, but I don't believe we will get off until tomorrow or next day. We go to Winchester I believe, direct your letters to that place and when we move I will let you know. Tom has his commission.[20] Bradford is our major.[21] I don't know who will be our quarter master as he is not yet appointed. There is but little sickness in our regt., scarcely any in our company. Two or three cases of the measles the worst sickness we have. The boys are all in fine spirits. Uncle John has Alfred now waiting on him.[22] I cook nearly every day. We have bacon, corn-bread and coffee to eat, occassionaly a few cabbage and onions, but have them to buy. Our boy Buck has been sick for the last two or three days but is now well.[23]

We drew our arms and other accouterments at this place. We got the musket. We drill three and a half hours a day. I drill a squad. We very often have lady visitors when on dress-parade. John Crawford is in our mess and getting along finely. He is the best drummer in the reg't.[24] Nothing more at present. I am in fine health. Direct your letters to Winchester, Va., 10th Regt. Ala. Vols. care Capt. Wm. H. Forney. Give my love to all. Write soon.

Your brother,
John

P.S. Tom Renfro passed through here yesterday he was well.[25]

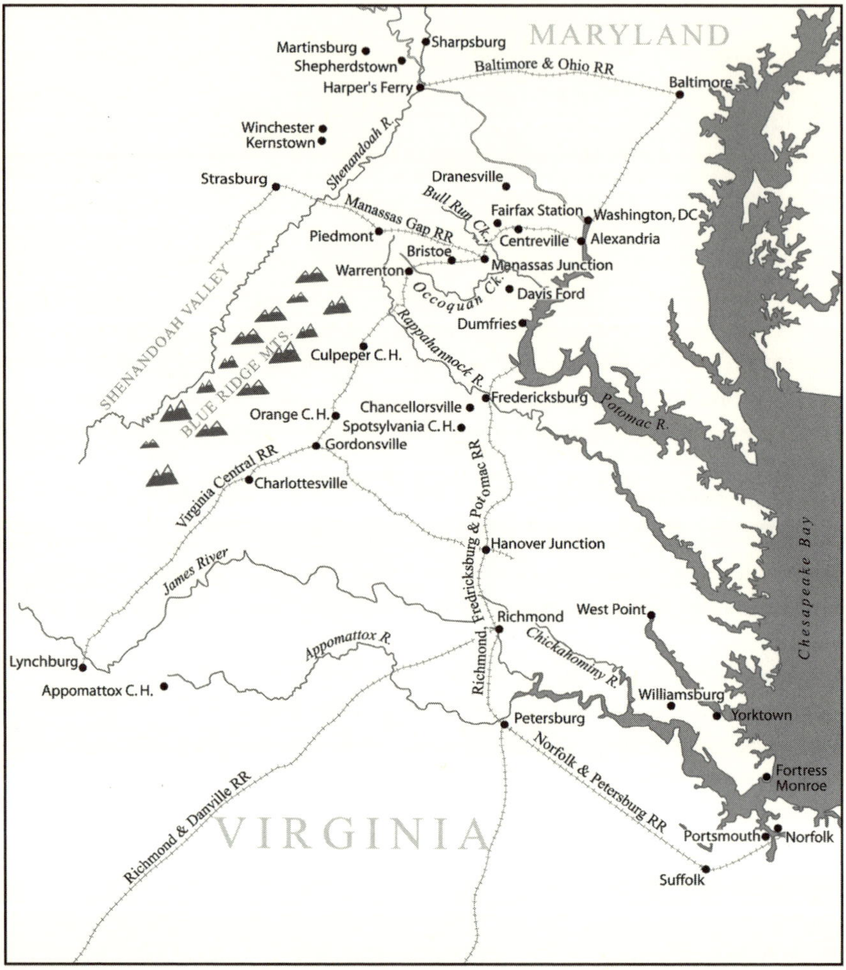

The War in Virginia

~

John C. Francis to James C. Francis
In Camp near Winchester, Va.
July 16, 1861

Dear Father,

I believe I have not written to you since I left Richmond. We started from that place on 11th and arrived at this place on the 14th. We had to walk with our knapsacks on our backs three miles. We had quite a weary some time getting here. We arrived at Strassburg on the 13th and on the 14th we started on a forced march to this place. We walked eighteen miles in about six hours.[26] We pitched our tents and stayed one night when we heard that the enemy were advancing and were within ten miles of this place. We then struck tents and came to this place, one mile from the city towards the enemy. We were expecting to have to march against the enemy last night but received no orders. Our col. gave us orders last night to cook three days rations and we were up nearly all night cooking. All of our boys are anxious to meet the invaders. There is but little sickness in camp, no one bad off.

We passed by Manassas Junction but did not see Miller. He wrote to Tom a few days ago from Fairfax Station he was getting along finely. Is reported here that Gen. Beaureguard has taken Alexandria and that he telegraphed to Gen. Johnston that he could send ten thousand men.[27] There is now stationed at this place about 25,000 troops though I am not certain about the numbers some say 35,000. We can't tell *how many* there are for they are scattered every where.[28] Tell Renfro that Mun is getting along finely, so is Lou Grant, George Turnley, Macon, Uncle John & c. I saw Jim yesterday he is doing very well in fine health so is Jim Adams.[29] I went over to see Pete Turney he is doing well.[30] We are in Smith's Brigade.[31] John Wyly is about leaving I must close.[32] I am in good health. Tom is well. My love to all.

Your son,
John

Miller W. Francis to James C. Francis
Camp near Bull Run[33]
Manassas Junction
July 24th 1861

Dear Father,

I am wearied & worn out from exertion. We have won the greatest battle that was ever fought. There are 12,000 of the Yankees killed, wounded & taken prisoners. We have over 50 of their cannon & all kinds of property. I have been over the field & such a wreck I never have witnessed. The enemy numbered about 80,000 men.[34] The best equiped of any army that ever went into the field. It is all ours. They commenced fighting at 8 o'clock in the morning & we whipped them at 6 in the evening.[35]

Four regiments of ours did the fighting. The 4th Ala. opened the fight & held a brigade of three regiments in check for 1½ hours by themselves.[36] They have crowned themselves with glory but are cut up dreadfully. They have 200 killed & wounded.[37] James has been wounded twice on the left shoulder by a bomb shell from Sherman's battery & in the left arm by two buck shot. I have them now in my possession. I saw him yesterday also Jim Adams he was in the fight but not hurt. Jim stayed with me a day or two, his wounds are slight & will soon be well.[38] I saw all the boys from our place yesterday on the battlefield. They are all well. John stood it finely & is in good health. I sent you a Minie musket that Jim got off the battle ground from an officer he shot.[39] I sent it to Montgomery by Mr. Benson, & he is to send it to Joe at Selma. You had better write to Joe about it. I also have a Yankee horse, saddle, & blanket & canteen & the surgeon of the 8th New York Regiment made me a present of a hospital knapsack.

I was close enough to the battle to hear it all & see the Yankees running. We made a march of 21 miles in 4 hours to be at the fight but got up in time to see them all running. If we had not been ordered to the support of our troops at Stone Bridge, we would have captured the whole army, as we had been ordered across Bull Run to attack the enemy in the rear & had got in ½ a mile of them & were ordered back to help our troops at the bridge & missed all the glory.[40] The federalists didn't have a single organised company in their retreat. We captured every thing they had, even to blankets & clothes.

Our loss is between 700 & 1000.[41] We captured 4 batteries, Sherman's, Patterson's, West Point & a Rhode Island battery.[42] I have seen them. The boys are about 6 miles from me at the battle ground, all well & c. I can't tell you all the news as I am tired out from hard exertion & c. Have been ever since our retreat from Fairfax, living on crackers & bacon, without a fire & without a shelter. Have just got up my tent & got my baggage here today. I don't feel sick but tired. No sickness with our troops at all, all got healthy & ready to fight. We are looking every day for orders to move to Washington, & when we do we will leave our tents & baggage behind.[43]

I will write to you again in a few days & give you more news.

M. W. Francis

John C. Francis to Amy I. Francis
Manassas Junction, July 25th 1861

Dear Mother,

I have not written to you I believe since I left. I hope you will excuse me for negligence. No doubt you have had some uneasiness since you heard of the battle at this place. We were stationed at Winchester expecting an attack from Gen. Patterson when we received orders from Gen. Johnson to move to this place.[44] We started on a forced marched at 2½ o'clock Thursday evening. We traveled across the Blue Ridge to the Shenandoah River, got there about twelve o'clock at night, slept on the ground until daybreak. We then waded the river and traveled in within twenty-five (25) miles of this place to a little place called Piedmont. We were delayed there until Monday morning 3 o'clock when we got a train for this place.[45] I believe we could have been here and *would* have been here if our officers had not sent their horses on. I believe that is the only reason they would not let us come.

When we were ordered to march Monday morning our captain told all those who were the least sick or thought that could not stand it, to step out. We thought then that we would be fighting in six (6) hours, not a single one of our men stepped out, all anxious to go. When we got here we heard every thing that could be thought of nearly. There were a great many killed & wounded. Our boys from Selma all came out safe. Jim was the only one that was wounded. Two buckshot struck him on the left arm about three inches above the wrist. One of the shot was burried in the flesh, the other stuck in the same place. He pulled one out with his fingers, and I believe Miller got the other out. It was only a slight wound. Did not injure any of the bones only a flesh wound. I visited the battleground yesterday and it is quite a bad spectacle. See the men laying dead all over the ground, some shot in one place with musket ball and perhaps torn all to pieces with a cannon ball. You can count from one place nearly one hundred (100) dead men and horses in proportion. They have buried all of our men and are now burying the Yankees. Jim got a minie musket that he will send to you. Gabe got him one. Miller got two or three. Jim got a fine horse he gave it to Miller.[46] Miller is busy fixing up the wounded Yankees.[47]

There are various reports of the killed and wounded. We have about

800 and I heard some one say that the Yankees report 13,000 killed, wounded and taken prisoners.[48] I expect you will hear all about it before you get this so I will close. Tom and I are well and doing well. You must excuse this paper for I have no better. We left all of our baggage in Winchester. Give my love to all. I have not received but one letter from home since I left and that was through Mr. Mitchell.[49]

Your son,
John

John C. Francis to James C. Francis
Camp Bristoe near Manassas
August 19th 1861

Dear Father,

Judge Walker,[50] Mr. Morague[51] & Crook arrived here yesterday evening.[52] I got the letters that Emma and Willie wrote. The only ones since you left. Was glad to know that all were well. There is no news of importance here now. We are in camp about four (4) miles west of Manassas.

The health of our regiment is about as it was when you left.[53] We have lost one of our men since our arrival at this camp, Doc Watkins.[54] There has been four deaths in the regt. All the sick boys in our company are on the mend. John Walker[55] & Keeling are considered now out of danger.[56] Macon Abernathy is a great deal better and thinks he will be up in a few days. He is staying in Tom's tent.[57] George Turnley, Lou Grant, Renfro and all the rest of the boys are doing finely. We concluded today that we could not get along in our mess well together and had a division and am now with Macon, George, Lou, Tom & Mun. We had everything to buy when we were with the other boys and besides that we had as much of the work to do.

When Judge Walker brought the letters to the boys it seemed to make them full of life, all in high spirits. It created a great change in the boys for we seldom get letters by mail. This is either because those at home don't write or the mails miscarry them.[58] Lieut. Whatley has gone out with Crook & Walker to show them the battleground. If anybody can give them the dots, Crog can, for he makes inquiry every where he goes about the battle who was engaged and all about it.[59] Uncle John is doing finely. Have me a heavy pair of boots made with the legs long for winter.

It has been raining off and on for four or five days and we have not had a single drill in that time.

I have not been to see Jim since I came over here but will go tomorrow. He has been in our camps twice since we came. Cy is getting along very well.[60] I have not seen Miller since you left. I think his reg't. is between Fairfax C. H. and Alexandria.[61] Tell Emma & Willie that I will answer their letters in a few days. I don't see what Pelham meant by publishing that letter from John.[62] I think it will injure him. I never want any extracts from my letters published. The boys think a great deal of a letter from home and I think they ought to write often. Letters for our company ought to be always directed in care of *Capt. Forney* because that is the only way that the P. M. knows where to send it.[63]

Your son,
John

John C. Francis to Mary Emma and Willie C. Francis
Bristoe near Manassas, Va.
August 22nd, 1861

Dear Sisters Emma & Willie,

I received both your letters by hand and am glad that you *do* send some by hand as it seems that you never start any otherwise. If you do I meet with the bad luck never to get any. Perhaps you are all out of ink if so take a pencil. If you can get no writing paper take some other kind. I don't see why you and can't write every week. I write home every week some time two or three times but don't get one once a month. You must do better than that.

Our major (Bradford) has resigned and left yesterday. We had an election today and Lieut. Whatley beat the formost man 70 votes but we will have to have another ballot tomorrow, as he did not receive a majority of the whole. If he is elected by the reg't. it may be that Pope Walker will appoint some one else.[64] I saw Jim the other day he was doing finely. They are in camp about mile from us. We can get off but seldom to see him as military laws are very strict. Pete Turney has been sick for several weeks with the typhoid fever but is now nearly well.[65] Macon Abernathy is getting well. George Turnley has been sick for a few days but is now nearly well, but he don't believe it. He is badly scared for fear he is taking the fever. I expect he will be up and going about tomorrow. There is but little sickness in our company now. John Walker is getting well. John Weaver died yesterday.[66] We have no other dangerous cases in our company. I am getting along finely having good health. Lou & Mun are both well. We have had six men to die in our reg't. since our arrival in this camp.[67] My love to all. Write soon.

Your brother,
John

~

John C. Francis to James C. Francis
Camp Bristoe near Manassas, Va.
August 29th, 1861

Dear Father,

As Judge Walker intends to start home tomorrow I concluded to write a few lines home.[68] I am in good health at this time so is Tom & Jim. Miller was over here a few days ago and was looking better than I ever saw him. He says that he has gained about twenty pounds since he left Ala. I was over to see him and Pete yesterday. Pete's health is not very good at this time. He is just recovering from an attack of typhoid fever. We have lost about twelve men in our regt. since our arrival at this place. Three of whom belong to our company. George Turnley is complaining a little, but is not much sick. He is nearly scared to death for fear he will be sick. Tatum was taken sick on Friday and died Tuesday.[69] Lou Grant is getting along finely. Mun R. is doing as well as he could anywheres. John Walker is still mending. There is none of our company dangerous now. Macon Abernathy is now sitting up writing home. Major Abernathy is still here and does not know at what time he will leave not until Macon is entirely well.[70] We are expecting marching orders tomorrow or next day. We don't know where we will go but perhaps to Leesburgs fifty (50) miles from our present camp. We march on foot as usual. Cy is as fat as a hog. We must get the major's stick for him by the time he gets back. Tell the little girls that they must write oftener and more at a time. My love to all.

Your son,
John

Miller W. Francis to Amy I. Francis
Sangsters X Roads, Va.
August 31st 1861

Dear Mother,

I have not written to you since I left. The reason is that it has been a difficult matter for me to find time to write to Father, Julia as often as I desired, not because they were uppermost in my affections, but because I knew you would see all the letters I wrote to Father. For you know dear Mother, I love you and have as much respect for you as a son could. If there is any thing on earth I adore, it is my kind and affectionate Mother. The person who gave me birth who trained, educated and who has watched over me, & through her tender regard for my well being since I was a child, has always advised me for my good. I know that I have in my wild & unthoughtful moments, given you trouble, have caused you sleepless nights, & troublesome thoughts, but I have always regretted those acts and if they were to do over again, the same cause would not exist for it.

Mother I am engaged in a cause, that we are all concerned in and one that will give you & has given you a great deal of trouble & anxiety, and you have cause for it. You in particular are deeply interested having 4 sons, who are liable at any time to die or be killed, but one of my brothers has passed through the terrible ordeal of a glorious victory. He has won for himself an undying reputation, he is worthy of his Mother, & of the cause. He is well & in excellent health. I was down to see him Tom and John last Monday & stayed all night with Tom. They are all in as good health as you ever saw them. All look stouter than they do at home. I think John will have better health than he would at home.[71]

Tell Julia I received her nice present of pickles & they are on my table at every meal & I am continually reminded of her by them. The socks were nice but John is only a private & I gave them to him, as he does not have the same chance to buy them that I have, & they may save the poor boy from suffering at sometime from cold.[72] Mother a privates life is a hard one. They are worse than Negroes, when they do not have kind officers, but the company John is in has kind and indulgent officers. He is well treated, and as much favor shown him as can be. Jim was in command of Goldsby's company the day I was there, as the officers were sick or off. I wish you could see us all at once, all in excellent health and me the healthiest looking one of all. I weigh 170 pounds, & am in as good health as I ever was.

Father wrote about winter clothing. I want 1 fine pair black pants for dress, 1 heavy pair of grey pants, two heavy woolen outside shirts, two heavy woolen drawers, two pair yarn socks, 1 heavy pair boots long legs stitch down soles, and a heavy overcoat of grey cloth if he can get it, of the Selma style, like the one he saw me have.[73] Gabe will want his blankets, two pair heavy kersey pants, a heavy kersey coat, a heavy overcoat, tolerable long, a heavy pair winter boots, two heavy flannel shirts, two pair heavy drawers.[74] He says his overcoat is too short. They are at home. When they are sent they must be directed to Fairfax Station by the Southern Express Company, and they will come safe.[75] The other boys are at 1 Bristow.

Now I will tell you what we are doing. Our troops are at Munson's Hill 5½ miles from Washington City and in full view of the White House & Georgetown. They are skirmishing there every day, & it would not surprise me if we had a general fight there before long. Our troops have all left Manassas but a few and are advancing towards the Potomac.

Tell Julia I saw Major Abernathy but didn't have time to write by him but will write to her tomorrow or next day. I will send some more money home, in a short time, as we are making out our pay rolls now & will get the money in a short time. Will send about $275 when we draw as the government owes me $324 today.[76] I am very comfortable situated in every way. Tell the little girls howdy for me, & tell them to write to me. Tell Tobe he must write, & tell Clark & Tom we have a brass band in our regiment that plays every day & night & we have fine music.[77] Dr. Clark and John are well. I am about 12 miles from them. Write to me dear Mother. It is a great deal of consolation to even hear that you are all well. Write often, direct to Fairfax Station. I hope we will all meet in health at our dear home once more. Goodbye.

Your son,
Miller

P.S. The time is passing off slowly, but I do not take note of the days as I am always busy with the poor sick soldiers. Tell Julia to keep in good spirits as it will not be long before we will be with each other to stay together as long as we live. I wish we had peace once more & we were free.

John C. Francis to Amy I. Francis
Camp Bristoe near Manassas, Va.
September 1st 1861

Dear Mother,

Major Abernathy intends to start home in the morning and I believe I will write you a few lines to let you know that I am getting along finely as well as Jim, Tom, & Miller.[78] I have not seen James in several days but know to be doing finely for we are in camp one half mile from each other. I have not seen Miller since I wrote last. Thomas is enjoying fine health. Lou Grant is doing as well as anyone in camp. Tom Walker is doing finely. Mun Renfro is as hearty as can be. George Turnley is complaining a little but is not very sick nor no likelyhood of it. All of the boys from about town are well and hearty. Most of the sickness is among the country boys. Hodges is pretty sick but not dangerous.[79] We have none dangerous in our company at the present time.

We have had quite a frolic since yesterday morning. Our colonel told us that he intended to pay us off but would have an inspection first. We proceeded to that about 12 o'clock at dress parade. In the evening orders were given to have a general inspection this morning at 8 o'clock. We then had to clean our guns, hunt up our haversacks, knapsacks and the like and see that they were in order so it kept us very busy all the time, but after all this there is no money yet. Each private gets about forty dollars ($40) in Confederate bonds. I suppose though it is the understanding that we receive our pay tomorrow morning but I doubt whether we get it then or not. We get plenty to eat and that very good. We can buy chickens, butter, eggs, cabage, onions and in fact almost any thing we want. We will not suffer as long as we stay about here. We pay 2$ for chickens, 2$ for eggs, 2$ for butter, 2 cents for cabage, 5 cents a dozen for onions and 10 cents for peaches and poor ones at that.[80]

We have not received orders yet to march. Blunn,[81] Fleishl[82] and several other Germans applied to Gen. Johnson for a permit to go to Richmond to attend some religious ceremonies but was refused. Johnson told them he could not spare any of his men as he did not know one day what would be done the next. Pete Turney is now nearly well of the fever. I am getting so I can cook a very good meals victuals. I have been making soup for our sick for several days. If you don't believe we know how ask Major Abernathy. He eat with us one meal. You will see Major Abernathy and he can tell you more than I can. Tell the little girls to write often and when they back their letters put "*Care of Capt. Forney 10th Reg't. Ala. Vols.*" or I will never get it. My love to all.

Your affectionate son,
John

Nathaniel D. Renfroe to James C. Francis
Richmond, Va., Sept 9th/[18]61

Dear Sir,

Admidst the confusion of some 3,000 soldiers, I make the effort to fulfill my promise made you the morning the Calhoun Sharp Shooters left Jacksonville.[83] Believing that you have our accounts of our journey up here, I pass that by. Two of our boys are in the hospital, viz. John Martin[84] & Thos Johnson.[85] They have the measles, are rapidly improving. James Crow,[86] Stephen Carter are also unable to drill but will likely recover without going to the hospital.[87] There is an excellent hospital provided in town for the accomodation of the sick from Ala. Tis a large, commodious neat brick building well furnished.[88] The rest of the company are well and well pleased. Exceedingly merry. In fact no one, who has any life at all, could become low spirited here, amid so may lively boys their jokes, puns, songs, hallowing, laughing & c., would keep the one most prone to despondency lively and courageous.

All express the greatest satisfaction with our capt., he is an excellent fellow. And I confess that I have been deceived in Capt. Bush. It is not usual for one of his age, to be possessed of so much cool, calm deliberation as he is. The military officer, of all other men should be a dispassionate thinker free from excitement this Capt. B. is just such a man.[89] With him to lead them, I feel safe in saying that the Calhoun S. S. if the war continues long will do deeds, and win laurels of which will reflect on their justly honored county much glory and which will make one of the brightest pages in the history of the present war. Our anxiety to move on to meet the foe is daily increasing but we know nothing as respects the time that we will leave here. Our guns are yet to be repaired. We are finely well drilled.

The more I see and learn of the Virginians, the less I like them. A vast majority of them refuse to be mustered into service for more than 12 months with the understanding too that they will not go out of the state to fight. Go into town and you can see hundreds of jack-leg-boys struting up and down the streets who evidently look with contempt on the soldiers.

Could we have this class separated from the patriotic citizens. I would glory in fighting the first battle in Richmond.

There is much sickness in the camp grounds and increasing. A bro. soldier seated by my side, writing, tells me that three have died in his company this morning and another is now dying. They die from the typhoid fever.[90] It may be expected for us all to die unless our fair is changed. The Calhoun S. S. have round tents about ten feet in diameter a little hole in one side, have to get on our knees and crawl in, fifteen men to each tent. The heat is very oppresive through the day and a greater part of the night. Any man with sense knows that fifteen men will soon fill this space with impure exhaled air it has no way of escape. This would kill alligators much less men.

There are some ten Yankee deserters here. They say that they were forced into service and that those who first volunteered in the North done so under the impression that a mere mob had risen up south to burn Washington. That when they discovered their delusion they all wished to ground arms. That many in all the battles that have been fought never fired a gun but run so soon as they could. That they will continue so to do that Lincoln may draft a large army but he can't get them to fight. That if we are victors in the next grand engagement the war will then close.

The city papers of this morning report that all the ports are open. This is generaly believed as true. The report has been current here for several days passed that Beauregard is in two miles of Washington throwing up breast works.[91] I cannot say that these reports are true.

We have preaching from three to four times per week in the fair grounds. Urge upon the Christians of Jacksonville to remember us in their approaches to the throne of grace. Should you find time I would glad to hear from you. You must excuse bad writing. I have written the greater part of this letter laying on my side with much noise and confusion. My respects to all friends.

Yours truly,
N. D. Renfroe[92]

~

John C. Francis to Joseph H. Francis
Camp Bristoe near
Manassas Junction, Sep. 9/[18]61

Dear Brother Jo,

You must excuse me for negligence as I have had nothing of interest to write and besides that you have never written to me since I left. We are now in camp about four miles (4) west of Manassas and one half mile (½) from Bristoe. We have been here about one month. Lieut. Col. Martin is now commanding this reg't. Col. Forney is acting brigadier gen.[93] I am now acting sergeant-major. There is some probability of me getting that position by promotion.[94] I saw Jim the other day. He was doing well. I have not seen Miller in some time he is stationed about 12 miles towards Alexandria from us. He is with the advance reg'ts. Our pickets and the federalists have a skirmish occasionaly. I was noticing a letter you wrote to Tom a few days ago and you made a mistake by putting the word "over" at the bottom of the page which you ought to avoid.

There is someone nearly every week from Ala. Hon. J. L. M. Curry is here now from Richmond.[95] Bob Wynne left here this morning on an errand for the boys for Richmond and will return tomorrow.[96] Black, Hall & Johnson are here now. We are on suspense all the time. We know not what hour we may be called on to march. Thomas is not very well at the present time. Our boys are doing as well as they can. George Turnley is getting well. We drill twice a day about 2 hours each. I am enjoying fine health and have ever since I came into camp. *Why* have you not written to me? We never hear any news here is the reason I don't write oftener. Give my regards to all. Write soon.

Your brother,
John

John C. Francis to Amy I. Francis
Camp Bristoe near Manassas
September 11th 1861

Dear Mother,

Mr. Hall will leave for Jacksonville in the morning and I will send a few lines by him though I wrote the other day by Mr. Curry. I am enjoying fine health. Can eat as much as any Negro. I made a peach pie today and it was as nice and good as any I ever eat. We get plenty of almost everything here now—peaches, apples, melons (few), milk, butter, eggs & c. Thomas' health is not very good. He has obtained a furlow of thirty (30) days and will start to Richmond tomorrow morning. He thinks that he will go on to Jacksonville in a few weeks.[97] Jim was over here yesterday, looking well. We are expecting orders every day to leave. Can't tell when we will go. All the boys are improving who are sick. The well ones are doing as well as they can. Lou & Tom are well. I don't know that I ever had better health. I don't know any news therefore will close. Give my love to all.

Your son,
John C. Francis

~

John C. Francis to James C. Francis
Camp Bristoe near Manassas
Sept. 17th 1861

Dear Father,

I hardly know what to write as we are here where we get no news and it is the same thing with us one day after another. I am getting along very well. I am still acting sergeant-major and don't know when I will get the appointment but not long. For I am almost confident from what the adjutant & col. says, that I will get it. All of our boys are getting along finely.

We had orders yesterday evening to cook one days provisions for we expected marching orders last night or this morning but as yet we have not received them and Capt. Forney thinks there is no probability of us getting them soon. We are ordered to keep one days provisions ahead don't know at what moment we may have to start. Tom is now in Richmond. He left here a few days ago for Richmond on a furlow of thirty days. We reported sixty-five men ready to march. Ponder died yesterday[98] and Plixco today both of fever.[99] Macon Abernathy is now at Orange CH doing very well. George Turnley is about well. I never get any letters from home by mail. I don't know why it is. Uncle John is well so is Lou Grant and Renfro. Tell Mother I am very much oblige to her for my haversack as it is very useful. Tell the *maker* it is very nice and I apreciate it very highly. Col. Forney is now out on the Potomac. Give my love to all and tell the little girls to write. I must close as my candle (rather Capt. F.'s, we don't get any now) is nearly out. Nothing more at present.

Your son,
John

~

John C. Francis to James C. Francis
Centerville, Va., October 3rd 1861

Dear Father,

I have now a favorable opportunity of writing you a few lines as Mr. Sisson,[100] Burton[101] & Nesbit intend starting this morning.[102] There is nothing of interest I believe. I am getting along finely. I saw James just before we left Camp Bristoe. He is now out on the Potomac somewhere. I have not heard from him since he went out there. I went up to Miller's camp the other day. He was out on picket. I received the goods you sent by Sisson day before yesterday. I received three jars of pickles, three cans preserves, seven pipes & three cakes of soap. I received the other day by Mr. Wiles two shirts & pr. of socks. The boys are in fine spirits and anxious to get a fight out of the Yankees. I reckon Miller will be down as soon as he gets off pickett. Tom I suppose is at home now. I saw Tom Renfro the other day he was doing well.[103] What did you do with the stick I sent to Major Abernathy? I must close as Mr. Sisson will leave in a few minutes. Nothing more.

Your son,
John

John C. Francis to Amy I. Francis
Camp near Centerville
Nov. 7th 1861

Dear Mother,

The cause for me not writing more is I have nothing of interest to write. I received a note from Jim this morning stating that he was on his way to Richmond. He was sick while at Dumfries but was improving.[104] I know he is improving from the fact that he wrote to me from Dumfries a few days ago and stated that he was hardly able to sit up and the last note I received he was at Bristoe and he could not have written from there unless he was up. He says that he will be back in a few weeks. I saw Miller a few days ago and he was doing well. I am looking for Tom up every day though I have not heard a word from him in some time. My health is very good could not ask better. Miller is stationed six (6) miles from us on Bull Run.

Col. Forney is with his reg't. now. Wilcox is our general.[105] The health of our reg't. is pretty good at the present time. We are now stationed between the suspension bridge on Cub Run and the Stone Bridge on Bull Run. I expect our reg't. will go out on pickett tomorrow and stay five days. Col. Martin is now in Richmond on business for the reg't. The government gave our reg't. a flag and our company had the honor of presenting it to the reg't. Uncle John is still attending to Tom's business.[106] If you see Miss Marion tell her that I saw John Marion today and that he was well.[107] George Turnley is a little sick but nothing serious. Nothing more at present. My love to all.

Your son,
John

John C. Francis to James C. Francis
Camp near Manassas, Va.
Nov. 17th 1861

Dear Father,

I have now a good chance of writing as Mrs. Martin[108] and Mr. Bush intends to start in the morning. I am getting along as well as I would wish. My health is better than it ever was before. We are looking for Tom here every day. Don't know when he will be in. Bush & Farmer have got up their suttler establishment and are selling a great many goods to our brigade.[109] Lt. Whatley is still commanding Capt. Hughes' company.[110] We moved our camps a few days ago from "suspension bridge" to within a few hundred yards (west) of Centerville. We get our mail at the Junction.

Our company is doing well at present. Some of our boys saw Miller at the Junction the other day he was in fine health. Jim is now in Richmond on a sick leave. He was improving the last time I heard from him. The weather is getting pretty bad here. We have had, for the last three days, some very cold weather and up to this time there is no change. Jo Farmer is now sick, I don't know the nature of his disease.[111]

We will draw our pay in a few days. Centerville is now well fortified on every little hill. There are batteries for flying-artillery and also breast works for infantry. Our company built one battery. Our regt. has to go out on picket about once in three weeks. There are supposed to be about forty or fifty thousand troops encamped in sight of our camps.

Serg't. McDaniel of our co. is pretty sick.[112] Brooks is not in good health.[113] P. Turney's reg't. is now stationed in Dumfries. I have not heard from them since they left us at Bristoe. The country about here is almost ruined. We have to carry our wood and water about ¼ of a mile. Our bedding consists of polls laid on two others with straw upon them. While out on pickets we have no tents nor straw. We stay out from four to six days. My boots fit me well and will do me service.

John C. Francis

Thomas W. Francis to James C. Francis
Centerville, Va., Nov. 27/[18]61

Dear Father,

I wrote you from Richmond enclosing $310 in a check on N.O. $70 for Grant, $100 for yourself, and the bal. for my use at home. I send you now $300 by Lt. Castleberry[114] and I wish you to pay my note to Col. Jno. R. Clark whitch is about $175, and you must pay my *taxes.*[115] The balance you can use as you please.

I heard from Jim today he is improving and is up. I got a note from Miller today and I look for him over every day. I understand he is in fine health and looks larger than any of the family. My health is not very good, but I am not exposed any as I do not ride. All were glad to see me, especially cols. Forney & Martin. The former is more social with me than he ever was. I am bound to stay it out if my health does not get worse and Forney says I shall not resign, that I can allways take a leave of absence. He certainly does think a great deal of me.

I will write more in a day or two. Be certain and pay Col. Clark on sight.

Your true son,
T. W. Francis

John C. Francis to James C. Francis
Camp near Centerville, Va.
Dec. 1st 1861

Dear Father,

I believe I wrote home a few days ago but as I have an opportunity now I will write you a few lines. There is nothing of interest about camp now. There is little talk of a fight at this place now but one more likely to take place at Dumfries as the enemy are building batteries on the opposite shore. They feel the effects of the blockade now greatly and I think they will try to raise it. Miller is here tonight. He is in fine health and doing as well as possible. I have heard nothing from Jim in some time but understand he is in a private house at Richmond.

The health of our reg't. & comp'y is pretty good at the present time.

Tom Rowland & Ben Brooks are a little sick now but think they will be up in a few days.[116] Tom's health is improving. He is attending to his business now with promptness. Uncle John is in fine health. We have sent all of our goods except our blankets, one over suit, two undersuits and an overcoat, to the Junction. Jo Farmer is up and going about. Lt. Whatley is again with our company since Captain Hughes' return. In a few days Capt. Forney will make application to get me a furlow to go to Calhoun for the purpose of raising a company. I don't know for certain that he will get it as the generals are so peticular about giving furlows. Luke Mitchell has a substitute and will start home tomorrow morning. Horace Stevenson arrived here yesterday.[117]

I and Swan have written to several of the citizens about Jacksonville concerning a company.[118] See them & speak to them on the subject. They are Dr. Hoke & Judge Woods.[119] Write and let me know about it, and do what you can for me either as capt. or 1st lt.

Thomas is writing to Fannie and will tell you more about things than I can. I have spoken to Capt. Forney about getting a company. He says that (I don't suppose he wants it made public) he intends to raise a reg't. and wants me to have a company to form a part of it. Tell Hop if he can find a leisure moment to drop me a few lines. Tell the little girls to write oftener. I have not received a letter from Emma in sometime. My love to all.

Your son,
John

~

James C. Francis, Jr. to James C. Francis
Richmond, Dec 5th 1861

Dear Father,

I wrote you on the 2nd and as "Col. Martin" is "in rout" for "J.V.", I thought I would drop you a line. I would not be surprised this letter did not reach you first. I am improving in health slowly I begin to feel tolerably strong. The atmosphere about "Richmond" is the meanest in the S. C. There are men here & one (1) from our company that had fever & has been here ever since August & they are not now fit for duty.[120]

I think there is some prospect for a furlough now but this you *must not* let *any one* know, as it was told to me in secrecy & should it get out before it is published then the party divulging would be expelled from his position & a heavy fine imposed.

Congress has passed an act granting furloughs to day. It has not been ratifyed by the "President." Unless he vetoes the measure I think I will get off. The probability is that he will endorse it.[121] My regards to all.

Your son,
Jim C. Francis, Jr.

Thomas W. Francis to James C. Francis
Camp near Centerville
Dec. 13/[18]61

Dear Father,

I have just seen your letter to John by Maj. Bush and was very much surprized at not getting a letter by him. I wrote you from Richmond enclosing check on N. O. for $300 or $310. I do not recollect whitch. I also sent you by Lt. Castleberry of Capt. Truss Company for $300 and by Luke Mitchell $110 to Fannie, and by Jim Martin $140 to you or to Fannie,[122] and I wish you to write me certain about it if it all came. I wrote you to pay Col. Clark my note, also to pay my *taxes*.

You have no idea how much uneasiness I have about the matter as I am afraid that some of it has gone by the board. I sold my horse and Jim Martin's yesterday for $450, mine for $300 and his for $150, and as he is not here I thought it best to send it home by Jno. Henderson.[123] I added $50, making $500 sent by him. Jno. will not be back before my next pay account will be due and then I shall pay him here. I wish you to pay John Easterwood $200 or $300 on the note he holds on me,[124] and then pay Z. Henderson our note due him for land and stop interest.[125] If you have not got the money to spare to pay your half, pay it all out of my money and place a cr. on the note you hold on me for your half. He holds my individual note for the land but half of it is yours. The ballance of the money you can keep for me or use on my debts, or do with it as you may think best. I am doing all I can to save evry cent I get so as to get as near out of debt as I can. I have not heard one word about the farm since I left home. I do not know why Hop could not write occasionally as he has but little to do on Sunday at the plantation.

I hope you have bought plenty of meat for us, and do not forget to furnish Hop with the money to pay for the meat I bought from "Autry."[126] I would buy meat at 12½ ¢ if I had the salt as I think it will be very high next summer and fall.[127] Tell Fannie to pay her Pa for my half of the pork if she got the money by Mitchell & Jim Martin. If she did not you can settle for it. I will write her the same to day. You will of course pay for my part of the pork out of my money. As I before said after paying the debts I have written about I wish you to do with the balance of my means as you think best and as you would with your own.

I wish you would see Nat Cobb and have him to pay you the $36 due me for ballance on settlement.[128] Uncle Dick also owes me $21.12 on our settlement but I have no note for it.[129] I suppose Jim is at home or Selma, and if he is at Selma please send the enclosed letter to him or if he is at home you can give it to him. I wish him to have it certain, for it is on business of importance to me in Selma. When you get the letter be certain and get it to him as soon as possible for I am afraid Hagood will try to chissel me out of the house rent he owes me and Jim can settle with him as he knows how the a/c stands.[130]

I am afraid you give John too much encouragement about making up a company as I think it extremely doubtful about any one being successfull. Be certain and write me about all I have written you particularly about as soon as this letter is recd. Perhaps this letter will reach you before the money reaches you by Henderson. My love to all the family.

Your son,
T. W. Francis

John C. Francis to James C. Francis
Camp near Centerville, Va.
Dec. 13th 1861

Dear Father,

I received yours of the 5th inst. by Mr. Bush contents noted. Capt. Forney told me that there would be no chance for a furlow until we got into winter quarters but if there is a company raised in Calhoun and they elect me as lt. I can come as soon as the company is mustered into service. It matters not if the company is for only twelve months I can be transferred to it as though it was for the war, so Col. Forney says.

There is nothing of interest in camps at the present time. All the boys seem to be in fine spirits. It seems that we will not have a fight at this place during this season. There is no signs of winter quarters yet. I find that the weather is as changeable here as in Ala. I have plenty of blankets I believe though if you see any one passing that can easily bring it send me a quilt. I don't want it until we get into winter quarters. I have plenty at this time. While I think of it, when you see Jim Martin get my watch from him. I will write to him to leave it with you. I will try and send you some money by Major Vernon.[131] I have made a bargen with Tom to let me have money when I need it and settle with him on next pay day and by this means I can send more than I could otherwise. We draw $37.00 and Tom owes me twenty $20.00. I will try and send you fifty $50.00. It does not take much to do us out here as we can buy nothing except at the sutlers and they have nothing that I need.[132] We get the Richmond papers here the morning after they are published for ten cents a piece. I suppose you will hear all about Ben Brooks before this letter reaches you. Nothing more. Write soon.

Your son,
John

Thomas W. Francis to James C. Francis
Centerville, Va.
Dec. 14/[18]61

Dear Father,

I have this day sold to Kahn & Fleishel of Jacksonville, Ala. our crop of cotton at 10¢ on a credit of twelve mos. without interest.[133] I have made this trade because I believe it to be the best thing we could do. The note for the cotton is to be due on the 14th Decr. 1862, less what I owe them & what you owe them ading no interest after today. I have thought over the matter and did not know what was best to do but you not being present I concluded to risk it. By getting that price I can pay very nearly out of my land debt to Hez Ingram. Joe says you can take the Hez Ingram note up if you wish.[134]

I have made this trade for our mutual benefit and if you think it not a good one write me so and I will agree to pay you for your half the cotton in *cash* at the market price when ever you may wish to sell, or I will furnish you as many bales of as good cotton from some other source. Joe further agrees to let me deliver my half the crop if you object to the trade and furnish as many bales as you take out from some other source, to be of like kind. So if you do not like it write me at once and I can get either from Capt. Hanna[135] or Woodruff[136] the amt. that your half is and they will take them for it. By this we can easily pay Hez and I am satisfied that it will be a long time before our cotton will bring 10¢ as it is like evry one else' not very nice on account of so much rain.

I would rather of course you would agree to the trade but if you do not I shall buy as much as your half for them. I want the amt. to go to the payment of the Hez Ingram note for land. I sent you $500 by Jno. Y. Henderson. My health is pretty good.

Your son,
T. W. Francis

James C. Francis, Jr. to James C. Francis
Selma, Decr. 20th/[18]61

Dear Father,

Enclosed I hand you $218.25/100. I sold the gold for 22½ ¢. I send this by "Col. Stevenson."[137] Business is quite dull here. Flour & molasses hold the sway. Molasses so high I can't doe a thing. My opinion is they are obliged to fall, but how soon I can't form an opinion; not very soon, holders say.

"Jo" is in good health. I find my business all strait, but sales are dull. I think if I were to remain here I could swell matters *sharply.* Since my return I have made 2 good bills, I hope & think I will continue as I opened. I shall mark all my stock up. I expect "Mr. Becker" each boat. My health is improving. I send by "Col. Stevenson" some notions for the children, a horn for "Jimmey & Tom," send Julia some of the oranges. There are no fresh nuts in market & I thought it best not to buy the old ones. You will find "Mrs. Clark's" box marked.[138] I hope to here from you occasionally. My love to all in haste.

Your son,
Jim C. Francis

Thomas W. Francis to James C. Francis
Head Quarters 10th Ala.
Centerville, Va.
12 o'ck. A.M., Decr. 21, 1861

Dear Father,

Our regiment & three others were ordered on night before last to Drainsville on a foraging expedition, and when they arrived at the place they were attacked by a large force and suffered very seriously.[139] There is 86 killed wounded and missing. Not many cases mortally wounded. Col. Forney was wounded in the arm four inches below the shoulder, and the ball passed through the musel of his shoulder back of his arm.[140] Miller got here this morning and has just returned from his place of confinement and reports that the medical men say that they hope to save his arm. Col. Martin is dead and left on the field. He fell at the head of division cheering the men on to victory or death. He died like a man at his post.[141] Capt. Forney is slightly wounded in the right leg, about half way from his foot to his knee. It is a very slight wound he never stoped for it.[142]

Jes Harris is rather severely wounded in the neck, but not mortally.[143] Jas. Moragne in the shoulder.[144] Wm. Moragne in the foot.[145] R. A. Wiley slightly in the face.[146] Wm. Mohon, slight in the mouth.[147] Brother Jno was shot through the arm about half way from the hand to the elbow, no bone broken. He suffers a good deal—nothing serious. He will go to Richmond to Doct. Clark, until he gets well.[148] He will soon be able for duty. Miller will advise us for the best about him. Henry Smith from Ball Play is missing supposed to be dead.[149] It was a hard fight but the regiment had to give way. Every one else is safe. Macon was not hurt nor Lou Grant, in fact no one else in the Pope Walker Guards.

Col. Forney & Col. Martin stood up like soldiers. Capt. Forney was brave as any one and has the entire praise of the whole regiment. After Col. Martin fell Capt. Caldwell took charge of the right wing and stood up like a "Pea Cock."[150] The boys say he will do to fight. Evry one speaks highly of his bravery. I have not heard of any flinching in the engagement.

All wished for Doc. Clark but he left us a few days too soon. I will write more tomorrow.

Your son,
Tom

[Margin note] Gutman got a ball shot through his cap.[151] There was a great many narrow escapes.

3 / *Looking for a Fight Every Day*

New Year's Day 1862 found Confederate armies stretched thin, their defensive positions reaching from northern Virginia westward to Tennessee and into the trans-Mississippi. Stricken with typhoid, Union commander George B. McClellan seemed satisfied with a stalemate in Virginia. Even after McClellan's recovery, President Lincoln seemed unable or reluctant to prod him to action. In the West, three disjointed Union armies moved haltingly against their undermanned Confederate counterparts. Under the command of Major General Albert Sidney Johnston, the inadequately armed Rebel forces, with command problems similar to those of the enemy, occupied a thin defensive line that spanned the varied terrain from Columbus to Bowling Green, Kentucky, eastward to Cumberland Gap. Johnston's scattered forces had the awesome task of protecting the "heartland" of the Confederacy while much of the Confederate leadership focused on the war between Washington and Richmond.[1]

Finally, the impasse ended when Brigadier General Ulysses S. Grant moved against Fort Henry on the Tennessee River on 1 February 1862. After a five-day siege, the fort fell on 6 February. This loss opened Alabama to invasion via the Tennessee River. Immediately thereafter three gunboats under Lieutenant S. L. Phelps were ordered up the Tennessee to destroy all Confederate supplies and steamboats. Within two days they reached Florence, burned several steamboats, destroyed large quantities of supplies, and returned downriver to augment the assault on Fort Donelson on the Cumberland River. Fort Donelson surrendered to Grant's force on 16 February, and Nashville was occupied by Brigadier General Don Carlos Buell's Union army on 25 February 1862.[2]

While John and Jim Francis continued their furloughs in the warmer clime of Alabama, Miller and Tom Francis remained with their regiments in the cold of northern Virginia. Miller remained at his post at Davis Ford, where he and Gabe lived comfortably in a small two-room house despite the unpleasant winter weather. In the meantime, his brother Tom escaped the Virginia winter altogether after receiving orders on 12 February 1862 to report to Chattanooga, Tennessee, to serve as assistant commissary of subsistence.[3]

With his brother Jim attending to his business interests in Selma, John Francis, recovering from his wound, used his furlough in Jacksonville to raise a volunteer company. His recruiting efforts continued when his furlough was extended through 20 March 1862 on the recommendation of Dr. Courtney James Clark, family friend and Miller's brother-in-law.[4] Governor John Gill Shorter's proclamation on 12 February announcing President Jefferson Davis's call for twelve additional regiments from Alabama gave John the final boost he needed to raise his volunteer company.[5] Eight days later he formally announced his plans to establish a company in the *Jacksonville Republican* under the headline "To Arms! To Arms!!" He promised each private and noncommissioned officer a $50 bounty when they mustered into service and arms and equipment when they entered camp.[6]

John's volunteer company, dubbed the Sallie Walker Boys, was mustered into service at Jacksonville on 5 March, and nineteen-year-old John Francis was elected captain. Sarah "Sallie" McGehee Walker, wife of state senator Thomas A. Walker, a generous contributor to the Confederacy throughout the war, donated $500 to outfit John's company. When the company was organized as Company B, Thirtieth Alabama Volunteers, at Camp Curry, near Talladega, its muster roll listed ninety-four men: fifteen officers, noncommissioned officers, and musicians and seventy-nine privates.[7]

The Thirtieth Alabama, commanded by Colonel Charles Miller Shelley, numbered 1,100 men in ten companies from Calhoun, Clay, Coosa, Franklin, Jefferson, Randolph, St. Clair, Shelby, and Talladega counties. After several weeks of drilling and training, the regiment marched off to war, cheered by a crowd of onlookers and well-wishers at Talladega, on 7 May 1862.[8] When they arrived at Knoxville, Tennessee, three days later, several of John's men had contracted mumps. The Sallie Walker Boys set up their tents at the Fair Grounds outside Knoxville, where the regiment waited to be armed with Enfield rifles.[9]

With brother John Francis drilling and training his company at Camp Curry, Jim Francis became the focus of a second round of letters promoting his appointment as a commissary in one of the new Alabama regiments. Three prominent Alabama jurists and politicians—Chancellor John Foster, Chief Justice Abram J. Walker, and Senator Thomas A. Walker—wrote letters in March 1862 to Confederate Congressman William P. Chilton and

George W. Randolph, Confederate secretary of war, requesting Jim's appointment as a commissary or quartermaster. Dr. James Carrington Francis also lobbied Congressman Chilton with a similar request. To this barrage of letters, Lieutenant Colonel Thomas J. Goldsby of the Fourth Alabama added a final letter to Secretary Randolph, citing Jim Francis's gallantry at the battle of First Manassas and recommending his appointment as a lieutenant of artillery.[10]

Ironically, despite this second letter-writing campaign to Richmond politicians, Jim's commission and new assignment came through Chattanooga via brother Tom. When John H. Forney was appointed commander of the Department of Alabama and West Florida, he requested that Tom Francis be promoted and transferred from Chattanooga to Mobile. Tom's promotion to major and reassignment to Forney's staff caused his commander at Chattanooga, Brigadier General Danville Leadbetter, to ask him to recommend a replacement as post commissary.[11] He quickly recommended his brother Jim. Leadbetter, in turn, immediately honored Tom's recommendation and requested Jim Francis be commissioned and appointed post commissary. This request was approved by the Confederate adjutant and inspector general, Samuel Cooper, in Richmond on 19 May 1862. A month later, on 11 June, Jim Francis assumed his new position as captain and assistant commissary of subsistence for the District of Chattanooga.[12]

A couple of months before Jim Francis's commissioning in Tennessee, his older brother Miller's fortunes were altering as well. In Virginia, Miller's mounting frustrations with his fellow officers and the medical department and his overall dissatisfaction with the political atmosphere convinced him to submit his resignation on 6 March 1862. Though he gave no specific reason for this action, he sided squarely with a pro-Beauregard faction that was part of a growing anti-Davis, anti-administration sentiment. This faction had emerged in the Confederate army after the first battle of Manassas and had been growing steadily since. Despite his bold take-it-or-leave-it rhetoric, Miller obviously had a plan: he was determined to join Colonel John Tyler Morgan's new Partisan Rangers regiment.[13] His resignation from the Sixth Alabama was finally approved on 7 May, and he returned to Jacksonville in early June 1862. After an extended furlough, his transfer as senior surgeon in Morgan's Fifty-first Alabama Mounted regiment was approved by special order on 25 August.[14]

While these developments were brewing, John Francis plodded on. He and his Sallie Walker Boys prepared for an active campaign in East Tennessee. Hop Francis left Jacksonville intent on joining his brother John's company at Knoxville. But on the way, he stopped at Chattanooga to visit Tom

Francis, who persuaded his younger brother to join the commissary service. Undaunted by Hop's defection and the loss of several men too stricken with measles and mumps to travel, Captain Francis and his comrades in the Thirtieth Alabama marched from Knoxville on 17 May 1862. By late May the Thirtieth Alabama and other elements of Carter L. Stevenson's command occupied the area around Cumberland Gap on the Tennessee-Kentucky border.[15]

As Confederate forces moved through East Tennessee, Union troops under Brigadier General Ormsby McKnight Mitchel occupied much of the Tennessee River Valley in North Alabama. Following Grant's victory at the battle of Shiloh on 7 April 1862, Mitchel led some 8,000 Yankee troops who occupied Huntsville, Alabama, on 11 April and established control over 100 miles of the Memphis & Charleston Railroad. Within days Mitchel also occupied Athens, Decatur, and Tuscumbia and sent his division to run roughshod over several smaller towns while capturing railroad equipment, cutting telegraph lines, and freeing slaves. From late June until the beginning of the Kentucky campaign in August 1862, Major General Don Carlos Buell used Huntsville as headquarters for his Army of the Ohio. This first Union occupation spurred the growth of peace societies and organized opposition to the Confederacy across the North Alabama.[16]

Thomas W. Francis to James C. Francis
Camp 10th Ala. Reg.
Near Lewis House
Jan. 9, 1862

Dear Father,

I have read your letter about the cotton trade with Kahn & Fleishel. I sent you by mail a copy of the agreement between Joe Fleishel and myself. I expect you have received it before this time. Your note and a/cs and my notes & a/cs were to be taken up by us and no interest to be added after the day of sale here but Hez Ingram's note if taken up by us was to be with interest up to the date their note was to come due for our cotton. You and Kahn can agree as to the delivery the best you can.[17]

I believe I would have the gin house fixed up and Hop can get Mr. Rowland's gin. He has a very fine one. There will be but little to do to fix to gin our own cotton, and Rowland will help to do it he wants some place to gin his own crop.[18] I believe I would not plant a seed of cotton or if I did I should not plant more than the 50 acres by the gin house for if that field is planted and well cultivated it will produce more than twice the amount and cultivated as it was last year.[19] I hope Hop will do as much plowing as he can before the spring comes in. I think you had better buy another good yoke of cattle as one yoke is very little service by themselves.

I hope you will buy plenty of pork if it can be had at 10¢ so that we can sell the hams and use the sides and shoulders, for I really believe that bacon will sell for 20¢ in the summer.[20] If you will you may buy 1000 lbs. for me and bacon it up at home or for us both and bacon either at the plantation or your house, but do as you think best. You are there to manage it. I wish you would write to me exactly what you have received and what you have paid out and to whom for me, and what Fannie has paid for pork so I may know exactly how much I have on hand. I sent home gold to you or Fannie one and I do not wish it disposed of at all. It is worth here 50 & premium or three for two.[21] I hope you can pay Zimeria Henderson the land note for if he don't get his money he will have a fit and I want to be out his sort of hands.

I do not know what I think of my health for I am not in condition to ride on horse back and I have some very hard spells that last me two or three days. I am afraid that I shall have to resign and go home, though I have told no one as yet nor do I intend to do so long as I think I can keep up. The surgeon thinks I should have a furlough but I am not going to take a furlough again but if I see I am not able to perform I will resign. I sent $100 by Jno. He would use what he wished and pay back when he got home. I have not heard a word from him since he left Wilmington, nor have I heard from Jim. I wrote to him about business of importance in Selma. I have not seen or heard from Miller since the 21st Decr., I have no idea where he is located, I wrote to him only a day or so since. Tell Jno. that we do not know whether Capt. Forney will be made Lt. Col.[22] or not but if he is there will three or four candidates for the vacancy of Lt. Jno. Cobb,[23] Mon Renfrow[24] & McDaniel,[25] & I think Bill Finley.[26] If he was here he would make a good race, and if I see any chance for him I will have his name run, but we cannot tell anything about it.

I hope you will write often and give me all the news. Half the regiment is on pickett and the weather is very bad, worse than I expected so early in the winter. My love to Mother and tell her to write to me. Love to all the children & to Jim & Thom. I will write to Emma & Willie soon.

Your son,
T. W. Francis

Thomas W. Francis to James C. Francis
Camp 10th Ala. Regt.
Near Lewis House Va.
January 18, 1862

Dear Father,

Joe Kahn got here a few days since and I received the bundles, and your letter by him.[27] I was glad to get the articles for I was really wanting some good sausage. I wrote to the little girls a day or two since by mail. I gave to Joe Kahn on yesterday $130.00 that Miller left with me to send to Julia. He said he was going to try to get a furlough in a few days to go home for a short time but I have no idea he will be able to get a furlough for any length of time for the Yankees have not struck a lick toward going into winter quarters nor do we expect them to go at work for a good while yet if they do at all.

Genl. Johnson was at Col. Forney's room the other day and he said to Col. Forney that he expected some very hard fighting this winter and that nothing but sick furloughs would be granted under the present circumstances. We are rather expecting the Burnside fleet to go into the Rapahannoc and attack on line at Evansport.[28] If that is done it will be a general movement of both armies but if we are not attacked then I have no idea when it will commence. The whole army has been for several days ordered to have three days rations of hard bread when it can be issued at a moments warning & from that order and other facts that we have we are led to believe that our forces will have a fight yet during the winter.[29] If the fight should come I rather fear the consequences for our troops are very much in need of discipline. I know that our regiment is in a very bad condition perhaps worse than any regiment in this portion of the army.

I got a letter on yesterday from John dated the 4th inst. in which he says he thinks he could raise a company if he could get the authority to do so. I have my doubts about his success but I have written to Mr. Curry & Doc Clark at Richmond & asked them to call on the sec. of war and get permission from him for John to raise the company. I think the Doc will stir Curry up to it and he will get permission if it is possible to do it. Capt. Forney will probably be at home by the 1st Feby. and if he is he could do a great deal for John & I know he would be willing to do all he could.[30] Col. Forney is doing very well and I have no doubt but what his arm will be very nearly as good as it was. He is growing very impatient and wants to get back to his regiment, and perhaps his anxiety will operate badly on him.[31]

Joe Kahn does not bring much news from Ala. except as to the times. He reports plenty of money in the hands of the people, but that none of them pay their old debts, but will buy *goods*. Did you ever see or write to Natt Cobb about the ballance he owes me on the cotton? If you have not done so please attend to it as soon as you can for if the matter lies too long I shall loose it all. And when you settle with Uncle Dick Ingram don't forget the ballance he owes me. He did not give me any note for it. I wrote you the amt. of it, and he will recollect it.[32]

My health is not very good but I still hope it will improve so that I can stand the winter. You must write often and give me all the news. My love to all the family.

Your son,
T. W. Francis

~

Thomas W. Francis to James C. Francis
Camp near Lewis House, Va.
Jany. 21/[18]62

Dear Father,

As Joe Kahn leaves in the morning I will write you on my business matters. You will find enclosed Wm. Henry's recpt. in full for the ballance of rail road stock due him. He promised to deliver the obligation that he had on me for the stock, but if he does not do so you must hold this recpt.[33] I do not know but what Esqr. Douthit may have some paper connected with the matter.[34] If he has you can show the recpt. and get the paper. I thought it best to settle it with the cash in the way I did.

You have not wrote about the money I sent by Jno. Y. Henderson. I sent $500, I wrote you to pay Easterwood two or three hundred dollars. If you have not done so pay him two hundred and the note we owe Henderson, for the Dulaney land ought to be paid[35] and I want my a/c to Blun & Frank paid it is not a great deal.[36] I shall need all the money I have at home during the next two months and I would like to know exactly how it stands.

I understand that Rowland has made a new rise in the way of money & Negroes, and will either have to sell or buy more land. Suppose you were to send him word that you would sell him half of our place and make the line where I spoke of making it between you and I, or even the section line. I would be willing to sell all on the lower half at $15, but do as you please and if we could make that trade and buy Downings place we would be well fixed, and have a fine mill seat, and I should like to have a first rate mill.[37]

We are having very bad weather indeed. I think Henry Forney will not be made Lt. Col. but that Maj. Woodward will be Lt. Col. & Henry will be Major.[38] You must write often.

Yours truly,
T. W. Francis

John C. Francis to Joseph H. Francis
Jacksonville, Ala.
Jan. 21/[18]62

Dear Brother Jo,

You must excuse me for not writing to you sooner. I would have done so, if I had not thought that Maj. Bush would see you and tell you what I desired him to.[39] I don't know of anything of interest to write you more than I am doing as well as I could wish. My arm is improving very fast I think. I want to start back to Va. in about three weeks. My furlow is out on the 23rd of February. I am very fearful that I will not be able to do my duties in that time.

Think I will come down to Selma in about 6 or 8 days if I can get off. Dr. Clark arrived at home last night.[40] I have not heard from camps since the 3rd. The boys were all getting along very well at that time. Dr. Clark says that Capt. Forney has been appointed Major of our regt. and Woodward Lt. Col., contrary to the wishes of the men. The men wanted Forney to be made Lt. Col., but a recent law prohibited it. Get acquainted with Dr. Rivers of Summerfield he is the pres. of the female col. there.[41] Nothing more at present.

Your brother,
John

Miller W. Francis to James C. Francis
Davis Ford, Va.
January 28th, 1862

Dear Father,

I have not written to you for sometime. It is not for any disrespect or anything of that kind, but from being very busy. Since our move to this point the sick list has gradually increased from 30 or 40 to as high as 158 very near every case diarrhoea. Have had but 3 deaths in 2 months, one away from the regt. & the other 2 from causes that were uncontrolable, aneurism & tetanus. Our present sickness is from the water we are of necessity compelled to use, but we are remedying that as rapidly as possible. My health is excellent. Gabe is quite sick from diarrhoea but is better than he has been.[42]

There is a good deal of excitement here in regard to reenlistment. A large majority of our 12 months men will go home when their time is out. If the system of furloughs that Genl. Beauregard attempted to establish had been carried out almost all of them would enlist for the war. It was this, he sent an order that he would grant 30 day furloughs to 10 privates in each company & 2 capts. & 5 lieuts. in each 12 months regt. but as the furloughs were going to him the order was suspended. That number of men would have comprised almost every man that wanted to go home, instead of that now, they will all or a large majority of them go home in May. We will be compelled to fall back from the position we hold at this time & God knows where we will take up another.

The department at Richmond has acted very unwisely in regard to the bill they have pursued. It is very unsatisfactory to the volunteers and the few that have enlisted for the war, have been refused their furloughs and they have determined, to remain until their time is out & then go home when their time is up.[43] They will go in spite of all remonstrance & entreaty on the part of government, & they will leave at the time their services are most needed. It will be in the midst of active operation, & when they leave there will be no more troops to take their places, & if they do, they will have to undergo all that we have done, all on account of the manner in which they have been treated in this army by superior officers. How easy it would have been to retain our troops here, that have become veterans, that no troops in the world could whip. One of our regts. that are here now are equal to any 3 new ones that can be sent here. They have passed through all the sickness & acclimation, drilling, & all little things that tend to make an army, such as sickly men. They are picked troops now, & the world can't beat them.

What an oversight, what a blunder was committed by heads of departments. It seems that they have considered that they were the masters & the men were slaves. They have not taken into consideration, that they were no more interested in this war than the poorest private. They have not considered that they were placed at the head of this government by the people, & that they have come out to endure it all, to keep them in their places. The reasoning of the men is this, what is the difference between masters if we are to be slaves & trampled underfoot, what is the difference whether it is Lincoln or Jeff Davis?[44] Stevens is the man for the volunteers, he it seems is the only one in power that takes the proper view of the matter.[45]

The 4th Ala. will go home to a man, no reenlistment, the expression here is let the *damned* scoundrels that are at home, come out & try it awhile, instead of remaining at home and growing rich off of our wives & children.[46] I am solicited by the medical director to remain in the army.[47] If they let me go home before spring I am willing to accept of my present position if not I shall be home in May. Genl. Beauregard leaves in a few days for Columbus, Ky. with the express understanding that he comes back here in time for the spring campaign.[48] He says he would not leave under any other considerations. He doesn't think there will be a fight here before spring. They will give the 12 months men hard work to do before their time is out.

I am in a comfortable house, good floor in it, fireplace & windows two rooms. Gabe is in one room & cooks there.[49] I don't know what I shall do, yet, unless I can go home before the time of the enlistment of our regt. is out I shall go home with them, as I am very anxious to see my dear wife & little children & my dear old Mother & Father, little sisters & brother. I have undergone troubles & hardships that nothing but feelings for my family & relatives as well as country would have made stand it this long. Nothing but indomitable will & conscience would have made stand it. It has been an arduous undertaking, but character & reputation is at stake & it is a full determination of mine to carry out my part with credit & honor to myself & name.

My kind regards to all friends. Write soon.

Your son [Miller]

Furlough Extension for John C. Francis
Jacksonville, Alabama
Feb. 15, 1862

I certify that I have carefully examined John C. Francis a private in Capt. Wm. H. Forney's Company (G) 10th Alabama Regiment and find him incapable of performing the duties of a soldier because of a gunshot wound of the left fore arm received in the fight at Drainsville Va. Dcr. 20th 1861.

It is my opinion that his arm, wrist, and hand, will not be in a fit condition for him to resume his duties, with safety before the 20th day of

March next and I therefore respectfully recommend an extension of his furlough to that time.

C. J. Clark[50]
Surgeon, P. A. C. S.

~

John C. Francis to John T. Montgomery[51]
Jacksonville, Ala.
Feb.16th 1862

Dear Cousin John,

I am now raising a volunteer company *for the war* and wish you to do what you can for me about Spring Garden.[52] I will be furnished with arms as soon as we are mustered into service. Tell them that we expect to get off in about three or four weeks. We only commenced a few days ago and have now about thirty or thirty-five. If you wish to go we would like very much to have you go with *us* as we have very nice men to go with us. We elect our officers when organised.[53] My love to the family. All well.

Yours & c.,
John C. Francis

~

Sallie Walker to John C. Francis[54]
Jacksonville, Ala.
March 6, 1862

Sir,

Your note of this date is at hand informing me that in organizing your company on yesterday, it received the name of "Sallie Walker Boys" in honor of myself.[55]

I can assure you and each one of your command, the unexpected and undeserved compliment, is highly and duly appreciated, by one whose ardent hope is, that you and your company may have a bright and brilliant future in the defense of your native land. I trust that each one of you, will press forward to meet the heaviest mettle of the enemy, with a pace as steady as time and with a conviction and firmness as secure as the base of your native mountains.[56]

I trust you all will ever bear in mind that your country-women look with confidence to the gallant and patriotic men and boys of Alabama to shield, protect and defend them from a wicked and heartless invading foe. In your march forward, let your trust be in the Great Ruler of the destinies of men, and with the prayers of your country-women, the patriotic cause of your sunny South will certainly prevail and your arms crowned with victory.

For the purpose of aiding you in obtaining an out-fit for your company, herewith I enclose 500 dollars. You will please present my grateful acknowledgments to each and everyone of your command, for the honor conferred in naming your company for me.[57]

I am sir, truly your obt. servt.,
Sallie Walker

~

John C. Francis to James C. Francis
Camp Curry near Talladega, Ala.[58]
March 15th 1862

Dear Father,

We arrived here on Thursday morning about eight o'clock and found everything in readiness for us.[59] Though we had a rather bad time for a commencement as it had been raining and the ground was damp we pitched tents. I then made the boys cut pine polls for their tents and about twelve I managed to get two loads of straw which when properly fixed made the boys very comfortable. All the boys seem to be well satisfied and are getting along very well. Manning Kimbrell was slightly sick from his drunken spree.[60] I only had one drunk man on our way down here they all behaved very well. We have had only two drills since our arrival on account of the bad weather. There are only three companies here besides my own. I think there is a very good chance to make Henry Forney our colonel.[61] I will write you again in a few days.

Your son,
John C. Francis

~

John C. Francis to James C. Francis
Camp Curry
April 3rd 1862

Dear Father,

I have nothing of importance to write you now as you have heard the news through those passing. My boys are doing very well. Dan Beacham is a little sick this morning nothing but cold.[62] Chamness[63] & Wolfe have been sick for a day or two but are now up and about.[64] Gober is complaining some.[65] Thos Finch is in town at the hospittel is getting well I saw him yesterday.[66] Col. Shelley left here this morning for Richmond.[67] Johnson is recommended for AQM of the regt.[68] Story for commissary.[69] Capt. Patterson for surgeon[70] & Gorman for assistant.[71] I wrote a few lines to Jim by Col. Shelley and told him if he wanted to I would assist in getting him run for his battery & Col. Shelley said that he intended to have a battery attached to his regt. I then asked him to write Jim from Richmond he said that he would do so and take him in to this regt. My co. is the 1st in the regt. The boys are all very well satisfied & have no complaints. My love to all. I will be up the first of next week.

John

James C. Francis to William P. Chilton[72]
Jacksonville, Ala.
April 3rd 1862
Hon W. P. Chilton[73]
Richmond, Va.

Dr Sir,

From my long acquaintance with you I take liberty of addressing you this note asking you if not drafting too much upon you take an interest in behalf of my son James C. Francis. I wish him appointed either quarter master or commissary of one of the 12 regiments now forming in Ala.

I will not say any thing as to his qualifications for the position but will say if appointed he will not disappoint the expectations of his friends. The enclosed letters are from our mutual friends. All of the writers having known James from childhood.[74]

I now have four sons in the army and expect another to go in a short time. My all is staked in this resolution. I hope we will triumph, but sink or swim live or die I am hand & heart in defense of Southern rights.[75]

Hope you will find it convenient to aid me in this matter and by so doing you will place me under the greatest obligations.

Very respectfully,
Your obt. servant,
James C. Francis

John C. Francis to Amy I. Francis
Camp near Talladega, Ala.
April 24th 1862

Dear Mother,

Lt. Carpenter is going up to day and I wish you would make me a bed tick and send it down by him.[76] Make it wide enough for two to sleep on. I wish you would also send me one nice white shirt. There is nothing of importance going on here. I think we will leave here in about ten days, probable that we will go to Va.[77] Excuse brevity as I have to go out on drill, and will not have time after drill. My love to all.

Your son,
John

Mary Emma Francis to Hopkins T. Francis
Jacksonville
April 24, [1862]

Dear Bro.,

As Mr. Fleishel is coming down tonight I will write you a few lines on the back of this letter. I guess you would like to hear from Bro. John & I will not be at the trouble of getting more paper.[78] We are all well at present. We received a letter from Bro. Miller this morning. He was at Yorktown.[79] He was well & the Yankees were close to them & he understands the 4th Alabama were there but he had not heard from Bro. Jim since the 15th of last month. If you hear from him write to us. Tom is at Chattanooga acting as commissary.[80] Xcus this write soon.

Emma

John C. Francis to James C. Francis
Camp near Knoxville, Tenn.
May 12th 1862

Dear Father,

We left Talladega, Ala. on last Wednesday morning on open cars.[81] Done very well all day arrived at Selma about three o'clock P.M. found the

"Southern Republic" waiting for us. I found Joe & Uncle Hugh there both doing well. We left for Montgomery about five P.M. I managed to get very comfortable quarters for my boys during the night though we were considerably crowded.[82] We arrived at Montgomery about day light marched up near town and there remained until evening. In the meantime we drew knapsacks, canteens, haversacks, cartridge boxes, belt & cap boxes, blankets, shirts & c. We left Montgomery, six companies under Lt. Col. Bradford,[83] about 7 P.M. for Chattanooga expecting to be overtaken at West Point by the remaining four companies but when we arrived there (W. P.). The superintendent said that we would have to go on as he could not take the whole regt. on one train therefore we started out for Atlanta.[84] By this time our bread rations were getting short as we left it with Col. Shelley.

When we came to Atlanta we managed to get a little bread & meat & proceeded to Dalton, Ga. where we received orders from Gen. Ledbetter to come to this place.[85] We arrived here about 8 o'clock Saturday night & managed to get something to eat for our men. They eat one days rations at one meal. I went to town yesterday and procured more for them. Col. Shelley has not arrived yet though we expect him every hour. We have no tents now but will get them when Shelley comes. I left Bill Alexander, Reaves, Turner, Niman & Jim White. All have the mumps except White who has the measles.[86] Those that have the mumps are numerous. Beacham & Warren, all the other boys are doing well & in fine spirits.[87]

We are stationed about three miles north east of town near the Fair Ground. There is considerable Union sentiment about here.[88] I saw Jas [Olerum] yesterday, he is clerk at one of the depots.[89] There is nothing of importance going on here. I understand since writing the above that Col. Shelley has arrived. We will get the Enfield rifle for our regt.[90] My love to all.

Your son,
John

Miller W. Francis to James C. Francis
In pine thicket near
Bridge on Chickahominy River
20 miles from Richmond
May 12th, 1862

Dear Father,

You are aware of our late evacuation of Yorktown & our subsequent fights.[91] I sent in my resignation from Yorktown to go into a partisan regt. with Col. J. T. Morgan who I learn this evening has been commissioned.[92] He wants me to raise a company in Kirby Smith's division.[93] I want a company, they will have to arm themselves & furnish their own horses, but government pays for them, after they are furnished by the men. The other officers are elected by the regt. Have the company raised for me & I will be able to get to it before it goes into service.[94]

Communicate with Col. Morgan at Selma or Cahaba, on the subject & he will give you all the information you will need. The men are raised from all classes whether the conscript law applies to them or not as I understand it.[95] Write to Morgan immediately about it, I am resolved not to remain in this regt. if I can get out of it. No difficulty with any one, only I am tired of the Medical Department & am not satisfied to serve under the officers we have here any longer than I can leave. If I can't get out I shall be transferred to Morgan's regt. as surgeon as he is anxious for me to go with him. I shall write to him by the same mail I do to you. Get the company, pick the men those that will do to depend on. I don't care what county they are from, so they are men that will not shrink from danger or hard service. Get Tom Rowland into it & Hop & such men as they are.[96] If you can't get me a company I shall join the regt. any how.

We are here looking for a fight every day, but it may be delayed some days. I don't want to leave until the fight is over here. I left Henry Forney at Williamsburg with his arm badly fracture in the same place John Forney was shot & same arm, tried to bring him off but he would not travel.[97] He will be taken good care of by the enemy, some of our surgeons went back under a flag of truce, will see them as soon as they return & write again. Caldwell & the other officers are safe, all the P W Guards are safe as they were not in the fight.[98] Our loss was 700 killed & wounded. The enemy acknowledge 4,000 in the papers.[99] We have had a hard time of it, but have made a successful retreat, am strong & hearty as ever, never felt better. Saw Jim a few days ago was well.

Your son,
M.W.F.

~

Miller W. Francis to John T. Morgan
In woods at bridge on
Chickahominy River 20 miles
from Richmond, Va.
May 12th, 1862

Col J. T. Morgan
Dear Sir,

Have just seen Whitely, told me of your success & c. Have not heard a word about my resignation yet, if it is not accepted I want a transfer to your regt. I have written to Father to raise me a company, and I will join you, with it. Write to him on the subject as I am overanxious to be with you let him know the terms & c. If I can't get a company & c., I shall join the regt. as a "Private Striker" as I am fully determined to be with you in that service.

We have had a retched time on our retreat, fought all day at Williamsburg. Our brigade was not in it, men on the field however &, under fire, the 10th Ala. won glory enough. Henry Forney arm was badly broken same point John's was shot, left him at Williamsburg, lost 700 men there killed & wounded. Col. Ward, 2nd Fla.,[100] Mott 19th Miss.[101] & Lt. Col. Irby 8th Ala. were killed.[102] Early wounded, all his brigade were farmed out,[103] Terry was badly wounded, but got off.[104] Lt. Col. Hairston same regt. shot in several places but not serious.[105] Dressed Early's wounds, gave him enough whiskey to make him tight & started him to Richmond, where he is now. Our troops fought well, McCrea came off unhurt but lost very near all his officers,[106] cursed Hardee soundly for not going into the fight with his regt.[107] Write to Father & also drop me a small note as soon as convenient. Direct to Richmond.

Resply.,
M. W. Francis

~

John C. Francis to James C. Francis
Camp near Knoxville, Tenn.
May 15th 1862

Dear Father,

Thinking it would not be amiss to let you know something of our doings at this place. I take the present opportunity of stating that we are doing as well as we could wish. It is true that we have a few sick but they are mostly measles and mumps.[108] We have the Enfield rifle for our regt. with accouterments, a few English blankets, knapsacks, canteens (cedar), havesack, shoes & c. Billie Alexander, White, & Niman have caught up with us. They were left in Montgomery.[109] I am Co. B at present, would not contend for the first as Patterson expects to become surgeon and then I go up.[110]

I received a letter Hop yesterday. He stated that he and Tom were doing well & that Gen. Ledbetter had telegraphed to the department to commission Jim A. C. S. of that post[111] & Tom would go to Mobile.[112] He starts there in a few days. I will give you a list of the sick and disease. I don't know when we will leave here. I would not be surprised to be ordered off at any time & I expect it soon. Warlick,[113] Mattison[114] & Clark are doing fine.[115]

Give my love to all write me at this place. If there is any one man wishes to join my company send him here if he is a healthy, able bodied man. As Hop will stay with Tom & I can take one in his place.[116] Reaves pretended to want to go with us but would not therefore goes back home as he came.[117] Nothing more at present. Write soon.

Your son,
John

~

John C. Francis to James C. Francis
Camp near Clinton, E. Tenn.
May 18th 1862

Dear Father,

We arrived at this place this morning about eight o'clock after a march from Knoxville of about eighteen miles.[118] We started from Knoxville on the morning of the 17th about six A.M. and marched about fifteen miles before night when we stopped for the night. The day was very warm though the boys did very well. This morning about daylight it commenced raining & has continued all day. We had a march about 5 miles through the whole of it. It was very hard marching, yet we all got through safe. Struck tents and had no more than gotten under our shelters until we received orders to be ready to march tomorrow morning at eight o'clock with one days rations.

We will go to Big Creek Gap I think about fourty miles from this place.[119] I will have about sixty (60) men able to march. I suppose we will be gone eight or ten days. The boys from town are all right none sick except Johnson. He is not much sick as he is up attending to his business. Reynolds is our brig'd.[120] Gen. Kirby Smith is at Knoxville. We left our extra baggage with Jas. [Olerum] in Knoxville. He is a clerk at the E. Tenn. & Ga. R. R. depot. I saw your old friend Campbell Wallace a few days ago.[121] He told me to remember him to you. I have not heard from Thos in some time. I suppose he has gone to Mobile. When you write direct your letters to Knoxville as they will be sent to us from there. This is only a small village. My love to all.

Your son,
John

Thomas W. Francis to James C. Francis
Chattanooga, Tenn.
May 19th 1862

Dear Father,

I received a dispatch from Genl. Forney a few days since from Mobile informing me of my appointment on his staff, and that I should report to him.[122] I showed the report to Genl. Leadbetter and said that he did not wish me to leave here, but that he would relieve me just so soon as he could have a commissary appointed, and asked me to recommend some one, and I recommended *James*. He said the name was sufficient and that he would telegraph, and did so, asking the department to commission him and order him to report for duty as post commissary. I suppose he will be appointed. I got an order from the genl. commanding here this evening ordering me to Richmond on special duty with the commissary general. And it would not surprise me at all if I was kept in Tennessee for some time to purchase supplies. From a conversation with the genl., I think that is the intention of the department.[123] I feel certain that I will get Jim the appointment at this post.

Hop is doing very well. John has been sent to the gap above Knoxville. Henry Forney is certainly a prisoner, so I see by the *Richmond Whig*.[124] I will not be gone long to Richmond.

Your son [Thomas]

4 / *A Very Hard Time*

By June 1862, the war in the west focused on Middle Tennessee and the lower Mississippi River, and John Francis and his Sallie Walker Boys were encamped at Cumberland Gap. With roughly 30 men on furlough or recovering from measles and mumps, his company's strength had dwindled to 63 men, the Thirtieth Alabama itself reduced to some 400 men. Those soldiers not ill with measles or mumps were exhausted by marches over the rugged countryside.[1]

The Thirtieth Alabama was now in the Second Brigade under the command of Brigadier General Carter L. Stevenson. On 18 June 1862, Stevenson's forces inexplicably withdrew from the Gap despite its strategic importance, allowing Union forces under Brigadier General George W. Morgan to occupy Cumberland Gap. The youthful infantry captain, John Francis, was sorely disappointed by this tactical decision, and his dissatisfaction spread to the men under his command. Despite their dwindling numbers, John was convinced that the Confederate forces in the Gap could have held their position if given the opportunity to fight.[2]

Equally frustrating to John Francis and his fellow officers was the rampant absenteeism. Many soldiers failed to return to active service after sick leaves or furloughs. The problem was serious enough for the *Jacksonville Republican* to publish a "Notice to Absentees of the 30th Regiment Alabama Volunteers" on 14 August 1862. This directive ordered all absentees to report to specified men assigned in their respective counties. To put teeth into this notice, a six-man detachment under Lieutenant Sam C. Kelly, Company E, Thirtieth Alabama, was sent to Alabama to enforce it. Kelly's efforts to arrest and bring back all able-bodied deserters and absentees met with limited success.[3] Desertion and absenteeism eventually became widespread as the war dragged on and expanded across the Confederacy. For his part, Captain John Francis developed a hard-line toward deserters and those who shirked their duty.

While desertion reduced his units, General Stevenson's forces encountered only limited action as they operated in the Clinch Mountains from Morristown to Tazewell, Tennessee. Stevenson was biding his time until he could seize an opportunity to reoccupy the Confederate "Gibralter" in the Cumberland Mountains.[4] That opportunity arose during a skirmish on 5–6 August 1862 near Tazewell with a Union force commanded by Colonel John F. De Courcy.[5] But the opportunity was missed when the Union foraging party was allowed to retreat safely to Cumberland Gap. Once again the youthful Captain Francis expressed his profound dismay that decisions made at the brigade level had prevented the capture of the entire Union force.[6]

While John struggled with these command issues, seventeen-year-old Jo Francis did his duty. Fully equipped with a horse, new uniform, and cavalry saber, Jo enlisted as a private at Oxford, Alabama, on 11 August 1862.[7] Then he joined brother Miller in John Tyler Morgan's Fifty-first Alabama Mounted Regiment. After a brief stint in North Alabama, the Fifty-first was sent to Tullahoma, Tennessee, in early September and on 9 October 1862 joined Brigadier General Nathan Bedford Forrest's cavalry division.[8] By late October 1862, Jo and Miller Francis were together in Middle Tennessee, Jim and Hop Francis were at Chattanooga, and Tom Francis was busy with his new assignment at Mobile.

Meanwhile, the Thirtieth Alabama moved to within three miles of Morgan's Union forces at Cumberland Gap. In a letter to his sister Emma, John speculated on possible Union ration shortages and their effect on impending operations. Two weeks later a letter from John to his father reviewed recent tactical developments. The Confederate invasion of Kentucky by Bragg and Kirby Smith forced Morgan's Union troops to abandon their camps, and Captain Francis personally commanded the first soldiers to reoccupy the Gap on 18 September 1862. After a brief sojourn at Cumberland Gap, the Thirtieth Alabama marched into Kentucky pursuing Morgan's retreating Union forces, with plans to rejoin Kirby Smith's army in central Kentucky.[9]

Despite marching and countermarching over 500 miles, the Thirtieth Alabama fought no skirmishes or battles during the Kentucky invasion. The battle of Perryville on 8 October 1862 effectively ended the Kentucky campaign, and Bragg and Kirby Smith withdrew their forces toward Cumberland Gap.[10] Their forces reached the Gap on 19 October 1862 and completed the retreat into Tennessee four days later. The only losses suffered by the Thirtieth Alabama were four men left in private homes in Kentucky because of sickness and exhaustion.[11] Although none of John Francis's letters from Kentucky survived, his correspondence to his father from East Tennessee on 24 and 25 October 1862 provide some details about his experiences in Kentucky.[12]

In November 1862, Miller, Jo, John, and Jim Francis were with Bragg's Army of Tennessee in Middle Tennessee. Miller wrote to his father on 23 November, nearly a month before his thirtieth birthday, informing him of his status as both the senior surgeon and the oldest surgeon in John Tyler Morgan's brigade. After Bragg established his temporary headquarters at Tullahoma in mid-November, Jim Francis moved there as depot commissary for the Department of Middle Tennessee.[13] According to company muster rolls, Jo Francis, detailed to the commissary department through December 1863, moved with Jim to Tullahoma.[14] John Francis was with the Thirtieth Alabama at Readyville twelve miles east of Murfreesboro.[15] With his brothers encamped near Murfreesboro, Hop settled down with Tom and his wife, Fannie, in Mobile. There he remained on special assignment while he assisted Tom Francis with his duties as commissary for the District of the Gulf.[16]

From late November through December 1862, Miller, John, Jo, and Jim Francis participated in Bragg's campaign to thwart the Union advance through Middle Tennessee.[17] Miller's letters to his father from Joe Wheeler's cavalry headquarters in November and December recounted the constant skirmishing between Nashville and Murfreesboro during which Miller furiously tended the sick and wounded of Morgan's brigade.[18] Yet, incredibly, no Francis letter survived to record the visit of Jefferson Davis to Bragg's army on 13–15 December 1862, when Davis ordered Bragg to send Stevenson's division to reinforce John C. Pemberton in Mississippi. Three days later John Francis and the Thirtieth Alabama started their circuitous trek to Vicksburg, a journey traveled by some 7,500 men in Stevenson's division between 18 December 1862 and early January 1863.[19]

Bragg's army fought a two-day battle of Stones River against a Union army commanded by Major General William S. Rosecrans. Despite a poorly coordinated Confederate attack on 31 December, Bragg telegraphed Richmond claiming a brilliant victory. After a New Year's Day hiatus, the second day of fighting on 2 January 1863 proved even more haphazard than the first, and Bragg's Army of Tennessee suffered heavier casualties in killed and wounded.[20] After an indecisive night followed by a morning filled with more equivocating, Bragg finally opted to abandon Murfreesboro on 3 January. His army slogged southward through miserable winter conditions to form a new defensive line along the Elk River near Winchester, Tennessee. Although Miller Francis was kept busy attending the sick and wounded, Bragg's retreat allowed him and his brothers Jim and Jo Francis a warm respite with their kinsmen in Franklin County, Tennessee, and finally relocation to the safety of Chattanooga by 16 January 1863.[21]

John C. Francis to James C. Francis
Camp in Cumberland Gap
May 28th 1862

Dear Father,

After a march of about seventy miles we are at Cumberland Gap. I can't tell how long we will stay here. I got to this place with sixty three men. Had to leave six on the road at Big Creek Gap, viz. Turner, Bagley, Moore, Stephens, Pitts & Seiber, John Rutledge.[22] All slight fatigue more than anything else. We left several at Clinton, viz. Wylie Carpenter, John Carpenter, Reynolds, Powers, Woodruff, T. Finch, R. P. Alexander, Marion Smith, Page, Harmon, Shurbutt, Champion, Beacham, Baird & Kimbrel, Hollingsworth, none very sick.[23] In camps we have sick Garvin, Poss, Dowdle, Clem, Milner, Roberts & Warren with measles & mumps all doing very well.[24]

Our regt. numbers for duty about four hundred (400).[25] I wish you send word to all my sick men at home that they must come on immediately or I will have to send for them and punish them as deserters. There are several at home on furlow that can come & must come. Let Redman know this if you can.[26] I think he is well enough to come. We are under Brigdr. Gen. Stephenson.[27] There are about five thousand troops at this place so I am informed.[28] We can whip a large force at this point. Our gen. is confident, if the enemy comes, of whiping them. I am doing very well I have hired the free boy Bill at ten dollars a month.[29] I must close as the mail is nearly ready to start out. Give my love to all. Direct your letters to Knoxville. Miss No. 1 is flourishing.[30]

Your son,
John

John C. Francis to James C. Francis
Cumberland Gap, E. Tenn.
June 1st 1862

Dear Father,

I know of nothing of interest to write at this more than we are all getting along as well as possible at this time. We are stationed on the eastern side of the Cumberland Gap, get good water both sulpher & limestone. Though I understand that we will have to go on top of the mountain, we will not do as well up there as we would if we remained here. None of my boys are dangerously sick. We left John Carpenter at Clinton.[31] I understand that he has been very sick though he is improving now. Those left at Clinton are Lt. Carpenter severe cold, settled on his lungs.[32] Marion Smith weakness in the back.[33] T. J. Powers cold. Reynolds cold.[34] R. P. Alexander a mule hurt his leg not very bad though.[35] C. Woodruff cold. W. Walker & a few others.[36] They are coming into camp every day or two. Champion is there also a little sick.[37]

Those sick in camp, are as follows Serg't. Glover cold,[38] John Milner—mumps, D. Roberts mumps,[39] J. Bagley cold,[40] R. F. Allen billious fever,[41] J. Whaley chills,[42] N. D. S. Culbreath cold,[43] T. Downing mumps,[44] L. Moses mumps, J. Harmon mumps, Poss mumps, W. Gennings mumps,[45] J. Kirby cold, Hutchinson rheumatism, Copeland diarrhoea, & Clem fever nearly well.[46] None of them are much sick. We number 46 for duty & 10 on detached service. We had an inspection & review yesterday. We have I suppose 5 or 6 thousand troops here. We get nothing to eat except bacon & bread. We are under Gen. Stevenson. I have received only one letter from home since I left that was from Sue.

Direct your letters to Cumberland Gap, E. Tenn. My love to all.

Your son,
John

~

James C. Francis, Jr. to Amy I. Francis
Chattanooga, Tenn.
June 11/[18]62

Dear Mother,

I have nothing of importance to communicate to you more than we are well. I was with our battery during the bombardment last Saturday. It was rapid for a time the shot & shell fell around my department thick, two shells entered my store room.[47] I received a letter from "Jno" this morning. He is well the health of his company is not good. They are at Cumberland Gap. "Tom" does not know what day he will leave. Soon though I think.

The enemy did us but little damage, killed 1 man, wounded 5 or 7. We killed several of them 7 were found in two graves.[48] They have fallen back. I think our forces will pursue them or force an engagement. Gen. "E. Kerby Smith" is here in person. My love to all.

Your son,
Jim C. Francis

John C. Francis to James C. Francis
Camp near Clinch Mountain
June 22nd 1862

Dear Father,

When I wrote to you last I was at Cumberland Gap. I believe since then there has been great change with us. When we left we went down the valley ten miles with the expectation of meeting the enemy who crossed over at Wilson's Gap (Wilson's Gap was eight miles below us).[49] We stayed at that place for four or five days laying on arms all the time. For some cause or other we left that place at the same time Cumberland Gap was evacuated, and fell back near Morristown on the R. R. After staying there one night we came back to this place about twelve miles from Morristown & are now guarding a gap in the Clinch Mountains.[50] The enemy I am told continued after us to Tazwell thirteen miles from us. They fired on our cavalry pickets yesterday with their artillery but did no damage. There are various rumors about them. I don't know what to believe therefore will not write them.

There is dissatisfaction about our giving up C. Gap. We could have held that point against almost any odds.[51] I don't know what will be done in a day or two. We may stay here on our arms or we may be ordered to an other point. We had to leave a great many sick in the country we passed over though I did not leave a single man from my company. I have eighty with me, all doing well. Baugh, Gidley & Champion was sent back yesterday to Morristown.[52] I suppose the remainder of my sick have been sent either home or to the different hospitals. I have no very sick men till now. I have one or two men in Calhoun Co. who will have to be reported if they don't appear soon. I can hear nothing from them at all. They are Redman,[53] Putman[54] & one or two others. About twelve of our sick men fell into the hands of the enemy. We have not heard from them since. We have no tents with us nor have not had for nearly two weeks. Though the weather has been very favorable to us. We only have two cooking vessels to each company. Nearly everything was destroyed at the gap. All the artillery was saved except two of our largest pieces. They were spiked and thrown down the mountain a great many muskets were broken up. All of the tents were cut to pieces. The magazine was blown up. All the clothing except one pr. of pants, two shirts, two prs. of drawers & one coat to each man was cut up. The commissary stores were destroyed. The cooking utensils were broken up. In fact every thing was destroyed and nothing except a few sick men left in the hands of the enemy. John Whaley had one of the small bones in his arm broken while coming on.[55] He was riding on a piece of artillery and turned over, it is slight he has gone to Knoxville I believe.

I understand that there was two companies formed in Tazwell for the enemy when they arrived at that place.[56] The Holston River is between us and Morristown six miles from here. The Clinch is about six miles in front of us. The wheat is pretty good in this part of the country. The corn is not so good. My clothing was sent to Morristown two weeks ago. I have not had a change of clothing in that time. I don't know when I will have a chance to change again. I have with me one blanket, my Indian rubber [cloth] & over coat. The nights are cool yet I sleep very comfortable. Baugh has the mumps and is in a house two miles this side of Morristown.[57] I don't know when I will get to send this off as we have no mail nearer than Morristown. I have only had one letter from home since I left & that was from Sue. I don't know what is the matter. The boys get letters nearly every day but I get none. Our surgeon has no medicine with him at all.[58] There is great complaint among the men about it. Everything seems to be badly managed & we can't help ourselves. It seems as though there was something wanting. We draw two days rations at once & they keep us cooking all night every other night. I detail the cooks and make them take it time about & then divide it out the next day. We sometimes have to cook our bread without salt. We occasionally get corn bread from the citizens near us.

This is much harder than I ever experienced before. Our men hold out amazingly well on forced marches. Ed Clark holds out much better than I expected. He has been with us all the time & is still with us. There is one brigade at this place, also two batteries one from Eufaula the other from Rome.[59] Bob Alexander has gone on to Knoxville he is nearly well.[60] Dan Beacham left his drum and carried a musket through the rounds. There is considerable sensation among the troops about the intervention of foreign powers. They don't know whether to place any confidence in the report or not. My sick men come in nearly every day. I have more with me now than I have had since I left Talladega. I am very well pleased with them. I try to do my duty toward them. I don't know that they are displeased with me, if they complain I never hear it. Lt. Carpenter is sick again he was just taken. I have the biggest company in the regt. The adjt. told me the other day that my men kept up better than any in the regt. The seniority in the regt.

has not been decided between Patterson & myself yet & I don't know when it will. My love to all.

Your son,
John

~

John C. Francis to James C. Francis
Camp near Clinch Mountain
June 24th 1862

Dear Father,

I wrote to you yesterday by mail but as Lt. Carpenter starts home this morning I will write you a few lines. Will tell you nothing of our travels as I stated those before. Lt. Carpenter has resigned & will start home today or tomorrow it was on account of his health. We are doing nothing now except eat & sleep. We only have one small oven to the company. We cook all the time day & night to get enough, have no salt nor soda. The boys take it very easy. Each one has a single blanket on which he sleeps at night without any protection from the dew whatever. I reported seventeen (17) not fit for duty this morning out of seventy nine (79). Thos Powers is the worst one we have. He is no ways dangerous. I have sent him to a house & have his brother waiting on him.[61] We have one or two cases of mumps. The rest is colds. I have a very severe cold myself but am still doing duty. The enemy sent over a flag of truce yesterday with several dispatches for Gen. E. K. Smith. We don't know what the purport of the flag was.[62]

Lt. Carpenter can tell you all the general news. My love to all.

Your son,
John

~

John C. Francis to James C. Francis
Camp near Rutledge, E. Tenn.
July 11th 1862

Dear Father,

I am again with the boys and getting along as well as I could wish. Lt. Vansandt is going home having resigned. The circumstances are these. Col. Shelley received orders to report every officer incompetent to hold his place. According to orders he [Vansandt] with six or eight others were reported incompetent being notified of the fact & ordered to stand an examination. He refused to so do because he thought that the report was partial to some & immediately sent in his resignation.[63] I tried to find out about the matter as I wished to see that we were treated right. I asked an explanation which was granted and that satisfactorily. I think he could have stood his examination if he had gone before the board. He did as I would have done under the same circumstances. It may be that Bradford had a hand in reporting.[64] I would like for you to explain this matter to all enquiring friends, so that they may know exactly what is going on. I will hold an election for the vacancies & not fill them by appointment although we are required to do so.

I have about eighty men for duty. Eleven sick in camps none dangerous nor very sick. We are now about ten miles below Bean's Station at Rutledge a small village near Clinch Mountain.[65] Col. Rains commands our old brgde.[66] We are under Barton & Gen. Stevenson commands this division from Bristol to the junction of the Clinch.[67] There is prospects of a good rain, here to day. You will please settle the accounts with the Selma, Talladega & Jacksonville papers, for that advertisement & send it to me so that I can settle with you. My love to all.

Your son,
John

John C. Francis to James C. Francis
Camp near Tazwell, E Tenn.
August 8th 1862

Dear Father,

Since I wrote you last we have had quite a hard time of it. We left Blain's X Roads on the 4th arrived at the Clinch River the same day stayed all night & until 12 o'clock the next day at which time we started on our march crossed the river without stopping to take off any clothing whatever. Marched all day in our wet clothing until about 9 o'clock at night when we were order to lay down and take a few hours rest being then in three miles of the enemy.

About two (2) o'clock we started slowly toward the enemy. At 9 o'clock we heard the artillery open and could occasionally hear a ball whistle. We move slowly on until eleven (11) when the musketry opened on the Yankee pickets. We were then ordered up to the scene of action. On getting there we found the enemy to be from four to nine hundred yards off. Our regt. opened on them with their rifles & before long they felt the effects of the minie balls. They could not stand it but took to their heels. We were then ordered to charge. With one shout we started it being nearly a mile to the point we were to go to. When within about two hundred yeards of the point our gen'l. being behind we had no orders therefore had to stop. This did us great injury for a great many of the men were already broken down & stopping made it worse. I was at that time about fifty yards in front with a squad of men. After stopping here for about fifteen minutes, I became so near dead that I could not move. The regt. move up on the side of the hill about one hundred yards, stop a few minutes & came back by order of Gen. Barton. There was no firing scarcely after we started on the charge & after we stopped there was none atall. The men acted nobly, obeyed every command without any hesitancy.[68]

I went into the action with fifty seven men. All came out safe, some few had their clothing shot was the only damage done in my company. Old man Warren was with us.[69] There was one man killed & four wounded in our regt. There was in the brigade five or six killed and about thirty wounded. The enemies loss was more than ours. I think that there has been found about fifteen killed & the same number wounded. They took a great many of their killed & wounded off with them. They left on the night of the sixth. We had only four regts. engaged. They had from four to six regts. I myself saw two full regts. & two detachments. I suppose they were full regts. also six pieces of artillery. We had no artillery nor cavalry engaged. We took fifty one prisoners, they only got one. That was Lt. Col. Gordon of the 11th Tenn.[70] We captured some commissary stores.

Nothing more of great importance. The only thing I regret was we had plenty of troops here to capture the whole concern if our genl. had of known what they were doing. I think it was badly managed on the part of some of our gen'ls. We had nearly four brdgs. here and only four regts. were brought into action: two of Genl. Taylor's & two of Genl. Barton's.[71] The engagement lasted about two hours & twenty minutes. Capt. Johnson was not allowed to go into the engagement because of having with him ten or twenty thousand dollars of the pay for the regt. Col. Shelley told him that he could not go in. This accounts for his not being in it. I am willing to risk my men in any place where they can get a chance to do execution. Nothing more at present.

Your son,
John

P.S. I started to telegraph you but Col. Shelley asked me to let him telegraph to the *Selma Reporter* for all. He did that yesterday.[72] J. C. F.

~

John C. Francis to Mary Emma Francis
Camp Investment near Cumb. Gap
September 3rd 1862

Dear Sister Emma,

I received your letter sometime ago & have not had time to answer it before this. Mr. L. C. Mitchell starts to Ala. tomorrow & I will send this by him, he is now sutler of our regt. & is going home to make preparations for it.[73] We have been here over two weeks & there is nothing more accomplished than when we first came. We are about three miles from the Gap & are so concelled in the woods as to prevent the enemy from seeing us. While out on pickett we can see the enemy at various points. Occasionally they come to their pickett lines & get green corn for their stock. We have taken several prisoners since our arrival. They report the rations at the Gap short.[74]

We have one or two brigades on the other side of the mountain & four or five on this. It is generally believed that they will either evacuate by squads or capitulate in a short time. I don't know what they will do, though I suppose a few days will decide what they will do. Occasionaly they throw bombs at us but have done no injury to our regt. There was seen a very large smoke to day in the Gap. We can't tell for certain what it was they were burning, or what they were burning for.[75]

We received the news today of the fight in Va.[76] Did not have any particulars though. The health of my company is very good now. There were only eight excused from duty morning. I go out on pickett every five days with my company. The boys from about town are all well I believe. We get flour, bacon & beef to eat. Apples & peaches sell for ten to fifteen cents per dozen, very poor at that. I am now writing by a tallow candle made in camps, for which I paid twelve & a half cents. Every thing sells for an enormous price with us now on account of the scarceness in this country. There is one good feature about it we can't spend much money here. We have eaten nearly all the green corn in this whole country. I expect we will soon have Kentucky in our possessions again, from all appearances now.[77]

There is nothing of importance going on here now. Tell Willie and Sue I will write to them in a few days. I would have written before now but we have been so much on the watch that I had not the time to write any thing. My love to all. Write soon & often.

Your affectionate bro.,
John

Alexander Woods to John C. Francis
Jacksonville, Ala.
Sept. 15th, 1862
Capt. J. C. Francis
Knoxville, Tenn.

I herein enclose you a power of attorney for David L. Roberts, he wishes me to say to you, that you will do him the favor to draw his money & send it to me by the first safe private conveyance.[78] This leaves myself & family in good health, your Pa's family are well & the health of the people generally are good. We are in pretty good spirits just now, at this late Virginia news, and hope we shall hear soon of the capture of the Yanks at C. Gap. We have but little news of the casualties in the 10th from the late battle of Manassas. The news comes in by scraps. Jesse Harris[79] & Neel Littlejohn were killed.[80] Capt. Moses was killed.[81] My respects to the boys, and accept for yourself my best wishes.

Very respectfully,
Yr. obt. servant,
A. Woods

P.S. Capt. please send me a descriptive list & pay account for any of your men that have died. I am making out claims to draw the pay due them.[82]
A. Woods

John C. Francis to James C. Francis
Cumberland Gap
Sept. 19th 1862

Dear Father,

Since writing you last the enemy have evacuated the Gap & we now have it in our possession.[83]

Night before last Gen'l. Barton sent me with a party of fifteen men to see what was going on in this place & if they had evacuated. I proced with my party, consisting of Lt. Finch,[84] Serg't. Skelton[85] & fourteen privates, beyond our own pickett lines & near the enemys sent out four men to see where their picketts were. The night being so dark they could not be found, when they came up I sent them back again so as to be near their lines by day light. I remained until about 7 o'clock A.M. (18th) they did not return (believing that the enemy had evacuated from their movements during the night) & I concluded to go with my whole party either to the Gap or at least until I came to their picketts. Capt. Anderson with three or four of his men being on pickett asked that they might go with me.[86] A second capt. ask the same. I did not refuse them but with this party I proced in this direction having thrown my men in line of skirmishers I came within a half a mile of the Gap. I then sent out five or six in front of the line to see whether they had gone or not. It was very evident at this time for we could see no one & also their tents were cut to pieces. We came on then between eight and nine o'clock, & took possession of the Gap the rear *march* of them having being gone about one or two *hours.*[87]

Col. Shelley & Lt. Col. Phillips[88] came in about a half an hour after we did seeing us come in they then came. *Mine was the first command,* by two hours, *that entered the Gap.* The enemy went out the Ky. road. We had no troops on that road. They blew up their magazines, burnt a portion of their small arms & everything else that could be were either burnt or cut up. We found several very large guns. Col. Phillips & I found two thirty-two pounders. I understand that several more were found. We took between five & ten thousand small arms, collurs, writing paper in abundance, gear for horses, a great many shovels and picks, and some of nearly everything needed in camps. We found the place well fortified at every point.

I have with me now 75 men. Corpl. Allen, privates Allen[89] & Stephens were sent back to Tazwell yesterday none of them are bad sick. Stephens has been very sick but is improving.[90] Some of our troops have gone to Ky. We are expecting marching orders soon.[91]

Your affectionate son,
John

~

Thomas W. Francis to James C. Francis
Mobile, Oct. 18, [18]62

Dear Father,

Mr. Snow will give you $189.80 for me the amt. I paid for 4 bales hides for him.[92] I am afraid they are not as heavy as he wished but I got every one I could get & the very best. They could have been sold before they were shiped for 20¢ per pound advance.

I have sent Hop up in the middle part of the state in Perry & Dallas to buy corn for this post under orders from Genl. Forney. You may expect to hear of a fight here any day for I am satisfied that it is close at hand. "*I expect Mobile will fall.*"[93] This you need not say.

Your son,
T. W. Francis

~

John C. Francis to James C. Francis
Tazwell, E. Tenn.
Oct 24th [1862]

Dear Father,

I wrote you last in Ky. I believe but don't know whether you ever received them or not.[94] I came on ahead of the regt. today from Cumberland Gap and have only a short time to write in. We left Camp Dick Robinson in Ky. on the 18th & have been traveling every since.[95] Our division covered the retreat, suffered a great deal for want of rations.

A great many of my men are a little puny none of them dangerous. I left four in Ky. Sam White & McAlreath at a private home at Nickolasville.[96] Tom Poss between Harrodsburg and Bryantsville.[97] Champion was left at a house on our way out there & went on to Richmond.[98] It is the last I have heard of him. Tell their friends that they need not be uneasy as they will be paroled & sent over to us. White and McAlreath had the fever but nothing but a bilious attack. Poss was tired down & had to stop on the way.

We go on to Rutledge & go into camps I suppose. Perhaps we will winter there. We were in no engagement at all in Ky. My men are all worn out but if they can get a rest of a few days will be on their heels again. I will write you again when I get to Rutledge. My love to all. I am in good health. Tell Col. Clarke that Ed went through like a man. The boys from about town are all well.

Your son,
John

John C. Francis to James C. Francis
Camp near Rutledge, Tenn.
Oct. 25th 1862

Dear Father,

I wrote by mail yesterday at Tazwell & will write a few lines to night as Serg't. Baugh starts home in the morning for the purpose of getting cloathing for the company.[99] I understand since I came back from Ky. that we have some cloathing in Knoxville. I don't know whether I have any or not, if not, I would like for you to send me, two good quilts or blankets as I have but two blankets the others were lost when we first left the Gap, two linsey shirts or something on that order, two pr. of drawers the same kind, one or two pr. of socks, one pr. of pants.[100] Buy these things with the money I sent you. You must use that money in any way you see proper. I have but little use for it in the army & I always keep enough for my use. Don't hesitate to use it in whatever way you see proper wherever it is needed most place it there. I want nothing more in the cloathing line except the above.

We had quite a hard time in Ky. We marched every day (and several nights) from the time we started until now with the exception of four or five, distance traveled about five hundred miles. For the first forty or fifty miles after you leave the Gap the land is very poor and mountainous, after that you see as pretty country as you ever saw. Good pike roads, neat villages & plenty of stock & provisions. I was very much please with Ky. & was very much surprised at leaving there. Our division went as far as Frankfort, stayed a few days in Versalles, went to Lawrenceburg, Harrodsburg & Camp Dick Robertson from thence to Tenn.[101] I can't tell how long

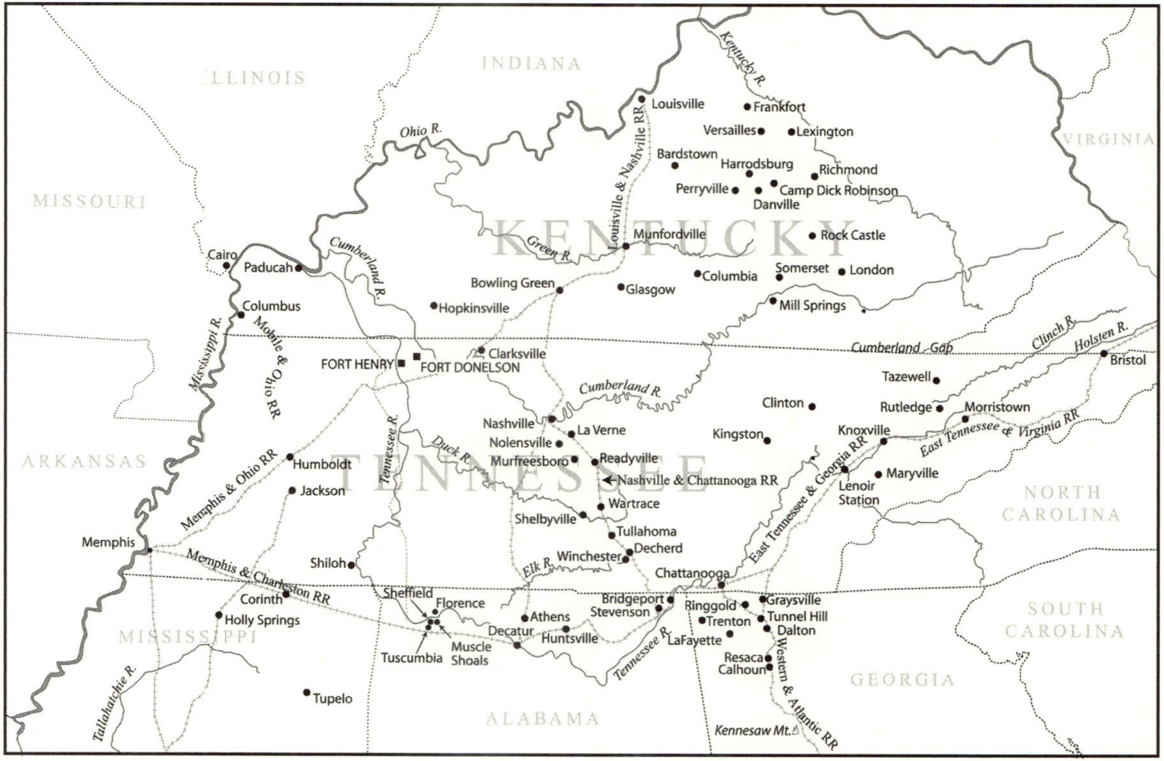

The Kentucky-Tennessee Campaigns

we will stay here. We have just had orders to make requisitions for everything need full for an active campaign. Where we will go from here I can't tell nor no one else as circumstances guides all of our movements. You will please assist Baugh in getting up the cloathing for my company. I am tired tonight & will not be able to write much more. I am doing well, with nothing more to do for a few days. My love to all.

Your son,
John

James C. Francis, Jr. to James C. Francis
Office Com. Post
Chattanooga, Oct. 25 [1862]

Dear Father,

I have just been informed that orders have been issued for me to go immediately to Murfreesboro, Tenn. & take charge of the comsry. Dept. of Middle Tenn. Genl. Bragg's army will I am informed make Murfreesboro the base line of operations.[102] This point is my preference but Genl. Bragg's chf. of subsistence says he is not satisfyed to trust the present comsry. with the responsibility that would naturally fall upon him. I will leave Bud's poney with Major Brooks at the Academy Hospitle subject to your order.[103] "Jo" is now with me.[104] Miller is well. Write me at M. Will send the money soon or come down myself. My love to all.

Your son,
Jim C. Francis

P.S. Will send some wheat soon to Rome, Ga. I hope you will start Emma as soon as possible.[105] J. C. F.

Hopkins T. Francis to Amy I. Francis
Selma, Oct. 27 [1862]

Dear Mother,

I wish to write you a few lines this morning. I have not rec. a letter from home since I left for Mobile. I left Mobile on the 17th of Oct. left Thomas & Fannie well. I am buying corn for the Department of Mobile.[106] I expect to remain here for some time. Where is Jno? I have not heard from him since I left Chattanooga. I heard that Jos. was with James. I send by to days train a pair of French rabbits for the little children. I wrote to Father on my arrival here but have rec. no answer as yet. My health is very good. My board is costing me $25 per month. Give my love to all. Write soon, tell the children to write also.

Your obedient son,
Hop

John C. Francis to James C. Francis
Camp near Lenoir's Station, Tenn.[107]
Nov. 11th 1862

Dear Father,

Mr. Weir I understand is to start home in a few days & I thought I would write you a few lines by him & send a little money for some of my men.[108] He will give you twenty dollars ($20.00) for Wm. Jerral's wife I think she lives down about Mr. Skelton's. *You will please see that she gets it* for I have no doubt but what she is suffering, as he lost all the money he started to her while we were at the Gap (he sent that by Wm. Wright who never got there).[109] I also send twenty-two dollars for Marion Smith which you will please pay him.[110] It is clothing money he never drew while in Knoxville. I send you also fifty nine dollars & fifty eight cents ($59.58) for David L. Roberts. This you will please deliver to Judge Woods, as I was ordered to send it to him, through Judge Woods.[111]

I received Emma's of the 30th last night. I am glad you have concluded to send her to Summerfield to go to school.[112] I was vaccinated this morning.[113] How much money have you received from me. You don't write me whether you get it or not. Emma wished to know whether I wished yarn or cotton socks. I prefer the cotton. We had orders this morning to be ready to march by 12 o'clock. The orders have been countermanded & we are to be ready to start at one hours notice. I don't know where we will go some think we will go to Kingston, Tenn. I can't say for certain. Tell Emma that I need both those books she spoke of but can't tell her where they are now. They are somewhere about the house. It is getting so dark I can't see how to write. I will write you more when I stop again. Weir is detailed with Johnson I suppose he is going to send him home. Nothing more at present.

Your son,
John

~

John C. Francis to James C. Francis
Camp near Lenoir's Station
Nov. 13th 1862

Dear Father,

We all are sending our money home by Capt. Wood to Judge Woods for distribution.[114] We send a little over two thousand. We have already sent a great deal off by others passing.

I have not time to write more at this time. The men are sending something over half of their money home.[115] My love to all.

Your son,
John

~

Miller W. Francis to James C. Francis
Camp Stewart's Creek[116]
Nov. 23rd 1862

Dear Father,

I have not written to you for some time. We got back to camp again 2 days since after being out 87 days, all tired out. We have been resting ourselves & horses & having them shod for another time can't tell where nor when. Col. Morgan has command of a brigade of Ala. cavalry.[117] I am in my old post senior surgeon of brigade being the oldest in it. We are going to hold our position at Murfreesboro. I was down there yesterday & day before.

Saw Jim he is in excellent health, & is in high standing with the officers. He is depot commissary there, has an easy time of it. I deposited $560 with him to be sent to you to pay for the lot I am on, pay yourself and make the titles out to me & have them properly fixed. I only drew my pay up to the 1st of Nov. The government owes me 125 dollars yet which I can get at any time I try. I am very anxious to get the other half of the Earle lot.[118] At the end of a years service I can pay for it as I think I can save out of my salary for 12 months at least $1,500 as my expenses are very little here. Don't buy anything but something to eat. I have been out of money for 1 month until I drew yesterday. See what is the least money he will take for the lot & let me know. I want to pay all my debts as fast as I can get money & improve my lot afterwards. My health is excellent never better have not had a days sickness, neither has Gabe. My horses are in fine condition, all standing it well. Joe is with Jim, but I did not see him as he was at Wartrace on business.[119] I saw all of Pete Turney's co. they are all well. All our Jacksonville boys are well.

Jack Roberts is doing tolerable well but it will be a long time before he can move & I don't think he will ever have a straight leg of it, as it was never set.[120] I did not see him until next morning after the fight & it was not set as he could not bear it. We have had a great many men wounded. Regt. is healthy as could be expected, only 1 died with the regt. Several more dies at home & in the country on our line of march near Ala. & in Ala. We will be thrown with Forrest & J. H. Morgan & they are to operate entirely outside our lines.[121]

Write me soon at Murfreesboro, regards to all & c. I sent Emma a piece of music sometime since.

Your son,
M. W. Francis

Thomas W. Francis to James C. Francis
Mobile, Nov. 24, [18]62

Dear Father,

I recd. your letter in reference to Mr. Snow's hides and wrote to him today about them. I hope to get the matter fixed for him. I have not heard whether you have paid Uncle James & Jno. Easterwood the money I owed them or not. If you have not done so I hope you will do it for I do not wish to pay interest. I have written Uncle James to call on you for the money but I suppose he will not do so.[122]

If you want Hop at the plantation he can go after Christmas. I need him now. I am now paying him 100$ per month and his traveling expenses. If you could get a good man even at a big price I think it best to let him remain in the army. I sent him orders the other day to go to Tennessee after flour and bacon but do not know that he was at Selma. He might have been in the country. I suppose if he has not gone he will do so in a few days. I would like to know how the farm is progressing, the hogs and cattle. I would put all the pork I could buy so long as I had salt for the army and the people will need it.[123]

I heard from Jno., Jim & Joe a few days since but have not heard from

Miller. I am having a good deal of work to do now. The command here has increased very much.

Your son,
T. W. Francis

~

Miller W. Francis to James C. Francis
Stewart's Creek
Dec. 4th 1862

Dear Father,

Mr. Stewart is here, brought my coat, came last night.[124] We had just got out of a fight & off 5 days duty in front. The Yankees attacked on the pike. We had about 150 men at that point they were a regt. of infantry. The fight commenced at 10 o'clock & continued until 3½ in the evening. They drove us back 1½ miles to some cedars. We then were reinforced when we started them back & drove them 2½ miles & occupied our old position killing 5 or 6 & wounding a good many.[125] They wounded 3 men & killed 1 in the first Ala. cavalry.[126] There was not a man in our regt. hurt & only 3 horses hurt. We fight every day we are out. Have had about 40 wounded, & not one killed yet. Have been in 25 or 6 skirmishes. Since we arrived here, have had but 2 men to die here in the state that we know of. They were from Talladega, Carter[127] & Meadows.[128] Jack Roberts will die from his leg. He is delirious from it & in one of his paroxysms jumped up & broke it over. I don't think he can live.[129]

My health is excellent never better. I send you by Stewart bushel Hungarian grass seed, sow it in the spring like oats. You can sow it on my lot. There is about ½ bushel to the acre, it is the best feed we can get & the farmers here prefer it to any other grass. Cut it just before it ripens & cure it & put it up like oats or hay. I sent Jim $560 to send to you the first chance, & I suppose he sent it by Lt. Bush. Pay yourself out of it for the ballance of the lot & make out the titles to Julia & have it recorded. If there is any over, pay any other debt I may have. Government owes me now over $180 & I can draw that as soon as I choose to do so. I am going to try and buy the ballance of that lot from Earle, if it can be bought for anything like its worth. I can save at least $1,000 more from 1 years wages if nothing happens. My horses are doing well. Everything going on smooth nothing of interest up here. Don't want anything at present. Regards to all.

Your son,
Miller

John C. Francis to James C. Francis
Camp Selby near Readerville, Tenn.[130]
Dec.10th, 1862

Dear Father,

I received yours of the 2nd of Dec. a few days ago & would have answered it by Mr. Nunnelley but was very busy at that time fixing to move.[131] I wish you to state to Mr. Rutledge that the best thing that he could, is to come immediately to camps for they are getting very hard on deserters & I have no doubt but what some will be shot for desertion. I have never been notified officially from Atlanta that he has deserted. Therefore will take no notice of it until I am notified & then I will be obliged to report him. This is why I stated that it would be best for him to come to camps. If after he is in camps I am notified that he has left the hospital, then there will be nothing done. I received a letter from him on the subject. Tell him what I have stated above also that it is impossible for me to get him a furlough & send to him.[132] I was a little sick when the regt. left Lenoir's Station, stayed there a few days, bought a horse for Johnson & came on and overtook the reg't.

I received the clothing sent by Capt. McBee.[133] Tell Mother that I have a sufficient number of overshirts for the present. If you have my gray jeans, you can have it made up at your leisure. I will need the coat & perhaps the pants this winter. Get R. J. Martin the tailor to cut my coat as he has my measure.[134] I want it double brested. I want you to use my money for any purpose you may wish. Tell Mr. Hays that I have no objections to his joining my company & for him to start before he is conscripted.[135] He will have to bear his own expenses & if he is not stout he will run some risk of being rejected by the surgeon. You need not be affraid that I will give up my place for another if I did this I would have the other secured first. I have nothing of that kind in contemplation at this time.

The clothing that Baugh started with have not reached here yet. They are at Bridgeport trying every train to get here.[136] We are stationed twelve miles east of Murfreesboro. I intend, if the gen'l. is willing, to go & see him tomorrow. Capt. Patterson is now major of our reg't. I am senior captain. I have not heard from Winchester since I left there. My love to all.

Your son,
John

Thomas W. Francis to James C. Francis
Mobile, Decr. 11, [18]62

Dear Father,

I shiped you the other day care Capt. Woodruff[137] at Selma a rood of goods containing one bolt of osnaburg & one bolt of brown drilling for Mother and the ballance & one blk. dress for Fannie.[138] Will you please let her know that it is there so that she may send after it. I have had your box of tobacco for some time & Fannie wrote me that you said that you did not wish it now as you had got some from some other quarter. If you still wish it or any part of it I will send it. I have heard nothing from you for a long time. What have you done about the notes I wrote you about held on me by James Montgomery & Jno Easterwood. Has Emma gone to Summerfield to school if she has not when will she go? I wish to send her some things when she gets there. I have heard nothing from home for a long while I heard from Hop at Montgomery today. He was with Jim & Jno & Joe while he was at Murfreesboro, Tenn. He will go to Lynchburg, Va. as soon as he gets through at Montgomery. I sent a pair of pigs up several days since did you get them? They are very fine stock.

Your son,
T. W. Francis

Miller W. Francis to James C. Francis
Camp Stewart's Creek
Dec. 12th 1862

Dear Father,

Mr. Allen leaves for home in the morning.[139] I was at Murfreesboro yesterday saw Jim & Joe both well & in good spirits. Jim tells me he sent $560 to Selma to my credit by Mr. T. Brown of our regt. but has not been notified as yet if it [is] at the bank.[140] As soon as he is notified of it, he will send you a check on the bank & I want you to place it to my credit for the remainder of the lot my house is on & have the titles made to me. I will send some more money home shortly, sometime after the 1st of January next as there will be 2 months pay due me then & I can pay all I owe here & send you at least $200.00. I am anxious to save enough out of my salary to purchase the other part of that lot and have me a good home. My health is as good as when I was a boy, never better in my life, am stouter than you ever saw me, am getting along finely, no trouble at all. We have a very hard time of it in the way of duty & fighting.[141] I wish you would write to me when you get the money.

I got Gabe's boots & my coat. My horses are all fat & in good order in every way forage is abundant. I sent you by Dave Stewart 1 bushel of Hungarian grass seed enough for 2 acres of ground. You can if you wish sow it on my lot, sow like you would oats & at the same time. The farmers here think more of it than any hay they can get. The 2 acres will make enough hay to do you all the year & the seed are no trouble to sow. John is in 12 miles of Murfreesboro at Readyville, is in good health. I saw Uncle Hugh & Tobe Turney at Murfreesboro.[142] I will go over to see John in a short time. My regards to all our kin & c. Tell the little fellows howdy for me.

Your son,
Miller

Joseph H. Francis to James C. Francis
Murfreesboro, Tenn.
Dec. 27th/[18]62

Dear Father,

Cannonading was heard here from 11 1/2 A.M. until nearly night on yesterday & was renewed again today. It is one general attack all along our line. The result is unknown. The heaviest part of the fight was on the Nolensville Pike.[143] Large reinforcements was sent out from this place yesterday evening & a general move of the whole army is reported this evening. The Yanks are out in a very strong force. Bragg says he will bag them all. Jo Johnson planned this battle before he left here (this is the general opinion). I have just had a talk with one of Morgan's staff. Morgan's men all safe except two or three prisoners.[144] Miller is in fine health. Will write again soon.

I started to write to Julia but thought it best to wait until the fight was over. Joe

5 / *Heroes of Vicksburg*

Little celebration attended New Year's Day 1863. The North and South remained deadlocked in a conflict whose only promise was new losses, deaths, sorrow, and sufferings. At least for the Francis family the holiday season offered some solace: that their sons were safe, for now. James and Amy Francis did their best to provide for their younger children and also to reach out to those less fortunate families, many driven from their homes by invading or occupying enemy forces.

In the meantime, John Francis, in command of five companies of the Thirtieth Alabama, rushed to Vicksburg, Mississippi, on 28 December 1862 in time to witness the battle of Chickasaw Bayou. Vicksburg, a prosperous port city on the Mississippi River with a population of 5,000, was built on a series of bluffs and rolling hills below the mouth of the Yazoo River. Departing Memphis, Tennessee, on 20 December, Major General William Tecumseh Sherman moved his amphibious expedition downriver while his men placed wagers on celebrating Christmas in Vicksburg. By Christmas Eve his men, some 32,000 strong, were poised for the assault on the Chickasaw Bluffs, ten miles northeast of the town on the Yazoo. The major Union assault came five days later at the Devil's Triangle on Chickasaw Bayou, and furious fighting ensued through the thirty-first at Hayne's Bluff.[1] The first Union land assault against Vicksburg ended when Sherman withdrew his army up the Mississippi to Milliken's Bend on 2 January 1863.

Following Sherman's withdrawal, the Thirtieth Alabama moved into camps about four miles east of Vicksburg on the Southern Railroad of Mississippi.[2] The cold rainy days of early January caused a rash of sickness throughout the regiment. A smallpox outbreak was exacerbated by poor drinking water, continued exposure, and poor diet.[3] The Sallie Walker Boys were especially hard hit by smallpox. John Francis's men were placed under quarantine in a slave quarter about a mile from the regiment. Standing by almost helplessly, John witnessed more than fifty of his soldiers develop the disease. For the eight who died, he wrote obituaries published in the *Jacksonville Republican* in February and March. Some of those fortunate enough to recover continued to suffer from complications of the disease, especially from vision problems caused by pustules that formed on the eyelids or the eye itself.[4]

During February 1863, with most of his company quarantined with smallpox, John Francis encountered three former classmates from Florence Wesleyan University. Adam Naff, a private in the Sixtieth Tennessee Mounted Infantry, was detailed as a clerk in the commissary department of John C. Vaughn's Tennessee brigade at Vicksburg.[5] The others, Henry Edington, a private in the Sixty-first Tennessee Mounted Regiment, and John Irwin, a Vicksburg native and a private in the Twenty-first Mississippi Infantry Regiment, were on furlough at the time of their unexpected reunion.[6] Their reminiscences of happier times of college life along the Tennessee River near Florence, Alabama, must have offered welcome relief, albeit brief, from the burdens of command.

Despite the smallpox outbreak at Vicksburg and other challenges, the Francis brothers continued their correspondence, asking about the welfare of their loved ones at home and expressing concern for the education of their younger siblings. Sister Emma, and later Willie, received special attention from their older brothers, who were anxious that their education continue beyond the schooling provided in Jacksonville. They supported the decision to send Emma to Centenary Institute at Summerfield near Selma in Dallas County.[7]

Springtime 1863 restored optimism. While sister Emma struggled with her studies at Summerfield, and withstood her first pangs of separation from family, her six brothers remained healthy but scattered from Vicksburg to Bridgeport, Alabama, and Shelbyville, Tennessee. When his commanding officer, Brigadier General John H. Forney, was relieved at Mobile in December 1862, Tom Francis sought and received a temporary assignment in the Department of Mississippi and East Louisiana.[8] This new assignment included his younger brother Hop. Following a trip to Richmond in early March 1863, Jim Francis became the post commissary at Bridgeport, Alabama, and his brother Jo remained with him, detailed to the commissary service.[9]

Meanwhile, older brother Miller remained on active service as senior surgeon with the Fifty-first Alabama, in Morgan's brigade and Will Martin's cavalry division, near Shelbyville in Middle Tennessee. From January through July 1863, Martin's cavalry, in Joe Wheeler's cavalry corps, harassed and skirmished with Union soldiers and cavalry from Murfreesboro to Winchester,

Tennessee. The constant skirmishing kept Miller and his medical staff supplied with sick, wounded, and physically exhausted troops. It also caused health issues for Martin's staff, and on 22 April 1863 at Frazier's Farm, Tennessee, Miller requisitioned two and a half gallons of whiskey as "supplies for the sick of Brig. Genl. Martin's staff." Serving as acting surgeon-in-chief of the division, he certified that the "Strimbers" were required for the general's staff, "which are severely taxed by exertions, both mental & physical, consequent on the large amount of business constantly occurring in both field & office."[10]

With six sons involved in the war and Emma away at school, Dr. Francis and his wife, Amy, continued their participation in community and war-related activities. They assisted kinsmen, such as the doctor's widowed sister, Mary Theresa Francis Turney, and other refugees fleeing the ravages of war-torn Middle Tennessee. The Francis family opened their home or found shelter for them elsewhere in Jacksonville.[11] At a meeting at the courthouse on 10 January 1863, Dr. Francis joined with other community leaders to issue an appeal "To the Patriotic Citizens of Calhoun County" to assist the sick and wounded soldiers from the battle of Stones River. Thousands of Confederates wounded in the fighting at Murfreesboro were already being cared for in private homes and hospitals "from Murfreesboro to Chattanooga, Atlanta, and Rome." The leaders implored their fellow citizens to contribute money, bandages, clothing, bedding, food, and medicines for the care of sick and wounded soldiers. Despite his active medical practice and civic service, Dr. Francis also joined Amy and the women of Jacksonville in soliciting support for the Soldiers' Relief Society to provide clothing and blankets for soldiers and to aid soldiers' destitute families in Calhoun County.[12]

As Ulysses S. Grant's Union forces advanced on Vicksburg, the Thirtieth Alabama received orders to march to Grand Gulf on 29 April 1863. Two days later they occupied positions near Port Gibson. Grant's army of approximately 24,000 crossed the Mississippi River below Port Gibson at Bruinsburg on 30 April, while Sherman led a diversionary attack at Hayne's Bluff north of Vicksburg.[13] The Union troops heavily outnumbered the Confederate force of some 6,800 men under Brigadier John S. Bowen.[14] When fighting ended on 1 May, the Thirtieth Alabama counted 18 killed, 112 wounded, and 142 missing. Brigade commander Brigadier General Edward Tracy, was killed by a Union sniper.[15]

While Captain John Francis and his Sallie Walker Boys suffered defeat at Port Gibson, Colonel Abel D. Streight's Union forces forayed across North Alabama, marauding the countryside from Tuscumbia to Rome, Georgia. With Nathan Bedford Forrest's cavalry in pursuit, Streight's 1,700 Yankee raiders fought a series of skirmishes between 30 April and 2 May 1863.[16] The raid ended when Streight surrendered his numerically superior Union force to Forrest around noon on 3 May near Lawrence, Cherokee County, Alabama, about twenty-eight miles from Rome.[17] The *Jacksonville Republican* announced the "glorious news" that Forrest had ended the Yankee threat to their homes.[18]

Thirteen days after Streight's surrender, the Thirtieth Alabama was involved in the battle of Baker's Creek, Mississippi. Grant's forces, advancing from Jackson toward Vicksburg, engaged Pemberton's Confederate army at Baker's Creek, about halfway between the two cities.[19] Although several Rebel units withdrew in a disorderly fashion, the Thirtieth Alabama's performance was praised by Brigadier General Stephen Dill Lee, who concluded the "Regiment behaved with distinguished gallantry against heavy odds."[20] Lee became the commander of Tracy's Alabama brigade after Tracy's death at the battle of Port Gibson on 1 May 1863.

Then, on 18 May 1863, Grant's Union force began a 47-day siege of Vicksburg.[21] This ordeal was to prove the second of a dual blow to the Confederacy. As Robert E. Lee led his defeated forces from the bloody fields of Gettysburg, Pemberton surrendered at Vicksburg on 4 July 1863, capitulating to Grant's terms. Captain Francis, acting commander of the Thirtieth Alabama in Lee's brigade, surrendered the Thirtieth Alabama on 8 July and was paroled as a prisoner of war.[22] Equipped with four-mule teams, wagons, and Union rations, the paroled Vicksburg garrison marched either home or to parole camps on 11 July.[23]

Although his family knew of John's capture, they were not aware of his status until Tom Francis's telegram reported John's safe arrival at Brandon, Mississippi, on 13 July. Pemberton briefly established his headquarters at Brandon before marching his ever-shrinking army of parolees to a parole camp at Enterprise, Clarke County, Mississippi. Within a few days, John Francis and his comrades were issued furloughs and returned home to await their formal exchange as prisoners of war and return to active duty.[24]

John C. Francis to James C. Francis
Camp near Vicksburg, Miss.[25]
Jan. 3rd 1863

Dear Father,

I have not written to you since I arrived here because I had no time to write anything. Last Monday week we left Murfreesboro for Jackson.[26]

Our reg't. was without a field officer therefore the command fell to my lot. We were placed on three different trains. I went with the one which carried the first five co's. We came through Selma & stayed there one night.[27] I saw Hop while there, but only for a short time as I had no one to assist me in command of the reg't. I saw Weir also I sent him to Montgomery on business. He has not arrived here yet. I understand that he was taken sick while in Selma. Came from Selma to Demopolis a little town on the Warrior.[28] At this place, the ladies had prepared for us a nice dinner of which we participated freely as rations had been a little short with us on that day. While crossing the river I met with Gen'l. Forney.[29] I only had time to say a few words to him. Passed through Meridian from there to Jackson at this place we were ordered to go into camp. Was there but a short time when orders came from Br. Gen'l. Pemberton to move immediately to this place.[30]

When we arrived on last Sunday evening about sun down we threw our blankets down for a rest & had just gone to sleep & orders came for us to go to camps.[31] The next morning (Monday) we had orders to go out on the line. At this time the enemy were advancing & our boys were giving them all they had in their power. We heard the guns while at Jackson & all the time we were here it was only cannonading though, yet I believe there was an engagement on Sunday.[32] Our brigadier gen'l. was behind & I was ordered to report to Gen'l. Barton our old gen'l. He told me that he sent for the 30th to occupy a very important position.[33] We went to our post & stayed there until after night, under the fire of the enemy, but not close enough to do any injury. On that day there was a general engagement but few killed on our side, a great many on the enemy. Our men were behind breast-works & the enemy charged it but was driven back, that night we were ordered on the line of trenches.[34] At this point we could only keep ourselves out of sight of the sharp-shooters, who were fireing on everyone that passed in view. We continued on this line until this morning (the sixth) when we had orders to go to camps. The enemy having left on night before last. They passed down the Yazoo & up the Mississippi. I don't know their destination.[35]

During the siege we lost about thirty killed & fifty wounded, no prisoners. The enemy between three and four hundred killed & wounded in proportion & about six hundred prisoners.[36] Most of the fighting took place about five miles above town. The enemy having landed on the east bank of the Yazoo. I heard some one say, and I expect he is reliable, that the enemy lost since they came to this place about twenty-seven hundred (2,700) men.

We captured a considerable amount of commissary stores. Gen'l. Sherman was in command of the Yankee forces. Some of the same Yankees were here that we fought at Tazwell.[37] Col. Shelley came up with us about three days ago with two co's. of our reg't. The remaining three came in yesterday. My company was with the last three that came in. They went by way of Mobile.[38] It has been raining about twenty four hours. The ground is very muddy. The men suffer a great deal from it. I can't tell where we will be ordered. I would like to find Mary Francis but don't know who to enquire for as she has married. I may find her but would be more certain if I knew who she married. The health of my company is pretty good now. I wish you would tell any of my men who went home to come on to camps immediately. My love to all. I suppose Aunt Turney & family[39] are at Jacksonville by this time as they started the same day I came through Decherd.[40] Give them all my love.

I got my watch. Nothing more at present.

Your son,
John

~

John C. Francis to James C. Francis
Camp near Vicksburg, Miss.
Jan. 6th 1863

Dear Father,

I wrote by mail a few days ago, but as Col. Shelley goes home today I will write you a few lines by him. I am getting along very well at the present time. My company is in very good health some few complaining but none bad sick. I heard nothing of Bob Allen when we came through Atlanta.[41] Major Patterson is now in comd. of the reg't. Every thing is quiet about Vicksburg. Some few reg'ts. have gone to Port Hudson from this place.[42] We are expecting orders soon to go to Grenada or Mobile. There is nothing sure about it. I don't think Vicksburg can ever be taken. It is to well fortified. Capt. Johnson has not arrived. We are looking for him every day. We are camped four miles east of the city on the R. R.[43] My love to all.

Your son,
John

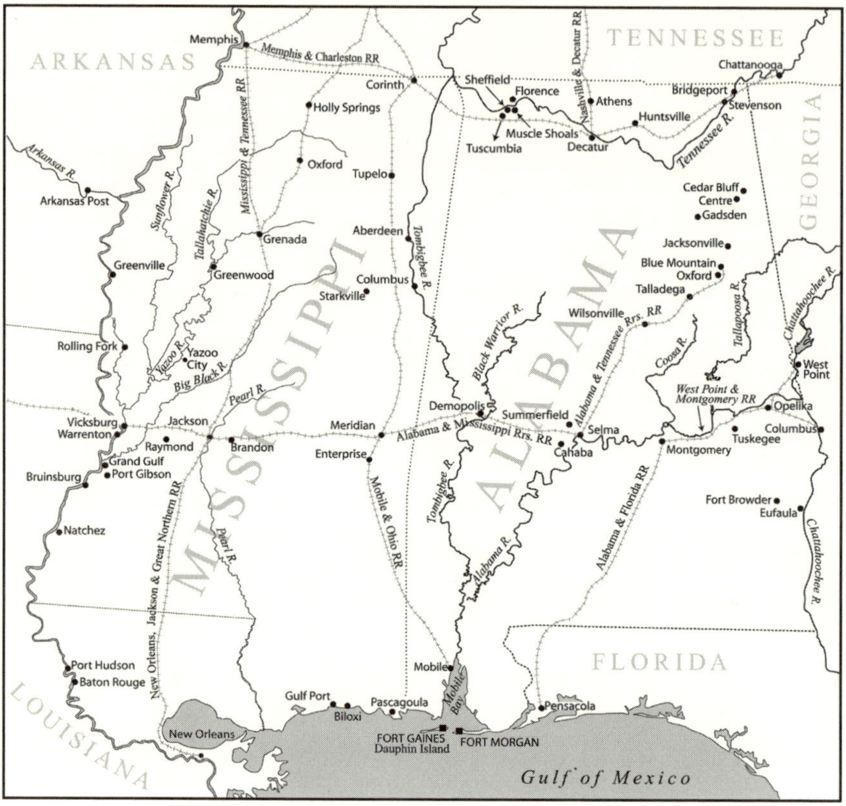

The Vicksburg Campaign

~

John C. Francis to Willie C. Francis
Camp near Vicksburg, Miss.
January 14th 1863

Dear Sister Willie,

I received yours a few days ago. What shall I write you & there is nothing about here that would interest you. We are stationed four miles east of Vicksburg on the V. & Jackson R.R. Our camps are in the woods, plenty of mud. It has been raining a great deal since we came here & is raining at this time. Our drinking water is very poor indeed & is from a little branch & a mud hole. I have a good many boys sick, viz. John Rutledge, Beacham, Smith, Bagly and a few others. Rutledge is pretty sick the others only a little.[44]

I have been to V. once or twice. Everything sells very high there. It is the one the most singular cities I ever saw. It is on the east bank of the Miss. River, the streets are up & down hill, the houses are on hills & there are nearly as many hills as there are houses.[45] So you can imagine how it is. You only told me in your letter that Aunt Finney & family had arrived without telling me anything, whether you went to see them often or not. You must go often. There are no girls I think more of than them & I have no doubt but what you will like them very much.[46]

There is nothing of interest here every thing quiet. There are a few gunboats in the river at this time, the remainder having gone up the river to some unknown point.[47] Col. Shelley has gone on sick furlough. Give my love to all. Write soon.

Your bro.,
John

James C. Francis, Jr. to James C. Francis
Chattanooga, Tennessee
January 16th 1863

Dear Father,

I am at this place for the present will remain here until the 25th. I have a short respite for the purpose of preparing my reports for the last quarter.

My stay in Murfreesboro was quite a pleasant one. Society good, the people hospitable & generous, while there my business was to contract & to purchase. I saved nearly all of my stores before leaving the place. I think I will be recalled to my old department (J. E. to Genl. E. K. Smith comd.). "Miller & Jo" are both in good health. "Jo" will be home soon.

If I were in your place I would buy Judge Woods house & lot.[48] If I could at any thing, like a fair price. It will be an investment that will pay finely. I wish you would purchase for me the lot adjoining "Miller's" & if he wants it I will let him have it.[49] Also the lot between the house built by Parson Smith & the fine house built by Jim Crook.[50] I understand it is for sale. I would prefer to have my money in lands than anything else during the war & at the close it can be sold for a handsome profit. If you cannot purchase either of the mentioned lotts, look around & see where you can invest in such property. If you will sell me George, I will promise to keep him always (unless some misfortune should befall me). I wish to take him & raise him to the house as he is perfectly honest. I will give you 900$ for him unless you think it more than his value.[51]

I have not herd whether Emma has gone to Summerfield yet or not. If not it is not my fault, I have at Keith's funds to defray any expense that may be connected with the trip, board, tuition & ca. ca. & in case more is requisite it shall be furnished. I hope for her sake that she may have some accomplishments when she is grown and that you will not post pone or delay any longer. I can't come down to attend to it for my duties are such as will not permit me to do so. I should think that "Hop" might carry her down at any time. I hope to get a long letter from you immediately on the receipt of this & if you conclude to let me have George send him by "Jo" before he returns. You can invest the same money in a larger boy & one that will make just as good a field hand. My love to all.

Your affectionate son,
Jim C. Francis

~

John C. Francis to Samuel H. Stout[52]
Camp near Vicksburg, Miss.
[February 8, 1863]

Dr:

You will confer quite a favor on me if you will inform me of the where abouts of S. V. Putnam a member of my company. He was sent to Morristown from Camp Investment near Cumb. Gap about the last of Augst. or the first of Sept. I understand he was sent from there to Knoxville. I know nothing of him therefore ask you to do me the favor of writing me a few lines concerning his whereabouts.[53]

I am your most ob't sev't,
John C. Francis, Capt.
Co. "B" 30th Ala. Reg't.

~

Adam F. Naff to John C. Francis
Commissary Dprt. Vaughan's Brigade
Vicksburg, Miss., Feb. 20th 1863

Dear Sir,

I recd. your note this morning informing me of your whereabouts and am pleased at the idea of getting to see another of my old Florence friends.[54] I am in the Commissary Dprt., Vaughan's Brigade, Tenn. Vols.[55] You will find our head quarters near Minl. Springs two miles from town, near the 4th Mississippi Regt. Our office is now in town on the street running parallel with the river, that the telegraph office is on. Tomorrow we expect to move out to our head quarters near the spring. I will be very glad to see you at any time. Come and see me.

Yours truly,
A. F. Naff

P.S. Henry Edwington is now in town on his way to his command in Tenn.[56] A. F. N.

John C. Francis to James Freeman Grant[57]
In quarantine, near Vicksburg Miss.
Feb. 26, 1863

Mr. J. F. Grant:

You will oblige me much by stating through your columns to the friends of my company that the company has greatly improved in health. Nearly all (50 in number) have had smallpox; eight of whom have died.[58] The remainder are now convalescing, and I think in a few weeks we will be ready to take the field.

Respectfully yours,
John C. Francis

Julia P. Francis to James C. Francis
[Monticello, Geo.] Feb. 28th 1863[59]

Dear Father,

Brother tells me there is no chance to get lumber to build the houses that I want at this time.[60] I can't live there without some sort of house for the Negroes.[61] I now want you if you please to hire some men to build a log house with stick and mud chimney. Have it set where it will not be in the way of building another when we get ready to build it. Please have the other room of my house finished and a chimney put to it. Let the old kitchen stand. Can put a great many things in there that I have in my dining room.

Minnie is very sick has been for three days.[62] Brother said her brain is in a great deal of danger. He will leave to day for Richmond. If she still keeps sick I will send for another physician. The rest ok. I had a letter yesterday from Dr. Francis he was very well.[63] Pa's family is tolerable well. I would be glad to come home before long if you can get the building done that is necessary for me. Give my love to Ma and the children. I will write again soon.

Your daughter,
Julia Francis

~

Susan H. Francis to Mary Emma Francis
Jacksonville, Ala.
Saturday, Feb 28th 1863

My dear Sister,

It has been raining all day long and I have been so lonesome I thought I would write. Bro. Jim came home Tuesday night and brought with him a Negro woman and 2 boys. The oldest boy is about as large as George and the youngest as big as Bill. The oldest is name Will and the youngest George. Bro. Jim hired the woman to Henry Earns.[64] Joe is going to take the oldest boy with him for Bro. Jim to the army. Bro. Jim started for Richmond last evening and Joe went to the plantation. He has been down there nearly ever since he came. We got a letter from Sister Julia & she says Minnie is walking. Mrs. Nancy Clark and Dr. Clark went to Georgia. Old Mr. Clark is about to die. We think Sister Julia will come with her. Gabe is at home now. Bro. Miller sent him after his clothes. I have been staying at home from school ever since you left. Willie has had the sore throat but is now well. We are going to school Monday. Cousin Mary & Harriet were here the other day.[65] We are all well. Bro. Jim says he is going to write to Mrs. Milton in Selma for you a spring bonnet.[66] Joe is going to start to Chattanooga on the 9 of March. We got a letter from Bro. John dated the 13 and they were still in quarentine yet near Vicksburg. I must close. Write soon, your sister.

Sue Francis

John C. Francis to Mary Emma Francis
Camp near Vicksburg, Miss.
March 11th 1863

Dear Sister Emma,

I learned sometime ago that you had gone to Summerfield to school. I am truly glad that you have a good opportunity of improving your mind. You must study hard & do all you can for cultivation. I don't want you to say that you have been off to school (in after life) & be as some that I have seen, only concerned to be more fashionable, no I have a better opinion of you than that. I believe you will do what is right as near as you can. Try & not be to easy to get mad for it often injures persons when they least think of it. You can make yourself popular with Dr. Rivers as well as all the other teachers by dilligence. I never saw a teacher but what he liked a good student. Tell the Dr. that I am getting along very well.[67]

The small pox has nearly run its course in my company. I have had about fifty cases eight of whom have died.[68] I have one other considered dangerous. The remainder are well or getting well. There has been about eight of other companies in the regt. Capt. Anderson I understand starts to Ala. today.[69] I don't suppose that I can send this by him as I will not get to see him. I wrote to Father & sent it by him. Joe Hoke I learn is coming to my co. but has not arrived yet.[70] I am looking for him every day. Gen'l. Forney has not arrived at V. yet. I learned indirectly that he was twelve miles above here at Big Black River. If he does not come down in a day or two I intend to go off & see Tom & Hop. I don't know where they are going.[71] I suppose Tom will come down or write me a few lines.

My company is still in quarentine I think I will be able to go to the regt. in a week or ten days. Lt. Warlick is doing very well he has a very bad eye caused from the s.p.[72] He has gone to town to day to be examined by the board for sick leave of absence. I don't know whether he will get off or not. All the boys from about town are doing well none of them much sick. We are five miles from the city. I go down every day or two. Col. Shelley has been quite sick, though improving. I saw Capt. Johnson this morning he was as well as usual. I sent you a piece of music a few days ago. I don't whether you will get it or not as the mails are so irregular. The weather is quite pleasant with us at this time. The trees are beginning to bud. The enemy are still laying off over the river occasionally they shell the town but don't do much damage. We have captured two of their gunboats.[73] I understand that two more passed down the river a few nights ago. I don't know whether there will be an engagement here or not. Some seem to think there will not be. I think it almost impossible for them to take V.

While at home did you get a gold pencil I sent you from Lenoir's Station, Tenn.? I sent it in a package of money to Judge Woods. I have seen several of the Miss. ladies since I came here. They are not like those in Ala. Perhaps though it is because I am not so well acquainted with them. Tell Dr. Rivers that I saw a few days ago John Irwin on furlough from Va.,[74] Henry Edwington on furlough from Tenn., & Mr. Naff who is in this army 60th Tenn. Regt. They were all well. Irwin has gone back to Va. The other two are here. Give him my kindest regards & tell him that I will write to him before long. There is rumor that our brigade is to go to Mobile. I do not credit it much.

You must be sure to improve your time while at S. You have an elegant opportunity. Dr. Rivers is a good man as well as a good teacher. You will learn to love him. I suppose you can get nearly all the books you will need from my lot. Miss Mary Abernathy is with you I understand.[75] Why did not Miss Annie Clark go also?[76] Give Miss Mary my kindest regards. You will be company for each other. Try & not get homesick for it injures one in studying. You must write to me as soon as you get this. My respects to Dr. Rivers & family. Nothing more at present.

Your affectionate bro.,
John

Joseph H. Francis to Willie C. Francis
Chattanooga, Tenn.
Mch. 14th [1863]

Dr Willie,

I arrived at this point day before yesterday evening, found Jim well. I was water bound at Huricane Creek & remained there until the next day. I saw Aunt Betsy Montgomery all was well.[77] After swimming in two places between Spring Guarden & Rome we took the train for Kingston

& from there to Chattanooga.[78] I tried to get on the cars this morning at Tullahoma but they were too crowded. We are ordered to that point. Will leave here in the morning. It is rumored that they are fighting at Tullahoma.[79] Also that our cavalry captured Rozencrances cavalry but it was taken back by the Yanks. I do not credit the report. There is two (2) deserters here. They have to walk the street every day with a large board on their back with—deserters—written on them, also a cannon-ball chained to their leg.[80] Nothing more at present write soon. Tell them all to write. I'll write to Emma when I get to Tullahoma. Give my love to all.

Your bro.,
J. H. Francis

Thomas W. Francis to James C. Francis
Edmond's Depot, Hinds Co., Miss.
March 18, [18]63

Dear Father,

I have not had a letter from home since I left. I have not written only to my wife. I have been waiting to see John before I wrote you. I went over to his camp and stayed two days with him and he came back with me and stayed two days. I saw the most of his men all in fact except those that were confined with small pox. Some of his men are very badly marked and others not so badly. John is in very fine health and looks as if he never would be sick. I sent Hop down today to him with flour, coffee, hams & soap for the use of his mess.[81] He will have enough to do him a good while. I gave him a nice pair of pants and I think he will not need those he wrote home for. Just now a dispatch is in from "Port Hudson" saying that Banks' army has fallen back to "Baton Rouge" in a state of demoralization.[82] They were advancing at the same time the gunboats attacked the forts.[83] It seems like a hard job for Banks to make his men fight wherever he goes.[84]

I bought a Negro man the other day and paid sixteen hundred dollars for him. He is a very fine boy twenty three years old. I see no chance for the Yankees to get Vicksburg unless they flank it by the way of Yazzoo City on the Yazzoo River.[85]

I am of the opinion that the canal will be a success but of course there is great difference of opinion about it.[86] I see in a Mississippi paper that the wheat crop is a failure. It does not say where. I suppose it means in this state. I have heard nothing from Ala.

I will promise to write in a few days a more interesting letter. I am hurried to get it off by to days mail.

Your son,
Thom

John C. Francis to James C. Francis
Camp near Vicksburg, Miss.
Mch. 22nd 1863

Dear Father,

It has been some time since I wrote to you I believe. Nothing of interest has transpired. I made application a few days ago to be released from quarantine. I went in to see Gen'l. Stevenson about it. Yesterday he ordered Dr. Compton to examine the co. & see if it would be prudent to join the command.[87] He will be out this morning. I think I will move in tomorrow. Warlick & Littlejohn have very sore eyes, with that exception we are nearly as good as we were before contracting this disease.[88] None of the bad cases have become stout yet.

I heard from my sick at the hospital yesterday. Harmon is about like he was. There seems to be no change.[89] Moore is improving very fast.[90] Reynolds[91] has erysipelas.[92] All the rest are nearly well. All the boys who were in the cabins near us have come into camps. Nothing more at present. I saw Tom & Hop a few days ago. They are both well.

Your son,
John

P.S. Mch. 24th 1863. The Yankees have knocked our batteries down at Warrington.[93] We had no guns up. I understand that we have surrounded two or three gun boats in Deer Creek. We have fallen trees in their front & rear.[94] My men are getting along very well. I am expecting orders all the time to go to my command. Your son, John

James C. Francis, Jr. to James C. Francis
Bridgeport, Ala.
March 27th 1863

Dear Father,

I find Bridgeport to be a pleasant place, through matter of choice I came to this post. I am getting a fine rest here I have nothing much to do. I hunt & fish most of the time. I hope to remain here about one or two months longer if they will permit me to.

I have been offered 6,000$ profit on my tobacco but will not sell yet. I have purchased 31 b/c in Selma running from 575 to 690# to the b. at 16½¢ & *strickly midlings.* I left 5,000$ to be invested in the same; cotton now I am told is worth 40¢ pr. #.[95] I intend to hold it as long as I can or as long as I think it safe. If I were in your place I would buy all the land I could that is near the farm. Invest any money you may have of "Hop's, John's or Jos." I give this as my prediction & you will see the day when it will be verifyed that you will regret that you did not invest every dollar you had on land when you had an opportunity. I intend to keep my last dollar invested in tobacco, cotton & Negroes. It is folly to think about keeping the 8% notes for the interest they call for, *invest* in lands at long prices. I can borrow as much Confederate money as I want for .o. & repay in the same & if you will make the investment I will get of J. M. Clay & Co. as much as you say & I will share the investment.[96] We are all well. My Love to all. Write me soon.

Your son,
Jim C. Francis

Amy I. Francis to Mary Emma Francis
Jacksonville, March 29th 1863

Dear Emma,

I received yours of the 15th on Friday night. I was glad to hear you was well and well pleased. We are all well and Mary Abernathy's family also as far as I know. Fanny is at the plantation. We received a letter from Tom last night written the 18th. He had been to see John and spent two days with him and John had went home with him and spent two days with him. He then sent Hop down to John's company with hams, coffee, and flower for his mess. They were all three well. His company were nearly all well. Some of them pock marked to some extent.

We heard from the other boys a few days since they were in good health. James and Jo are at Bridgeport. Miller near Shelbyville.[97] Gabe started back some time since is there before now if no bad luck. You wanted to know about studying French. I thought you was studying it. I have no objections to you studying any branch you see proper to study. It is hardly worth while to take painting lessons now, take up the French or any other study you want. Your Uncle Porter is here he has been a little sick with asthma. Your Aunt Susan came up on Thursday.[98] They expected to start down home to day. It is so cold I do not know whether they will start or not to day. They take dinner to day at Henry Forney's.

Nothing more worth your attention. You must remember your creator now in your youth for you know life is very uncertain. The salvation of the soul is worth more than all the world, besides may the Lord protect and save you is the prayer of your mother.

A. Francis

John C. Francis to James C. Francis
Camp near Vicksburg, Miss.
April 19th 1863

Dear Father,

Mr. Wells leaves this morning. I believe I will try & write you a few lines & send by him.[99] I have nothing of interest to write. I believe I wrote to Willie & Sue yesterday I gave them all the news. There is nothing going on of interest at Vicksburg except the Yanks continue to shell the city from a battery across the river.[100] I send you some old papers, that I wish you would lay a way some where as I don't wish to keep them here, also some books. The little girls must take care of them. Capt. Johnson is up on Sunflower.[101] I don't know when he will be back.

I went up to see Tom & Hop yesterday. They were both doing well. Tom told me that he was going to Richmond before long. I am fearful that he will not do for Hop what he said he would. Gen'l. Forney will comd. Maury's Divs. M. is going to Tenn.[102] I can't exactly tell what Tom is going to Richmond for. I heard from Jo yesterday by letter. I hear from Emma occasionly. Nothing more at present.

Your son,
John

~

Amy I. Francis to Mary Emma Francis
Jacksonville, Apr 22nd 1863

Dear Emma,

I received you letter dated Friday on Saturday. You cannot imagine how glad I was to hear that you had found the pearl of great price which is worth more to us than all the world besides. I hope and pray that you may never backslide but be a shining light that others seeing your good marks may be constrained to glorify our Father who is in Heaven.

We received a letter from Miller last night dated the 17th he was well. He went to Atlanta for medicine and went down on Thursday to see Julia and the children and stayed until Sunday morning. He found them well. Julia says she will be at home again the 15th May.[103] The boys were all well when we heard from them last at the same places as far as we know. Fowler's battery passed through here since I have been writing. Several guns and a good many wagons and men. They are from Mobile on their way to Tullahoma, Tenn.[104]

I have a good garden, have English peas large enough to eat, have plenty of vegetable. Your Aunt Martha sends her love to you. Abernathy's are well. You must write often. Nothing more. I remain your affectionate mother until death.

A. Francis

~

John C. Francis to Amy I. Francis
Camp near Vicksburg, Miss.
April 26th 1863

Dear Mother,

It has been some time since I wrote to you so I will write you a few lines by Lt. Warlick. For the last day or two I have been a little unwell though have been on duty all the time.

There is nothing of importance going on here at this time. I received a note from Tom this morning. He states that he was affraid that Hop was taken prisoner the other day between Jackson and Meridian.[105] I suppose Lt. Warlick will find out as he goes through. We are stationed ten miles below Vicksburg near a little place called Warrenton.[106] My co. is in very good health at this time. I have only one sick man. That is L. D. Moses.[107] He has erysipelas. I am fearful that it will be a long time before he will be able to do duty. I went to see my sick in hospital yesterday. They were all doing very well. None of them are at all dangerous. Tom is station just the other side of V. from us. I see him occasionally. The weather is growing quite warm here. I bought some linen pants yesterday. I hear from Emma occasionly. I believe she is well pleased.

Lt. Warlick can tell you all the news. Give my love to all. How is Aunt Turney's family. I have not heard from them in some time. Nothing more at present.

Your affectionate son,
John

~

Thomas W. Francis to Robert W. Memminger[108]
Hd. Qrs. 2nd Dist. Miss. & E. La.
Vicksburg, May 2, [18]63

Major:

I respectfully ask that I be ordered to report to Maj. Theo Johnson[109] chf. sub. Dept. Miss. & E. La. for "*Temporary Duty*" until I am requested by Maj. Genl. Forney, who having placed in command of this Dist. was ordered to maintain the staff officers of Genl. Stevenson on duty until he would return to this command.[110]

I have the honor to be very respectfully

Your obt. servt.
T. W. Francis[111]
Maj. & C. S.

Amy I. Francis to Mary Emma Francis
Jacksonville, May 3rd 1863

Dear Emma,

I received your letter a few days ago I was sorry to hear you was sick. I have been uneasy about you ever since and sorry I could not be with you to wait on you. When you kneed anything, you must not be backward in telling the girls to have it prepared for you. They certainly would have you any little thing prepared for you. I will fix up a box of cakes and a corset and send by John Wily to morrow.[112] I wanted to send you some things in Mary Abernathy's box. They did not let me know when they sent it. The corset is not firm but it is the best I can do. We are well. Julia Scales is very sick with erysipelas in the head and face.[113] Sargent's baby dyed yesterday. There is great complaint among the children, hooping cough mostly. We heard from the boys all well. Mary's relations all well.

We had quite a stir in town last night. News came about nine o'clock that the Yankees were at Gadsden, at twelve yesterday in large force with a battery of six guns. They destroyed the ferry boats, broke up all the guns they could find, took men prisoners and paroled them. Took all the horses and mules they could find then left and went on towards Rome.[114] There was a letter came this evening from Center stating that they burnt the iron works there last night and then went on towards Rome.[115] Their force is three regs. of cavalry and artillery.[116] It also stated that Forrest was in two hours march of them, it is thought he will capture them.[117] I hope he may.

This letter was misplaced but I will send it to you as it gives you some advice. Have not heard from the boys at Vicksburg since the 9th of this month. They were well then. When we hear from them we will write to you.

May 26th We have not heard from Vixberg yet. Have no letters or dispatches since they have been fighting.[118] Write often. May the Lord bless and save you is the prayer of your mother.

A. Francis

Willie C. Francis to Mary Emma Francis
Jacksonville, Ala.
May 5th 1863

My Dear Sister,

As Mr. Wily starts to night I will write you a few lines. I have a delightful place to write under the large snowball bush in the garden the shade is very refreshing & I prefer it to sitting in the house. Sue is sitting by me making a boquet to send you if she can get it in the box. The roses are now in their prime while the snowballs are fading. We had a good many spring flowers but they are all gone now. It is now about 2 o'clock in the evening & is almost as warm as June. You have no idea what a pleasant place I have while every breeze is laden with the fragrance of the blooming flowers. Mother has eighty four young chickens. I am afraid the Yanks will be here about the time they get large enough to eat.

We received news this morning that the Yankees were in seven miles of Rome, Ga. & that Forrest's cavalry were in full pursuit only two hours march behind them & that he sent a courier to tell the people to keep them in check until he came up.[119] I hope to gracious he will get the last hateful rascal of them. The stage has not been to Rome in two days. Mr. Wollum went up in a buggy yesterday & got back this morning. He says that they are fortifying the place.[120] About 20 men & boys started from here night before last to help drive them back, & 70 men from Talladega went through last night on their way & several of our citizens started this evening. I believe that Judge Walker, Jo Forney, & Dr. Nesbit were among them.[121] Every body is excited. I expect some of the women about town have been hiding their meat. I don't know.

Do you need any more clothes? If you do let us know. I am taking music lessons under Aunt Mat.[122] We are all well. Tell Mary I sent her two horses to be ready when the Yankees come as I recon you will want to skeedaddle when they come. Tell her she must loan you one, write soon.

Affectionately sister,
Will

[Margin note] Since writing the men have come back to bring the glorious news that Forrest captures 22 hundred Yankees without firing a shot at Cedar Bluff & has taken them to Rome as prisoners instead of conquerors as they anticipated.[123] Willie

John C. Francis to James C. Francis
Camp near Warrenton, Miss.
May 6th 1863

Dear Father,

As Lt. McGee starts for Talladega this morning I thought of writing you a few lines as it has been some time since I wrote to you caused by continued marching.[124] On the night of the 29th of April we received orders to take up the line of march for Grand Gulf. We marched all that night & next day until about sun down and found ourselves within a few miles of Port Gibson (about forty miles from Warrenton) was halted to cook rations. Just commenced when we were ordered into line & marched three miles beyond Port Gibson & took our position to wait the coming of the enemy.[125] About twelve o'clock at night they advanced on our left & was met by Gen'l. Green's Brigade.[126] About six o'clock in the morning our battery (Capt. Johnson's) opened on them (this battery was just behind our reg't.) it was only a few minutes until they made a reply, only a few minutes until we heard the report of rifles from our skirmishers, a short time only elapsed & they advanced on our position.[127] We opened on them with small arms, our position was quite exposed my co. was in a garden on top of a hill just before the fight commenced. I made the boys pile up a few rails by the side of the fence which gave us some shelter & made us able to hold our position while otherwise we could not have held it.[128]

We engaged them for ten hours. Gen'l. Tracey was killed early in the engagement (about 9 o'clock). He was struck with a minie ball just below the shoulder blade & came out through the brest.[129] About ten o'clock B. F. Garvin & Geo. Stephens were wound. G. had his left arm broken.[130] S. had a flesh wound in the arm.[131] This was done by a shell. About the same time J. M. Karr was wounded slightly in the head with a minie ball.[132] Luke Roberts was shot while laying down.[133] The ball entered near the neck in the shoulder. He lived a few hours & was in his right mind until he died. He refused to be carried off the field stating that he knew he could not live long & wished to die on the battlefield. He said that he was willing to die for his country. I was not able to talk to him any as I was needed at my post but those who saw say that he was perfectly willing to die. O. E. Langley was killed instantly while in the act of shooting.[134] The ball entered his head just above the eye. About the same time N. V. Stephens was wounded in the head.[135] I can't learn how badly. I saw the wound but did not examine it. Roberts & Langley were left on the field. We got all their papers before leaving. B. F. Garvin & N. V. Stephens were taken to the hospital & have not been heard from since. They were captured. G. W. Stephens & J. M. Karr, both came off & are safe. John Ford,[136] John Gidley,[137] Hughes Newton[138] & Ben Nunnelly are missing.[139] I am confident they were captured as I have not heard from them since we left.

We had to retreat about five o'clock in the evening. Gen'l. Tracey was buried at Port Gipson. A great many of our men were captured. The loss in our reg't. was I understand, seven killed, twenty eight wounded & fifty missing.[140] I sent you a dispatch the day after the fight. I don't know whether you got it or not. I had only thirty one men with me at the commencement of the fight, about twelve or fourteen came in during the engagement. Capt. Tom Patterson of our reg't. was wounded & taken prisoner.[141] My co. shot about thirty rounds apiece. They did as well as any men could do. *All* did well. None showed a disposition to leave their post until ordered. We have been on the retreat until now. We have take our position on the line from Warrenton to Jackson. I was not hurt at all. Lt. Col. Pettus of the 20th has got in having escaped after being captured.[142] He says that we killed half as many as we had engaged which would be over one thousand. Our loss was four or five hundred killed, wounded & missing.[143] The enemy I understand have not crossed Big Black. I will write you again soon. My love to all.

Your son,
John

Hopkins T. Francis to James C. Francis
Selma, May 26th 1863

Dear Father,

I left Meridian on last Sunday. I saw that there no chance to get through to Vicksburg & I returned to Selma. shall remain here untill I can get through. I will stay with Maj. Bowman Depot Camp.[144] I have heard nothing from Thos or John since I left home. I saw a gentleman from Vicksburg that was in fight at Big Black. He says that Stevenson's Division lost but few men.[145] It is almost impossible to hear anything from Vicksburg as all communication is cut off. I will write again in a few days. My love to all. I rec. the hundred dollars by Warlick.

Your obedient son,
Hop

Thomas W. Francis to James C. Francis
The Southern Telegraph Companies[146]
Jackson, May 29, 1863

Dr. J. C. Francis

Jacksonville
Arrived tonight, heard from Vicksburg. Up to Sunday John still safe, genl. & staff safe.

T. W. Francis

Charles M. Shelley to John C. Francis
Convalescent Camp
June 15th [1863]

Capt.:

I received the order from Genl. Lee ordering certain promotions in the regt.[147] I notice however that he has made a mistake by promoting Lieut. Beavers to the captaincy of Co. H[148] & neglects to promote Lieut. Spruill[149] or Turner.[150] Both of whom ought to be promoted & Lieut. Green being killed will make another change in the order.[151] I think you had better return the order to Genl. Lee & call his attention to the changes necessary to be made and ask in view of the smallness of the companies to allow you to defer the elections until the companies can be reunited or till we can get the men together who are now absent. My health is more feeble today than usual. Send Butler of Co. "K"[152] down to wait on Col. Smith.[153] He is not doing well and needs some one to lift him about. Send me word how you are getting on and whether you have had any casualties today. Have the enemy annoyed you much? Give me all the news in detail. There is a "Grape" here that a "Carier Pigeon" came in to day with a dispatch from Johnson to the effect that he would attack the enemy tomorrow or next day with an army of 75,000 men. So you may "look out for the cars when you hear the whistle."[154]

Yours & c.,
C. M. Shelley

Ada Barnett to John C. Francis
[Vicksburg, Miss. June 24, 1863]

Capt. Francis,

Since you have become one of the "heroes of Vicksburg," you have forgotten your old friends entirely. I send you a bouquet to remind you that in spite of the shells we are still alive and will be glad to see you whenever you can leave the trenches.
June 24th/63
37th Day of Siege of Vicksburg.

Sincerely your friend,
Ada Barnett[155]

Parole certificate for John C. Francis[156]
Vicksburg, Mississippi, July 8th 1863

To All Whom It May Concern, Know Ye That:

I John C. Francis a Capt. of Co. B 30th Reg't. Ala. Vols. C.S.A. being a prisoner of War, in the hands of the United States Forces, in virtue of the capitulation of the city of Vicksburg and its Garrison by Lieut. Gen. John C. Pemberton, C.S.A. commanding, on the 4th day of 1863, do in pursuance of the terms of said capitulation, give my solemn parole under oath -

That I will not take up arms again against the United States, nor serve in any military, police, or constabulary force in an Fort, Garrison or field work, held by the Confederate States of America, against the United States of America, nor as a guard of any prisons, depots or stores, nor discharge any duties usually performed by Officers or soldiers against the United States of America, until duly exchanged by proper authorities.

Jno C. Francis, Capt.
Co. "B" 30th Ala. Reg't.

Sworn to subscribed before me at Vicksburg, Miss., this 8th day of July 1863.

John C. Fry, 20th Reg't.
Ohio Vols.
Major and Paroling Officer

Thomas W. Francis to James C. Francis
The Southern Telegraph Companies
Meridian, July 13, 1863

Dr. J. C. Francis

Jacksonville

John safe at Brandon.[157] Don't know his loss if any.

T. W. Francis

6 / *Some Fighting and Retreating*

By July 1863, the war had dragged on two years with mounting death and ruin spawning cynicism in the wake of a faltering idealism. Both sides, North and South, now had disaffected citizens harboring growing discontent and scepticism. In some northern cities this violence flared into antidraft riots with the worst violence and lawlessness directed at free blacks. The worst of these, in New York City, subsided only after four days, resulting in 1,000 people killed or injured and property losses estimated at $1.5 million.[1] Both wartime governments confronted new grim realities. Although the North seemed to have the advantage, Lincoln's administration was hounded by the resistance and discord of a growing peace movement. Nor was the South immune. The Davis administration faced daunting opposition from its military and burgeoning discontent in its general populace. Southerners were increasingly concerned about holding off invading Union armies and rampant economic hardships.

In Alabama, the discontent manifested itself in the elections of 1863. The people, especially those in the Tennessee River Valley, were weary of war and want. They voted against President Davis, Confederate taxes, and Governor John Gill Shorter. Thomas H. Watts, a prewar Whig, defeated Shorter's reelection bid in August 1863 by a vote of 28,221 to 9,664. In the Fourth Congressional District, which included Calhoun County, Jabez L. M. Curry, the incumbent Talladega congressman, was defeated by Marcus H. Cruikshank, editor of the *Talladega Alabama Reporter.* Curry, a staunch secessionist, remained a strong war proponent and a vocal supporter of Jefferson Davis. However, a growing peace party, strong disaffection for the war in North Alabama, and hard times across the state combined to defeat Shorter and Curry.[2]

Through these winds of discontent, the Francis brothers soldiered on, unswerving in their commitment, persevering in their cause, especially John, still in the thick of the Confederate military effort. At the end of their furloughs, the men of the Thirtieth Alabama were ordered to report to a regimental rendezvous near Talladega, Alabama. John Francis arrived with orders promoting him to major. This promotion made him the highest-ranking officer in his regiment except for the still absent commander, Colonel Shelley. Shelley was not the only absentee. The Thirtieth Alabama, over the course of some fifteen months of fighting and retreating, had shrunk from 1,099 men in May 1862 to approximately 200 in late August 1863. Francis and his fellow officers attempted to collect their missing troops and published notices in papers statewide urging their return. These efforts were assisted by the Confederate government's declaration of a prisoner exchange for those captured at Vicksburg. The formal exchange was made on 11 September 1863.[3]

Within a few days of this declaration, the Thirtieth Alabama traveled from Talladega to Demopolis, Alabama, which was designated by the War Department as a reception center for Alabama troops.[4] Once mustered anew at Demopolis, the monotony of drill was broken only by religious meetings and parades. Clearly the most memorable parade occurred on 18 October 1863, when the Alabama troops formed in a line three and a quarter miles long for half an hour for a review by President Jefferson Davis. As the thin, graying war leader reviewed the formation, the men presented arms and gave him three cheers "with much enthusiasm."[5]

The Thirtieth Alabama, under command of Major John Francis, was assigned to an all-Alabama brigade under Edmund Winston Pettus and ordered to join the Army of Tennessee commanded by Braxton Bragg near Chattanooga.[6] Arriving on the west side of Lookout Mountain on 8 November 1863, the men of the brigade were assigned picket duty in a position that gave them a clear view of the Union camps down the valley. Although they experienced no active fighting for nearly three weeks, the regiment occasionally engaged the enemy in long-range artillery duels. Pettus's brigade was relieved of picket duty and moved to the east side of Lookout Mountain while Stevenson's division continued in its defensive position atop the mountain.[7]

On the foggy morning of 24 November 1863, the battle of Lookout Mountain began as 12,000 Union troops led by Brigadier General Joseph Hooker crossed Lookout Creek on the west side of the mountain. Moving through the cold mist, Yankee soldiers capitalized on their surprise and captured many of Edward C. Walthall's Mississippi brigade.[8] Pettus sent reinforcements who stopped the Union advance and relieved Walthall's dispirited brigade.[9] About noon Pettus deployed skirmishers to Smith's Trail on top of the mountain. There a scout party, under Major John Francis, observed the Union advance around the mountain. Ordered to withdraw to the valley between Lookout Mountain and Missionary Ridge about 7:00 P.M., Pettus's brigade completed its withdrawal after 1:00 A.M. on the twenty-fifth.[10]

Later that morning, the Thirtieth Alabama formed a line on the north end of Missionary Ridge on the right flank of the Confederate position.[11] Bragg's second corps occupied rifle pits at the base of the ridge, on the slope, and on the crest of the ridge on the Confederate left and center. Nearly 32,000 strong, they waited for Ulysses S. Grant to unleash his 60,000 Yankee troops against their strongly held defensive position.[12] The Union infantry struck the Rebel lines in waves across a two-mile front. John Francis, positioned on the right flank, thought his men had won a complete victory when Stevenson's and Patrick Cleburne's divisions repeatedly repelled Sherman's troops. In the late afternoon, however, the Confederate center was ultimately breached. The Union forces swept over the ridge during the late evening.[13]

In the early morning hours of 26 November, Bragg's broken army retreated over Chickamauga Creek toward Graysville and Ringgold, Georgia. Struggling through a cold rain over muddy roads, they reached Dalton, Georgia, on the Western & Atlantic Railroad the following night.[14] Writing to his father the next day, John Francis, now a battle-hardened veteran, expressed the bitterness felt by so many in Bragg's army over the defeat at the battle of Missionary Ridge.[15]

By early December 1863, the Thirtieth Alabama had entered winter quarters near Dalton, Georgia. The desertions of sixteen of his men on the night of 4 December revealed a mellowing of John's outlook. Although he condemned the deserters, his attitude had been tempered by war. An early champion of public execution, John Francis displayed a softer attitude toward the deserters. Sobered by combat, John probably understood the reasons for this continuing plague of Confederate desertions: low morale, discontent over the war, command problems, and the Davis administration's policies, including conscription and limited furloughs. Nevertheless, the Thirtieth Alabama persevered, as did the rest of the Army of Tennessee. They built winter quarters of makeshift cabins, stacked up stores of fuel, and received boxes of food and clothing from family and friends.[16]

The strain of the harsh winter and boredom of camp life were relieved by religious and Masonic meetings, visits from friends and family, furloughs, and massive snowball fights among the brigades. Although Dr. James C. Francis did not visit Dalton, his brother Hugh traveled to the encampment to see his sons, Joseph Hugh and Hopkins Turney Francis, and other Francis kinsmen, including Jim Montgomery, John Montgomery, and Miller Francis Turney.[17] The Montgomery brothers, sons of James and Elizabeth Ingram Montgomery and nephews of Amy Ingram Francis, were privates in the Nineteenth Alabama at Dalton.[18] Hugh's nephew Miller Francis Turney, known as "Tobe," served as a captain and assistant commissary for subsistence in the Twenty-third Tennessee Battalion there.[19] Despite the harshness of the winter camp, life became tolerable for the Confederate soldiers at Dalton when Joe Johnston, known affectionately as "Old Joe," assumed command of the Army of Tennessee on 27 December 1863.[20]

The 1863 Christmas season found the Francis family scattered from East Tennessee to southeast Georgia, from North Alabama to East Mississippi. Jim Francis enjoyed Christmas day with his fiancée, Sadie Whitehead, and her family at Ivanhoe, Georgia.[21] John and Jo Francis passed "a dull Christmas" at Dalton, where John's dinner consisted of oysters. Tom Francis, his wife, Fannie, and Hop were in Enterprise, Mississippi, where Tom continued to worry about his property, livestock, and slaves in Calhoun County. Miller Francis remained with Longstreet's corps in East Tennessee, and Emma, at Summerfield, spent her first Christmas away from her family.[22]

Thomas W. Francis to James C. Francis
Selma, Ala.
July 14, [18]63

Dear Father,

I wrote you a few days since and have heard nothing from you since. I hope you have bought the land at satisfactory prices, since I wrote you. I have sold my house and lot here for $10,280—cash and I am now more anxious than ever to get the land[23] and I am going to leave here in the morning for Jackson & c., Brandon where I understand our prisoners will be from Vicksburg and if I cannot get to them I will get where I can communicate and find out about Jno.[24] If Crow will take $2,000 for his place buy it for me, or if you can make any trade for a good piece of property in Jacksonville do so on your own judgement and I will risk it.[25] Write me here care M. J. A. Keith and I can get my letters.[26]

Your son,
Thom

Miller William Francis to James C. Francis
Trenton, Ga.
July 18th 1863

Dear Father,

Julia and Frank arrived here safe yesterday evening without accident. We were taken by surprise. Our brigade will move in a short time to the neighborhood of Alexandria or some where in the Coosa Valley near our county. We are waiting for our horses to be shod, only that is the present order, unless it is changed. I sent a list of killed, wounded & missing from our two co's by Uncle Hugh.[27] It is as correct as can be made and there is a list in a Yankee paper of all the captives.

I will give you a list of them as near correct as possible. Lt. Fain's name is among the captured not killed as first supposed, as soon as I see the Yankee list I will send it for publication.[28] Lt. Col. Webb dangerous wound in right side on 2 July at Elk River left at Pennington's house near Winchester.[29] Adjt. McCraw dangerous wound through right thigh left at Shelbyville a prisoner.[30] All the names that are missing are correct but we are not able to tell whether they are killed or captured but from the places where they were last seen it is probable there are very few lost. We have correct information that there was but 20 bodies obtained from the river & I think there were but few from other Regt that are missing that reached the river as they were sent off & captured before that time.[31] Lt. Fain, Burton, Pelham, Cowling & Major Dyes & Capt. Force are prisoners & neglected to put Dyes name amongst the field officers.[32] Tell Mrs. Bush that I feel confident that Dudley is only a prisoner & that we will have his clothes taken care of.[33] She told Julia to ask me about him. The loss from our Regt. is about 140 men & officers more than any other two Regts. in the Division. The Regt. fought well as I ever saw it but had but little assistance. As soon as I can get hold of the Yankee list I will send it home for publication. I feel confident there were but few of our men killed or wounded.

I saw the Regt. rallied and formed 3 different times. I saw men of the Regt. go back & meet the Yankee charge when they assumed before they went that their guns & cartridges were useless. There were numbers of personal deeds of daring amongst men & officers. The men & officers of the different Regts. are not to blame. The condition of their arms & ammunition was reported to Genl. Martin & he reported to Genl. Wheeler.

Nothing but fight would do & you see the end of it. There are some men that take a larger contract than they can carry out, that is the case with some officers.

We will move in short time to your county. I suppose I wish my bay horse fed so that I can ride him while there & not the sorrel. Gabe left the wagons unwell & suppose he started for home. Keep him there as I can get along without him. I spoke about covering my house with boards. Have it done with shingles. I am good health so is Julia & Frank & White.[34] You can give this list of names to Grant as it is correct as can be made. Our Regt. is in fine health but horses worn out.

Your son,
M. W. Francis

Joseph H. Francis to Amy I. Francis
Office of Purchasing Commissary
Augusta, Ga., July 24 1863

Dr Mother,

I recd. Willie's and Sue's letters today was glad to hear from John. You must excuse me for not answering you sooner. Tell Sue that I wrote her a letter the other day. I'll write to Willie soon. I wonder if Emma claims a letter of me. She has not written to me since she left Summerfield, & I am certain she was due me two or three before she left.

Our work is not quite so heavy as it has been. We are through with the big lots of sugar. I suppose you have learned before now, about the seizure of all the sugar at this post. Jim has about completed the impressment, it amounts to about three thousand (3,000) hhds. Some men has lost as high as forty thousand ($40,000.00/100) dollars by the seizure.[35] The rain is ruining the wheat & corn above here in Va. & Carolina, not a day has been missed in some time. We are having a thunder shower now, the lightening has struck some where near this block just then. It was the loudest I ever heard, & shook the building. It has made my head ache, it was like a 4 pounder turned lose over your head.

As soon as the raid on Rome is decided you will send my coat, blk. pants, janes vest & c. I'm sorry you can't find the colers & butiscal for my shirt. If you by chance get the colers, I want them some wider than two inches or two and a half. I'm much in need of the clothes. Send them to Rome in Mr. Wolum's care and from there by express, takeing receipt &

valueing the same at $75.00/100, the charges to be paid at this place.[36] I like to hear from home soon. My love to all. Jim is unwell today. Hop well. Excuse mistakes in haste.

Your son,
Jo

Joseph H. Francis to Amy I. Francis
Augusta, Ga., Aug 24th 1863

Dr Mother,

I recd. the package several days since. We have no news from Charleston of importance, except that a demand for the surrender of this place.[37] No papers from there today. I send you the *Chattanooga Rebel* with an account of the little shelling that occured last Friday.[38] Nothing more at present, you will excuse this letter as my arm is so soar that I have not wrote any in several days, (a boil). Did Charley get his piece of artillery I sent by Hop? Tell him to write me a letter.

You need not have any fears of its bursting for I gave it a fire test.

Your son,
Jo

Hopkins T. Francis to James C. Francis
Demopolis, Aug. 27th 1863

Father,

I have to day expressed you a bag of wool. It will be at Blue Mountain Saturday or Monday also a small sack for Thos.[39] I do not know how much yours contains. But I suppose some 25 or 30 lbs. Ask Lark where my calf skin is?[40] It is at Maj. Abernathy or Snow's Tan yard you can get it & have shoes made for the children.[41]

Where is Jno? I have not heard from him since I left. We are getting along finely. The weather is very pleasant. It is getting a little cool now of nights. I haven't a single blanket. I wish you would get me something in the shape of bed clothing & send by first opportunity. My love to all.

Your obedient son,
H. T. Francis

John C. Francis to Mary Emma Francis
Talladega, Ala.
August 27/[18]63

Dear Sister Emma,

I received yours a few days ago & have not had time to answer you before. I have been very busy since my arrival, keeping the regt. together. We have now in camps near two hundred men.[42] I will send Father's shirt by some one passing it is in wash now. We received orders a few days ago to await further orders at this place. I don't know how long we will be here. It may be only a few days & it may be months no one knows. I attended a pic-nic a few days ago at this place. Very few out. I wrote to Jim today about that picture of mine & give it to sister Fannie. Send my uniform down by Ed Clark.[43] I don't know whether I will come up soon or not. There is no field officer with the regt. but myself. Get me some ink & pens. There is only about twenty men of the 31st here.[44] My love to all. How is Jo doing?

Your affectionate bro.,
John

Thomas W. Francis to James C. Francis
Demopolis, Ala.
Aug. 31, [18]63

Dear Father,

I send Hop home to get some papers that I require in fixing up some reports and I send with him a young man by the name of Scott from Missouri. He is maimed and a cripple for life. I do not know how he will do but I thought I would give him home if nothing else. I told him that you would tell him how I wanted the crop planted and when and how to manage and that if you got no one that he would have to look after your hands too. But if you can get any one I would prefer it so that he can spend all of his time with my hands and taking care of my stock but I think with a white man on the place to protect them that Lark would make a good crop if you tell him that you make him accountable for every thing.[45]

I want you to rent out such of my lands as you think best I prefer some one to take it all. I think it best for me to sew the far Tramell field in oats and the Mill field in wheat and a part of the Downing place and the rest of the Walker place and the Downing place for rent at the usual rent. You can tell the young man whitch the young mules you intend for me to have, and I expect I will have to buy another mule.

I will try and get home before Christmas some time. I sent two bags of sugar by express to the depot marked in my name and I wish you would take charge of it and keep it until some of the family need it. I sent a sack of salt home some time since did you ever get it.[46] You can try the young man a while and if you think its best he can take charge of your hands as well as mine. I do not know whether he can manage them or not. See Jno Abernathy if he wants to rent the land give him the preference, but I don't think he will go down.[47]

Your son,
T. W. Francis

~

Hopkins T. Francis to James C. Francis
Enterprise, Miss.
Sept. 25, 1863

Dear Father,

I have not heard from home since I left. Thos rec. a letter from Fannie yesterday stating that all were well at home. I heard that Thos overseer had left. I am surprised at his leaving. I thought that he was very well satisfied. Thos is now issuing to the paroled prisoners stationed at this place.[48] We are getting along finely. We have comfortable quarters, a good tent, plenty to eat, and abundance of bedding. There is none of the prisoners stationed at this place exchanged yet that I have heard of.[49] I understand that the Ala. exchanged prisoners are ordered to report to Genl. Johnson.[50] Tell the children to write me how the boys from Jacksonville & vicinity came out in the late battle in Georgia.[51] Tell them it is almost impossible to hear anything from them any other way than by letter.

Thos & I are enjoying fine health. My love to Mother & the children. Write soon.

Your affectionate son,
H. T. Francis

Thomas W. Francis to James C. Francis
Enterprise, Miss.
Oct. 5, [18]63

Dear Father,

I wrote you soon after Hop's arrival but have heard nothing from you since I left except through Hop. I expect to be in the course of a few days but I may be disappointed again as before. If so I want you to direct my folks where to sew wheat and about how much. I think fifty acres will be about right and the ballance of my land that I cannot work I wish rented out. You can take what you wish and rent the ballance. I have not heard whether Scott is there or not or what arrangements you have been able to make for an overseer.[52] I wish we could get a first rate man if we had to pay him a large price. I have heard of Rowland's misfortune with his boy.[53] I am sorry for him but he is certainly a hard case.

I have heard nothing from Jo for some time. Hop is in fine health and is doing finely. I see no reason for any of you to be uneasy about him. He is all right and hard at work.

I hope I am able to come back home during next week. Emma I suppose will start to Summerfield on Monday. My love to all the family.

Your son,
T. W. Francis

John C. Francis to James C. Francis
Camp near Demopolis, Ala.[54]
Oct. 11th 1863

Dear Father,

Mr. W. Denman starts home tomorrow being on a visit to our reg't.[55] There is nothing of interest here. I suppose Tom is at home now. I wrote him to get one hundred dollars from you if he needed it. Pay it to him if he calls on you for it. If he has no particular use for it I will pay him at some more convenient time. I am getting along very well. Lt. Col. Patterson of our reg't. tendered his resignation a few days ago but the medical board refused to sign it & recommended a furlough of sixty days. He has sent on his furlough for sixty days. He does not think it will be approved by the medical director but a resignation recommended, but I can't believe that though it is possible. He seems to be very anxious to resign and was considerably mortified to find that they would not approve his papers. If he gets a furlough I think he will resign at its expiration.[56] My horse is doing very well. Send me my mare by the first good opportunity if you do not particularly need her as some accident might happen to my horse & I would be on foot. My love to all.

Your affectionate son,
John

Thomas W. Francis to James C. Francis
Enterprise, Miss.
Oct. 28, [18]63

Dear Father,

I have been unable to hear from John since I returned here. I saw him as I came through Demopolis and told him I would send him a boy if I could get one and I sent the boy a few days since and I suppose he will remain at camp with his mess until he returns to the camp. Should he not I think certain I can get him one in a few days.

I hope you have been able to go down to the plantation and see about sewing wheat & oats. I am very uneasy about the corn not being taken off of the Walker bottom in time. As I told you I think it much the best to seed down all the Walker bottom on each side of the creek and where there has been wheat put it in oats and the ballance of the oats either in the field around the Walker houses or Tramell field.[57] If you can rent all the ballance do so. There is 12 or 15 acres next to Rader's place that is cleared on the Walker tract. I expect Downing will take the ballance of the Walker place and seed it down.[58] He told me he had plenty of seed and time to do it. Hop will be at home next week for Fannie.

Yours affectionately,
T. W. Francis

Amy I. Francis to Mary Emma Francis
Jacksonville, Nove. 1st 1863

Dear Daughter,

I write you a few lines to let you know we are all well. I have your things all ready and will send them to you in a few days. Miller came home late Wednesday and left yesterday.[59] John left this morning for Tennessee. I would have sent your things last week if John had not been ordered to Tennessee. He was a going by to see you. The regiment he belonged to was ordered to Tennessee.[60] We heard from James and Jo a few days since.[61] They were well. We have heard nothing more from W. White. We suppose he is dead do not know.[62]

Fanny White bought you a delain dress in Selma cost $1.50, .15 dollars a yard. She left it with Miss Tully.[63] She Miss Tully said she was in Augusta and saw James and he told her to make up dresses for you and charge it to him. You can do as you please about it. The delain she bought was a piece you did not see. She says it is very pretty.

Your Father and Bud started to the plantation this evening.[64] Bud is highly pleased with his trip. Your home spun dress is very much admired. Willie wore it yesterday to hear the governor speak.[65] He made a very good speach. Study with one of the girls until your book gets there. You must study very hard and get good lessons, treat your roommates well, and remember your duty to your God. We are in his hands and he will with us as he sees fit. If we have God all things will work together for our good. Write often. May the Lord bless and save is my prayer from your affectionate mother.

A. Francis

John C. Francis to James C. Francis
Camp near Chickamauga, Tenn.
Nov. 4th 1863

Dear Father,

I arrived here yesterday & found everything quiet except an occasional gun from our lines. We have just received orders to report to Gen'l. Walker on the extreem left of our line.[66] We will start this evening or tomorrow morning. The enemy appear to be moving up from below. I am getting along very well. I saw Capt. Jim Martin yesterday he was doing very well.[67] I left Uncle John in Rome.[68] I will write you again as soon as we get our new quarters. My love to all.

Your son,
John

~

John C. Francis to Amy I. Francis
Camp near Chattanooga, Tenn.
Nov. 8th 1863

Dear Mother,

Since I wrote last we have been marching a great deal over rough roads. We left Chickamauga Station on the night of the 4th & came on the west side of Missionary Ridge to the foot of Lookout Mt. on the east side was there only a short time & was ordered on pickett across the mountain.[69] It was raining and dark which gave us a great deal of trouble. We are now on the west side of Lookout Mt. on pickett will be here for several days. The enemy occupy Raccoon Mt. & the valley to Chattanooga Creek.[70] Our picketts on one side of the creek theirs on the other. We have no talking on the line. The enemies picketts seem to be very anxious to communicate with us but it is disobedience of orders to communicate with them. From our position we can see their camps very distinctly. They run the railroad to within twenty seven miles of C. & haul in wagons to the city. Our batterys on Lookout Point are shelling their trains regular.[71]

My horse has not come yet. I don't need him much now as I am in the mts. There is nothing of interest going on here. I saw Adrian[72] & Beasley a few days ago.[73] A citizen came through the enemies lines yesterday to ours & he states that it is thought among the soldiers of the federal army that Sherman from Miss. will flank our position here and compel Bragg to fall back.[74] I think we will flank through East Tennessee.[75] It has been raining a great deal here of late but is very pleasant now. We look for our wagon train about tomorrow night. The health of the troops is presently good. Tell Father if my mare gets in good order soon, sell her if he can get a good price for her. My love to all.

Your affectionate son,
John

John C. Francis to James C. Francis
Camp near Chattanooga
Nov. 11th 1863

Dear Father,

There has nothing of interest happened since I wrote you last. We are still on pickett on the west side of Lookout Mt. The enemy have their supplies down the valley in front of us & our batteries on top of the mt. are shelling them continually. Occasionly they shell our men on this side of the mountain. A few days ago they killed one man and wounded ten of the 42nd Ala. is all the damage done us.[76] Four of our reg't. (Co. "H" from St. Clair) deserted night before last & went to the enemy.[77]

It is very hard to get rations here especially meat. Though, I understand that we will be supplied tomorrow. We drove up a beef this morning from the picket line which will do us for a while. The Masons of the reg't. have secured a charter for a lodge. They desire that I should join. It is my intention to do so. I don't know what our forces are doing I don't believe there is any prospect for an engagement here. Our wagons have not come yet we look for them today. The weather is quite cool here now.

If you can get me a "boy" send him to me as it will be impossible to get the one that Tom spoke of. I have not heard from Miller since I came here. I don't know where he is. I have been unable to see but few acquaintances since I came here. W. P. Becker came to see me a few days ago.[78] I have not seen Johnson in several days. He is on the other side of the mt. Lt. Thomas has resigned & is going to start this evening.[79] I will send this by him. I don't know how the mails are I have not received a letter since my arrival. I am getting along very well. My love to all.

Your affectionate son,
John

John C. Francis to James C. Francis
Camp near Chattanooga, Tenn.
Nov. 18th 1863

Dear Father,

Nothing of interest has happened I believe since I wrote you last. Yesterday morning there was very heavy cannonading on the right. It was our men shelling the enemys camp.[80] We have been relieved from duty on the west side of Lookout Mt. & are now on the east side on the left of our army.[81] We are expecting orders to move up the valley. We get plenty to eat now. Some think we will have to fall back on account of forage. I don't know whether we will or not.

I understand from someone that Mr. Land is very mad about me taking a "guitar" out of his shop.[82] His lady was there when I got it. I told her that I would return it. It properly belongs in his shop. You will please see that it is returned to him. I don't see any chance of getting a boy here. You will please send me one by the first chance. I am in need of one very much. I have not heard from home in some time. I think Willie ought to go to Summerfield next session as she will be with Emma but if she waits she will not have that advantage which will be of great benefit to her. My horse is looking well. I am paying Lt. Warlick as I draw. I am very well pleased with my saddle. Was there any clothing left in the shop? I have not had an opportunity of seeing Miller since I came. Tell Sister Julia that I am very much obliged to her for the coverlet. Talladega done much better than Calhoun.[83] She gave nearly all of her blankets & money to buy more. My love to all.

Your son, John

John C. Francis to James C. Francis
Dalton, Ga., Nov 28th 1863

Dear Father,

This is the first time I have had an opportunity of writing to you for several days. I don't know when I will send it off. Since I wrote you last we have had some fighting & retreating to do. On the morning of the 24th it was very foggy. The enemy was seen crossing Lookout Creek on the west side of Lookout Mt.[84] We had only one brigade on that side of the Maj. Walthall's.[85] The enemy drove him around the mt. a few hundred yards this side of the Cravens house on the bench of the mt.[86] Then we stopped there. A portion of our brig. (20th, 31st regts.) went to their assistance from the top of Lookout Mt.[87] Our regt. was ordered to Smith's trail on top of the mt.[88]

I was ordered on a scout to the point of Lookout Mt. When I arrived there I could very plainly see the enemy moving around the mt. and did some execution from the top of the mt. though I had so few men I could do but little. I sent back for more men & got four co.'s to guard the point. The enemy started up but soon found that we occupied it & they retired. After dark we were ordered off of the mt. & stayed in the valley between Missionary Ridge & Lookout Mt. that night.[89] The next morning we took position on Missionary Ridge on the right of our army. (I forgot to mention that I lost one man on Lookout, M. T. Sewell, Capt. Kelly's co. killed).[90] We formed line of battle on the ridge. We skirmished with the enemy until about ten o'clock A.M. when they advanced in four columns on our right a few hundred a column came in our front and lay down about four hundred yds. from us. They made a charge two or three different times & were repulsed every time. They went of in the wildest confusion, there was no two together, every man for himself. This was a complete victory. It lasted until nearly night.[91] About dark we learned that they had broken our center (Day's & Vaughan's brigades).[92] This caused us to fall back and we have been going ever since, stoping to rest occasionly.

We have been here since last night. I don't know whether we will go on to day or not. We lost some artillery & some wagons. I don't know the number. I don't know where our line will be.[93] Our loss in B & E are as follows, 24th—M. T. Sewell Co. "E" killed, Jos. Hollingsworth Co. "B" wounded severely in arm;[94] 25th—Co. "B" Serg't. J. K. Landers mortally in brest was left behind,[95] Sergt. M. T. Durham slight in shoulder,[96] J. P. Cook severe in hand,[97] Barney Baxter Co. "E" slight in leg.[98] I was not injured a ball cut my coat. The regt. lost about twenty (20) in all. Lt. Warlick comded. Co. "B" & did himself credit.[99] John Glover was accidently shot this morning near the spine.[100] I am fearful that he will not recover. Johnson, Mattison, Ed Clark & Weir are safe and well. The enemy are only persuing us with cavalry. We captured a good many of them. My brigade is safe. The reg't. lost no baggage at all. My love to all.

Your son,
John

P.S. Tell Aunt Kate that I saw Jo the morning before. I don't think he was hurt in the fight he was in the pioneer corps. I will hunt him up today & if he is hurt I will write her. John

[Margin note] Direct your letters to Dalton. Joe Francis is safe.[101]

John C. Francis to Mary Emma Francis
Dalton, Ga., Nov 28th 1863[102]

Dear Sister Emma,

I will write you a few lines this evening to let you know that I am safe. Did not get hurt in the fight near Chattanooga on the other day. I had a ball to strike my coat was the nearest thing came to me. We are in this place I think only for a while. I think the army will fall back to Rome. I don't think the enemy will follow us though. They are following very slow only with cavalry. I am doing very well. The reg't. lost about twenty men in killed and wounded.[103] You don't know any of them. When I have time I will write to you again. I have not heard from you since I left home. Why don't you write to me? Tell Dr. Rivers that I saw Winston this morning. My regards to him & family. Direct your letters to Dalton & I will get them. Write to me as often as you can. I did not loose any of my baggage. There was no officers in the reg't. killed only one wounded a Lt. of Co. "H".

Your affectionate bro.,
John

James C. Francis, Jr. to Mary Emma Francis
Office of Purchasing Commissary
Augusta, Ga., Nov. 30th 1863

My Dear Sister:

Your letter of the 24th inst. to hand. I am glad to hear from you but my dear sister you should not view things in the way you do. I am somewhat surprised at you. You should not think that your brothers do not love you. Yes they all care very much, probably it was not convenient for Sister to come to tell you goodbye. You should not judge rashly my sister.[104]

I am very sorry that it does not meet with your approval (I mean my marriage). I do not know the exact time "Emma" that we will marry. I expect not before "April." When the time is set you of course will get an invitation. Miss "Sadie" will love you so much and you will love her when you meet her.[105] I know you will. My darling "Emma" you must change your way of thinking about your brothers. I know you are mistaken. I will always love you this you know & so will all the rest. I will remain in "Augusta" during the war if it is possible. After that I will spend my winters south of this. I hope you may be able to come on and see me married if possible.

When this evil war is over if I should be spared & can have a home, you must come and stay with me. I live for my little sisters as well as for this lady of my choice and it will always give me pleasure to add to their happiness when I can. My time is very much absorbed with my business.[106] I have much to do. I hope it may slackin soon and then I can write you oftener. You must forget any seeming neglect my dear sister from your brothers. They may not write you often but that is no evidence that they do not love you very much. Won't you write to Miss "Sadie"? She will appreciate the letter so much and will reply on receiving it. She will be proud to correspond with you. She is a sweet lady of 19 years, one of the 1st familys in the state, a good Christian.[107] This you will be proud of and she says she will make one of me soon. I pray she may, and then you will love me better.

I must close now dear "Emma." Won't you write Miss "Sadie"? Send the letter to my address and I will deliver it to her for you. Write me on receipt of this. "Jo" is well.[108] With much love your devoted brother.

J. C. Francis, Jr.

John C. Francis to James C. Francis
Camp near Dalton, Ga.
Dec. 5th 1863

Dear Father,

Mr. Wright will come by this morning on his way home.[109] I will send by him a saber & four yards of cotton goods. Tell Mother that she can use it any way she wishes. Some of the boys gave it to me. It was captured in a sutler's wagon. We are all doing very well at present, get plenty of beef and bread. There was sixteen of our regt. left camps last night. We suppose they have gone home. I think this could all be remedied if they would try those that we have in arrest for desertion & shoot a few of them. There is no excuse in the world for men's desertion at this time.[110] I don't see what they can hope for.

I received a letter from Jim yesterday. He was doing well. I wrote you some time ago about the fight. I have not had a single letter from home since the wagons passed through Jacksonville. I wrote to Willie and Sue a few days ago. I don't think there will be any move in this army before spring. The most of the troops are building winter quarters. If you can get a good trade for my mare let her go. Don't take less than eight hundred. Horses are worth a great deal here. I don't know what to write you about a boy as I have written you so often about it.[111] I am very much in need of one. My love to all.

Your affectionate son,
John

John C. Francis to James C. Francis
Camp near Dalton, Ga.
Dec. 10th 1863

Dear Father,

Nothing of interest has happened since I wrote you last. I am now on the road between Dalton & Resaca with five hundred men from the brigade working the road. I suppose that I will be relieved in a day or two. I saw Jo at D. today. He has been here several days. I think he was ordered to field duty. He came here & is staying with the post commissary until his command gets here. I think he intends to send his papers up to get a permanent detail with Jim. I think he wrote to you about it.

I have not had a single letter from home since the wagons passed through. I don't know what is the matter. I write home about twice a week & it is something strange that I can't hear from home. I have had one letter from Emma since I came here & one from Jim. He is doing very well. He wrote me about his engagement. I am getting along very well.

Col. Shelley told me yesterday that Capt. Patterson had received a letter from Lt. Col. W. C. Patterson, who ordered him (Capt. P.) to tender his (Lt. Col.) resignation. The Col. directed him to write to him to go before the board in Talladega & send the certificate from the board & that it would be forwarded.[112] They have not had time to hear from him since. I saw John Rowland today he said that he thought that Morgan's command would be here in a few days.[113] I don't know what will be done here. Some think we will fall back. The enemy are making no demonstrations in our front. The boys from about town are doing very well. My love to all.

Your son,
John

P.S. I think Willie ought to go to Summerfield next session. It is true she will labor under some disadvantages by being there at the middle of the session but I think that she should be there while Emma is there. I think that I shall join the Masons soon. We have a lodge with our regt.[114] John

~

Joseph H. Francis to James C. Francis
Dalton, Ga., Dec. 16th/[18]63

Dear Father,

Uncle Hugh has procured for you a permit to visit Dalton, which he requests me to forward immediately.[115]

With this you will have no difficulty in making the visit. John is 1½ miles of this place. I think Miller will be here shortly, but I'll write you tomorrow again. I saw Col. Hill of Tenn.[116] Nothing more at present. My love to all. Write soon.

Your son,
J. H. Francis

P.S. I'm still in Capt. Glover's office.[117] I think I'll get a permanent detail.[118] Jo

~

Thomas W. Francis to Amy I. Francis
Enterprise, Miss.
Decr. 20th [18]63

Dear Mother,

I have not written you for a long time but have been waiting to have something to write about but I fear that I will have nothing to write about now.

I received a letter from Jim yesterday and he says he will marry on the 16th February. Before I received his last letter I supposed he would not marry before April. I hope to be able to go and see him married but I am afraid I will not get off.[119] If I can go I want to take Fannie with me. I suppose you all are fully posted about who the young lady is. I do not know anything about her. Jim has not said much to me about her. He only said that she was a very nice lady and of a very fine family. Which of course must be true or he would not marry her. We have had a letter from John since the fight of course he has written home. I will write to him in a day or two.

I wrote to Emma today. I suppose she will miss home Christmas as she has never spent a Christmas away from home yet. I have a nice Christmas present for her but I fear that I will be unable to get it to her before Christmas but will send it the first chance I have. Tell Willie that I have one for her in the shape of a very fine calico dress but that I will not send it until I get a good chance and then it will be a Christmas present delivered after Christmas.

I wrote Father last week about killing my pork and if he has not received my letter tell him I wish him to have it brought up to town and leave the bones at the plantation for the Negroes and not to have any sausage made for us but to let Julia have what may be necessary for her, and if he thinks I will have more pork than I need to let Julia have some or whether I will have any over or not to let her have some if she needs it. But just to do as he thinks best in the way of saving the meat and killing it & c.[120] I thought possibly that Fannie would get home by Christmas in time to attend to it but I suppose she will not come until I get off but I do not know when that will be. I have written Father a half dozen letters in the last three months and have not had a line from him yet. I do not know what fields are sowed in wheat or oats or what he has done about renting my land. In fact I am in a state of blissful ignorance about my affairs at the plantation. I suppose he has just forgotten to write to me. You must tell him to write to me.[121] I will send you a box of beef tongues in a few days.

Hop is very well and I think getting along finely. He spent the evening with Fannie this evening. He was quite lively. Fannie is a little sick for the past two days but nothing of a serious nature. My love to all the family.

Your son,
T. W. Francis

John C. Francis to Amy I. Francis
Camp near Dalton, Ga.
Dec. 20th 1863

Dear Mother,

I understood some time since that Father was coming up. I have been looking for him for some time. The weather is very cold here now. Our men have all built their winter quarters & are now doing very well. They are getting plenty of clothing. I am doing very well, get plenty to eat & have plenty of clothing. I think I shall send some clothing home by Ed's boy Bill who will start home day after tomorrow.[122]

I had a letter from Jim a few days ago. He gave me his intentions. I will try & be in Augusta in Feb. if I can get off & have time, I will come by home for a few days. I don't know whether or not I will get off. Jo is here. I saw him yesterday. He was doing well. I have had one letter from Emma since I came to Tenn. I think Willie ought to go to Summerfield soon. I don't think you will have a better opportunity.

I saw Jim Montgomery a few days ago, he was doing well.[123] Uncle Hugh's Jo is in good health.[124] I wished Father would send me a boy if possible for I need him very much. I can furnish him with some clothing & after he stays here a while I can get him all he will need. I have not heard from him or Hop since I came here. I will send the children a pack of nice envelopes by Capt. Thompson.

Tell the little girls to write to me. I am in good health. I have not heard a word from Miller since I came here. I was at Wheeler's hdqrs. a few days ago. They were looking for them. My love to all.

Your affectionate son,
John

~

John C. Francis to Mary Emma Francis
Camp near Dalton, Ga.
Dec. 26 [18]63

Dear Sister Emma,

I have written to you two or three times since I came here & have had only one letter. Perhaps you never received mine.

There is nothing of interest going on here. We are all doing well. Have plenty to eat & the government has given us plenty of clothing. We have gone into winter quarters. The men all have comfortable huts built & are doing well. We have very little sickness now. I hear from home occasionly. They were all well at last accounts. I see Jo occasionly. He is with Capt. Glover in Dalton, is doing very well. I have not heard from Miller in some time. He is with Longstreet.[125] Tell Miss Clark that I saw her bro. Robt. about two weeks ago he was doing very well & was making application for furlough. I learn that he has received a furlough & gone to Mobile, Ala.[126] The weather is very bad. It is now raining & very cold.

Quite a dull Christmas with me. Had nothing but a few oysters Jo gave me. Jo took dinner with me yesterday. I think I will get a furlough in Feb. If I do I will go to Augusta & attend Jim's wedding & go by Summerfield & see you & from there home. We have orders to furlough one man for thirty present for duty, one officer for every three co. officers & one field officer when the whole field & staff are present.[127] I think more than probable that I will get one under that order. Will not get more than twenty days, if that. I will write you in the mean time. From what Jo tells me I think the lady Jim expects to marry is very nice & well worthy of anyones affections. Our army is doing nothing at this time. I hear nothing from the federals. Every body appeared to be drinking yesterday. Nothing unusual happened amongst them. All are sober today.

I think Jim intends to take his bride to Ala. after his marriage. I don't know to what part. I will send you a few nice envelopes I don't know whether you have plenty or not. The boys from J. with me are all doing very well. Several of the citizens of our county have been up to see us since we came here. I understand that Father intended to come up but I suppose he has been so busy that he could not get off.[128] Has Willie concluded to go to school in Summerfield this next session?

Study hard & acquit yourself with honor. Tell Dr. Rivers that what few of his old students that are here are doing well. My regards to him & his family. I think you will find Miss Clark a very nice girl if she is like her brothers. They were both members of our secret society at school.[129] I liked them very much. Present her with my compliments. Also my friends who are with you. Write when you have an opportunity.

Your affectionate bro.,
John

1. James Carrington Francis (1810–1888). Original photograph by Clinedinst, Staunton, Virginia, c. 1870. Courtesy of Mrs. Clara Jackson Martin, Birmingham, Alabama.

2. Amy Ingram Francis (1811–1868), c. 1861. Courtesy of the Alabama Department of Archives and History, Montgomery, Alabama.

3. Miller William Francis (1833–1877). Original photograph by Fredericks' "Knickerbocker" Family Portrait Gallery, New York, c. 1869. Courtesy of the Alabama Department of Archives and History, Montgomery, Alabama.

4. Julia Patterson Clark Francis (1833–1874). Original photograph by Fredericks' "Knickerbocker" Family Portrait Gallery, New York, c. 1869. Courtesy of Mrs. Clara Jackson Martin, Birmingham, Alabama.

5. Thomas Woodson Francis (1837–1890). Original photograph by C. D. Fredericks & Co., New York, c. 1880. Courtesy of the Alabama Department of Archives and History, Montgomery, Alabama.

6. Hopkins Turney Francis (1840–1926), c. 1870. Courtesy of the Alabama Department of Archives and History, Montgomery, Alabama.

7. John Clark Francis (1842–1864). Original photograph by Wilde & Son, Selma, Alabama, c. 1864. Courtesy of Mrs. Clara Jackson Martin, Birmingham, Alabama.

8. Joseph Hugh Francis (1844–1905). "At seventeen under Gen. Joe Wheeler 1865." Original by Fredericks of New York, c. 1862. Courtesy of Mrs. Clara Jackson Martin, Birmingham, Alabama.

9. Mary Emma Francis (1846–1918). Original photograph by Huntington & Clark, Detroit, Michigan, 1870. Courtesy of Mrs. Clara Jackson Martin, Birmingham, Alabama.

10. Willie Caroline Francis (1848–1878), c. 1870. Courtesy of the Alabama Department of Archives and History, Montgomery, Alabama.

11. Susan Hannah Francis (1851–1939), c. 1870. Courtesy of Mrs. Clara Jackson Martin, Birmingham, Alabama.

12. Charles Henry Francis (1853–1895). Original photograph by A. L. Banks, Birmingham, Alabama, c. 1880. Courtesy of Mrs. Clara Jackson Martin, Birmingham, Alabama.

7 / *Reinforcing at Dalton*

New Year's Day 1864 found weary soldiers on both sides huddled in makeshift quarters, in winter encampments, grateful for the temporary respite. The season granted no such clemency to the Davis administration, however; for it there was no respite from harsh reality. The Southern Confederacy had grave problems. Its infrastructure was in near collapse and its leadership in disarray. Indeed, the whole Confederacy faced a bleak, perhaps short, future.[1] Aware of the South's condition, Lincoln sought to hasten its demise. His first and most important actions in this direction were military. On 12 March 1864, the Union president promoted Grant to general in chief of the armies and named Sherman commander of the Military Division of the Mississippi. His orders gave Sherman free rein to wage total war in his theater, especially in Georgia and South Carolina.[2] President Davis continued his shell game of shifting generals in the face of overwhelming odds, hoping that one grand victory could reverse the tide flowing against the Confederacy.

As the politicians and generals planned and plotted, the Francis brothers awaited winter's end, poised for the next, perhaps last, season of fighting. At Dalton, Georgia, in late January 1864, John Francis and his men enjoyed the lull in the fighting. Throughout the winter his men's confidence in Joe Johnston, commander of the Army of Tennessee, had grown.[3] Johnston earned their good will. He provided regular rations, tobacco, and whiskey twice a week, as well as clothes, shoes, and hats. But the biggest boost to morale occurred because Johnston granted furloughs to one-third of the army at a time. With the boys from Jacksonville and Calhoun County in good spirits, John made plans to go to Augusta to visit Jim. Ever the modest veteran soldier at the tender age of twenty-two, John made no mention to his family of his recent promotion to lieutenant colonel, effective 28 January 1863.[4]

In February, John Francis traveled to Augusta for Jim's marriage to nineteen-year-old Sarah "Sadie" Galphin Whitehead. The wedding took place at Ivanhoe in the home of Sadie's sister and brother-in-law, Mr. and Mrs. John Richard Wilde. The death of the Wilde's five-year-old daughter, Clara, that morning muted the wedding celebration. Nevertheless, the wedding party was an impressive group with twenty attendants, ten women and ten men. Five men wore civilian clothes, and five wore uniforms, including John Francis in his new colonel's uniform. Most of the men had their hair frizzed by Balzeau, a hairdresser from Augusta, and according to Sadie's sister, Catharine Barnes Rowland, "They all looked most ridiculous." The new couple received a number of presents, and Jim Francis presented his new wife with an elegant watch studded with diamonds. The wedding party spent the night and departed the following day in bitter cold weather.[5]

On 28 March 1864, after months of active duty in East Tennessee with Will Martin's cavalry division in James Longstreet's army, Miller Francis returned to Jacksonville. Miller's brigade was no longer an effective fighting force. As Morgan's Fifty-first Alabama moved into encampments near Oxford and Blue Mountain, Alabama, the troops appeared as gaunt and skeletal as their emaciated horses. For the next thirty days, they recruited men and horses and replenished arms and equipment in preparation for their new assignment in North Georgia. Before breaking camp in late April 1863, they issued an invitation in the *Jacksonville Republican* to the public to attend a "tournament" at 11:00 A.M. on 21 April featuring "horsemanship, target shooting and sabre exercises." Within a few days, Miller, veteran and senior surgeon, was back in active service with his comrades on the left flank of Johnston's army. Unfortunately, his candid, gruff commentary on this final phase of the war is missing.[6]

As springtime approached North Georgia in March and April 1864, Lieutenant Colonel Francis, his fellow officers, and the men in the Army of Tennessee awaited the imminent Union offensive. John's letters to his family, couched in his reserved upbeat prose, assured them that the army was in good fighting trim.[7] With spartan austerity, John's only requests were for sole leather for his boots, a pair of buck gauntlets, and news about Emma and Willie at Summerfield.[8] John also mentioned that his brother Jim's sister-in-law, Catherine Barnes Rowland, was there visiting her husband, Charles Rowland, with the Forty-third Georgia regiment. Conspicuously absent from this correspondence, however, was any mention of the pageantry of the grand review of the Army of Tennessee on 18 April 1863. Thousands of spectators, including women and children, were treated to a sham battle with maneuvers involving some 40,000 troops with many generals and officers present.[9]

With John and Miller within the range of Union guns, Tom, Jim, and Hop continued their commissary duties behind the lines. In fact, Hop Francis, on furlough, traveled between Selma and Jacksonville on family business. Brother Tom's commissary duties took him from Selma to Mobile and then on to Montgomery and Augusta, where he visited with Jim and Sadie Francis. Although far removed from the battle lines in his commissary office at Augusta, Jim remained supremely confident of Confederate victories in North Georgia and Virginia. Meanwhile, Emma and Willie Francis continued their studies at Summerfield, which pleased their soldier brothers, who sent them money, gifts, and advice.[10]

By early May 1864, Sherman's army, consisting of three large divisions totaling nearly 100,000 troops, was poised to move against Joe Johnston in North Georgia. Johnston's Army of Tennessee, numbering approximately 60,000 men, held defensive positions in the mountainous terrain near Dalton.[11] Three days before the Union assault, John Francis informed his father that he expected active operations soon. Also in this correspondence appeared a muted and regretful reference to the impending execution of seventeen deserters from Brigadier General Alexander W. Reynold's brigade.[12]

As the opposing armies skirmished near Rocky Face Ridge on 11 May 1864, John Francis was mortally wounded in the abdomen, while engaged in conversation with Brigadier General Pettus. Family oral tradition suggests he was shot by a Yankee sniper, although no records have been discovered to validate this story. John died in the early hours of 12 May, surrounded by a coterie of friends and family, including his first cousins Joseph Hugh Francis and Hopkins Turney Francis. His cousin Joe Francis dispatched a hastily written note to his uncle, Dr. James Carrington Francis, urging him to "come immediately."[13] Later that day, the news of John's death reached Jim Francis by telegram in Augusta. Jim immediately attempted to recover his brother's body and deliver it to his parents in Jacksonville. Johnston's evacuation of Dalton and retreat to Resaca thwarted his efforts. Sadly John Francis was hurridly buried at Kingston, Georgia.[14]

Although Jo Francis was reunited with Miller in the Fifty-first Alabama in North Georgia, the Union advance against Dalton found him on special detail, assigned to Johnston's wagon train near Calhoun, Georgia. Jo's letters reveal a growing maturity as he became the family's primary correspondent during the war's last year. Despite his youthful and spirited prose, his correspondence accurately reports the brigade's constant movement. After leaving its camps near Oxford, Alabama, Morgan's brigade was assigned to the left wing of Johnston's army, picketing the Oostanaula River from near Calhoun to Rome, Georgia.[15] As Jo retreated with Johnston's wagon train, he reported the bitter fighting, hard marching, and gloomy prospects of a retreat into Atlanta, but he remained ever hopeful of success.

Thomas W. Francis to James C. Francis
Enterprise, Miss.
Jany. 1, 1864

Dear Father,

I received yours & Mother's letters last night. I know very well how you feel after being left with such a small force to make your crop with, and especially to loose as valuable boy as Gabe was, but it is the beginning of what we may expect from our Negroes.[16] I predict that in less than twelve months that at least one half of the men in the county will leave and try to get with the Yankees, and I expect that a large portion of them will succeed. I am free to express that I have no confidence in any of them. I believe that they all are more than willing to try the Yankees to better their condition.[17] "Poor deluded wretches" will they never learn any better until it is too late.

You say that you left for me at the plantation about twelve hundred pounds of pork and that you will not have enough to do you. I can get along with the amount you left me and you had better take the ballance of the pork up to Jacksonville and put it away in your smokehouse. I think there will be enough to do you with what you have already killed, and if Julia needs any let her have it. I am certain whether you or Julia need it or not that it will be best for you to put it up at home, and if you need you can use it. For I have made arrangements to get 350 lbs. bacon certain, in fact I have already secured fearing that something might happen that we might be short of pork. If you think best for the bacon you left to stay at the plantation you can leave it or if best to carry it up home you can have it hauled up.[18] As for the corn I do not have any idea how much I have or what it will require to do me, but as a matter of course you can have whatever you want of it, and if Julia is out and cannot get any have my folks to haul her a load up.[19] In the name of God I do not want any thing when it is needed for bread by my family nor do I care to leave it on the plantation for the Negroes to destroy.

If you need any money I would be glad to let you have it as long as you wish it and if it is to come back to me from the younger children of course I do not want it. I am perfectly willing to let you have now or from time to time as much as you want without any obligation on your part to pay it back to me. Nor would I have it back if this war should terminate in such a way as to take from you your present means of supporting the family. I can tell you precisely how my financial affairs stand. You know all my property. I have in Confederate money and bonds about $10,000.00 and about 14 or 1,500 ozs. in gold & silver, and no one to live on except myself & wife and I certainly find that I could willingly give all of it to any member of the family that needs it.[20] For money I believe to be a curse to any man except to be used for the benefit of his family.

I hope you will not feel any delicacy in telling me at any time what I can do. For I think I am now under the same obligation to do for you as you were to me until I became a man to act for myself. I can give you a draft that will be honored for as much money as I have at any time. If you go to see Dick fix the land matter so as to pay him up no matter what the cost is for in my judgement it is an only safe course and we must pay Hezy up too.[21] And then let the worst come and if we are out of debt we cannot be annoyed. I wish you could arrange my debt with Montgomery in some way.[22] It troubles me no little. I wish you would diminish our stock of horses and mules in some way if you think best. I am certain we have too many but you are on the premises and can tell best what to do.[23] If I am called on for a boy send either Jim or Kit.[24] I don't care whitch.

I hope to come home before long but I cannot tell when. I will try and come in three or four weeks. I have a pair of blankets for John and if you go to see him you had better take two from home and when Fannie comes I will send these and Mother can use them on the beds in the place of them they are *white.* I do not know that he needs them atall, but I had a chance of buying a good lot of them and I bought them. They are very fine and large. I gave Hop a pair besides what he had and he now has plenty in fact more than he needs.

I do not understand why Joe has left Jim. I fear Jim has in some way mistreated the boy as he might think and Joe has left him. I fear Jim is too hasty in a great many sayings and especially with his brothers. I know well he is as quick as powder and he has on many occasions wounded my feelings when he did not intend it. I hope and trust my conjecture is wrong but from what Hop tells me I am afraid I am correct. I know but very little about Joe for I have never been with him but little, but I think he is a comet and a very high spirited boy. When you see him know all about it and try and have him go back to Jim. For such service as he will necessary be with, the cavalry will be more than he can stand. I know there is no trouble about Jim's keeping him as long as he wants him and certainly he should do it by all means. Hop received a letter from Joe some little time since and Joe complained that Jim did not trust him as respectfully as he should do at all times. Had I of had any fears of Joe's leaving Jim I would have written to Jim at once. Hop said to me to day that he expected that Jim & Joe had had a falling out, that he expected that Jim had pitched into Joe about something and that Joe had bundled up and left. I write to night to Jim to find out about it.

I do not know it but I think that Genl. Forney expects to go to the Tennessee army in a week or so.[25] If so we will come by home all of us & if not I will try and get a furlough to come home, for a few days. Hop & Fannie are both in good health. The weather is freezing cold now. In fact it is as cold as I ever saw it anywhere. I am expecting a letter from Emma evry day now.

My love to all the family,
Your son,
Thomas

~

John C. Francis to James C. Francis
Camp near Dalton, Ga.
January 13th [1864]

Dear Father,

I wrote to Willie yesterday advising her to go to Summerfield next session. I told her that if she needed any more dresses for her to get some of my money from you & buy. I am very anxious that she should go. I have not heard from Jim in several days. I saw Jo yesterday he said that he expected Martin's Div. in about two weeks.[26]

I am getting along very well. Lt. Col. Patterson sent up his resignation from Talladega.[27] It was forwarded from here this evening. The boys are all getting along very well. There is nothing unusual going on here at this time. Col. Shelley was sent up an application for furlough.[28]

Our provisions are lasting very well. I met Col. B. O. Ramey in town the other day he says that he intends to play the wild with deserters when he gets back.[29] Jo is doing very well.

My love to all.

Your son,
John

John C. Francis to Amy I. Francis
Camp near Dalton, Ga.
Jan. 26th 1864

Dear Mother,

I have not written home in several days for want of something to write about. There is nothing of interest going on here. Everything perfectly quiet. We have very nice weather now.[30] It appears that spring has commenced. I am getting along very well. We have just finished moving our camps. I have plenty of every thing at present.

I received a letter from Thomas a few days ago he was doing as well as usual. He said that he had a pair of fine blankets for me & that he would send them home. I have plenty of bed clothing with me now. If he sends them kept them I may need them. If you want them for any other purpose before I need them, use them. I think it more than probable that I will be at home next month for a short time. If I get off, I will go to Augusta & spend a few days with Jim. We have provisions enough to last us some time yet. Our army is getting in fine discipline. I hope you have decided to let Willie go to Summerfield. The boys from Jacksonville are all doing well. The army has great confidence in our present *leaders*.[31] My love to all.

Your affectionate son,
John

Sarah Galphin Whitehead to Mary Emma Francis
Ivanhoe, Feb. 4th 1864

[Dear Emma,]

You will doubtless be very much surprised to receive a letter from me, but I trust my dear little friend, that it will be a pleasure, for I assure you, that feelings of love prompt me to write you. I do not feel that I am writing to one that I have never seen, for I have heard your brother so frequently speak of you, and have read your sweet letters to him so often, that I have already learned to love you very dearly. I read your last letter to Capt. Francis, and assure you that I was much gratified to receive your sweet messages.

I wish that you could be at our wedding, for I am so anxious to see you, and would like as much to have all your family here. We will be very privately married, only our attendants. We expected to have a few friends but my sister has just lost a lovely little girl about seven years old, which has caused quite a blight in our usually cheerful household, and makes us all feel too sad to think of anything like a merry-making.[32]

I hope that your brothers will all be here, for it will be such a pleasure to Capt. Francis and myself to see them. I have seen Joe several times, and I feel as though I have known him for years. He has promised to love me a great deal, and I know we will always be good friends. I hope too that you will love me, if not for myself, for your brother's sake, and that when we are domiciled, in our own little house, that you will come and make a long visit. Augusta is a very small place, and I know that you will be pleased with it.[33]

You expressed a desire to have my photograph. As soon as I go to Augusta, I will get you a copy of the one I sent to your mother, and enclose it to you in a letter. I must tell you though that it is a very flattered likeness, and you must not expect to see me looking exactly like it. I see your brother every week. He comes down every Saturday night, and spends Sunday with us. I do not think that he looks as well as he did some time ago, because he has so much to do. He says, he writes every night until twelve or one o'clock. I wish that you would write and beg him not to do it, for my powers of persuasion have been of no avail.

I expect he thinks me a great scold, for I am always telling him how wrong it is to confine himself so closely to his business. He does not do it, when I am in Augusta, for he comes every night to see me, and calls occasionally to take me to ride. He promises faithfully to do better after a while. Capt. Francis has a splendid little horse, and when you come to Augusta, he will take you to ride very often. He loves you very devotedly and speaks very often of you. And now my very dear little friend I will say good-bye. Do write me when you can, I will be delighted to hear from you. And now, goodbye. God bless you my dear Emma and believe me with a heart full of love.

Yours very sincerely,
Sadie Whitehead[34]

[P.S.] Do not show this to anyone. Now, if you do I will never write you again. This is alone for your eyes. Sadie

John C. Francis to James C. Francis
Camp near Dalton, Ga.
Feb. 7th 1864

Dear Father,

I have just received a furlough for twenty days. I will start to Augusta on the 10th or 11th & will stay until after the wedding. I would not go to Augusta in four or five days but Jim wants me to be there by the 10th. I would prefer not staying in A. so long but it is Jim's wish. My love to all.[35]

Your son,
John

Joseph H. Francis to James C. Francis
Dalton, Ga., Feb. 18th 1864

Dr Father,

It has been some time since [I] wrote to you, but it has been delay on account of not having any thing to write about. I'm getting along pretty well, & think I shall go to E. Tenn. shortly by way of Augusta. I intend going up to see Maj. Wailes tomorrow or next day.[36] Wheeler's hd. qrs. have moved to Tunnel Hill.[37]

From the way they are maneuvering every body thinks a movement is on foot, which will commence in a day or two. I never saw better indications than there is now.[38] I think myself that the main army will go in direction of Rome, Geo. But of this no one knows except our genls. The weather for the last five days has been very cold. Nothing more. I suppose John will be at home by the time you receive this. My love to all.

Your son,
Jo H. Francis

Hopkins T. Francis to John C. Francis
Demopolis February 26th [1864]

Dear Bro,

I have just learned that you were at home. I suppose you was at Jim's wedding.[39] You must write me how the thing passed off. I am lazing here nothing to do & scarcely anything to eat. Tell Thos that there is nothing new here. We are just as we were when he left. Frank Ward has taken his papers to Selma & will wait the arrival of Thomas there.[40] How long will you be at home? Write me immediately care of Genl. Forney.[41] My love to all.

Your affect. Bro,
H. T. Francis

John C. Francis to James C. Francis
Camp near Dalton, Ga.
Mch. 6th 1864

Dear Father,

I wrote to you several days ago. Since that time nothing of importance has happened. Jo & Tobe Turney were out to see me this morning. Tobe starts for Jacksonville to night.[42] Jo is getting along very well he says. Our army is very quiet at this time. Nothing stirring at all. I had an opportunity of sending a letter to M. L. today. I wrote a few times to Dr. Estill's wife.[43] I am getting along as well as usual. I have not heard a word from Jim or Miller since my arrival. My love to all.

Your son,
John

John C. Francis to James C. Francis
Camp near Dalton, Ga.
March 10th 1864

Dear Father,

As every one is desirous of getting rid of the present issue of our money, perhaps you can get a good price for my mare if so, sell her. Don't take less than seven hundred dollars ($700) for her. If you sell her let me know immediately. If before Capt. Johnson starts back send the money to me by him.[44] Don't think by this that I am in need of the money, but money at this time is worth as much to me as it will be in the new issue.

I am getting along very well at present. Nothing of interest at this place. Our army is in good trim. Every body appears to be in good spirits. I understand that Gen'l. Forney has been relieved from command in Miss. & expects to be ordered here.[45] I hope it will be the case. Rumor says that Hindman has resigned.[46] I think it meets with the approbation of the whole army.

Jo is well. I saw him yesterday. We are expecting Martin's dvs. here soon.[47] My love to all.

Your affectionate son,
John

John C. Francis to Amy I. Francis
Camp near Dalton, Ga.
Mch. 13th 1864

Dear Mother,

There is nothing of importance in D. Tell Tobe Turney that I went to the adjt. gen'l. office for him yesterday. His commission had not come. I called to see Jo but learned that he had gone to Tunnel Hill to see Adjt. Wailes. Mr. Winston told me that Jo had a furlough & would start home on Monday next. I suppose that Jo will be out to see me to day & if he goes tomorrow I will send this by him. If not I will send it by Lt. Wyly.[48] Gen'l. Forney is here on business.[49] He thinks he will start back to day. He is here partly to get a command in this army. I don't know whether he will succeed or not. He will be in our camps this morning & will then know more about it. Maj. Gen'l. Hindman tendered his resignation a few days ago, but has with drawn it. His reason for resigning was that Gen'l. Hood, his junior, was promoted over him.[50]

I am getting along very well at present. Our army is in fine condition. All the boys from about Jacksonville are in good health. I wish you would speak to Thos and ask him about the boy he promised to get me at Demopolis. If he has him to send him up by someone passing. I have heard nothing from Jim since I came here. I am expecting Miller through here in a few days. I will write more during the day. Jo is here he starts to morrow morning. I give him a jacket. I send one to Miller. The one I sent home some time ago, you can give to Hop if he will wear it. I want them to have one apiece. I don't know how they will fit. I hope the girls have gone to Summerfield.[51] If Willie has not taken the money that I gave her & will not need it in two months, tell her to send it to me & I will give her at that time the new issue which will be of more service to her, but if she needs it at this time let her use it.[52]

I am getting along very well at present. I have not heard from home since I left. If Emma & Willie have gone to S. Tell that she must write to me often. I will write to E. & W. at S. as soon as they get there. I don't know when Gen'l. F. will go back as I have not seen him today. My love to all.

Your affectionate son,
John

Amy I. Francis to Mary Emma and Willie C. Francis
Jacksonville, Mar. 20, 1864

Dear Daughters,

I received your letter Friday night. You seemed to be rather desponding. I hope you have become better satisfied by this time and will try and be satisfyed and put up with a great many things for the sake of getting an education. You cannot expect to be as well satisfyed as if you were at home.

I want you to try and live in peace and love with all and try to have good lessons and obey your teachers. Each one do your part in cleaning up your room and be kind to each other. What did Pigeon leave you? How did you find your things? Were they all there? What sort of a room have you and what sort of roommates have you? Jo arrived home on Tuesday night and will leave Wednesday morning next for his regiment.[53] Have not heard from Miller since you left nor from James. Had a letter from John yesterday. He was well still at Dalton.

Jo went to the farm Thursday, came back yesterday. They have all returned from the farm but Hop he is there yet.[54] We are all well nothing more to relate. Write often and how you are getting along. Have you got your jewelry? May the Lord bless and save you. From your affectionate mother.

A. Francis

Thomas W. Francis to James C. Francis
Selma, Ala.
March 24, '64

Dear Father,

I send you your certificate for one thousand dollars. The treasure would not issue but one certificate.[55] I have left Miller's money & Downing's to be funded to be sent to you.[56] I expect 100$ of Downing's money is bad.[57] Maj. Keith will send it in a few days.[58]

I leave for Demopolis in the morning. It is impossible to get potatoes here.

Yours,
T. W. Francis

John C. Francis to James C. Francis
Army of Tenn.
March 27th 1864

Dear Father,

I received four hundred dollars ($400) by Capt. Johnson. I would like to know who it belonged to. If any of it belonged to Willie? I wish you would send my shoes by the first one passing also enough sole leather to go on my boots once. I am getting along very well. I have just learned that the enemy have been sending troops (two corps) from our front. The supposition is that they are going to Va.[59] I had a letter from Jim a few days ago. We draw one ration now & can buy one. Lt. Skelton got in yesterday. The boys are all doing very well. Send me a pair of those buck gauntlets. I have not heard a word from the girls since they left home. Jim seems to be delighted with house keeping. Tell Tom & Hop to write to me. I suppose Martin's command is now in Ala.[60] Tell Jo if you see him that I now have my repeater & wish to exchange with him so that he can sell mine. It is a good one & shoots *well,* but is too heavy for which reason, I wish to dispose of it. My love to all. Tell Jo he can take the note I have of Miller's if he has no objections.

Your son,
John

Amy I. Francis to Mary Emma and Willie C. Francis
Jacksonville, Mar. 29th 1864

Dear Daughters,

I received your letter Saturday morning, was glad hear you were well and satisfyed. We are all well. Miller arrived home yesterday in good health. The division will be on soon to go in camps near Blue Mt. for one month.[61] Thos. left last week for Demopolis. Hop will leave tomorrow night for Demopolis. Jo leaves for Blue Mountain tomorrow. Heard from John a few days since he was well. Have received no letter from James since you left. Your Uncle John starts to Virginia to night. Jim's Negroes go with him to Augusta.[62] Liza Tournies baby is very sick, is better than it has been.[63]

Mr. Perry married your father's cousin. Was Doctor Rivers willing to take the money and how mutch did you let him have?[64] You must both keep your clothes well mended and in good order. Each one do her part in cleaning up the room. No doubt you will be good girls, be kind to all, and get your lessons good.

Sue and Bud started to school yesterday. Last week was very cold. It sleeted and snowed. The snow was an inch and a half deep. The fruit is not all killed. You must write often. May the Lord bless and save you is my prayer from your affectionate mother.

A. Francis

John C. Francis to James C. Francis
Camp near Dalton, Ga.
April 9th 1864

Dear Father,

I wrote to Sue yesterday by mail. Today some of the boys from my old co. start home & I will write you a few lines by them. There is nothing of interest here. Everything appears quiet. I am getting along very well. Those articles you sent me by Serg't. Smith came safe.[65] My glasses were covered very nice. I will send two blankets home by Cap't. Allen. I have two coverlets one quilt & one blanket. This is enough for summer. Hon. J. L. M. Curry speaks to the brigade this evening. He is here now as Judge Advocate Gen'l. for this army.[66] We draw one ration now & are not allowed to buy anything in the provision line. My love to all.

Your son,
John

~

John C. Francis to Amy I. Francis
Hd. Qrs. 30th Ala. Reg't.
April 12/[18]64

Dear Mother,

Lt. Weir starts home tomorrow or next day & I will write you a few lines by him.[67] I am getting along very well since we have commenced drawing rations. We fare as well if not better than we did before. We get as much as we can use & just as good as before. My rations before cost me nearly one hundred dollars a month. Now it costs us nothing. The servants are reported as laundresses & we draw rations for them. I have plenty of clothing to do me. If any of the boys need any clothing that I have sent home let them have it. Everything appears to be very quiet in this vicinity.

I had a letter from Willie today she seems to be very well pleased. I have not heard from Jim in some time. The weather is very bad. We have rain nearly every day. The boys from J. are all in good health. I am very sorry to learn the Gen'l. Lorings troops have gone to our county.[68] I fear they will injure it very much. There are very few citizens living near here when the army stops, everything is laid waste. My love to all. Tell Sue that she must write to me frequently. I will write to Hop in a few days. I sent two blankets by Mr. Allen a few days ago.

Your affectionate son,
John

~

John C. Francis to Willie C. Francis
Hd. Qrs. 30th Ala. Reg't.
April 21/[18]64

Dear Sister Willie,

I send you a piece of music I found in town to day. I don't know whether you have it or not. I am getting along very well. We leave our winter qrs.

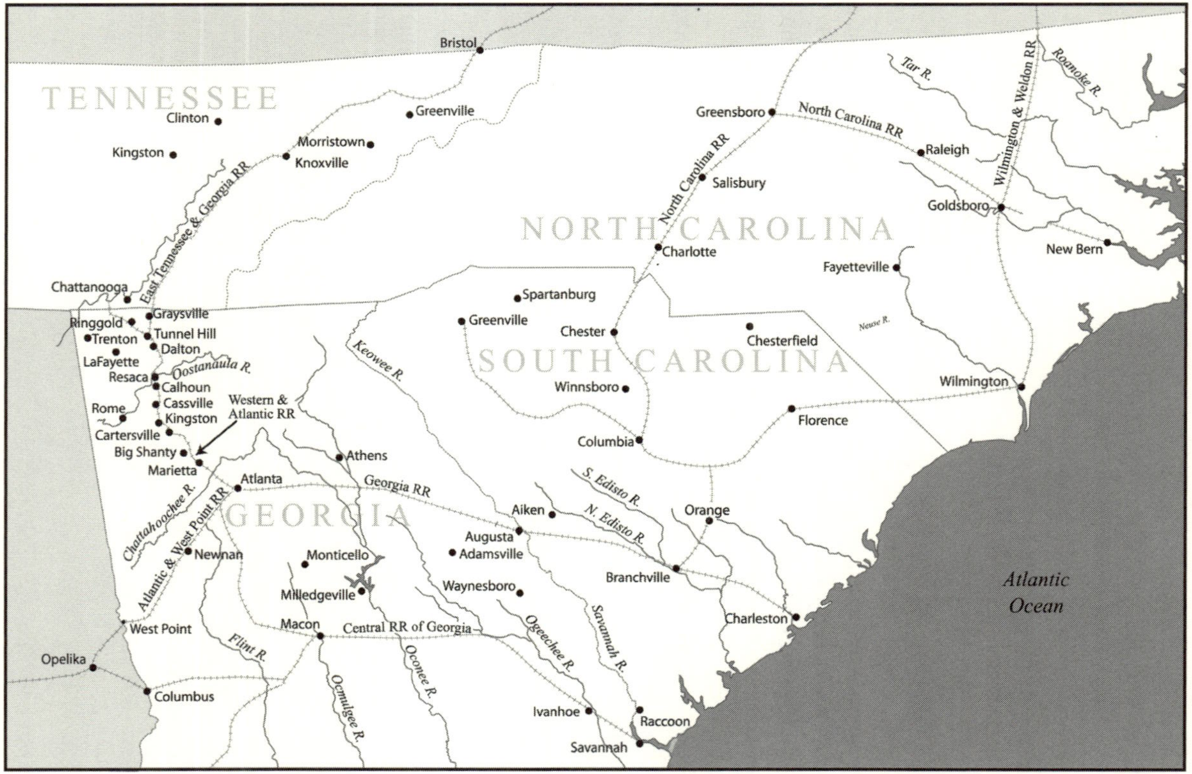

The War in Georgia and the Carolinas

to morrow & go to the front. The weather is getting so pleasant that I suppose our gen'ls. think we have no business in houses. Nothing of interest here.[69] Every thing appears to be quiet. Jim's sister-in-law, Mrs. Rowlin, is here with her husband.[70] I have met her several times. She is quite a nice lady. My love to Emma. Write to me when you have leisure.

Your affectionate bro.,
John

John C. Francis to James C. Francis
Hd. Qrs. 30th Ala. Reg't
April 21st 1864

Dear Father,

Lt. Airhurst of Capt. Kelly's co. has resigned & will start home tomorrow.[71] Nothing of interest about here. We leave our winter qrs. to morrow. We go to the front. I think our position will be on the Cleveland road.[72] Everything appears to be quiet in our front.

We draw rations for the servants at this time, but that will cease in thirty (30) days. I sent my pistol to Miller by Capt. Johnson. If Miller did not get it nor has no opportunity to get it, you can keep it & sell it. If anyone wishes to buy it at two hundred & fifty dollars ($250), it is so heavy that I cannot use it. When will Willie need more money & how much? I sent two blankets home a short time ago. Did you get them? We get bacon for meat rations now altogether & plenty to do. The army is well fed. Tell Capt. Johnson that everything is getting along very well in his dpt. My love to all.

Your son,
John

James C. Francis, Jr. to James C. Francis
Augusta, Apr. 24th /[18]64

Dear Father,

I have not written you in some time but "Sadie" writes occasionaly to Mother or some member of the family by this means you hear from me occasionaly. I have no news to relate. I am elated with the news from the

Trans-Mississippi Dept.[73] I think that the pending fight before Richmond will produce about the same results[74] and the one near Dalton is bound to be the greatest defeat the federals has ever sustained.[75] I think that peace will be proclaimed before the opening of another spring. I hope you are full of hope. Indeed you should be and quite cheerful and thankful for remember what you have done and are daily doing for your country. Six (6) sons in the service as yet no serious misfortune has befalen any of us. I hope you are enjoying good health. Can't you come to "Augusta" soon and see us? We would be delighted to receive a visit from any or all of the family.[76] My love to Mother and to Sue & Charlie.

Your affectionate son,
J. C. Francis, Jr.

~

John C. Francis to James C. Francis
Hd. Qrs. 30th Ala. Reg't.
May 1st 1864

Dear Father,

Nothing of interest has transpired since I wrote you last. Day before yesterday we were all drawn up in line of battle expecting the advance of the enemy. It turned out to be nothing more than a dash on our cavalry pickets.[77] Every thing in this army is ready. All heavy baggage has been sent to the rear. We have orders to keep on hand two days cooked rations. Everything quiet at present. Ed Clark is a little sick with dysentery.[78] I think it probable that he will be at home in a few days. Mattison is complaining a little.[79] I am doing very well. My health is good. My love to all.

Your son,
John

~

John C. Francis to James C. Francis
Hd. Qrs. 30th Ala. Reg't.
May 4th 1864

Dear Father,

I wrote to you several days ago by mail. I have an opportunity of writing today by hand. There is nothing of importance. We are expecting active operations in this army soon. I don't know what we will do. We are very fortified here & are still at work.

Ed Clark has a very bad spell of dysentery. Has been confined to his bed for four or five days. He does not seem to improve much. I sent up an application for furlough for him three days ago. It will return today or tomorrow. I am a little apprehensive that they will order him sent to a hospital though I hope not. I would have written to Col. Clark but Warlick wrote to him. I don't think Ed would be able for some time to ride on the stages. If he gets his furlough, Col. Clark had better send to Rome for him if possible. I am getting along very well. There is to be seventeen men shot today from Reynolds' brigade for desertion.[80] I suppose the whole dvs. is ordered out to witness it.

Col. Shelley's bro. will be in Talladega in a few days on his way to Texas.[81] I should think it would be a good opportunity to write if you desire it. My love to all.

Your son,
John

Amy I. Francis to Mary Emma and Willie C. Francis
Jacksonville, May 6th 1864

Dear Daughters,

I received a letter from Willie yesterday. We had not heard from you in two weeks. Was glad to hear that you were well and I hope getting along well. Jo and Miller left here more than a week ago. Have not heard from them since they left. Then ordered to Cartersville I suppose.[82] We got a letter from John last night. He was well. They were looking for a battle. Tom wrote from Selma last Wednesday. He and Hop were going to Demopolis on yesterday. Tom thinks he will be at home in a week or two.

Your father will have your shoes made as soon as he can. Are you kneeding them badly? I will try and have your dress in time. Nothing done towards your collar and cuffs. Nothing more to relate. All getting along as usual. Your Aunt Martha has a son a week old, has not named him yet.[83] You wanted to know about the chickens. It will some time yet before they are large enough to fry. I have about fifty, your lame one is about well. We have had green peas, will soon have potatoes. Vegetation is backward here. You must be good girls and try to have good lessons, be kind and agreeable to all. I believe you will.

You must write at least once a week. We wait for a letter from you and then answer it. We have answered all your letters. May the Lord bless and save you is the prayer of your affectionate mother.

A. Francis

~

Joseph H. Francis to Amy I. Francis
Camps near Calhoun, Geo.
May 10th 1864

Dr Mother,

We moved here yesterday & are encamped in one mile of Calhoun.[84] We had a rite nice time until we arrived at Cartersville on the 3rd inst. Since then the roads have been very disagreeable. We left Cartersville on the 6th and on the 7th camped one mile north of Rome.[85] Here Gen. Morgan established a line of couriers to Blue Mountain also a heavy picket in the direction of Lafayette, Geo. We left Rome at 12 noon the 8th and on the 9th came to this point where we are expecting orders at any moment. Our brig. is nearly all on duty. Gen. Morgan has a courier line from this place to Blue Mountain, Ala., a distance of 100 miles, also a heavy detachment for picketting the river. Movements are being made very rapidly, upon both sides.[86] We have all styles of rumors. I learned that one regiment of the Geo. brig. had a pretty heavy fight yesterday near Resaca.[87] Dispatchers are passing every five hours in great haste. We are reinforcing at Dalton. The roads are very dry & dusty. The prospect for a shower is fine.

I have nothing interest to write. We heard heavy guns yesterday. Nothing more. Miller is in fine health. My love to all.

Your son,
"Jo"

~

Joseph Hugh Francis to James C. Francis
Dalton, Ga.
May 11th 1864

Dr. J. C. Francis
Jacksonville, Ala.

Come immediately. John is wounded severly in the abdomen.[88] Turney & I are safe. I will send pass to Rome p. office.

Joe H. Francis[89]

James C. Francis, Jr. to Amy I. Francis
Office of Purchasing Commissary
Augusta, Ga., May 12th 1864

Dear Mother,

Ere this you doubtless have herd of the death of your *noble, gallant* son and my brother. John was wounded yesterday and died last night. I will not trust to my feelings now. Miller Turney I think was with him. I received intelligence of his death from him.[90] I will go up this evening for his remains. If it is possible to get a metallic coffin, I will bring his remains to you. If not will mark well the spot where he rests that he may be removed as soon as practicable. Be of good cheer my dear mother and father "Gods will not mine be done." His noble spirit is now in heaven sweetly conversing with our sister that went before him.[91]

Your affectionate son,
J. C. Francis, Jr.

Sarah Whitehead Francis to Amy I. and James C. Francis
Augusta, May 13th 1864

My beloved Parents,

"Bad news travels fast," and I know long before this reaches you you have heard of your irreparable loss. The death of your noble, gallant son. What can I say that will alleviate your pain one iota—nothing—no, at such an hour as this there is *no human consolation.* My heart never went out to any one so completely, as to Brother John and I had learned to love and esteem him for his many virtues and loveliness of disposition, and I feel in giving him up, that I too have lost one near and dear to me.[92] But my dear Father and Mother in this hour of deep distress there is a source from whence we may all derive comfort. May God bless you both and sustain you, and give you strength to bear this great trial.

Yesterday when Capt. Francis came in to tell me the sad news, my first thoughts were of you. Just two years ago I lost a brother, just as promising and interesting, as Bro. John and my poor heart broken parents were almost crazy.[93] Capt. Francis left last night for Atlanta where he hoped to meet the remains and take them to Jacksonville. Poor fellow!

His heart is completely crushed, but amid it all, he murmurs not, but exclaims "God's will be done." I most sincerely pray that it may be sanctified to his eternal welfare, that his noble heart may have possess the purifying influence of God's holy spirit, the only thing, which is requisite to make him a perfect character. He wrote you a few hurried lines on yesterday and says he will write all the particulars when he returns.

I know a father's pride was centered in that noble boy, and that you had cherished fond anticipations for his brilliant future. Yes, I know yours was the same disappointment, that my Father felt in giving up his boy. But oh! what a glorious death he died. Your noble boy was killed in the most sacred cause which any people ever fought for. Let this thought console us, and let us feel that our dear John is now in Heaven, where will be but a short separation. And now good bye. Capt. Francis requested me to write to Bro. Hop, from whom he received a letter on yesterday, and tell him all we knew of the sad circumstances. Give my love to each member of the family who may be with you, and with a heart full for yourselves believe me my dear parents.

Your affectionate daughter,
Sadie W. Francis

James C. Francis, Jr. to Amy I. Francis
Atlanta, Georgia
May 13th 1864

Dear Mother,

Enclosed I hand you a paper containing telegraphic notice of Jno being wounded. I could not get a metallic coffin in Augusta or at this place. I received a telegram from Capt. Johnston last night stating that John's remains would be at Kingston last evening. I will go to the front and if possible accompany his remains home.[94] I telegraphed you thro Maj. "Keith" also to "Emma and Willie" at Summerfield.

I trust dear Mother that you and Father will bear it with *that* fortitude that *he bore himself* on the many battlefields that it was his blessed privalidge and liberty to command upon. I will write you all the particulars when I get them. With much love,

Your devo. son,
J. C. Francis, Jr.

Joseph H. Francis to Mary Emma and Willie C. Francis
Hd. Qrs. Morgans Brig. Cavry
Near Calhoun, Geo., May 13th 1864

My dear Sisters Emma & Willie,

It has been some time since I last wrote you. I have come to the conclusion that your delay in answer is, that, you do not know my whereabouts. We have been moving about pretty constant since we left Oxford, Ala.[95] Our brigade is now stationed on the left wing of the army, and is picketing the river which forms our line. We have scouting parties from our brigade every day. We are picketing from here to Rome. Rome is now garrisoned by men from our brigade.[96] We can hear connonading every day. The wind is so high that we can't tell exactly at what point of our line it is.

Our brigade has been expecting to get into a fight at any hour. The fireing has been more regular to day than usual. I think there will be a general engagement tomorrow. All is confident of our success. All indications go to show that there is a hard fight on our right up near Dalton, the cannonading is very heavy indeed at the present.[97] No one doubts but that there will be a general engagement. Probily the engagement will be general this evening, the fireing is now getting in about five miles of us. I'm unable to tell you the strength of either armies, for I have not the most remote idea. Hoping that you will hear of a glorious victory in a few days I'll close.[98] If you direct your letters properly, they will follow us up wherever we are. Nothing more. Write soon.

Your bro.,
"Jo"

Joseph H. Francis to Amy I. Francis
Camp near Cartersville, Geo.[99]
May 20th 1864

My dear Mother,

You must forgive me for not writing more often. Tis useless for me to tell you of our movements. Our brigade has had some very hard fighting, and also hard marching.[100] I'm now with the wagon train.[101] I left Miller and Jim at Adaresville.[102] I have Millers bay horse with me he is very lame (the horse). I have Bro. Johns horse, saddle, bridle & c. with me also. Would that he could have lived to have seen this great fight over with. I have heard him often say that he wanted to live to see our army go into K'nty. this spring. The prospect is rather gloomy at present, as it is generaly believed that in a day or two we will be in Atlanta, Geo., but all seem confident of success.[103] All our cavalry is being massed on our right, for I suppose the purpose of making a raid on the enemys rear.[104]

Mother I have a few lines that I have carried in my pocket for some time. I think they are so sweet.

"Brother thou wast mild & lovely,
Gentle as the summer breeze,
  Pleasant as the air of evening
When it floats among the trees,
  Peaceful be thy silent slumber
Peaceful in the grave so low:
  Thou no more wilt join our number
Thee no more our songs shall know:
  Dearest brother, thou hast left us
Here thy loss we deeply feel:
  But 'tis God that hath bereft us
He can all our sorrow heal.
  Yet again we hope to meet the,
When the day of life has fled:
  Then in heaven with joy to greet the
Where no farewell tear is shed"[105]

I must close as it is getting late. My love to all. I have not received a letter from any one since I left home. I'm very anxious to send Bro. Johns horse & c. home. We move camps every day, tis useless to try to send for them. I gave his pistol to Jim to take care of. Good bye, dear mother, my warmest love to all.

Your son,
"Jo"

[Margin note] I will be more likely to get letters at Marietta but we know not where we will go.[106] Jo

8 / *House of Mourning*

By early summer 1864, the Confederacy's future was bleak; the most important condition for its demise, the defeat of its armies and the loss of its last heartland state, Georgia, seemed imminent. The Union, thrusting deeper into the state, had only to position its overwhelming numbers to ensure the defeat of the South. The deteriorating military situation limited personal correspondence. As a result the Francis family's war news at this time came primarily from son Jo and various newspapers, notably the *Jacksonville Republican.* Although the Confederacy's prospects seemed almost hopeless, the fighting and dying continued unabated.

With Sherman's Union troops pressing Johnston's line on the Chattahoochee River in early July 1864, Joe Wheeler's cavalry harassed the Union advance to cover Johnston's retreat. Wheeler succeeded, and Johnston retreated under the cover of darkness with his army intact over the Chattahoochee three miles from Atlanta on 9 July. As Johnston began to regroup, politics intervened, causing widespread controversy. On 17 July, President Davis replaced Johnston with John Bell Hood as commander of the Army of Tennessee. When the rank and file caught wind of this "treachery," the dismissal of their beloved "Old Joe," hundreds openly wept, and others threatened to quit the war. Private Sam Watkins of the First Tennessee was typical of Old Joe's men. In his memoir he saluted Johnston: "Farewell, old fellow! We privates loved you because you made us love ourselves." Despite Davis's confidence in Hood's ability to stop Sherman's armies, the fight for Atlanta ended with Hood's evacuation of this critical rail hub on 1 September 1864.[1]

Two days after Johnston's removal, Jo Francis escaped the Union advance on Atlanta. He was ordered to a camp near Eufaula, Alabama, on a special detail to care for the exhausted horses of Will Martin's cavalry division. Jo remained at Fort Browder through November 1864. No letters document Miller's activity during this period, and his service records are silent about his assignments following the fall of Atlanta. He remained with Morgan's brigade, then under the command of Colonel James Hagan. His brothers Tom and Hop Francis remained in Alabama with the commissary service. In the meantime, Jim Francis moved to his new commissary purchasing office at Athens, Georgia, in late July 1864 and welcomed the opportunity to demonstrate he could manage a larger district for the Confederate commissary bureau.[2]

While the Confederate forces were concentrating before Sherman in North Georgia, Sherman sent a Union cavalry raid deep into east Alabama. The Union commander ordered his raiders to cut the Montgomery & West Point Railroad at Opelika, Alabama. Passing through Sulphur Springs about eighteen miles below Jacksonville, the raiders under Major General Lovell H. Rousseau blazed a path of destruction across Calhoun County near the Francis plantation at Ohatchee. Along the way they torched over 100 bales of cotton near Middleton and destroyed the Morrisville Iron Works. They also burned the conscript camps and railroad depot at Talladega on 15 July 1864 but left the Alabama & Tennessee Rivers rail line intact. The raiders met only token opposition. They briefly skirmished with elements of Brigadier General James H. Clanton's cavalry at Ten Islands Ford on the Coosa River, crossing into Calhoun County, and again with the home guard, including cadets from the University of Alabama, at Chehaw Station, east of Montgomery. Between 17 and 19 July 1864 Rousseau's men destroyed thirty miles of track. The Yankee cavalry reached Marietta, Georgia, on 22 July, a full day before the general populace knew they were operating in the area. The *Jacksonville Republican* reported on the raid "from the great mass of rumors and floating news" in its 23 July issue.[3]

By early fall 1864, the brothers were again corresponding. Instead of pessimistic war talk, their letters were solicitous, written to and about their sisters. Doting on Emma and Willie and their education at Summerfield, the brothers offered money for music lessons and clothes and advice, even testimonials, on the importance of a good education. In the face of war, the tenor of the brothers' letters suggested gentility mixed with practicality, demonstrating an understanding of the value of their sisters' education in preparing them to face the challenges of the postwar world.[4]

The Christmas season 1864 found Sherman sealing Georgia's fate with his occupation of Savannah. Soon after, John Bell Hood retreated to the Tennessee River, following his defeat at the battle of Nashville on 16 December 1864.[5] Tom and Fannie Francis and Hop at Wilsonville, Alabama, were able to visit the family at Christmas. There was no such comfort for sons Jo and Miller, who were on active service with the Fifty-first Alabama in the Barnwell District, South Carolina. Jo's letter written on Christmas Eve provided the family with details of his long trip from Jacksonville to Macon, Georgia, and then to South Carolina. Obviously cloaking his loneliness, he commented that Christmas was like every other day in the army. Jo was not alone in his melancholy; the Confederacy found little to celebrate on Christmas day 1864. Meanwhile, Jim and Sadie Francis enjoyed the warmth and spirit of the holidays by visiting Sadie's sisters, Catherine Barnes Rowland and Anne McKinne Wilde, and her parents in Augusta and Ivanhoe, Georgia.[6]

Early in the new year 1865, Joe Wheeler's calvary corps attempted to disrupt Brigadier General Hugh Judson Kilpatrick's cavalry, who screened the advance of Sherman's army through South Carolina.[7] The pursuit of the Yankee cavalry gave Sadie Francis the rare opportunity to serve dinner to her brothers-in-law Miller and Jo Francis at her new home in Athens. Their reunion was brief. Miller and Jo had to scramble to rejoin Wheeler's cavalry as it retreated ahead of Kilpatrick's marauding horsemen into Aiken, South Carolina. Anxious to pillage Aiken, Kilpatrick rushed into an ambush on 11 February 1865, fighting a furious skirmish in the streets of Aiken, and barely escaped capture by Wheeler's forces. The Fifty-first Alabama, Hagan's brigade in Allen's division, was in daily contact with elements of Sherman's forces in South Carolina from 19 January through 21 February 1865. Despite occasional small-unit victories, the prospects for the Confederate forces in South Carolina by mid-February were dark and grew bleaker daily. As Sherman's veterans continued their campaign of total war, Charleston was evacuated by William J. Hardee's forces on 17 February. At the same time Union forces burned Columbia.[8]

Muddy roads and swollen streams and rivers made the retreat across South Carolina arduous and painful for Wheeler's cavalry, including Jo and Miller Francis with the Fifty-first Alabama, Hagan's brigade. At least one authority claimed that Wheeler's cavalry corps received no government rations near the end of the war. Wheeler's men, like Sherman's Yankee troops, were forced to forage the countryside for provisions. This tactic led to charges that his men were no more than mounted "chicken thieves." Heavy January rains and the bitter cold of February 1865 exacerbated the hunger, filth, and misery of thousands of Confederate soldiers. On 22 February 1865, Jo wrote his last wartime letter, from Chesterfield, South Carolina, near the North Carolina state line. In characteristic understatement, he glumly declared the past two weeks had been hard. Three days of continuous rainfall on 23–25 February and bitter cold weather intensified the discomfort felt by Confederate and Union soldiers in the Carolinas.[9]

In the midst of gloom and destruction, Jim and Sadie Francis announced the birth of their first child, a daughter with "rich brown" hair. Elizabeth McKinne Francis was born in Athens, Georgia, on 23 February. Her birth cheered the Francis and Whitehead families who had lost two young sons, a brother, two nephews, and countless friends over the last four years. Unfortunately, Elizabeth's young life, like that of the Confederacy, was brief. She died seven months later on 28 September 1865.[10]

With the Confederate territory shrinking and its armies reeling in the face of ever-increasing enemy numbers, springtime arrived in the South. In Jacksonville, Amy Ingram Francis announced in mid-March 1865 that some of her peach trees were blooming and beans and Irish potatoes were up in her garden. It was indeed a time for rebirth. Memories of the bloody battlefields began to fade, as did any Confederate war spirit, with Lee's surrender of his Army of Northern Virginia to Ulysses S. Grant on 9 April 1865 at Appomattox Court House, Virginia.[11] On 26 April at a modest farmhouse near Greensboro, North Carolina, Joe Johnston surrendered the remnants of his beloved Army of Tennessee to William Tecumseh Sherman. While a final formation of Johnston's army was scheduled for Salisbury, North Carolina, many soldiers departed for their homes before paroles were issued at Greensboro.[12] It was planting time in the South, and this bloody war was finally over for Old Joe's gritty fighters.

Now a shadow of the unit that had fought so gallantly, Pettus's Alabama brigade surrendered 1,017 guns at Salisbury on 3 May 1865. The Thirtieth Alabama had been consolidated with the Twentieth Alabama on 19 April, and only six members of John Francis's Sallie Walker Boys, Company B, answered the roll call at the final formation.[13]

~

Joseph H. Francis to Amy I. Francis
Camp near Atlanta, Ga.
June 2, 1864

My dear Mother,

Enclosed I send a letter which I wish you would back & send to Hop as I do not know where he is. I'm getting a long finely. I think I'll go to the front tomorrow if Uncle Hugh comes out for Johns horse.[14] I'm much afraid that some one will steal him but I sleep in ten feet of him every night. Upon two or three occasions I sat up all night watching him. This was while we were immediately in the rear of the army. Nothing more. Uncle Hugh delivered the boots for Miller. He was much in need of them. I hear from Miller every day, he is well.[15] My love to all, write soon.

Your son,
J. H. Francis

Hopkins T. Francis to Willie C. Francis
Montgomery, June 6th [18]64

Dear Sister,

I received your kind and interesting letter to day and was truly glad to hear from home as it has been some time since I received a letter from home. It seems that you all slight me in not writing oftener. I hear from home about once every two weeks. Thos sends me word to write to him but never answers my letters. Half the time I do not know where he is. James sent me some very nice clothes a few days ago whitch was very acceptable. I have a very good assortment of clothes now.

I have nothing of interest that I could write you today. I cannot think of anything to write. I am very well satisfied here but had much rather be with Thos.[16] Tell him he never writes me at all. I am in hopes if James has been removed that he is well pleased. He will certainly write me soon if he has been removed.[17] I want you to write me where Miller & Jo are so I can write to them. I have not heard from them since I came here. I do not know where they are. Emma wrote me that it was reported that John Montgomery was killed. I have heard nothing definite about him. Write me whether he is dead or not.[18] Tell Sue to write to me. Tell Father I have not heard from him in some time. Excuse misspelled words as I have been disturbed a great deal since I commenced this letter. Give my love to all. Write soon.

Your affectionate brother,
Hop

Joseph H. Francis to Mary Emma Francis
Camp near Atlanta
June 9th 1864

My Dear Sister Emma,

Your kind letters one of ___ date and the other of the 27th came duely to hand a few days since. Uncle Hugh delivered Miller's boots when I met him in Atlanta some days since, but said nothing of your letter. The contents of your letters noted & shall long be remembered. I went up to the front & stay three days. I'm really anxious to leave this camp there was nothing of much importance going on when I left. Our right wing fell back about three miles. They came in four miles of Marietta. Our division was ordered around to meet them which was the right wing of our army. Our command commenced skirmishing with them when they fell back to Big Shanty, about seven (7) Miles from Marietta.[19]

I think probably that Capt. Forney will go with the Gen. to the Trans-Miss. Dept.[20] I knew nothing as to Toms & Hops movements until you wrote. Jim told me when I saw him at Adaresville that he was going to move to Athens, Geo.[21] I have not yet made any exertions to be detached with him. I'll wait until things become a little quiet on the front. I went to Atlanta yesterday to attend to some business. We are now seven (7) miles from Atlanta. Miller's horse has not yet become able for service. We get plenty rations (corn meal and bacon). Our rations of corn for the horses has been cut down to seven (7) pounds per day. With no long forage. The loss of our brig. in men since the fight at Calhoun is very light.

Tell Mother to send me by the first opportunity one or two prs. of drawers, and two prs. socks. I learned from the post master in Atlanta that Uncle Hugh, has gone to Montgomery, but will return soon. I'm very anxious to send Johns horse & c. home. I suppose you all are not much frightened about the enemys raiders. We have had several rumors that the enemy had been to Blue Mt., but I did not credit them.[22] The weather is very pleasant. We have a very pretty camp. Our tent is in fifteen (15) feet of a red birds nest. While doing nothing I set & watch the old birds feed the young. They have become very tame. We have some right harty laughs over the capers they some times cut, apparently playing with the young. I must now write Father a small note. So goodbye for a short while. My love to all. Write soon.

Your bro.,
J. H. Francis

Hopkins T. Francis to James C. Francis
Montgomery, June 25, [18]64

Dear Father,

As Mr. Renfro leaves this evening I will write you a few lines by him.[23] I received Thos letter to day. I send you fifty ($50) dollars new issue by Mr. Renfro. I send it in fives for I expect they are scarce in Calhoun.[24] This is for the fifty I borrowed of you while at home. I also send Mother a pair cotton cards. Cousin Joseph Francis is here with a slight wound on the knee his wound is a very slight bruise on the knee from the bursting of a shell.[25] He is up and about. He says it was reported that Turney was killed before he left the front but he has heard nothing definite from him.[26] Tell Mother to send me 6 brass buttons to put on my coat, cut them off of some of old coats at home. Mr. Renfro can tell you all the news so I will not write any more. My love to all, tell the children to write to me. You must write soon.

Your son,
Hop

~

Joseph H. Francis to Mary Emma Francis
Reserve Camp Morgan's Brig.
Near Atlanta, Geo., June 27th [1864]

Dear Sister,

What a beautiful morning this is. What a pleasant breeze, but there is one thing that prevents all from enjoying it, the distinct roar of artillery has been very distinct all morning. It has been growing more fierce as the day advances. I imagine there will now be a general engagement as the firing seems to be all along the line, but from this point we cannot tell. I shall not mail this letter before evening as I hope to hear something of today's fighting, but it is not an uncommon thing to hear artillery every day, but this is more fierce than it has been for some time.[27]

Our reg. has quite a hard time for the last week. The has been a number killed & wounded. Among the killed are Geo. Harrison of Co. D. He was Miller's courier while in E. Tenn.[28] Jno Prater was shot through the abdomen and left in the hands of the enemy (supposed dead).[29] A courier came down from brigade hd. qtrs. yesterday, Miller was well. I'll go to the front tomorrow or next day. Bur Neighbors went home yesterday, if I had of known it in time I could have sent Johns horse.[30] I am exceedingly anxious to get him home. He has been very sick, is not well yet. We get only (5) pounds corn per day (no long forage), our horses are all on the decline.

Tell Father that Gen. Morgan has been ordered to report to Gen. Wright at Atlanta to await his trial.[31] All feel confident that he will be cleared. The whole brigade is very much displeased with Gen. Allen.[32] They all want Morgan back. Morgan is more popular this day than he ever was in the brigade. Gen. M. has been in camp with us here for a week. He has quit drinking all together, and says that he will give no one a chance to accuse him of being intoxicated again, that he will not touch another drop while in the army. He is going to show that a gentleman has been making false reports concerning him ever since he was made Brig. Gen. He is very anxious for the trial to come off soon.[33]

It is reported that our regt. has been ordered to the coast in Fla. I don't know how true it is. All say that it will be a desirable place. When Mother sends my drawers I wish you would find in my trunk a pair of dove colored gaiter tops, that has steel strips at the side one of the strips are broken. Send them to me they will keep off the dust while I'm wearing shoes. My boots are about worn out. Tell Father that I want if he can have made a pr. of neat heavy boots. Tell Sister Julia that Miller is with the 51st Reg., but can go where he pleases in the brigade. Tell Sue, Willie & Tobe to write. I'm anxious to have a letter from them. It is now about ten o'clock. The firing continues more fierce. It must certainly be a general engagement. The firing is as heavy as it was at Resaca. I'll close until evening. My love to all. I forgot to say your letter by Capt. White has been received.[34] I sent it to Miller. I have been amusing myself in reading, some quite interesting books published in the Confederacy. I'm now on the history of Jacob in the Old Testament.[35] Write soon.

Your bro.,
J. H. Francis

Hopkins T. Francis to Mary Emma and Willie C. Francis
Montgomery, June 30, [18]64

Dear Sisters,

I have written you all but you seem to not answer. You must all write to me often. I saw Cous. Jo Francis to day and he seemed to be enjoying very good health. I suppose Cous. Turney's remains have arrived at home ere this. Joe told me that Turney was reported to be killed before he left the front but he was not certain whether he was killed or not.[36] I went down Saturday evening to the boat with Judge Woods and Mr. Renfro.[37] A friend of mine came up to me and asked me if the corpse on board of the boat was a relation of mine. I went on board and found it to be the remains of Cousin Turney. I went immediately and dispatched Uncle Hugh at Selma. I looked for Joe but could not find him. He had gone to the country. I sent him word as soon as possible. He came for him Monday night. He did not hear of the death of his brother until Monday evening.[38] I received a letter from Thomas a few days ago. He said he would be here this week. I am waiting patiently for him. Write to me often.

Your affectionate bro.,
H. T. Francis

Joseph H. Francis to Mary Emma Francis
In field 8 miles from Marietta
July 4th 1864

Kind Sister,

On the 1st we all fixed up for a raid, but in the evening it was countermanded. On the second we moved from our position on the right to the left. We halted about seven miles from Marietta went into camp.[39] In a very short time a very heavy thunder cloud came up, weting everybody. The lightning struck a tree near hd. qrs. of the 51st Ala. killing Lieut. Castleberry[40] & Pane.[41] We then received orders to return to Marietta which was accomplished in the night. We then went to the breast works of the infantry, relieving them. It was late in the morning before the enemy knew that Johnson was on the retreat. Our cavy. covered the retreat. This morning it seems that there will be a pretty heavy fight. There is pretty heavy firing all along the line.[42] The 3rd Ala. of our brigade charged into an ambuscade and was cut up rite badly.[43] Johns horse has been lame for some days. Miller is well. Tell Mother to send me some sort of a dark cotton over shirt when she sends the other clothes. I shall hate very much to hear that the enemy has been on our little town, but you must expect them now, but only as raiders.

Well I stoped to eat my breakfast. It was such an uncommon one that I feel very little like writing. We had boiled bacon, Irish potatoes, coosh (made of hard bread), and corn bread. I saw no wounded or slain in Marietta that could fall into the hands of the enemy. I'll write you again soon. Today is the 4th I suppose the feds will have a sullification in Marietta.[44] They said some time back that they would be in Atlanta on this day. Some of them have got there, (but had an escort). Well good bye. Write soon. My love to all.

Your bro.,
Jo H. Francis

Joseph H. Francis to James C. Francis
Recruit Camp Martin's Div.
Near Eufaula, Ala.[45]
July 19th 1864

Dr Father,

We arrived at this point after one weeks journey. Our camp is in two miles of town. I wish you would write me if you think it safe to bring the horses to Jacksonville. My mare will have a colt next month. Brooks is unfit for the service as one hoof of his fore feet will come off (that is they tell me so). It has cracked around near the hoof hairline. With gentle use he will not be injured by it, as another will grow out. It will be about one month before it comes off without an accident. He is not lame. Miller's horse has all of a sudden become lame in the hind leg from what cause no one can tell.[46] As my dutys are very light, how would it be for me to ride Jno little mare? Capt. White says I can go to Jacksonville with my horses if you think it safe to have them there. I wish you would pay Sister Julia one hundred dollars for me, as I borrowed that amount from Miller ($100.00). The enemy made a raid on Opalaca a few nights ago, tore up the R.R. track & c.[47]

Write to me in care of Capt. White. Tell Mother to make me a hunting shirt out of the shawl that is on left of the wardrobe in the back room. Without any fancy trimmings, just work button holes for the vest bottons. I have buttons on my vest that will do. The weather is very warm. I have been sick for a day or two. We get plenty corn bread & bacon. I must close for I write on my knee. My love to all.

Your son,
"Jo"

P.S. Have me a pair of good boots made if it is possible. Your predictions came true about our army falling back on Atlanta. I believe I wrote you that our brigade was in its brest works near Marietta. Capt. Forney and I are together. We have plenty to eat. Nothing new today at all. It has been raining all evening. Nothing more. Yr. son, Jo

James C. Francis, Jr. to James C. Francis
Athens, Ga.
Aug. 13th 1864

Dear Father,

I wrote Jo a short letter from Augusta before I left. I am now nicely situated at this place and am better pleased than when in Augusta.[48] I find that I am improved in health but I am never sick. Sadie is delighted here. Her father and brothers were educated and she has *many* warm friends.[49] I have a very large district and I think the dept. begin to believe that I can handle a dist. of large size better than most of the old major comsry.

We are delightfull situated. Col. Leipers family is boarding at the same hotel and are just across the hall from us.[50] If you remember I sent a little note by Col. Forney that I had shiped you some money express.[51] It will leave Augusta Tuesday. I hope to hear from you soon. Give my love to all the family. I would be so delighted to see and talk with you. I think a trip to Athens would improve you so much. If you and Mother will come to see us I will pay all expenses. If she cannot come, can't you? Give my love to all. Sadie sends much love.

Yr. affectionate son,
J. C. Francis, Jr.

Sarah W. Francis to Amy I. Francis
Athens, Aug. 25th 1864

My dear Mother,

I just finished a letter to Aunt Martha and will send you one by the same mail in reply to yours received last night. I was truely sorry to hear of Uncle John's death and have thought most constantly of his poor heart stricken wife.[52] He spent several days with us in Augusta on his way to Virginia, and his love for his wife which was so apparent in all his sayings had quite won my heart. Oh! When will this cruel war end, when will this carnage and bloodshed be stopped?

I wish now that we could go to see you, but it will be some time before I will be able for reasons which you can imagine. It is a great disappointment to me for I am so anxious to see and know all of my precious husband's relations. I hope that you will all love me, as much as I have learned to love every member of the family and will feel as near to me as I do to you. As soon as I am well again, my first desire and intention is to visit you.[53]

What have become of Sisters Julia and Fannie—if mistake not—they both owe me letters, and I would be delighted to hear from them. I suppose sister Fannie is with Brother Tom. I was surprised to hear that Emma was at home. Will she not return to Summerfield? I wish that I could be at home while Joe is there, do Mother, beg him to come and spend a few days with us. Tell him I insist. I would be perfectly delighted to see him and wish that he would come. There has been a great deal of excitement here about raids. The raiders did appear within a few miles of the place but were repulsed and I do not think will again appear.[54] And now my dear mother good bye. Give a heart full of love to each member of the family, in which my dear husband unites, and accept the same for yourself from

Your affectionate child,
Sadie W. Francis

James C. Francis, Jr. to Amy I. Francis
Office of Purchasing Commissary
Athens, Ga., Aug 26th 1864

Dear Mother,

Sadie received your letter night before last and answered it last night. You will get it by the same mail that bears this. We are well and pleasantly located. I regreted very much to hear of the death of Uncle John. I do hope that we have drunk as deeply of sorrow's cup as will be required of us. Point to a family that has not been called upon to give up a near relative? Our entire land is an vast house of mourning.[55]

If the little girls wish anything or need anything let me know and I will hasten to procure it. Do not think that it will not be a pleasure to me. I realize more pleasure from assisting my brothers & sisters with what money I have been so fortunate as to accumulate than from any other way of spending it. I know that you are ambitious and I am glad it is so with all of our family. *Yet* I wish this to be put aside. The time may come when I or my dear Sadie may want and I know we would be cared for. I have written Father often in relation to money I loaned Mr. Land[56] & Tom

Crow.[57] 100$ of the amt. loaned Crow was for Sister Julia. Please ask Father about it.

When does the Summerfield session begin? Let me know & I will remit funds. I wish Emma to continue so do not let her quit. Send Willie and Sue also. Give them up but for a little while and you will be glad of it. Woman will be more dependent on her education after the war than ever before. So make the sacrifice of their company for a little while. I wrote Aunt Martha. So did Sadie. I hope to hear from you all often. I believe sisters Julia & Fannie each owe Sadie a letter.

Your affectionate son,
J. C. Francis, Jr.

Thomas W. Francis to Hopkins T. Francis
Selma, Sept. 12, [18]64

Dear Hop,

I will try and come up on my way to North Alabama Wednesday or Thursday night. I have to wait here for Genl. Adams who will return on Tuesday.[58] I will want you to go with me. I will make arrangements to get you a horse. I send by Mattison a pigeon that I wish you would send out to Fannie as soon in the morning as you can. I want you to send Fred to me by Wednesdays train.[59] I want to send him to Meridian.

Tell Fannie to give him some provisions to do him two or three days. Give him a pass to come to me at Selma. Go out and see Fannie and tell her I had not time to write before the train left.

Yours,
T. W. Francis

[Margin note] Give Fred the order to Maj. McMinn for the transportation.[60]

Joseph H. Francis to Mary Emma Francis
Musquita Retreat Ft. Browder,
Sept. 23rd [18]64[61]

Fond Sister,

I imagine from the quantity of paper you have placed in this envelope you expect quite a lengthy letter. Well to make it so, I'll have to enter into the full details of my trip. Ragin stood it finely. The first day I arrived in the neighborhood of Talladega. Rode two miles off my road to get my knife. I had but little hopes of ever finding it. I paid the servant boy two dollars ($2.00) as a reward for his honesty. Staid all night with quite a clever gentleman. I opened a crib door and let Ragin stick his head in and eat. Made my bed down near him, don't think he stoped eating during the night. Well in short I made my trip with but little difficulty. Sent Tobe's knife by Mr. Douthit.[62] I suppose you have heard the song of "The old dog lay on the barn floor." Whether that was true or not I cannot say, but can assure you that I now *write* on the barn door. I found Capt. White & Ed well. Capt. White went to Eufaula this morning before I arrived.[63] This being the sixth day of my journey. I got in about 11 o'clock went out this evening & gathered quite a nice lot of muscadines. They are very plentiful all over the swamps here. Also grapes in the greatest abundance. Don't know when we will leave here. You can continue to write to this point.

I think of making a visit to Glenville soon, in the shape of a pleasure trip.[64] It is only fifteen miles. I may enjoy myself, but not so well as if I was at home. Don't think that I am at all homesick, but I can assure you that I appreciate home as much as any one. Ed says tell his family he is in fine health & is enjoying himself very much.[65] Well I'll have to postpone my writing until morning.

Morning has come (this the 24th). Capt. White came back very late last night. Mr. Driskil & lady arrived safe at Eufaula.[66] Tell Father my boots are finely. The luntch you fixed up for me was of much value. I eat five meals off of it. Well it is time for me to close. I don't know when you will get this. If I don't send it to Eufaula by hand, it will not leave here before next Wednesday, as that is the first mail day.

Goodbye. I have an opportunity of sending this to be mailed now. My love to all. Write soon.

Your bro.,
J. H. F.

James C. Francis, Jr. to Amy I. Francis
Athens, Ga.
Sept. 24th 1864

Dear Mother,

Your letter to hand by yesterdays mail. It pains me to hear of the death of so many of our friends & relations, but more of us may go ere the struggle is over. I know it was a severe blow to Aunt Betsey.[67]

I will send to Maj. M. J. A. Keith in a few days 2,000$ subject to Father's check. I wish Emma to make herself a *good* schollar. Let her take music lessons and anything else she may desire, anything that would be useful to her in after life. I am glad she did not graduate last session. I wish Emma to have 300$ for spending money & Willie 150$. At any time that money is needed for the purposes above mentioned (educating the little girls), tell Father to write me and I will send it. I wish to return any funds that Father may have advanced for them. Have they plenty of clothes? If not let me know what is wanting and I will send it. Has Emma any *nice* clothes? If not write me.

Sadie is quite anxious to hear from you. She is now in Augusta and has been for 10 days. When you write direct your letter to this place. Give my love to all. Tell the little girls to write me. Tell Father that I have not heard from him. If he will open a regular correspondence with me I think he would feel much better. I cannot tell when we can come to Ala. I am collecting about 300 hd. beef cattle per week.[68] Write me often. My love to all.

Your affectionate son,
J. C. Francis, Jr.

Joseph H. Francis to Mary Emma Francis
Musquita Retreat
Ft. Browder, Oct 2nd 1864

Fond Sister Emma,

No letter from home yet. Ed received one yesterday. I really don't know what to think of the mails for I know some of you have written.

We have no news at all. Had a picknic yesterday, spent quite a pleasant day. A large crowd have attended three parties since my return. Will have a supper at Mr. Bates tomorrow night.[69] They are surprises without a doubt. We get together of an evening about one hour before sunset, go after the young ladies and arrive at the house without giving them any notice whatever. Our party always consists of about twelve or fifteen young ladies and seven or ten boys. Capt. White attends pretty regularly. He is very anxious to tell me something to write, but it is some of his nonsense about our "sweetharts," as he calls them.

Went to church today but heard no sermon as the minister failed to come. Had prayer meeting.[70] Ate quite a large watermellon this evening. What shall I write? Suppose I draw you an apple cart on it as I can't write. A number of the boys are sick (chills & fever). I'm feeling pretty hungry. I must go and cook something. Goodbye for a while. My love to all. Write soon. Tell Willie & Sue to write.

Your bro.,
J. H. Francis

~

Joseph H. Francis to Mary Emma Francis
Musquita Retreat
Fort Browder, Ala., Oct. 10th 1864

My Fond Sister,

Seated with the Cowikee Church Bible in my lap as a portfolio.[71] I'll run a few dull lines over this sheet for the purpose of informing you of my condition. As to the knowledge of affairs at home. How long since I left that dear old spot it seems months. Not a simple scroll of the pen have I ever seen since I left. Was it not that Capt. White & Ed received letters every few days I would not really know what to think. Tis true the mails are very uncertain, but then it is strange that they should get letters almost every mail and me none at all.

I feel very little like writing this evening. I and Capt. White went out to take a parting meal with two boring lady friends. They live in Geo. Have been out here for some weeks. They started home this evening. When we got back to camp it was 3 o'clock, found the boys had served up a large "posum" & a large fine turkey that we were so fortunate to capture yesterday. We have a mess of this kind every few days.[72] Have attended three (3) paryties in the last week. Enjoying myself finely have nothing to do but take care of my own horse, been suffering a little with the tooth ache. The last two nights have been very cold slept cold both nights. Will sleep in the church to night. I'm doing finely would feel better if I could get a letter from home ever now & then. Heard that Miller had been home but went with Wheeler again.[73] Why have you not written? Will go to the church tonight. Had quite a poor sermond this morning. This pencil is so miserable and it puts me out of patience to write. I fear we will have to move our camp fifteen (15) miles on account of forage.

I have written every thing I know, but that I expect to go "posum" hunting again in a few nights. Excuse this. Write soon, tis sunset.

Your bro.,
J. H. F.

[Margin note] Spend my leisure moments on reading *David Copperfield,* a very interesting book.[74] Jo

Joseph H. Francis to Mary Emma Francis
Ft. Browder, Nov. 10th 1864

My Fond Sister,

Your very kind letter of the 31st came to hand yesterday. I was sorry I did not start home some time since. I'll start home on the 13th but will not find you there.[75] I must say that your letter was of that style that I really desired, for I really wanted to know if they had undergone any change since I left. I should not let such things trouble my mind in the least. If this war should ever close there will be quite a change in the world. I'm really glad to see that it was not your desire to attend such parties as you mentioned in your last letter. I think I am fully awake as to the feeling of certain ones. Never seek acquaintance with such characters as those that were floating around Jacksonville when you left, but I know it is useless to mention this, for your letter explained fully to me your ideas upon this subject.

Friday night Nov. 11th 1864

You will have to excuse this letter. While writing it yesterday about 12 o'clock I took a chill, which lasted me two hours. The fever lasted me six. My head has not quit aching yet. I missed my chill today. I don't apprehend any danger as Miss Cade is as kind as any one could be. I shall never forget her.[76] Will start home on Monday next. It will take us five days to make the trip. Cousin Jo is going to Uncle Porter's from here.[77] I receive letters from Athens ever now & then. Jim & Sister Sadie is very anxious for me to make application to be detached in that department. You will have to excuse me for writing on this paper, as I have none other convenient, and I'm fond of writing on large paper.[78] My love to Willie. Will look for a letter from you both at Jacksonville. You will make all due allowances for this as I feel very stupid & dull. Goodbye. Write soon.

Your bro.,
J. H. F.

Hopkins T. Francis to Mary Emma and Willie C. Francis
Wilsonville, Dec. 21st [1864]

Dear Sisters,

I have not heard from you since you left home. I suppose you did not know where I was. I am now stationed in this place with Thos.[79] I heard from Sister Susan a few days ago. All were well at home. Sister Fannie will be down here on next Saturday. She & Thos will stay at Mr. Hanley's about 8 miles from here. You must be studious & try & obtain an education now while you are young. Perhaps you do not see the necessity of a thorough education now but it will not be long before you will see the necessity of a good education. Now is the time do not put it off untill it is too late. I used to think that going to school was an irksome task but now I see my error. Write to me soon for I do not know how long I will remain here. My love to all. Goodbye.

Your affectionate brother,
Hop T. Francis

Joseph H. Francis to Willie C. Francis
Wagon Camp Allen's Div.
Barnwell District, S.C.
Dec. 24th 1864

My Sister Willie,

I wrote Emma some time since but have not heard from her. I have not heard from home since I left there. I wrote two letters home while in Augusta. Our train is now in twenty five (25) miles of the command.[80]

We have had quite a time of it. Capt. White & I went from Jacksonville to Macon. There we found the wagon train. Remained there one week. We left there with the train for the command, passed through Milledgeville, Wainsboro & Augusta.[81] I visited Mr. Whitehead's & spent several hours very pleasantly with his family, was very kindly treated, took dinner with him also. The enemy damaged him to the amount of thirty thousand dollars.[82] We stoped two days in Augusta. I found Mr. Wilde there. He is one of Mr. Whitehead's sons-in-law and quite a nice fellow too. He carried [me] down to his residence where I met his lady.[83] Tis useless to speak of the kindness shown me here, for they did all in their power to make me *feel* at *home*. Jim was expected down every day while I was there but did not come. I was much disappointed in not seeing him.

We are now about seventy five miles below Augusta not far from the Savannah River. We had some very unpleasant weather on our trip. The country that we are now in is very poor. It is what is called the wiregrass country.[84] I have suffered very much from a *cold* that I have had for three weeks. I'm going down to the command tomorrow. Heard from Miller today he is in fine health. Savannah was evacuated by our forces on the night of the 20th none of our forces were captured with the place.[85] I have heard very heavy cannonading for the last three days. The enemy are supposed to be moving on Branchville. If they take this point all communication with Richmond will be cut off, but they can't hold it long, if they get it.[86] I write by a camp fire which affords a very poor light.

News is *news*, and long letters are sometimes interesting, but I must close. Tomorrow is Christmas. Many may enjoy it & feel gay, but it is no more than any other day in the army. It seems as though the fire is consious of my intentions, & seems to burn with a new spirit, as though it was interested in my writing you a lengthy letter but no I must close. Good night. My love to Emma. A long letter from each of you will be looked for soon. You will make all necessary allowances for this & commit it to the flames.[87]

Your bro.,
Jo

Amy I. Francis to Mary Emma and Willie C. Francis
Jacksonville, Dec. 27th 1864

Dear Daughters,

I received your letter by Mary Grant was glad to hear that you were well and getting along well and pretty well satisfyed.[88] We are all well not much sickness in town.

We received a letter from James Sunday.[89] He and Sadie were well. He said he had written you a long letter. I hope you have received it. We received a letter from Jo last night. He was at Augusta. He was looking for James down that day. He thought they would leave there for Adairsville near Savanna the next day. Heard from Miller a week ago. He was well had been to Mr. Whitehead's, was very much pleased with the old people. They treated him very kind.[90] Thos and Fanny left here on Sunday night for Willsonville. She will be gone eight or ten days on a visit to Mr. Hanley's.

Julia has given out moving down to the plantation. We have not killed our pork yet, will kill as soon as it turns cold. It is now warm and raining. We had a severe hail this evening the most singular I ever saw. The hail was not round but in every shape you could imagine, some with bills like birds, some like stars, spiders, craw fish, and almost every animal and creeping thing you could think of. The icicles were from two to three inches long. It was a form of icicles in the place of hail. It was a beautiful sight. They almost covered the ground.

You wanted to know how they were all pleased with your cousin Maries choice.[91] They are all very well pleased not a desenting voice. They will have onely a marriage, will not make a wedding. No doubt he will make her a good living and a good husband. I will send you a few candles by Mary Grant, be saving of them as tallow is high and hard to get.[92] I send you a box for Christmas, started it on last Wednesday night, expressed it to the care of Maj. Keith. Hope you got it. A very dull Christmas. Will write by M. Gr.[93] Your Father and Sue, Bud send their love. May the Lord bless and save you is my sincere prayer.

A. Francis

~

Mary Emma Francis to James C. Francis
Summerfield, Ala.
Jan. 8th 1865

My dear Father,

We received your short but interesting letter by Mary Grant. We were agreeably surprised on receiving it. Mary Grant delivered the money you sent to the amount of $(500), five hundred dollars. I did as you directed. I gave Dr. Rivers $(300) three hundred[94] and Mr. Garrett ($200) two hundred dollars. Mr. Garrett said I need not pay him any more before the close of the term.[95]

Willie received a letter from Joe last week written on the 24th of Dec. He was at Branchville S.C.[96] He said he was going to the command the next day. He heard from Brother Miller the day he wrote. He was in fine health. He said he had not heard from home since he left. I have written to him several times but I suppose he has received none of them.

We would have written by Lou Grant but he left sooner than we expected and we did not have time to write.[97] I suppose Cousin Mary is to be married next Thursday night. Please tell her to send me a piece of her wedding cake. I would like very much to attend but it is impossible for me to do so.

Mrs. Rivers has been quite sick, but has entirely recovered.[98] She often inquires when we heard from home and asks about the different members of the family. School is about as large as it was last session. Tell Bud he owes me a letter. If he don't write to me I won't have him as one of my correspondents but will write to Clark and I know he will answer my letters.

Willie and I are enjoying fine health and are getting along very well. We both join in sending much love to all the family. Hoping to hear from you soon. I am,

Your devoted daughter,
Emma Francis

~

Amy I. Francis to Mary Emma and Willie C. Francis
Jacksonville, Jan. 12th [18]65

Dear Daughters,

I received your letters some days since was glad to hear that you were well and getting along well. I hope you are satisfyed with your boarding house. We are all well. Your Aunt Turney is not going to Flourada.[99]

Gid and Mary are boarding at Eliza Forney's.[100] Julia will not move to Bitnose.[101] Hop is not paying any attention to any young lady as I heard of. He is at the plantation. Thos has a furlough of 40 days. He will be assigned duty at some post as he is not fit for field duty.[102] Have not heard from the other boys for some time. I will send the things you wrote for by Lon in a short time. We are all getting along very well. The white rabit dyed, old Ben cat is still alive, your Simon turkey hen grows finely. Maybe she may raise a brood of turkeys.

When you get your ink you must shake it up before using it. Your Uncle Griffith[103] is in partnership with your Uncle Woodward,[104] Hugh Ford and Carrol in a store and scarcly anything to sell, nothing that you would want.[105] You have some very small quilt buttons here your Brother Tom bought for you. Do you want me to send them to you? Your delain dresses are very pretty, very light, will only do for spring or fall. Lon goes down the 18th I suppose.

You must be good girls, treat kindly. The family all join in sending you much love. May the Lord bless and save is the prayer of your affectionate mother.

A. Francis

Sarah W. Francis to Mary Emma Francis
Athens, Jan. 18th [1865]

My dear Emma,

I have been intending for some time past to write you, but I have not been feeling very well, for some weeks, and have not been able to write anyone.[106] Capt. Francis has written both Willie and yourself two or three times, but the mails are so irregular now I doubt if you have received them. How do you feel about the Yankees? Are you afraid they will get us all? It seems so. When taking human aid into consideration, but it is a precious thought, that God does all things well and every thing is in his hands.

I believe that this war will last until we are thoroughly scourged and purified from the evil that now predominates in our land. It will not last always however, and we can alone trust in God. If my precious husband and brothers can be spared 'tis all I ask, and I do pray that God will see fit to bring them safely through this war. We have both given up a noble brother both killed on distant battle fields, where none were near to soothe their last hours, and bear to loved ones at home their last message of love, but God doeth all for the best.[107] His will be done and all will be perfectly right in the end. The Yankees have payed my father a visit and took almost everything from him.[108]

Bro. Miller and Joe were with Wheeler when he was in pursuit of Kilpatric and his men. They stayed at our house to dinner.[109] We had a letter from Joe last night. He was quite well and in fine spirits. When do you have vacation? Do my dear sister study hard and improve, now the golden opportunity, apply yourself diligently to your books, treasure up every hour and improve it well, and you will never regret it. I only wished that I had studied more diligently, and improved my advantages more, at your age, for I would have been a far more useful woman if I had, and I want you and Willie, my dear sisters, to profit by my experience. You will be rewarded far more than you dream of now, I must bring my letter to a close, as I am not feeling well at all today. Capt. Francis is not here or would I know send love. With a heart full for both Willie and yourself. I am,

Yours devotedly,
Sister Sadie

Joseph H. Francis to Willie C. Francis
On the field near Aiken, So.Ca.
Feby. 13th 1865

My Fond Sister,

Your kind letter of the 8th of Jan. came to hand yesterday, tis torn. Our mail is quite irregular, but the letters generaly turn up some time or other. I have been absent from the brig. for some time. I left it on the 2nd inst. returned on the 12th. I went to Augusta with the ambulances of our brig. for the purpose of having them repaired also to purchase a supply of medical stores. My trip for the last two weeks would be quite interesting to you but I have not the patience to relate the whole.[110]

On the 8th inst. the enemy with three brigs. charged less than two hundred of our men & caused a great retrograde movement (stampeed).[111] There has been occasional fighting for several days. The enemy moved in force on us yesterday, came up in our front, but did not fight. They retreat about one [P.M.]. We gave them a good floging on the 11 inst., drove them five miles.[112] This morning they have moved on us with a heavy force of infantry & cavalry. The strength of the enemy has caused us to fall back on a position one & a half miles from the little town Aiken, which is seventeen (17) miles from Augusta on the R. Road.[113] We fought them day before yesterday in the streets of Aiken, our loss small. There has been no fighting this morning, except skirmishing. Gen. Beauregard is in Columbia.[114] Infantry from Hoods army has gone there. There is no troops confronting the enemy at this point except our division. Gen. Wheeler with two divisions moved out last night, supposed to be in the rear of the enemy.[115]

All the cotton in Augusta has been removed from the ware houses for the purpose of being burnt if the place is given up. A great deal of excitement prevails among the citizens. Heard from Jim while in Augusta.[116]

Enclosed I send you a nice pen that I found yesterday. Received a letter from Tom & Hop yesterday. The first from home in some time. I suppose every body has given up the hope of an early *peace*. The proceedings of the abolitionists at Fortress Monroe is hoped to give those at home a new spirit.[117] The president says there is no other hope for us than to fight.[118] Stevens is coming to Geo. to arouse the people to a speedy prosecution of the war.[119] I shall close this so as to give room for a P. S. on the next page when I send it off. My love to Emma. Have written her several times & recd. several letters from her. Must write Hop & Tom today. I will look for letters from you both soon.

Your bro.,
Jo

P.S. The enemys movements today were similar to those of yesterday. They did not fight. We are still in Aiken. They retired about 12. All is quiet once more. The weather is very cold. Jo

~

Joseph H. Francis to Amy I. Francis
Camp Hagans Brig.
Near Chisterville, S. C.[120]
Feby. 22nd 1865

My dear Mother,

I suppose you are aware that we have no mail communication. Our only chance of writing is to send letters by hand to Augusta. Some one will start tomorrow for Geo. or Ala. so I'll write a short note by them. We are living fine on fowls, honey & c.[121] I believe there is nothing of interest to write. Have seen quite a hard time in the last two weeks. Miller is in fine health. I'm quite dirty, & feel miserable this morning.[122] I can't tell you anything about our future movements. Jessey Ingram has been a little sick.[123] All are in fine spirits. Miller recd. a letter from Emma three days ago. The man is waiting to carry my letter. Goodbye. My love to all.

Your son,
Jo

P.S. I wish you would send this to Emma & Willie, for I have not time to write to them. The prospects are fine for bad weather.[124] Nothing more. Yr. son, "Jo"

James C. Francis, Jr. to Mary Emma and Willie C. Francis
Athens, Ga.
Feby. 23rd [18]65

My dear Sisters,

It gives me pleasure to announce to you the arrival of a little niece for you. It weighs 9 1/2# *full.* I send a lock of hair taken from its little head.[125] I will write you again soon. Good bye with much love from S. & J. Your much attached and affectionate bro.,

J. C. Francis, Jr.

Amy I. Francis to Mary Emma and Willie C. Francis
Jacksonville, March 19th 1865

Dear Daughters,

I received a letter from Willie a few days since, was glad to hear from you. I wrote to you a week since we are all well. Have not heard from the boys since I wrote you. We are all getting along very well. I have nothing new to write you. How are you getting along with your studies? How did you stand your last examinations?

Susan is going to school to Carrie.[126] Mrs. Calwell has never been able to teach yet and it seems that Carrie will have to teach alone.[127]

Spring is very backward, very few peach trees in bloom yet my hot bed is getting fit for use. Have a few beans up. Think the frost will ketch them. Irish potatoes are up, will plant corn and beans tomorrow. Have nearly forty young chickens, will try and have plenty of young chickens to fry when you come home. We hear no talk of a raid here now. Gen. Hill's head quarters are here, his wife is here.[128] They are keeping house in Crawford's old house. Write me any thing you need and I will try and get it for you. Mr. Yeats folks are all well.[129]

You must study hard. Charlie is writing at school and when he can write a little better he will write to you. Remember your Creator in your youth. May the Lord bless and save you is the prayer of your affectionate mother.

A. Francis

Edmund Winston Pettus to Pettus Brigade[130]
Hd. Qrs. Pettus Brigade
Salisbury, April 28th [18]65

Soldiers:

You have now served your country faithfully for more than three years. On many hard fought fields your steady determined valor has been proved. In camp, and on the march your cheerful endurance of privations and labor, has won the admiration of the army and the country.[131]

Your prompt obedience of orders has justly won the admiration of your commanders. You have won a reputation, as regiments and as a brigade of which you and your dear ones at home are and ought to be proud. Now you are to be subject to a new trial.

The fortune of war has made you prisoners. You are to be marched in a body to your state, and there disbanded on parole. Your valor and good conduct has been my greatest joy and pride; and it is confidently expected that the reputation of this command will be still preserved in this new trial![132]

Though others may desert and disgrace themselves, & their kindred, let us stand together and obey orders! In this way we best contribute to our safety, and comfort; and preserve our characters untarnished.

Let our motto be "Do our duty trusting in God."

E. W. Pettus[133]
Brig. Genl.

Epilogue

While the American Civil War officially ended with the formal surrenders of springtime 1865, the Francis family concluded its wartime experiences with John's reinterment in the Jacksonville City Cemetery on Tuesday, 16 January 1866. War veterans, members of his Masonic order, and his extended family escorted the casket bearing his remains from his family home, to the subdued accompaniment of a band. The band was led by Ira Webb, a distinguished musician, and included "Walter Caldwell, Capt. McGregor, Capt. Farmer, Wright, Stevenson, Mitchell & Crawford." Although Lieutenant Colonel Francis's burial followed Masonic ritual and good Methodist doctrine, he also received military honors for his service in the Confederate army from former comrades and other veterans.[1] Perhaps the service helped other families and residents of Jacksonville and Calhoun County to heal from the loss of 741 friends and family members—267 killed in battle or from their wounds and 474 dead from sickness during the war.[2]

John's brothers and kinsmen ended their Confederate service under widely varying circumstances. Miller Francis, major and senior surgeon in Hagan's brigade, was paroled on 26 April 1865 near Durham Station, North Carolina.[3] Private Jo Francis, who had remained on detached service from the Fifty-first Alabama in the medical department, was paroled on 3 May at Charlotte.[4] Captain Jim Francis was captured and became a prisoner of war but received an expedited parole on 8 May at Athens, Georgia.[5] Major Tom Francis and Hop Francis were apparently issued paroles at Montgomery in late April or early May 1865.[6]

While life could never be the same for the Francis brothers, their fortunes were brighter than most Southerners. With relative ease the brothers either returned to their former careers or established new ones in the postwar South. Although Jim and Sadie Francis continued to reside in Georgia following the war, Miller, Tom, Hop, and Jo returned to Jacksonville following their paroles. By November 1865, Miller Francis had returned to his prewar partnership with his father, and, together, father and son practiced medicine in their apothecary office in Jacksonville until Miller's death on 2 May 1877. His wife, Julia, had died some three years earlier on 6 November 1874 at the age of forty-one.[7]

Following the war, Tom Francis rebuilt his fortunes and landholdings near Sulphur Springs, operated the Francis Mill below Ohatchie for several years, and served as a representative for three New York commercial houses. He also established a successful mercantile business with John F. Cobbs in Montgomery before his retirement. He died at his home at Francis Mill on 23 October 1890 at the age of fifty-three. His wife, Fannie, passed away in Jacksonville nearly thirty years later, on 14 August 1920.[8]

Hop Francis became a successful planter and merchant in Calhoun County. On 22 November 1872, he married Suphena Sims of Newton County, Georgia, the niece of his sister-in-law Julia Patterson Clark Francis. Although Hop lived at Polkville, he also served as a postmaster in the Shady Glenn community for several years before his retirement. He died on 27 March 1926 in his eighty-sixth year and was interred with his brothers and other kinsmen in the Jacksonville City Cemetery.[9]

After a brief postwar residence in Selma, Jo Francis, now known as "Joe," moved to New York City in 1869, where he worked for Tefft-Weller Company and became a successful dry goods salesman. A world traveler, he remained a debonair bachelor who occasionally visited his family and friends in Jacksonville. He died on 29 November 1905 and was buried in the Francis family plot.[10]

During his postwar career, Jim Francis engaged in farming and business activities in Georgia and New York. Tragically, he and and his wife, Sadie, suffered the loss of their four children before they reached adulthood. His wife died on 2 October 1882 at age thirty-seven, and he died less than three years later, on 1 January 1885.[11]

The other Francis family members and wartime correspondents also shared a mixed postwar heritage. Mother Amy Ingram Francis died on 20 July 1868 at the age of fifty-six, and daughter Willie Caroline, who never married, passed away ten years later, on 25 February 1878 at age twenty-nine. Willie continued her letter writing in the postwar years, keeping in touch with her brothers and other kinsmen. She also wrote poetry, a novella entitled *The Star of Blood,* and other works.[12] Sister Emma, who also never married, was, as of 1880, engaged in domestic concerns. She remained in the family home after the death of Dr. Francis at age seventy-eight on 20 March 1888, but she later made her home with her sister Susan Francis Martin in

Jacksonville. Although Hop and Susan survived her, she died at St. Vincent's Hospital in Birmingham on 7 January 1918, having outlived her other siblings, including her youngest brother, Charlie, who died in Birmingham on 14 February 1895. He had been in the shoe business in Birmingham for twelve years before his death, and his brother Joe Francis of Brooklyn, New York, arranged his burial in Jacksonville.[13]

Susan Hannah Francis continued the Francis tradition of educating their women and gave the salutary address when she graduated from Wesleyan Female Institute in Staunton, Virginia, in June 1870. She married John Thomas Martin, a lawyer and son of Lieutenant Colonel James Benson Martin, who had been killed at the battle of Dranesville, Virginia, on 20 December 1861. Susan's death on 6 November 1939 in Jacksonville at the age of eighty-eight silenced the final voice in the James Carrington Francis family Civil War correspondence.[14]

Appendix A

Muster roll of Captain William H. Forney, Company "G" the "Pope Walker Guards" of the 10th regiment, Alabama volunteers, Lewis House near Manassas, Virginia, 20 February 1862

William Henry Forney, Capt.
George C. Whatley, 1st Lieut.
James B. Farmer, 2nd Lieut.
John [W.] Francis, 2nd Lieut.
James M. Renfro, 1st Sergt.
Thomas R. Rowland, 2nd Sergt.
Thomas J. Walker, 2nd Lieut.
Isaac N. Roden, 1st Corpl.
Wyatt McDaniel, 3rd Sergt.
Shelton J. Stevenson, 4th Sergt.
Luke C. Mitchell, 2nd Corpl.
Dave F. Shuford, 3rd Corpl.
William R. Pirkle, 4th Corpl.
John R. Crawford, Musician
Robert H. Holmes, Musician

Privates

Abernathy, Macon
Alexander, A. F.
Allsup, John R.
Belton, James F.
Belton, Newton J.
Beach, Ira W.
Blun, Elias
Bonds, Norval W.
Brady, James L.
Brooks, Benjamin A
Browning, James Y.
Campbell, John A.
Carpenter, Jacob G.
Carruth, A. P.
Cleveland, James G.
Clark, John P.
Cobb, John A.
Earns, Henry A.
Findley (Finley), William M.
Francis, John C.

Francis, Thomas W.
Fleishl, Joseph
Garmany, James H.
Garrett, Benjamin F.
Glover, Asa S.
Glover, Hampton W.
Glover, Joseph M.
Goodman, David
Grant, Leonidas W.
Green, James L.
Green, John D.
Green, William B.
Griffith, Vardy S.
Gutman, Henry
Haglin, James
Hall, John D.
Harris, Jesse
Hayden, Marcellus
Hodges, Benjamin F.
Hodges, Samuel K.
Hodges, Thomas M.
Huckaby, Littleberry
Humphries, Asberry
Jackson, William B.
Johnson, Americus F.
Keeling, Edwin M.
Keller, James M.
Kimbrell, Archibald
Littlejohn, Cornelius
Littlejohn, William J.
Love, Andrew J.
McAdams, Abner G.
McCollum, Samuel A.
McGlatney, Samuel H.
Martin, [Radomanthens] M.
Martin, William A.
Miller, Luke C.
Mohon, William W.
Moragne, Augustus W.
Moragne, James M.
Moragne, Macinus W.
Moragne, William M.
Murry, Hugh
Murry, James
Neal, Francis M.
Neal, William M.
Peace, Jesse
Pirkle, Isaac L.
Plexico, James L.
Ponder, Malachi
Prater, Wiley T.
Read, Asa
Robertson, Francis M.
Rutledge, William A.
Sisson, Charles B. Jr.
Smith, William H.
Steed, William C.
Stephens, Newton J.
Stevenson, Horace L.
Stewart, Franklin J.
Stone, William M.
Swan, Isaac L.
Tatum, Carter B.
Thompson, John W.
Thompson, William P.
Turnley, George J.
Vernon, Henry F.
Walden, Hamilton G. G.
Walden, Henry
Walker, John D.
Walker, Thomas J.
Watkins, Doctor Franklin
Weaver, John W.
Wells, Thomas T.
West, John P.
Wharton, Richard T.
Wharton, William C.
Wharton, William M.
Wiley, Ransom A.
Williams, Richard D.

Woodley, William G.
Woolsey, Nathaniel F.
Wright, John W.
Wright, Wesley J.
Wyly, John M.
Yeager, James Y.

Recruits and Substitutes

Andrews, J. D.
Bailton, John J.
Belton, William
Bonds, John T.
Browning, Robert W.
Bryson, Jackson R.
Bryson, Samuel
Champion, W. M.
[Collum], David M.
Cornelius, John M.
Crawford, Alfred M.
Crawford, Slater
Dondy, John W.
Farmer, Joseph H.
Gault, Thompson
[Glenn], James M.
Hale (Hall), Ezekial A.
Hampton, Robert I.
[Hendon], William E.
Hennessy, John
Huckaby, James B.
Huckaby, John G.
[Lisely], George C.
Luttrell, [Harry] W.
McCain, Richard H.
McDaniel, John C.
McKey, John W. J.
Mead, John
Meyers, August
Mitchell, William A.
Nabors, John F.
Nabors, Thomas S.
Neal, Wesley A.
Nolen, George B.
Palmer (Parmer), Joseph
Patterson, Thomas A. B.
Pirkle, Zilman M.
Plexico, Henley E. D.
Rhodes, John A.
Sappington, James A. T.
Smith, Francis M.
Smith, Hardy L.
Smith, New Jersey
Talbot, J. J.
Teague, Robert W.
Van Dan [Corput], Julius H. J.
Walden, George P.
Walden, Newton
Watson, Elias
West, Andrew J.
Williams, A. S.
Wilson, Francis M.
Young, David

Appendix B

Muster Roll of Captain John C. Francis, Company "B" Alabama Volunteers, 30th Regiment (P.A.), Camp Curry near Talladega, Alabama, 29 March 1862

John C. Francis, Capt.
Wylie Carpenter, 1st Lieut.
Joseph H. McCain, 2nd Lieut.
George W. Vanzant, Jr., 2nd Lieut.
J. N. Baugh, 1st Sergt.
John W. Smith, 2nd Sergt.
Mark Driskill, 3rd Sergt.
John W. Glover, 4th Sergt.
Hugh McFadden, 5th Sergt.
E. P. Davis, 1st Corpl.
John S. Thomas, 2nd Corpl.
W. R. Moore, 3rd Corpl.
M. Thomas Durham, 4th Corpl.
William A. Champion, Musician
Daniel W. Beacham, Musician

Privates

Alexander, William T.
Alexander, Robert P.
Arnold, J. D.
Allen, Robert F.
Blun, S. A.
Baird, E. B.
Baird, W. W.
Bagley, James N.
Clark, Edward T.
Copeland, R. J.
Culbreath, N. D. S.
Carpenter, John W.
Cook, James B.
Cook, John P.
Chamness, John
Crawford, Slater
Denman, William C.
Dowdle, James W.
Dowdle, John F.
Driskill, James H.

Finch, Thomas S.
Finch, W. T.
Ford, John
Garvin, Benjamin F.
Gober, Bradford
Gordon, W. P.
Gray, Thomas
Hill, Andrew
Hill, Floyd G.
Hollingsworth, Joseph S.
Humphries, M. T.
Hutchinson, W. T.
Johnson, Euclid
Kimbrell, Manning K.
Kirby, Johnson R.
Kerr (Karr), J. M. M.
Kerr (Karr), James S.
Landers, John K.
Langley, Oliver E.
Littlejohn, Thomas
Martin, R. J.
Matheny, J. F.
Marable, T. A.
Mattison, J. L.
Matthis, M. R.
Milner, John
Moore, James B.
Moses, L. D.
Newton, William H.
Niman, J. H.
Norris, J. E.
Nunnelly, Joseph
Nunnelly, Benjamin F.
Pinson, Peter
Pitts, H. H.
Powers, Thomas J.
Poss, Thomas E.
Reaves, David R.
Reaves, J. W.
Redman, William B.
Reynolds, William J.
Roberts, David L.
Roberts, Luke R.
Roberts, Thomas B.
Rutledge, John
Rutledge, William R.
Seiber, J. E.
Skelton, Green B.
Skelton, W. A.
Smith, J. M.
Stephens (Stevens), Namon V.
Thompson, T. J.
Turner, Calvin C.
Warlick, Daniel W.
Warren, Thomas
Weaver, R. P.
Weir, William M.
Whaley, John
Whatley, W.
White, Thomas H.
White, James M.
Willingham, Geo. J.
Willingham, William
Wilson, George W.
Wolfe, Henry
Wright, Wiley

Appendix C

Muster Roll of Captain John C. Francis, Company "B," 30th Alabama volunteer regiment, Vicksburg, Mississippi, 5 July 1863

Jno. C. Francis	Capt.	Present for duty
J. H. McCain	1st Lieut.	Present for duty
J. M. Smith	1st Sergt.	Slightly wounded in leg 23rd May. Present for duty
W. M. Cantrell	2nd Sergt.	Present for duty
G. B. Skelton	3rd Sergt.	Severely wounded in head 16th May at Baker's Creek is out of danger
H. McFadden	4th Sergt.	Severely wounded in heel 16th May at Baker's Creek and missing
J. S. Thomas	5th Sergt.	In hospital at Vicksburg as nurse. Present
S. Crawford	1st Corpl.	Missing at Baker's Creek
M. T. Durham	2nd Corpl.	Present for duty
J. D. Arnold	3rd Corpl.	Missing at Baker's Creek. On duty at Brandon
L. R. Roberts	4th Corpl.	Killed at Port Gibson May 1st 1863
J. K. Landers	5th Corpl.	Present for duty
D. W. Beacham	Musician	Present for duty

Privates

Alexander, W. T.	Present for duty
Alexander, R. P.	Present for duty
Allen, H.	Wounded on 22nd May, died 6th June, siege of V.

Allen, O. P.	Present for duty
Bagley, J.	Severely wounded in leg and head at Baker's Creek and missing
Blun, S. A.	Present for duty
Baird, W. W.	Present for duty
Clark, E. T.	Present for duty
Copeland, R. J.	Present for duty
Culbreath, N. D. S.	Wounded severely in leg at Baker's Creek and missing
Carpenter, J. W.	Missing at Baker's Creek
Cook, J. B.	Present for duty
Cook, J. P.	Left at Baker's Creek, very sick not expected to live (went home on parole).
Crossley, J.	Left at Warrenton, not heard of
Crossley, E.	Nurse at Vicksburg, well
Clem, W. T.	Left in Tenn.
Davis, E. P.	Present for duty
Denman, W. C.	Present for duty
Driskill, J. H.	Missing at Port Gibson
Downing, E. B.	Present for duty
Downing, T. J.	Present for duty
Emerson, H. S.	Present for duty
Finch, W. T.	Ensign for regt., killed 22nd May
Ford, John	Missing at Port Gibson
Glover, John	Absent on sick leave
Gordon, W. P.	Wounded May 19th, died 25th June
Gidley, John	Missing at Port Gibson
Gidley, Rich	Missing at Baker's Creek
Garvin, B. F.	Wounded severely in arm and missing at Port Gibson
Hill, Andrew	Wounded slightly in hand at Baker's Creek
Hollingsworth, J.	Nurse in hospital
Jarrel, Wm.	Captured at Baker's Creek
Karr, J. S.	Left in Tenn.
Karr, J. M. M.	Wounded slight in head at Port Gibson, with leave absent
Kimbrell, M. K.	Present for duty
Kirby, J. R.	Present for duty
Langley, O. E.	Killed at Port Gibson
Littlejohn, Thos.	Present for duty

Martin, Wm.	At convalescent sick
Moore, W. R.	At hospital
Matheny, J. F.	Present for duty
Marable, T. A.	Present for duty
Moses, L. D.	Died in hospital at Vicksburg
McElreath, J. R.	Present for duty
Nunnelly, B. F.	Missing at Port Gibson
Nunnelly, Jos.	Wounded severely in head June 9th 1863
Norris, J. E.	Missing at Baker's Creek
Niman, J. H.	Present for duty, slight in head May 22nd
Newton, W. H.	Missing at Baker's Creek
Powers, J. E.	Present for duty
Pinson, Pete	Died 17th June in hospital No. 2
Pitts, H. H.	Present for duty, wounded in thigh 22nd May
Poss, T. E.	Left in Ky.
Putman, S. V.	Left in Tenn.
Putman, J.	In hospital
Roberts, Wm.	Present
Rutledge, W. R.	Died at home
Reynolds, W. J.	Sick leave
Reaves, J. W.	Wounded slight in arm 25 June 1863
Reaves, D. R.	Wounded slight in foot 22nd May
Redman, Wm.	Missing at Port Gibson
Satterfield, J. H.	Missing at Port Gibson
Seiber, Jno.	On sick leave
Skelton, Wm.	Nurse in hospital, wounded slight in hand 22 May
Stephens, Geo.	Wounded in arm at Port Gibson
Stephens, N. V.	Wounded in arm at Port Gibson
Thompson, T. J.	Missing at Big Black
Weir, W.	Present for duty
Wright, W.	Present for duty
Warren, Thos.	Wounded in left hand at Baker's Creek, left arm shot off by shell 24th May
Whatley, John	Wounded in chin and arm 11th June. Died 15th June
Whatley, W.	Present for duty
White, Thos.	Present for duty, wounded in head slight May 22
White, J. M.	Killed May 29th 1863
White, S. B. P	In hospital

Weaver, [R. P.]	Present for duty
Wolfe, H.	Wounded at Baker's Creek and is nurse in hospital
Wilson, G. W.	Missing at Baker's Creek. On duty at Brandon
Walker, Wm.	Sick in convalescent camp
Woodruff, C. H.	Present for duty
Woodruff, S.	In convalescent camp

Notes

Introduction

1. Malcolm C. McMillan, ed., *The Alabama Confederate Reader,* 1, 4–7; William Warren Rogers et al., *Alabama: The History of a Deep South State,* 181–82.

2. *Jacksonville Republican,* 19, 26 January 1861; Malcolm C. McMillan, *The Disintegration of a Confederate State,* 11.

3. *Jacksonville Republican,* 1, 22 March 1860.

4. Ibid., 26 July 1860; McMillan, *The Alabama Confederate Reader,* 7–8; Rogers et al., *Alabama,* 182–83.

5. *Jacksonville Republican,* 31 May, 26 July 1860.

6. Ibid., 20 December 1860, 2 January 1861; McMillan, *The Alabama Confederate Reader,* 26–35; Rogers et al., *Alabama,* 183–84; William Warren Rogers, Jr., *Confederate Home Front: Montgomery During the Civil War* (Tuscaloosa: University of Alabama Press, 1999), 19–20.

7. McMillan, *The Alabama Confederate Reader,* 22–24.

8. *Jacksonville Republican,* 31 January, 14 February 1861.

9. Ibid., 14 February 1861; McMillan, *The Alabama Confederate Reader,* 47–49, 55–56.

10. Confederate Alabama Militia by Companies & Counties (1860–1865), Confederate Regimental History Files, Alabama Department of Archives and History, Montgomery; *Jacksonville Republican,* 6 June 1861.

11. Francis-Martin Genealogy Collection, Mrs. Clara Jackson Martin, Birmingham, Alabama; Francis-Martin Family Papers, ADAH.

12. Francis-Martin Genealogy Collection.

13. U.S. Bureau of the Census, *The Population Schedule of the Eighth Census of the United States, 1860: Alabama,* 2:285 (hereafter *Eighth Census/Alabama*); *Eighth Census/Alabama, Slave Schedule,* 1:265.

14. *Jacksonville Republican,* 15 November 1860; McMillan, *The Alabama Confederate Reader,* 7–8.

15. *Jacksonville Republican,* 15, 22 November 1860.

16. Ibid., 13 December 1860, 3 January 1861.

17. *Compiled Service Records of Confederate Soldiers Who Served in Organizations from Alabama,* 122:579, 158:789, 193:516 (hereafter *CSR/Alabama*).

18. Francis-Martin Genealogy Collection; Henry William Clark, *Genealogies of the Clark,*

Parks, Brockman and Dean, Davis and Goss Families (Montgomery, Ala.: n.p., 1905), 29–30; Marriage Records, 1850–1865, Calhoun County, Alabama, Book 2:126.

19. *Eighth Census/Alabama,* 2:285; ibid., *Slave Schedule,* 1:265.

20. Francis-Martin Family Papers; Miller W. Francis, Report of Sick and Wounded, July 1861–March 1862, Sixth Alabama Infantry Regiment, Confederate Regimental History Files (hereafter Miller Francis, Report of Sick and Wounded).

21. *CSR/Alabama,* 158:789.

22. *Eighth Census/Alabama,* 2:297; *Jacksonville Republican,* 8 November 1890; Marriage Records, 1850–1865, Calhoun County, Alabama, Book 2:131.

23. *Eighth Census/Alabama,* 2:297; ibid., *Slave Schedule,* 2:142; Francis-Martin Family Papers.

24. *CSR/Alabama,* 193:514, 516; Willis Brewer, *Alabama: Her History, Resources, War Record, and Public Men from 1540 to 1872,* 604–5.

25. Francis-Martin Family Papers.

26. *Eighth Census/Alabama,* 4:801; *CSR/Alabama,* 122:579; Alston Fitts III, *Selma: Queen City of the Black Belt,* 45–47.

27. *Jacksonville Republican,* 19 December 1861, 30 January 1862. See ibid. and *Selma Times* in 1862–63.

28. William Lindsey McDonald, *Beginnings . . . of the University of North Alabama: The Story of Florence Wesleyan University,* 33–35; Francis-Martin Family Papers.

29. *CSR/Alabama,* 193:514; Francis-Martin Family Papers.

30. *Jacksonville Republican,* 2, 16 January 1862.

31. Bailey George McClelen, *I Saw the Elephant: The Civil War Experiences of Bailey George McClelen Company D, 10th Alabama Infantry Regiment,* 21.

32. *Jacksonville Republican,* 2, 16 January 1862.

33. Ibid., 27 February 1862; *CSR/Alabama,* 333:401.

34. *Jacksonville Republican,* 21 May 1864; Francis-Martin Family Papers.

35. Francis-Martin Genealogy Collection; Francis-Martin Family Papers.

36. Francis-Martin Genealogy Collection; Francis-Martin Family Papers.

37. Unfiled Papers and Slips Belonging in Confederate Compiled Service Records, National Archives and Records Service, Microcopy 347, Roll 135, No. 5573 (hereafter Unfiled Papers & Slips); Francis-Martin Family Papers.

38. *CSR/Alabama,* 445:443.38.

39. Francis-Martin Family Papers.

40. Ibid.

41. Ibid.; Catharine Barnes Whitehead Rowland, Journals, iv, 2–3, 10, 50 (hereafter Rowland Journals).

42. Francis-Martin Family Papers.

43. Miller Francis, Report of Sick and Wounded; *Jacksonville Republican,* 19 February, 19 March 1863.

44. Francis-Martin Family Papers; Rowland Journals, 41–42, 50.

45. *Eighth Census/Alabama, Slave Schedule,* 1:265; Richard Rollins, ed., *Black Southerners in Gray: Essays on Afro-Americans in Confederate Armies,* 1–28.

Chapter 1

1. *Jacksonville Republican,* 3 March 1861; *CSR/Alabama,* 122:579, 158:789, 191:19, 193: 513, 514, 516, 194:549; McDonald, *Beginnings . . . of the University of North Alabama,* 35.

2. *CSR/Alabama,* 122: 579; Alton Fitts III, *Selma: Queen City of the Black Belt,* 45–47.

3. Brewer, *Alabama,* 594–96; Kenneth W. Jones, "The Fourth Alabama Infantry: First Blood," 36–41.

4. *CSR/Alabama,* 122:579.

5. *Jacksonville Republican,* 6 June 1861; Lee Forney Crawford, *Forney Forever,* 2.

6. *CSR/Alabama,* 158:789; *Jacksonville Republican,* 23 May 1861; Brewer, *Alabama,* 459; Robert K. Krick, *Lee's Colonels: A Biographical Register of the Field Officers of the Army of Northern Virginia* 338.

7. W. Todd Groce, *Mountain Rebels: East Tennessee Confederates and the Civil War, 1860–1870,* 33, 47.

8. *CSR/Alabama,* 193:514, 516; McClelen, *I Saw the Elephant,* 4–8.

9. McClelen, *I Saw the Elephant,* 9–12.

10. George C. Whatley to Cynthia Whatley, Strasburg, Virginia, 13 July 1861, Whatley Letters (hereafter Whatley Letters); *CSR/Tennessee,* 111:1574; *Jacksonville Republican,* 8 August 1861; Joseph H. Parks, *General Edmund Kirby Smith, C.S.A.,* 130–32.

11. *Eighth Census/Alabama, Slave Schedule,* 1:265.

12. Rollins, *Black Southerners in Gray,* 1–28.

13. *Jacksonville Republican,* 16, 23 May 1861.

14. The Florence Wesleyan University campus consisted of two buildings, Wesleyan Hall, a three-story brick building completed in 1856, and a large barn used by the students and faculty to stable their horses. *Florence Gazette,* 19 May 1855; McDonald, *Beginnings . . . of the University of North Alabama,* 23–24.

15. A student roster for 1859–60 listed 182 students, 133 in the University and 49 in the Preparatory Department. See McDonald, *Beginnings . . . of the University of North Alabama,* 35, 76–80.

16. Dr. Richard H. Rivers, FWU President and Professor of Moral Philosophy and Belles Lettres, taught mental and moral philosophy, political economy, rhetoric, and logic. Ibid., 19, 72.

17. Septimus P. Rice, a native of Virginia and Professor of Pure Mathematics, taught through the war years and served as de facto president from 1865 until 1868. Ibid., 19–21.

18. Norman F. Briggs, a native of Dallas County, Alabama, became Professor of Chemistry, Geology, and Mineralogy in 1859 after receiving his degree. He died of wounds received at the battle of First Manassas. Ibid., 19, 22, 35, 73.

19. Morgan was one of four FWU professors who joined the Confederate army when hostilities broke out in April 1861. Ibid., 35.

20. William E. Forbes enlisted in the Lauderdale Volunteer Dragoons, Company H, 4th Alabama Infantry Regiment, and mustered into service on 7 May 1861 at Lynchburg, Virginia. Ibid., 21–22, 35.

21. Ashley D. Hurt became the commander of the University Grays which included several FWU students. He joined the Confederate army with Briggs, Forbes, and Morgan and approximately 100 FWU students. Ibid., 33–35, 72, 77–78.

22. E. August Prouskoski, a native of Poland, taught ancient and modern classics and was noted as a scholar and painter. Ibid., 31, 73.

23. Florence, county seat of Lauderdale County, had a population of 1,395 in 1860. Thomas McAdory Owen, *History of Alabama and Dictionary of Alabama Biography,* 1:596.

24. The Tuscumbia Railway Company built a road from Tuscumbia to Sheffield and completed the first railroad bridge to cross the Tennessee River, at Florence in 1858. Ibid., 1:596, 2:1340.

25. The steamboat *Muscle Shoals* operated on the Tennessee River. It was seized by federal gunboats after the fall of Fort Henry in February 1862. Jill Knight Garrett, *A History of Lauderdale County* (n.p., 1964), 94.

26. LaGrange Military Academy was located near Leighton, Alabama, about fifteen miles southeast of Florence. It had an enrollment of 171 cadets, 47 from Alabama, in 1861. McDonald, *Beginnings . . . of the University of North Alabama,* 11–13; Owen, *History of Alabama,* 2:838.

27. "Hancock from Winchester" was one of two brothers, seventeen-year-old Charles Hancock or nineteen-year-old William Hancock, who were listed in the 1860 census for Winchester, Franklin County, Tennessee. *Eighth Census/Tennessee,* 6:70.

28. Slater Crawford was listed in the 1860 census as the eighteen-year-old son of John Crawford, a Jacksonville cabinetmaker. William Wright was listed in the 1860 census as a sixteen-year-old living with R. H. Wynne, a Jacksonville tailor. *Eighth Census/Alabama,* 2: 286, 291.

29. The Tuscumbia fair was typical of county or state fairs prior to the Civil War. They featured exhibits of prize farm animals; awards for the biggest watermelons, best corn, or tastiest baked goods; plowing or pulling contests; and amusements such as horse racing and brass bands. Daniel E. Sutherland, *The Expansion of Everyday Life, 1860–1876* (New York: Harper & Row Publishers, 1989), 259–60.

30. John Francis's grade report for the 1860 fall quarter at FWU listed grades of "A" in mathematics, natural sciences, Belles-Lettres, French, and deportment. He also made fifty recitations in each course without any absences, received no demerits, and had perfect attendance for chapel and church. Francis-Martin Family Papers.

31. Leonidas William Grant, "Lou," was the seventeen-year-old son of Elizabeth L. and James Freeman Grant of Jacksonville. Tom remains unidentified. *Eighth Census/Alabama,* 2:291.

32. John Foster was listed in the 1860 census as a forty-two-year-old chancellor judge living in Jacksonville with his wife and teenage daughter. Ibid., 300.

33. The Florence Guards was a volunteer company organized under the command of Captain Sterling A. M. Wood (1823–91) following the election of Lincoln in November 1860. *CSR/Alabama,* 170:1054; Brewer, *Alabama,* 569, 599–600; McDonald, *Beginnings . . . of the University of North Alabama,* 33; McMillan, *The Alabama Confederate Reader,* 127.

34. James Freeman Grant was the fifty-one-year-old editor and publisher of the *Jacksonville Republican,* and his son Lou Grant, was John Francis's roommate and classmate at FWU. *Eighth Census/Alabama,* 2:291; Glover Moore, *A Calhoun County, Alabama, Boy in the 1860's,* 19.

35. The FWU students lived or boarded in private homes or in public housing. One source cited board expenses at $70 for "Board, per ten month session, including washing, fuel, room, rent, and servant's hire." McDonald, *Beginnings . . . of the University of North Alabama,* 18, 25, 31.

36. The *Jacksonville Republican* of 22 November reported on the "Southern Rights Meeting in Jacksonville" on Saturday evening, 19 November 1860, where Dr. Francis was one of several speakers.

37. The receipt of a box from Jacksonville on Wednesday, 19 December 1860, a week prior to Christmas 1860, was a special event for the three young college students. It probably contained a ham, canned fruit and jellies, and baked goods to carry them through their Christmas vacation. Francis-Martin Family Papers.

38. South Carolina was the first southern state to secede from the Union when its secession convention passed an ordinance of secession on 20 December 1860 by a unanimous vote. Emory M. Thomas, *The Confederate Nation, 1861–1865,* 42–43.

39. John Francis joined one of two FWU companies, either the University Grays or College Grays. McDonald, *Beginnings . . . of the University of North Alabama,* 33–34; *Florence Gazette,* 3 April 1861.

40. The purchase of a Dialectical badge indicates that John Francis was a member of the Dialectic Society, one of two debating societies at FWU. McDonald, *Beginnings . . . of the University of North Alabama,* 29–30.

41. Kerosene or "coal oil" was used in oil lamps throughout mid-nineteenth-century America as the primary lighting source. *Encyclopedia of Chemical Technology,* 4th ed., 25 vols. (New York: John Wiley and Sons, Inc., 1994), 12:156; Sutherland, *Expansion of Everyday Life,* 33, 42.

42. Mary Grant was Lou Grant's fifteen-year-old sister. John Francis, exhibiting a certain amount of southern chivalry, apparently had a special interest in her. *Eighth Census/Alabama,* 2:291.

43. The University Grays commanded by Ashley D. Hurt and the College Grays commanded by Alfred Moore O'Neal were made up of FWU students. McDonald, *Beginnings . . . of the University of North Alabama,* 33–35; *Florence Gazette,* 1, 3 April 1861.

44. James C. Francis, Jr., a private in the Governor's Guards, left Selma, Alabama, on 12 January 1861 for Fort Morgan. Fitts, *Selma,* 45–47; McMillan, *The Alabama Confederate Reader,* 22–24, 26.

45. John Francis's report for the 1861 winter quarter included grades for natural science, natural philosophy, Belles-Lettres, and modern language. Francis-Martin Family Papers.

46. Margaret A. Cobb, Susan's teacher, also served as the head mistress or superintendent of the Jacksonville Female Academy. *Jacksonville Republican,* 3 January, 6 June 1861.

47. Lark was listed as a thirty-five-year-old slave in the 1860 Alabama slave schedule. He was listed in the 1870 census as Lark Francis, an Alabama native, Jacksonville resident, and forty-five-year-old farmer. *Eighth Census/Alabama, Slave Schedule,* 1:265; *Ninth Census/Alabama,* 3:532.

48. The Francis plantation was located near Ohatchee, Calhoun County, Alabama. According to the 1860 slave schedule, Dr. Francis owned two slave houses and thirteen slaves, six males and seven females. *Eighth Census/Alabama, Slave Schedule,* 1:265.

49. Jim Francis was assigned to a gun crew from 1 January to 23 February 1861. He received $25.50 for one month and fifteen days at the rate of $17 per month. 4th Alabama Infantry Regiment, Confederate Regimental History Files.

50. The two Selma companies at Fort Morgan were Captain Thomas J. Goldsby's Governor's Guards and Captain James Kent's Selma Blues. Ibid.; Fitts, *Selma,* 45–47.

51. Fort Morgan remained unfinished, and U.S. engineer troops were working to strengthen it when it was seized by two Mobile companies on 4 January 1861. Arthur W. Bergeron, *Confederate Mobile,* 7.

52. The 32-pounder gun was traditional seacoast artillery pieces or columbiads employed in the seacoast defenses of the United States between 1841 and 1860. It was a smoothbore, cast of iron, and fired a 32.6-pound shell approximately 1,922 yards. Harold L. Peterson, *Round Shot and Rammers: An Introduction to Muzzle-Loading Land Artillery in the United States* (Harrisburg, Pa.: Stackpole Books, 1969), 101, 106; *War of the Rebellion: A Compilation of the Official Records of the Union and Confederate Armies* (hereafter cited as *OR*), Ser. 4, 1:227.

53. Casemates are masonry or fortified chambers in which cannon were placed to fire through embrasures. Batteries are emplacements where artillery are mounted.

54. The 24-pounder howitzers were muzzle loaders with an effective range of 1,325 yards.

They were bronze smoothbore guns that fired solid shot, grape, cannister, and shell. Peterson, *Round Shot and Rammers,* 91, 96.

55. Winfield Scott (1786–1866), hero of the War of 1812 and the Mexican War, was general in chief of the U.S. army from 1846 through 1862. Mark Mayo Boatner III, *The Civil War Dictionary,* 728.

56. Henry Maury (c. 1827–69), a Virginia native and lawyer/politician in Mobile, commanded a ship in William Walker's last attempt to conquer Nicaragua in 1858. He was elected colonel of the 2nd Alabama Volunteer regiment organized at Fort Morgan in April 1861 and replaced William J. Hardee as commander of Fort Morgan in June 1861. Bergeron, *Confederate Mobile,* 12, 18–20, 88, 154; Rex Miller, *Wheeler's Favorites: A Regimental History of the 51st Alabama Cavalry Regiment,* 36; Brewer, *Alabama,* 420–21, 591, 640.

57. Fort Gaines on Dauphin Island at the mouth of Mobile Bay was seized by two Mobile companies of the 1st Alabama State Troops on 4 January 1861. Bergeron, *Confederate Mobile,* 7.

58. The Sand Island Lighthouse was one of several lighthouses seized by the state of Alabama in January 1861. It was located southwest of Fort Morgan near the main ship channel into Mobile Bay. Ibid., 63–64; J. Thomas Sharf, *History of the Confederate State Navy: From Its Organization to the Surrender of Its Last Vessel* (1887; reprint, New York: The Fairfax Press, 1977), 21–22; Brewer, *Alabama,* 398–99.

59. The Governor's Guards were reorganized as Company A, 4th Alabama Volunteer Regiment, and mustered into Confederate service for twelve months at Lynchburg, Virginia, on 7 May 1861. *CSR/Alabama,* 122:628; Brewer, *Alabama,* 594–95; James G. Hudson, "A Story of Company D, 4th Alabama Infantry Regiment, C.S.A.," 142–45.

60. Jabez Lamar Monroe Curry (1825–1903), a Georgia native, served in the Alabama legislature (1847–48 and 1853–57) and in the U.S. Congress (1857–61). He resigned his seat in Congress on 21 January 1861 following Alabama's secession from the Union. Richard N. Current, ed., *Encyclopedia of the Confederacy,* 1:439; Owen, *History of Alabama,* 3:444–45.

61. Curry was a member of the Montgomery Convention which inaugurated Jefferson Davis as provisional president on 18 February 1861 and became the provisional Congress of the Confederate States. Current, *Encyclopedia of the Confederacy,* 1:392; Owen, *History of Alabama,* 3:445; Thomas, *The Confederate Nation,* 56–62.

62. Samuel F. Rice, Curry's old law mentor, was elected to the Alabama senate, and John Tyler Morgan enlisted in the Cahawba Rifles, later Company G, 5th Alabama Infantry Regiment. *CSR/General & Staff,* 182; Owen, *History of Alabama,* 4:1435; Fitts, *Selma,* 45.

63. Curry, a staunch States Rights Democrat, received the support necessary to win election to the first Confederate Congress. Owen, *History of Alabama,* 3:445.

64. Benton was the name of Calhoun County until 29 January 1858 when it was changed to honor John C. Calhoun of South Carolina. Calhoun County in 1861 included the current Calhoun and part of Cleburne and Etowah counties until 1866. Ibid., 1:191, 277, 549.

65. Cherokee County is located to the north and contiguous to Calhoun County. Ibid., 235.

66. Edward L. Woodward, a Virginia native, was Dr. Francis's brother-in-law, married to his sister Malinda Jane Francis, and a prominent Jacksonville merchant. Francis-Martin Genealogy Collection; *Eighth Census/Alabama,* 2:287; *Jacksonville Republican,* 26 January, 18 October, 1 November 1860, 24 October 1861, 7 August 1862.

67. The Alabama & Tennessee Rivers Railroad Company completed laying track from Selma to Blue Mountain, present-day Anniston, Calhoun County, Alabama by 1861. Owen, *History of Alabama,* 1:505–9; W. Craig Remington and Thomas J. Kallsen, eds., *Historical Atlas of Alabama: Historical Locations,* 1:35–36.

68. John W. Lapsley was one of the commissioners of the Alabama & Tennessee Rivers Railroad Company who received a charter from the Alabama legislature, 4 March 1848, to construct a railroad from Selma to the Tennessee River. Owen, *History of Alabama,* 1:505, 4:1012.

69. Camp Seibels, near Corinth, Mississippi, was named for Colonel John Jacob Seibels (1826–99), commander of the 6th Alabama Volunteer Regiment. Brewer, *Alabama,* 597–98; Krick, *Lee's Colonels,* 338.

70. The 6th Alabama numbered approximately 1,400 men from Autauga, Henry, Jackson, Lowndes, Macon, Montgomery, Russell, and Wilcox counties. They were lead by Seibels, Benjamin Hurt Baker from Russell County, and John Brown Gordon from Jackson County. Brewer, *Alabama,* 598–99; Jon L. Wakelyn, *Biographical Dictionary of the Confederacy* (Westport, Conn.: Greenwood Press, 1977), 205.

71. Dr. William M. Nisbet was listed in the 1860 federal census as a twenty-five-year-old physician with a personal estate valued at $3,000 and living in St. Clair County, Alabama. He was appointed an assistant surgeon with the 10th Alabama on 17 February 1862. *CSR/General & Staff,* 187; *Eighth Census/Alabama,* 12:205–6.

72. Bristol, Tennessee, and Bristol, Virginia, sprang up as railroad towns during the construction of the East Tennessee & Virginia Railroad on either side of the state lines. Groce, *Mountain Rebels,* 15, 32, 39; Robert C. Black III, *The Railroads of the Confederacy,* 68.

73. The 6th Alabama traveled from Corinth, Mississippi, on the Memphis & Charleston Railroad, to Chattanooga, and to Bristol, Tennessee, via the East Tennessee & Georgia Railroad and the East Tennessee & Virginia Railroad (approximately 350 miles). Black, *Railroads of the Confederacy,* 5–6, 38, 68.

74. John B. Gordon (1832–1904), a Georgia native, organized a volunteer company, the Raccoon Roughs, which was mustered into Confederate service as Company I, 6th Alabama Volunteer Regiment, on 15 May 1861. *CSR/Alabama,* 159:891; Wakelyn, *Biographical Dictionary of the Confederacy,* 205; Current, *Encyclopedia of the Confederacy,* 2:696.

75. William Gannaway Brownlow (1805–77), a Virginia native and Methodist circuit rider, turned to journalism and openly opposed the Confederate government as the Unionist editor of the *Knoxville Whig.* Groce, *Mountain Rebels,* 26–27, 47, 129–36.

76. East Tennessee Unionists actively opposed the Confederacy and in November 1861 destroyed five of nine major railroad bridges between Bridgeport, Alabama, and Bristol, Tennessee. Ibid., 81, 110–11; Charles F. Bryan, Jr., "Tories Amidst Rebels: Confederate Occupation of East Tennessee, 1861–1863," *East Tennessee Historical Society's Publications* 60 (1988): 9–10.

77. Fanny Rebecca Harelson married John B. Gordon on 18 September 1854. She used her nursing skills to help Gordon recover from five wounds he received in the battle of Sharpsburg on 17 September 1862. Current, *Encyclopedia of the Confederacy,* 2:697; Wakelyn, *Biographical Dictionary of the Confederacy,* 205.

78. Gabe was Miller Francis's body servant and was owned by Dr. James C. Francis. Francis-Martin Family Papers; *Eighth Census/Alabama, Slave Schedule,* 1:265.

79. Pneumonia often followed in the wake of measles and other diseases. It was an important cause of morbidity and mortality among Civil War soldiers. Horace H. Cunningham, *Doctors in Gray: The Confederate Medical Service,* 190, 202–3; Paul E. Steiner, *Disease in the Civil War: Natural Biological Warfare in 1861–1865,* 16; Bell I. Wiley, *The Life of Johnny Reb,* 254–55.

80. The 6th Alabama traveled from Bristol to Manassas Junction, Virginia, via the Vir-

ginia & Tennessee, Orange & Alexandria, and Manassas Gap railroads. Black, *Railroads of the Confederacy,* 6–7, 14, 57, 60–61.

81. At Manasssas Junction, the 6th Alabama joined the Second Brigade under Lieutenant Colonel Richard Stoddert Ewell (1817–72). *OR,* 2:61, 63–64, 896; Wakelyn, *Biographical Dictionary of the Confederacy,* 181.

82. Maxcy Gregg (1814–62), a South Carolina native, was commander of the 1st South Carolina Infantry Regiment. *OR,* 2:62, 128–30; Current, *Encyclopedia of the Confederacy,* 2:717.

83. Dr. Courtney James Clark was Miller's brother-in-law and senior surgeon with the 10th Alabama Regiment. *CSR/General & Staff,* 56; Owen, *History of Alabama,* 3:328.

84. The thirty-four-year-old James B. Farmer, a Georgia native and Jacksonville resident, was listed in the 1860 census as a tin and copper smith with real estate valued at $3,000 and a personal estate valued at $44,080. *Eighth Census/Alabama,* 2:294.

85. Brigadier General Joseph E. Johnston (1807–91) was commander of the Army of the Shenandoah near Winchester. *OR,* 2:470–78, 844–45.

86. Pierre G. T. Beauregard (1818–93) was commander of the Army of the Potomac near Manassas Junction. *OR,* 2:440–47, 896; T. Harry Williams, *P.G.T. Beauregard, Napoleon in Gray,* 66–72.

87. The 6th Alabama moved up the Orange & Alexandria Railroad and encountered scouting parties in advance of Irwin McDowell's Union army. Black, *Railroads of the Confederacy,* 60–61.

88. Maxcy Gregg with his 1st South Carolina Regiment, "70 of Capt. Terry's horse," and two guns from Kemp's battery ambushed the First Regiment of Ohio Volunteers near Hunter's Mill, Virginia, about 6 P.M. on 17 June 1861. Gregg's forces captured a train, left six Union dead and one wounded, and generally embarrassed McDowell's forces. *OR,* 2:128–30; E. B. Long, *The Civil War Day by Day: An Almanac, 1861–1865,* 86.

89. The 4th Alabama left Harper's Ferry, Virginia, on Saturday morning, 15 June 1861, and arrived at Winchester on Monday, 17 June. Hudson, "A Story of Company D," 153–54.

90. Robert Emmett Rodes (1829–64), a Virginia native and 1848 graduate of Virginia Military Institute, was commissioned colonel of the 5th Alabama Volunteer Regiment on 11 May 1861. *CSR/Alabama,* 146:1758; Current, *Encyclopedia of the Confederacy,* 3:1344; Wakelyn, *Biographical Dictionary of the Confederacy,* 372.

91. Hall Lewis and John T. Morgan joined Company E, 5th Alabama Volunteer Regiment, at Montgomery on 5 May 1861. The company was raised in Talladega County and commanded by Captain Charles M. Shelley. Brewer, *Alabama,* 596–97.

92. Richard S. Ewell, a Virginia native and 1840 West Point graduate, was commander of the Second Brigade on the right wing of Beauregard's army at Union Mills Ford on Bull Run Creek on 18 July 1861. Vincent J. Esposito, ed., *The West Point Atlas of American Wars,* 1:20; Wakelyn, *Biographical Dictionary of the Confederacy,* 181; Williams, *Beauregard,* 82–83.

93. William Thomas Renfro (1841–63) enlisted for twelve months in Company E, 5th Alabama Volunteer Regiment, at Talladega, Alabama, on 1 May 1861. *CSR/Alabama,* 146:1723.

94. Camp Porter enlisted in 1861 in one of several companies raised in Calhoun County, but his service records were incomplete. He later enlisted as a private in Company A, 51st Alabama Mounted Infantry, at Alexandria, Calhoun County, Alabama, in August 1863. Ibid., 447:1084.

95. Miller Francis listed 75 cases of *catarrhus epidemicus* among the 1,244 men in the 6th

Alabama in July 1861. *Merck's 1901 Manual* described catarrah epidemic as "A contagious inflammation of the air passages known as 'influenza' or 'grip.'" Miller W. Francis, Report of Sick and Wounded, July 1861, Union Mills Ford, Virginia, 6th Alabama, Confederate Regimental History Files; *Merck's 1901 Manual of the Materia Medica; A Ready-Reference Pocket Book for the Practicing Physician and Surgeon.* (New York: Merck & Co., 1901), 125.

96. A large number of wounded Confederate soldiers were sent to Culpepper Court House, Culpepper County, Virginia, for medical treatment following the battle of First Manassas. Robert T. Coles, *From Huntsville to Appomattox: R. T. Coles's History of the 4th Regiment, Alabama Volunteer Infantry, C.S.A., Army of Northern Virginia,* 30, 50–51.

97. While some medical colleges required nine-month or six-month sessions, most doctors North and South attended medical colleges that provided a four- or five-month course of lectures to doctoral candidates. Many young doctors started careers having never observed an operation, and medical quackery was not uncommon in antebellum America. Cunningham, *Doctors in Gray,* 9–17.

98. Richard S. Ewell apparently received a wound in a skirmish at Fairfax Court House, Virginia, on 1 June 1861. Long, *The Civil War Day by Day,* 81; Boatner, *The Civil War Dictionary,* 268–69.

99. Miller Francis was the proud owner of one of the most popular handguns of the Civil War, a Navy Colt Model 1851. It was a .36-caliber, six-shot weapon with a 7½-inch barrel, weighing 42 ounces, and featured a naval engagement motif engraved on the cylinder. Robert L. Wilson, *Colt: An American Legend* (New York: Abbeville Press, 1985), 43

100. The Pope Walker Guards traveled by freight cars to Selma on 20 June 1861 and reached Montgomery by steamboat, the *R. B. Taney,* on 21 June. *Jacksonville Republican,* 4 July 1861; McClelen, *I Saw the Elephant,* 6–8.

101. Hampton W. Glover, a private in the Pope Walker Guards, shot himself in the thigh while "examining a pistol in his tent." Muster Roll, Company G, 10th Alabama, 20 February 1862, Confederate Muster Roll Collection; L. W. Grant to J. F. Grant, Montgomery, Ala., 25 June 1861, in *Jacksonville Republican,* 4 July 1861.

102. David Goodman enlisted as a private in the Pope Walker Guards at Jacksonville on 4 June 1861. He was detailed as a nurse or ward master for much of the war. *CSR/Alabama,* 194:585.

103. John Horace Forney (1829–1902), an 1852 West Point graduate, was appointed colonel of the 10th Alabama on 4 June 1861. Ibid., 193:504, 516; *CSR/General & Staff,* 96, 98; Current, *Encyclopedia of the Confederacy,* 2:604–5.

104. George Isbell Turnley enlisted as an eighteen-year-old private in the Pope Walker Guards at Jacksonville on 4 June 1861. *CSR/Alabama,* 198:1579.

105. James "Mun" Renfro enlisted in the Pope Walker Guards at Jacksonville on 4 June 1861. Ibid., 1319.

106. Thomas J. Walker and Macon Abernathy, privates in the Pope Walker Guards, enlisted at Jacksonville on 4 June 1861 for the war. McClelen, *I Saw the Elephant,* 8; *CSR/Alabama,* 191:19, 200:1620.

107. John Clark enlisted as a private in the Pope Walker Guards at Montgomery in June 1861. *CSR/Alabama,* 192:293.

108. William Henry Forney (1823–94) was elected captain of the Pope Walker Guards, Company G, 10th Alabama, and his law partner, James B. Martin, was elected lieutenant colonel in the 10th Alabama. Ibid., 193:505; Brewer, *Alabama,* 154–55, 604–5.

Chapter 2

1. Esposito, *West Point Atlas,* 1:18–21; *OR,* ser. 1, 2:187, 484–505.

2. McClelen, *I Saw the Elephant,* 9–12; Parks, *General Edmund Kirby Smith,* 130–32.

3. *OR,* 2:484–505.

4. Coles, *From Huntsville to Appomattox,* 19–24.

5. *CSR/Alabama,* 122:579.

6. J. L. Swan to A. Woods, Army of the Shenandoah, 7 miles north of Manassas Junction, Va., 24 July 1861, *Jacksonville Republican,* 8 August 1861; Charles T. Jones, "Five Confederates: The Sons of Bolling Hall in the Civil War," 145; McClelen, *I Saw the Elephant,* 15.

7. *OR,* 2:316–25; Esposito, *West Point Atlas,* 1:24.

8. *Jacksonville Republican,* 12 September 1861; George C. Whatley to Cynthia Whatley, Camp near Manassas, 2 August 1861, Whatley Letters; Owen, *History of Alabama,* 4:1237, 1714.

9. George C. Whatley to Cynthia Whatley, Camp near Manassas, 2 August 1861, Whatley Letters; McClelen, *I Saw the Elephant,* 16–17.

10. Miller W. Francis, Report of the Sick and Wounded, July–November 1861, 6th Alabama, Confederate Regimental History Files; *Jacksonville Republican,* 14 November 1861.

11. *CSR/Alabama,* 122:579, 193:516; *Jacksonville Republican,* 26 September, 19 December 1861.

12. Francis-Martin Family Papers; *Jacksonville Republican,* 12, 26 September, 24 October, 19 December 1861.

13. *OR,* 5:473–94; McClelen, *I Saw the Elephant,* 20–21.

14. *CSR/Alabama,* 193:504, 514, 196:973; *OR,* 5:490–94; McClelen, *I Saw the Elephant,* 21; *Jacksonville Republican,* 2 January 1862; Crawford, *Forney Forever,* 22.

15. *Jacksonville Republican,* 2 January 1862.

16. Patterson's Union forces fought a series of skirmishes with Johnston's troops in his advance on Martinsburg. *OR,* 2:160–61, 179–87, 472–73; Long, *The Civil War Day by Day,* 90–92.

17. Organized as the 8th Regiment of Alabama Volunteers at Montgomery in May, 1861, the regiment's designation was changed to the 10th Alabama at Richmond, Virginia, on 3 July 1861. McClelen, *I Saw the Elephant,* 4, 8, 11.

18. John Francis was apparently referring to the .69-caliber smooth-bore musket which were changed from flint to steel percussion locks and widely used in the first year of the war. Ibid., 8; Wiley, *The Life of Johnny Reb,* 290.

19. Fairfax Station, a few miles north of Manassas Junction, was located where the Manassas Gap Railroad intersected with the Orange & Alexander Railroad that connected north to Washington, D.C. McClelen, *I Saw the Elephant,* 15; *OR,* 2:440–48, 469–70, 484–507.

20. Tom Francis was commissioned captain and assistant commissary for subsistence of the 10th Alabama on 8 July 1861. *CSR/Alabama,* 193:516.

21. Taul Bradford (1835–83) served briefly in the 10th Alabama and later as lieutenant colonel in the 30th Alabama Volunteer Regiment. Owen, *History of Alabama,* 3:196; *CSR/Alabama,* 332:152.

22. John W. Francis (c. 1833–64) was apparently recovering from the measles in Virginia with the assistance of Alfred, one of the Francis slaves. *CSR/Alabama,* 193:513.

23. Buck was another of Dr. James C. Francis's slaves. *Eighth Census/Alabama, Slave Schedule,* 1:265.

24. John R. Crawford joined the Pope Walker Guards as a thirteen-year-old drummer at Jacksonville on 4 June 1861. *CSR/Alabama,* 192:367; Muster Roll, Company G, 20 February 1862, 10th Alabama, Confederate Muster Roll Collection.

25. William Thomas Renfro, a second lieutenant in Company E, 5th Alabama, was granted a sick furlough for 5–25 June 1861. *CSR/Alabama,* 146:1723.

26. The 10th Alabama traveled from Richmond to Manassas Junction via the Fredericksburg & Potomac, Virginia Central, and Orange & Alexandria railroads. From Manassas Junction, they traveled aboard the Manassas Gap Railroad to Strasburg in the Shenandoah Valley and rode baggage wagons and marched the final eighteen miles to Winchester. Black, *Railroads of the Confederacy,* 6–7, 37, 60–61, 66; McClelen, *I Saw the Elephant,* 11–12.

27. Rumors were rampant, and Alexandria remained under Union control. *OR,* 2:303–8, 314–15; Esposito, *West Point Atlas,* 1:19.

28. On 21 July 1861, Joe Johnston reinforced Beauregard's Army of the Potomac at Manassas with 8,334 men and 20 guns. *OR,* 2:187, 484–505; Esposito, *West Point Atlas,* 1:19.

29. James L. Adams enlisted as a private in Company C, 6th Alabama Volunteer Regiment, at Montgomery, Alabama, on 17 May 1861 for twelve months. *CSR/Alabama,* 155:20.

30. Peter Turney (1827–1903), John Francis's first cousin, practiced law before the war with his brother, Miller Francis Turney, in Winchester, Tennessee. He raised a regiment known as Turney's First Tennessee and was elected colonel on 8 May 1861. Francis-Martin Genealogy Collection; *CSR/Tennessee,* 111:1574; *Tennesseans in the Civil War: A Military History of Confederate and Union Units with Available Rosters of Personnel,* 2 vols. (Nashville: Civil War Centennial Commission, 1964), 1:170; Clement A. Evans, *Confederate Military History: A Library of Confederate States History,* vol. 10, *Tennessee,* 762–63.

31. Edmund Kirby Smith (1824–93), a West Point graduate and Mexican War veteran, commanded the fourth brigade which included the 9th Alabama, 10th Alabama, 11th Alabama, 19th Mississippi, and 38th Virginia. *OR,* 2:476–78; Parks, *General Edmund Kirby Smith,* 130–32.

32. John M. Wyly enlisted as a private in the Pope Walker Guards at Jacksonville on 4 June 1861. He was assigned as an orderly to John H. Forney in October–November 1861 and served as his aide-de-camp through 1864. *CSR/Alabama,* 200:1758.

33. In 1861 Bull Run Creek was a small stream running west to east from its source in the Bull Run Mountains to its confluence with the Occoquan Creek, twelve miles from the Potomac River and about halfway between Centreville and Manassas, Virginia. Esposito, *West Point Atlas,* 18, 20.

34. McDowell's Union army numbered approximately 35,000. The Union losses numbered 2,896 killed, wounded, and captured, compared to Confederate losses of 1,982. Williams, *Beauregard,* 77–79; Esposito, *West Point Atlas,* 1:24; Long, *The Civil War Day by Day,* 99.

35. McDowell's artillery commenced firing the morning of 21 July north of Bull Run Creek, and the first fighting began on the Confederate left flank. About four o'clock in the afternoon, the tide of battle turned with the arrival of Kirby Smith's brigade from the Shenandoah Valley and Jubal Early's brigade from the Confederate right flank near Blackburn's Ford. *OR,* 2:316–20, 331–34, 367–69, 382–86, 402–8, 440–48, 484–505; Esposito, *West Point Atlas,* 1:22–4; Williams, *Beauregard,* 88.

36. Barnard E. Bee (1824–61) led Confederate forces at Henry House Hill, including the

4th Alabama, two companies of the 11th Alabama, 2nd Mississippi, 7th and 8th Georgia, and Capt. John D. Imboden's battery. His forces, numbering approximately 5,000, attempted to halt the flanking attack of about 17,000 Union soldiers. *OR,* 2:382–83, 395–98, 402–4, 558–60; Coles, *From Huntsville to Appomattox,* 19–22; Esposito, *West Point Atlas,* 1:22–3.

37. The 4th Alabama lost "40 killed and 170 wounded" out of the 558 men engaged. Several brigade commanders and officers were killed or wounded between Sudley Springs and Henry House Hill, including Bee, Col. Egbert J. Jones, 4th Alabama, and Col. Francis S. Bartow (1816–61), 8th Georgia. *OR,* 2:489–99; Coles, *From Huntsville to Appomattox,* 22–25; Extract of letter from Capt. William H. Forney, Manassas Junction, 23 July 1861, in *Jacksonville Republican,* 8 August 1861.

38. Jim Francis received buckshot wounds to his left arm and a shrapnel wound to his left shoulder in fighting near Henry House Hill. *CSR/Alabama,* 122:579; J. L. Swan to A. Woods, Army of Shenandoah, 7 Miles north of Manassas Junction, Va., 24 July 1861, in *Jacksonville Republican,* 8 August 1861.

39. The "Minie musket" was a reference to the Model 1861 Springfield rifle which became the standard issue for Union soldiers. It was a .58-caliber rifle-musket that fired a minié bullet, a hollow-based, conical-shaped lead bullet, with deadly accuracy up to 500 yards. William C. Davis, *Rebels & Yankees: The Fighting Men of the Civil War,* 50, 54–56.

40. The Stone Bridge spanned Bull Run Creek on the Warrenton Turnpike between Centreville and Warrenton, Virginia. McDowell's forces retreated across the bridge in the late evening of 21 July 1861. *OR,* 2:316–25; Esposito, *West Point Atlas,* 1:20–24.

41. The Confederates lost 387 killed, 1,582 wounded, and 13 missing for a total of 1,982. Long, *The Civil War Day by Day,* 99.

42. The captured Union equipment included 28 field guns, 37 caissons, some 500,000 rounds of field ammunition, and tons of other valuable military equipment. *OR,* 2:328, 347, 385, 403, 405–8, 410, 502–3, 567.

43. Despite Miller Francis's optimism, Confederate indecision and heavy rain the following day prevented an attack on Washington, especially a quick, vigorous strike against a beaten Union army. Williams, *Beauregard,* 89–90; Long, *The Civil War Day by Day,* 99.

44. Patterson's forces outnumbered Johnston's troops in the Shenandoah Valley, but he failed to engage Johnston and was mustered out of service on 27 July 1861. *OR,* 2:157–79, 607, 611.

45. The 10th Alabama left Winchester on 18 July and arrived at Piedmont Station around 11 A.M. on Friday, 19 July. They boarded boxcars on the Manassas Gap Railroad on Monday, 22 July, and arrived at Manassas Junction later that morning. McClelen, *I Saw the Elephant,* 14–15.

46. For several days after the battle, soldiers, servants, and civilians poured over the battlefield, robbing the dead and choosing equipment or souvenirs. Davis, *Rebels & Yankees,* 54–56, 229, 235.

47. Miller Francis's treatment of the wounded Union soldiers became a common practice by the medical staffs on both sides. Union commanders were allowed to send medical supplies for their wounded. Cunningham, *Doctors in Gray,* 127–29.

48. Confederate losses numbered 1,982, and Union losses totaled 2,896, including 460 killed, 1,124 wounded and 1,312 missing. Long, *The Civil War Day by Day,* 99.

49. Lucius C. Mitchell enlisted in the Pope Walker Guards at Jacksonville on 4 June 1861. *CSR/Alabama,* 197:1089.

50. Abram Joseph Walker (1819–72), a former Jacksonville resident, was chief justice of the Alabama supreme court (1861–68). *Jacksonville Republican,* 12 September 1861; Owen, *History of Alabama,* 4:1714; Brewer, *Alabama,* 474.

51. Isaac P. Moragne (1817–87) was a forty-three-year-old farmer from Cove Creek, Calhoun County, Alabama. His son, Augustus W. Moragne, and two nephews, James M. and William W. Moragne, were in Company G, 10th Alabama. *CSR/Alabama,* 197:1110–11, 1113; *Eighth Census/Alabama,* 2:606; Owen, *History of Alabama,* 4:1237–38.

52. John M. Crook, a resident of Alexandria, Calhoun County, Alabama, served as a delegate from Calhoun County to the special Alabama convention in 1860 that voted for secession. His son, James Crook, enlisted as a private in the Pope Walker Guards on 4 June 1861. *Jacksonville Republican,* 13 December 1860, 3 January 1861; *Eighth Census/Alabama,* 2:647; *CSR/Alabama,* 192:371; Owen, *History of Alabama,* 3:428–29; Rogers et al., *Alabama,* 183–84, 188–89.

53. Dr. James C. Francis visited his sons in late July and returned to Jacksonville in early August 1861. George C. Whatley to Cynthia Whatley, Camp near Manassas, 2 August 1861, Whatley Letters.

54. Doctor Franklin Watkins enlisted as a twenty-five-year-old private in the Pope Walker Guards at Jacksonville on 4 June 1861. He died of "brain fever" on 15 August 1861 at Camp Bristoe, Virginia. *CSR/Alabama,* 200:1622.

55. John D. Walker enlisted as a twenty-nine-year-old private in the Pope Walker Guards at Jacksonville on 4 June 1861 and was elected 5th sergeant on 18 December 1861. Ibid., 1618.

56. Edwin M. Keeling enlisted in the Pope Walker Guards at Jacksonville on 4 June 1861. He was reported absent on sick leave in Alabama on a muster roll dated 20 February 1862. Ibid., 195:833; Muster Roll, Company G, 10th Alabama, 20 February 1862, Lewis House near Manassas, Virginia, Confederate Muster Roll Collection.

57. Macon Abernathy, Tom Francis's brother-in-law, was probably recovering from measles. *CSR/Alabama,* 191:19.

58. Walker and the other visitors not only brought letters to the Virginia camps but also returned to Alabama with large numbers of letters. *Jacksonville Republican,* 12 September 1861.

59. George C. Whatley, a native of Georgia and Jacksonville resident, was listed in the 1860 census as a thirty-nine-year-old lawyer with real estate valued at $7,000 and a personal estate valued at $20,000. His nickname was apparently "Crog," but his middle name was actually Craghn. *CSR/Alabama,* 200:1664; *Eighth Census/Alabama,* 2:290–91; McClelen, *I Saw the Elephant,* 30; Owen, *History of Alabama,* 4:1749.

60. Cy was another of Dr. James Francis's slaves. *Eighth Census/Alabama, Slave Schedule,* 1:265.

61. Miller Francis was in camp at Sangster's Crossroads from August through mid-October 1861 with Beauregard's brigades. *CSR/Alabama,* 158:789; Williams, *Beauregard,* 99–100.

62. John Pelham (1838–63), a native of Calhoun County, left West Point in April 1861 prior to his graduation and commission. He apparently published a letter written by John W. Francis. William Woods Hassler, *Colonel John Pelham: Lee's Boy Artillerist,* 13–23; Brewer, *Alabama,* 156–58; Owen, *History of Alabama,* 4:1439–40.

63. "P. M." was a reference to postmaster or the Confederate postal service. Letters to Confederate soldiers were commonly delivered through various messengers, such as servants, soldiers on furlough or sick leave, discharged soldiers returning home, or the numerous visitors

to the camps. Wiley, *The Life of Johnny Reb,* 192–94, 199–200; James M. McPherson, *For Cause and Comrades; Why Men Fought in the Civil War* (New York: Oxford University Press, 1997), 132–33.

64. George C. Whatley was elected captain and served as commander of Company G, 10th Alabama, until he was killed at the battle of Sharpsburg, Maryland, on 7 September 1862. *CSR/Alabama,* 200:1664; McClelen, *I Saw the Elephant,* 30.

65. Peter Turney, commander of the 1st Tennessee, recovered from his bout with typhoid fever only to suffer wounds to his face and neck at the battle of Fredericksburg, Virginia, on 13 December 1862. *CSR/Tennessee,* 111:1574.

66. Private John W. Weaver, Company G, 10th Alabama, died of "brain fever" on 21 August 1861 near Bristoe, Virginia. *CSR/Alabama,* 200:1652.

67. The camp diseases—diarrhea, dysentery, malaria, and typhoid fever—reached endemic or epidemic levels in virtually every unit and continued to the end of the war. Typhoid fever accounted for one-fourth of the wartime deaths attributed to disease. Stewart M. Brooks, *Civil War Medicine,* 6, 45, 118; Cunningham, *Doctors in Gray,* 194–95; Steiner, *Disease in the Civil War,* 12–26.

68. Abram J. Walker arrived in Jacksonville on Thursday, 5 September 1861, where he visited with relatives for several days. *Jacksonville Republican,* 12 September 1861.

69. Carter B. Tatum, an eighteen-year-old private from Jacksonville, died of "camp fever" at Camp Bristoe, Virginia, on 27 August 1861. *CSR/Alabama,* 198:1527; Muster Roll, Company G, 10th Alabama, Lewis House near Manassas, 20 February 1862, Confederate Muster Roll Collection.

70. Miles W. Abernathy traveled to Virginia in late July 1861 to visit his sick son, Macon, at Camp Bristoe and returned to Jacksonville on Sunday, 8 September 1861. *Jacksonville Republican,* 12 September 1861.

71. Tom and John Francis were at Camp Bristoe, and Jim Francis was at Bristoe Station on the Orange & Alexandria Railroad about four miles southwest of Manassas Junction. Coles, *From Huntsville to Appomattox,* 30–32.

72. A box from home was a very special treat for the Civil War soldier. See Philip Van Doren Stern, ed., *Soldier Life in the Union and Confederate Armies* (Bloomington: Indiana University Press, 1961), 154–55.

73. Requests for clothing from home was another common theme in letters written by Confederate soldiers. Neither the Confederate government nor the states could supply the quantities of uniforms and other clothing described in their regulations. Wiley, *The Life of Johnny Reb,* 108–21.

74. Kersey cloth was a coarse heavy wool or wool and cotton cloth woven in a plain or twill weave and was commonly used for uniforms, work clothes, and coats. *Fairchilds' Dictionary of Textiles,* ed. Isabel B. Wingate (New York: Fairchild Publications, Inc., 1967), 315.

75. The Southern Express Company operated weekly routes between the major southern cities from the eastern seaboard to Texas. It delivered payrolls, munitions, military supplies, and packages and mail to Confederate soldiers in hospitals, prisons, and camps. Current, *Encyclopedia of the Confederacy,* 4:1511.

76. The rate of pay for surgeons was $162 per month, and it appears that Miller Francis was paid for the months of July and August. *CSR/Alabama,* 158:789.

77. Clark and Tom were Miller's two young sons, James Clark and Thomas Woodson, ages six and four. Francis-Martin Genealogy Collection.

78. Miles W. Abernathy arrived back in Jacksonville on 8 September 1861 with a large

number of letters and approximately $8,000 forwarded by men in the 10th Alabama to their families in Calhoun County. *Jacksonville Republican,* 12 September 1861.

79. Benjamin F. Hodges, a native of Pickens County, Alabama, enlisted as a private in the Pope Walker Guards at Jacksonville on 4 June 1861. *CSR/Alabama,* 195:750.

80. Despite the relative abundance of food in September 1861, a Confederate congressional investigating committee reported inadequate supplies of vegetables, milk, and molasses in Virginia by January 1862. Wiley, *The Life of Johnny Reb,* 90.

81. Elias Blun, a native of Germany, enlisted as a twenty-eight-year-old private in the Pope Walker Guards on 11 June 1861 and was discharged in March 1863. *CSR/Alabama,* 191:173–74.

82. Joseph Fleishl (Fleishel), a native of Bohemia, enlisted as a twenty-six-year-old private in the Pope Walker Guards on 4 June 1861 and was discharged on 3 April 1862. Ibid., 193:500; *Eighth Census/Alabama,* 2:286.

83. The Calhoun Sharpshooters were organized by Thomas B. Bush at Jacksonville on 10 August 1861. They were mustered into Confederate service as Company B, 5th Alabama Battalion, with three other volunteer units from Calhoun, Mobile, and Sumter counties. *Jacksonville Republican,* 13 February, 20 March 1862; *CSR/Alabama,* 150:102; Brewer, *Alabama,* 689–90.

84. John T. Martin enlisted in the Calhoun Sharpshooters on 19 August 1861. *CSR/Alabama,* 152:430.

85. Thomas B. Johnson enlisted in the Calhoun Sharpshooters on 19 August 1861 and served until paroled at Appomattox Court House, Virginia, on 9 April 1865. Ibid., 356.

86. James P. Crow enlisted as a private in the Calhoun Sharpshooters on 19 August 1861 for the war. Ibid., 150:181.

87. Stephen S. Carter (Cartee) enlisted in the Calhoun Sharpshooters on 19 August 1861 and was paroled at Appomattox Court House, Virginia, on 9 April 1865. Ibid., 126–27; *Eighth Census/Alabama,* 5:113.

88. Dr. Courtney James Clark served as director of the Alabama hospitals in Richmond, and Juliet Opie Hopkins (1818–90) was appointed superintendent of the Alabama hospitals by Governor John Gill Shorter in November 1861. McMillan, *The Alabama Confederate Reader,* 367. See also Lucille Griffith, "Mrs. Juliet Opie Hopkins and Alabama Military Hospitals."

89. Thomas B. Bush was elected captain in the Calhoun Sharpshooters when mustered into the Confederate service as Company B, 5th Alabama Battalion. *CSR/Alabama,* 150:102.

90. Typhoid fever became a killer disease in both armies. Cunningham, *Doctors in Gray,* 194.

91. In early August 1861, Beauregard moved several brigades north of the post-Manassas line to the south side of the Potomac River opposite the heights above Washington, D.C. *OR,* 5:778–79; Williams, *Beauregard,* 99–100.

92. Nathaniel D. Renfroe, a former Baptist minister in Jacksonville, enlisted as a private in the Calhoun Sharpshooters on 19 August 1861. He was killed at the battle of Fredericksburg, Virginia, on 13 December 1862. *CSR/Alabama,* 153:607; *Jacksonville Republican,* 1 January 1863.

93. John H. Forney was one of several officers mentioned by Joe Johnston as potential brigadier generals in a report on 2 February 1862, and his promotion was confirmed on 10 March 1862. *OR,* 5:1058; *CSR/General & Staff,* 96; *CSR/Alabama,* 193:504.

94. John Francis's promotion to sergeant-major was never confirmed. *CSR/Alabama,* 193:514.

95. Jabez Lafeyette Monroe Curry (1825–1903) was a member of the first Confederate

Congress and a strong supporter of President Davis and the Confederate war effort. Owen, *History of Alabama,* 3:444–45; Current, *Encyclopedia of the Confederacy,* 1:439–40.

96. Robert H. Wynne, a Jacksonville tailor, made uniforms and other clothing for the men of the 10th Alabama. *Eighth Census/Alabama,* 2:291; *Jacksonville Republican,* 17 January, 28 March 1861.

97. Tom Francis received a thirty-day sick furlough which was extended to two months. He remained at Jacksonville until early November 1861. *CSR/Alabama,* 193:516.

98. Malachi Ponder, a thirty-five-year-old private, died of "camp fever" on 16 September 1861. Ibid., 198:1269; Muster Roll, Company G, 10th Alabama, 20 February 1862, Lewis House near Manassas, Va., Confederate Muster Roll Collection.

99. James L. Plexico, a twenty-three-year-old private, died of "camp fever" on 17 September 1861 in Prince William County, Virginia. *CSR/Alabama,* 198:1266; Muster Roll, Company G, 10th Alabama, 20 February 1862, Lewis House near Manassas, Va., ibid.

100. Charles B. Sisson was listed in the 1860 census as a forty-five-year-old farmer living near White Plains, Calhoun County, Alabama. His son, Charles B. Sisson, Jr., was a private in the Pope Walker Guards. *Eighth Census/Alabama,* 2:389; *Jacksonville Republican,* 24 October 1861; *CSR/Alabama,* 198:1435.

101. John H. Burton was listed in the 1860 census as a forty-eight-year-old farmer living near White Plains. His son, William D. Burton, was apparently a member of a unit from Calhoun County, but his service records list only his later service in the Dudley Snow Rangers, Company D, 51st Alabama Mounted Infantry. *Eighth Census/Alabama,* 2:388; *Jacksonville Republican,* 24 October 1861; *CSR/Alabama,* 445:192.

102. James G. Nesbit was listed in the 1860 census as a thirty-nine-year-old proprietor of mills and lived with his family in Jacksonville. *Eighth Census/Alabama,* 2:402; *Jacksonville Republican,* 24 October 1861.

103. William Thomas Renfro (1841–63) served with the Talladega Artillery at Fort Morgan for six weeks. He returned to Talladega and enlisted in Company E, 5th Alabama Volunteer Regiment, under Captain Charles M. Shelley. *CSR/Alabama,* 146:1723; *Jacksonville Republican,* 19 December 1861.

104. The 4th Alabama was sent to close the navigation of the Potomac River below Washington and to support siege guns near Dumfries, Prince Henry County, Virginia. Coles, *From Huntsville to Appomattox,* 32; Jones, "The Fourth Alabama Infantry: First Blood," 51.

105. Cadmus Marcellus Wilcox (1824–90), a native of North Carolina and an 1846 West Point graduate, was the new brigade commander. He was commissioned colonel of the 9th Alabama Volunteer Regiment and led his regiment at the battle of First Manassas. *CSR/General & Staff,* 96, 267; *CSR/Alabama,* 193:504; Current, *Encyclopedia of the Confederacy,* 4:1718.

106. John W. Francis served as acting commissary for the 10th Alabama while Tom Francis was on furlough. *CSR/Alabama,* 193:513.

107. Lina Marion was a widow and her son, John Marion, was a member of a company raised in Calhoun County, Alabama. *Eighth Census/Alabama,* 2:292.

108. Mary Elizabeth Nisbet Martin was the wife of James Benson Martin (1825–61) of the 10th Alabama. Their eldest son, John Thomas Martin, married Susan Hanna Francis, the daughter of Dr. James C. and Amy Ingram Francis, on 5 February 1873 in Jacksonville. *CSR/ Alabama,* 196:973; *Eighth Census/Alabama,* 2:424; Francis-Martin Genealogy Collection.

109. William F. Bush and James B. Farmer, Jacksonville residents, were sutlers to the 10th Alabama. Sutlers were traveling merchants who provided a variety of goods to the unit they served. *Eighth Census/Alabama,* 2:294, 298; *Jacksonville Republican,* 2 January 1862; Wiley, *The Life of Johnny Reb,* 76, 100.

110. George C. Whatley, Company G, 10th Alabama, served as commander of the Company I until Capt. Abner A. Hughes returned on 27 November 1861. *Jacksonville Republican,* 17 October 1861; A. A. Hughes to George C. Whatley, Camp of the 10th Ala. Regt. (near) Centreville, Va., 19 December 1861, in *Jacksonville Republican,* 19 December 1861; *CSR/Alabama,* 200:1664; George C. Whatley to Cynthia Whatley, Centreville, 26 November 1861, Whatley Letters.

111. Joel H. Farmer, a private in Company G, recovered from his illness at Centreville but was killed at the battle of Gettysburg on 2 July 1863. *CSR/Alabama,* 193:491; *Jacksonville Republican,* 22 August 1863.

112. Wyatt McDaniel recovered from his illness at Centreville. He was later wounded in fighting near Richmond and died on 22 July 1862. *CSR/Alabama,* 196:1022; *Jacksonville Republican,* 31 July 1862.

113. Benjamin A. Brooks enlisted as a thirty-two-year-old private in the Pope Walker Guards at Jacksonville on 4 June 1861. He developed erysipelas and died on 9 December 1861. *CSR/Alabama,* 191:172; *Jacksonville Republican,* 19 December 1861.

114. John R. Castleberry was elected second lieutenant in Company F, 10th Alabama, at Cropwell, St. Clair County, Alabama, on 4 June 1861 and resigned on 18 November 1861. *CSR/Alabama,* 192:266.

115. John R. Clark was listed in the 1860 census as a forty-year-old farmer with real estate valued at $6,800 and a personal estate valued at $42,570. *Eighth Census/Alabama,* 2:292.

116. Thomas R. Rowland enlisted as a twenty-seven-year-old second sergeant in the Pope Walker Guards at Jacksonville on 4 June 1861. *CSR/Alabama,* 198:1378.

117. Lucius C. Mitchell furnished eighteen-year-old Horace L. Stevenson as a substitute in accordance with Confederate army regulations. Stevenson enlisted as a private in Company G, 10th Alabama, in Fairfax County, Virginia, on 30 November 1861. Ibid., 196:1496; Muster Roll, Company G, 10th Alabama, Lewis House near Manassas, Va., 20 February 1862, Confederate Muster Roll Collection.

118. Isaac L. Swan enlisted as a thirty-two-year old private in the Pope Walker Guards at Jacksonville on 4 June 1861. *CSR/Alabama,* 198:1579.

119. George Hoke was listed in the 1860 census as a fifty-four-year-old merchant with real estate valued at $6,000 and a personal estate valued at $24,000. He and Alexander Woods, probate judge in Calhoun County, were leading citizens in Jacksonville and very active in support of the Confederate cause. *Eighth Census/Alabama,* 2:285, 288; *Jacksonville Republican,* 30 May 1863.

120. Jim Francis's reference to the Richmond atmosphere being the meanest in the Confederacy was directed at the widespread sickness that reached epidemic proportions from late summer through early December 1861. See Steiner, *Disease in the Civil War,* 3–45.

121. President Davis signed the act granting furloughs, and Jim Francis was granted a thirty-day furlough starting on 7 December 1861. *CSR/Alabama,* 122:579.

122. James B. Martin, Jr., enlisted in the Talladega Davis Blues, Company E, 10th Alabama, at Talladega on 4 June 1861. He was elected second lieutenant and served as acting adjutant general for the 10th Alabama. Ibid., 196:974; *Jacksonville Republican,* 12 December 1861.

123. John Y. Henderson, a native of South Carolina, was listed in the 1860 census as a twenty-five-year-old merchant living with his brother Zimri Henderson near Sulphur Springs, Calhoun County, Alabama. *Eighth Census/Alabama,* 2:684.

124. John Easterwood, a native of South Carolina, was listed in the 1860 census as a thirty-four-year-old farmer living near Morrisville, Calhoun County, Alabama. Ibid., 667.

125. Zimri Henderson was a thirty-two-year-old merchant who lived near Sulphur Springs, Calhoun County, in 1860. He owned real estate valued at $2,000 and a personal estate valued at $14,000. Ibid., 684.

126. James H. Autrey was listed in the 1860 census as a thirty-eight-year-old farmer living near Morrisville, Calhoun County, Alabama. Ibid., 682.

127. Southerners consumed large amounts of pork prior to the war. The absence of men to supervise the butchering and curing, the scarcity of feed, and an insufficient supply of salt for curing the pork helped to produce a shortage that grew as the war spread through the Confederate states. Mary Elizabeth Massey, *Ersatz in the Confederacy: Shortages and Substitutions on the Southern Homefront,* 60–61.

128. Nathaniel Cobb, a native of South Carolina, was listed in the 1860 census as a fifty-seven-year-old farmer living near White Plains, Calhoun County, Alabama. He owned real estate valued at $6,000 and a personal estate valued at $21,000. *Eighth Census/Alabama,* 2:358.

129. Richard Avery Ingram (1819–69) was one of Amy Ingram Francis's brothers. He married Sarah Barksdale McLendon on 10 February 1842 and was buried at Ohatchee, Calhoun County, Alabama. Francis-Martin Genealogy Collection.

130. C. R. Hagood, a native of South Carolina and a Selma resident, was listed in the 1860 census as a forty-year-old warehouse merchant with real estate valued at $24,000 and a personal estate valued at $2,500. *Eighth Census/Alabama,* 4:802; Fitts, *Selma,* 47.

131. Henry F. Vernon enlisted as a thirty-eight-year-old private in the Pope Walker Guards at Jacksonville on 4 June 1861. He was discharged on 15 December 1861 after hiring James Y. Browning as his substitute. Muster Roll of Captain William H. Forney, Company G the Pope Walker Guards, 10th Alabama, Lewis House near Manassas, Va., 20 February 1862, Confederate Muster Roll Collection.

132. Sutlers often became semi-official members of a regiment and provided an important service despite their exorbitant prices. Wiley, *The Life of Johnny Reb,* 76, 100; Stern, *Soldier Life in the Union and Confederate Armies,* 159–64.

133. Joseph Kahn and Joseph Fleishl were partners in a dry goods business in Jacksonville until Kahn's death in April 1862. *Eighth Census/Alabama,* 2:286; *Jacksonville Republican,* 26 January, 26 April 1860, 4 April 1861, 24 April, 3 July 1862.

134. Hezekiah B. Ingram, a native of Georgia, was listed in the 1860 census as a twenty-year-old farmer living near Morrisville, Calhoun County, Alabama. *Eighth Census/Alabama,* 2:667.

135. Woodford R. Hanna, a resident of White Plains, Calhoun County, was commissioned by Governor A. B. Moore as captain of the Choccolocco Rifles on 27 April 1861. The Choccolocco Rifles were mustered in as Company H, 10th Alabama, in June 1861. Ibid., 373; *CSR/Alabama,* 194:648; Confederate Alabama Militia by Companies & Counties (1860–65); Brewer, *Alabama,* 606.

136. Franklin Woodruff, a resident of Alexandria, Calhoun County, was commissioned by Governor A. B. Moore as captain of the Alexandria Rifles, dated 4 May 1861. The Alexandria Rifles were mustered in as Company D, 10th Alabama, at Alexandria, Alabama, on Tuesday,

11 June 1861. *Eighth Census/Alabama,* 2:648; *CSR/Alabama,* 200:1726; Confederate Alabama Militia by Companies & Counties; McClelen, *I Saw the Elephant,* 4–5, 49.

137. James Ainsley Stevenson, a native of South Carolina, was a successful farmer and merchant who operated a dry goods business and a large grocery store on the Jacksonville public square. *Eighth Census/Alabama,* 2:312; Owen, *History of Alabama,* 4:1622; *Jacksonville Republican,* 26 April 1860, 6 June 1861.

138. Nancy Clark was the wife of Dr. Courtney James Clark; she remained in Jacksonville with their four young children while he was stationed in Richmond. *Eighth Census/Alabama,* 2:288; Owen, *History of Alabama,* 3:328.

139. J. E. B. Stuart (1833–64) led the Confederate forces at the battle of Dranesville, including the 10th Alabama, 1st Kentucky, 6th South Carolina, and 11th Virginia, 150 cavalry, and four pieces of artillery. *OR,* 5:473–94; *Jacksonville Republican,* 2 January 1862; McClelen, *I Saw the Elephant,* 20–23.

140. John H. Forney received a severe wound to his right arm while leading the 10th Alabama at Dranesville. *Jacksonville Republican,* 2 January 1862; *OR,* 5:490–94; *CSR/Alabama,* 193:504; *CSR/General & Staff,* 96; McClelan, *I Saw the Elephant,* 21.

141. James B. Martin was mortally wounded by a minié ball to his left side during a charge by the 10th Alabama. *Jacksonville Republican,* 2 January 1862; *OR,* 5:493; *CSR/Alabama,* 196:973; McClelen, *I Saw the Elephant,* 21.

142. William H. Forney received a two-month furlough and was promoted to major on 22 February 1862 at Manassas, Virginia. *Jacksonville Republican,* 2 January 1862; *CSR/Alabama,* 193:505; *CSR/General & Staff,* 96; Crawford, *Forney Forever,* 2.

143. Jesse Harris recovered from the neck wound he received at the battle of Dranesville, but he was killed at the second battle of Manassas on 30 August 1862. *Jacksonville Republican,* 2 January, 18 September, 13 November 1862; *CSR/Alabama,* 194:670.

144. James M. Moragne recovered from his wound, served four years with the 10th Alabama, and was paroled at Appomattox Court House, Virginia, on 9 April 1865. *Jacksonville Republican,* 2 January 1862; *CSR/Alabama,* 197:1111; Owen, *History of Alabama,* 4:1237–38.

145. William M. Moragne recovered from his leg and foot wounds, but his service records ended with a muster roll dated 20 February 1862. *Jacksonville Republican,* 2 January 1862; *CSR/Alabama,* 197:1113.

146. Ransom A. Wiley was apparently driving one of the foraging wagons when fighting broke out on 20 December 1861. He recovered from the wound above his left eye and was paroled with the 10th Alabama at Appomattox Court House, Virginia, on 9 April 1865. *Jacksonville Republican,* 2 January 1862; *CSR/Alabama,* 200:1682.

147. William W. Mohon recovered from his wound and served with the 10th Alabama until paroled at Appomattox Court House on 9 April 1865. *Jacksonville Republican,* 2 January 1862; *CSR/Alabama,* 196:955.

148. Three days after being wounded at Dranesville, John Francis was recommended for a sixty-day furlough by Dr. J. William Walls, surgeon for the 10th Alabama. *Jacksonville Republican,* 2 January 1862; *CSR/Alabama,* 193:514.

149. William Henry Smith, Company G, 10th Alabama, escaped serious injury at Dranesville but was killed at Gaines' Mill, Virginia, on 27 June 1862. *Jacksonville Republican,* 2 January 1862; *CSR/Alabama,* 199:1463.

150. John H. Caldwell (1826–1902) was commander of the Ashville Guards, Company A, 10th Alabama, from St. Clair County, Alabama, at the battle of Dranesville. *CSR/Alabama,* 192:235; *Jacksonville Republican,* 2 January 1862; Krick, *Lee's Colonels,* 79–80.

151. Henry Gutman, a Jacksonville resident, was part of the German contingent in Company G, 10th Alabama, and served until his "retirement" on 5 October 1864. He was paroled at Talladega on 18 May 1865. *CSR/Alabama,* 194:628.

Chapter 3

1. Thomas Lawrence Connelly, *Army of the Heartland: The Army of Tennessee, 1861–1862,* 50–55, 63–68; Long, *The Civil War Day by Day,* 156–58.

2. Connelly, *Army of the Heartland,* 106–8, 117–25, 133–39; Esposito, *West Point Atlas,* 1:25–30; McMillan, *The Alabama Reader,* 140–44.

3. *CSR/Alabama,* 193:122, 514, 516, 579, 158:789; *CSR/General & Staff,* 98.

4. *CSR/Alabama,* 193:514; *CSR/General & Staff,* 56; *Jacksonville Republican,* 30 January 1862.

5. "Proclamation by the Governor of Alabama," Executive Department, Montgomery, Alabama, 12 February 1862, in *Jacksonville Republican,* 20 February 1862; McMillan, *The Alabama Confederate Reader,* 233–34.

6. *Jacksonville Republican,* 20 February 1862.

7. Muster Roll of Captain John C. Francis Company Ala. Volunteers, 30th Regiment (P.A.), Camp Curry near Talladega, 29 March 1862, Confederate Regimental History Files; William Milner Kelly, "A History of the Thirtieth Alabama Volunteers (Infantry) Confederate States Army," 119–23; *Jacksonville Republican,* 13 March 1862.

8. Samuel C. Kelly to Amie P. Kelly, Montgomery, 8 May 1862, Kelly Letters; Kelly, "A History of the Thirtieth Alabama Volunteers," 124.

9. The British-made Enfield rifle musket fired a .577-caliber minié ball and was very similar to the .58-caliber Springfield rifle musket used by the Union armies. Samuel C. Kelly to Amie P. Kelly, Knoxville, 11 May 1862, Kelly Letters; Wiley, *The Life of Johnny Reb,* 286, 291.

10. The letters written by John Foster, Abram J. Walker, Thomas A. Walker, Thomas J. Goldsby, Dr. James C. Francis and others were found in the compiled service records for Jim Francis. *CSR/Alabama,* 122:579.

11. *CSR/General & Staff,* 98.

12. Danville Leadbetter (1811–66), a native of Maine and a West Point graduate, was commander at Fort Morgan before his promotion to brigadier general on 6 March 1862 and command at Chattanooga. Boatner, *The Civil War Dictionary,* 473–74; *CSR/General & Staff,* 98; Francis-Martin Family Papers.

13. The Partisan Ranger Act passed on 21 April 1862 by the Confederate Congress authorized the organization of partisan ranger units to conduct guerrilla operations against the Yankee invaders. Morgan's Partisan Rangers were formally organized as the Fifty-first Alabama Mounted Infantry at Oxford, Calhoun County, Alabama, on 11 August 1862. Bertil Haggmann, "Confederate Irregular Warfare, 1861–1865: Partisan Ranger Units and Guerilla Commands" (unpublished manuscript, Helsingborg, Sweden); *CSR/General & Staff,* 182; *Jacksonville Republican,* 1, 8, 15, 22, 29 May 1862; Brewer, *Alabama,* 663.

14. *CSR/Alabama,* 158:789; *Jacksonville Republican,* 5 June 1862.

15. Unfiled Papers and Slips Belonging in Confederate Compiled Records, Roll 135, No. 5573.

16. Long, *The Civil War Day by Day,* 198–200, 202–6; McMillan, *The Alabama Confederate Reader,* 144–85.

17. While their principal business was "Staple & Fancy Dry Goods" in 1860, Joseph Kahn

and Joseph Fleishl became commission merchants and served as brokers in numerous business transactions. *Jacksonville Republican,* 26 January, 26 April 1860, 24 April 1862.

18. Thomas R. Rowland was listed in the 1860 census as a twenty-six-year-old merchant who lived in Jacksonville with his twenty-three-year-old wife, Mary E., and their three young children. He owned real estate valued at $1,700 and a personal estate valued at $24,450. *Eighth Census/Alabama,* 2: 293; Muster Roll of Captain William H. Forney, Company G, Pope Walker Guards of the 10th Regiment, Alabama Volunteers, Lewis House near Manassas, Va., 20 February 1862, Confederate Muster Roll Collection.

19. While Tom Francis does not mention shortages of grains and food crops, his advice to his father to limit his cotton acreage was obviously motivated by the need to raise these crops for the family and the market. See Massey, *Ersatz in the Confederacy,* 55–77.

20. Pork shortages were reported in several areas of the Confederacy by 1862 because of military consumption, hog cholera, feed shortages, and shortages of salt for curing the meat. Ibid., 61, 63; Paul W. Gates, *Agriculture and the Civil War,* 90–94.

21. Inflation had become a problem by January 1862 and had a dramatic impact on the Confederate economy and treasury. While a dollar in gold in May 1861 cost $1.10 in Confederate currency at Richmond, it was up to $3.00 by December 1862. John Christopher Schwab, *The Confederate States of America, 1861–1865: A Financial and Industrial History of the South During the Civil War,* 166–67; Long, *The Civil War Day by Day,* 727–28.

22. William H. Forney was promoted to major on 22 February 1862, lieutenant colonel on 15 March 1862, and colonel on 27 June 1862. *CSR/Alabama,* 193:505; *CSR/General & Staff,* 96.

23. John A. Cobb enlisted as a thirty-two-year-old private in the Pope Walker Guards at Jacksonville on 4 June 1861. He was promoted to second lieutenant 30 July 1864 and paroled as a captain at Talladega on 25 May 1865. *CSR/Alabama,* 192:305.

24. James "Mun" Renfro, first sergeant in Company G, 10th Alabama, was elected second lieutenant on 6 December 1862. Ibid., 198:1319.

25. Wyatt M. McDaniel was elected third sergeant in the Pope Walker Guards at Jacksonville in June 1861. He was wounded in the left arm near Richmond on 30 June 1862 and died on 22 July. Ibid., 196:1022; *Jacksonville Republican,* 31 July 1862.

26. William M. Findley enlisted as a twenty-five-year-old private in the Pope Walker Guards at Jacksonville on 4 June 1861. He was detached as a clerk in the second auditors office at Richmond on 30 April 1862. *CSR/Alabama,* 193:498.

27. Before the war, Joe Kahn operated a confectionary business at Middleton, Calhoun County, Alabama, and a mercantile firm in Jacksonville in partnership with Joe Fleishl. *Jacksonville Republican,* 26 January, 26 April 1860, 4 April 1861; *Eighth Census/Alabama,* 2:286.

28. Ambrose E. Burnside (1824–81) was given command of the Department of North Carolina in January 1862 and sailed out of Hampton Roads, Virginia, with approximately 15,000 soldiers and about 65 ships. From mid-January through June 1862, his seaborne expedition struck the coastal areas of North Carolina instead of the Rappahannock and Evansport, Virginia. *OR,* 9:74–343; Long, *The Civil War Day by Day,* 158–63, 168, 184–85, 187, 237.

29. The 10th Alabama left its position in northern Virginia on Saturday, 18 March 1862, when Joe Johnston moved his Confederate forces southward and established a new line on the Rappahannock River around mid-March. McClelen, *I Saw the Elephant,* 21; Long, *The Civil War Day by Day,* 180–82.

30. William H. Forney was still recovering from his leg wound received in the battle of Dranesville on 20 December 1861. *CSR/Alabama,* 193:505; Crawford, *Forney Forever,* 2, 22.

31. John H. Forney's right arm was badly shattered by a minié ball at Dranesville; he

was promoted to brigadier general on 10 March 1862 following his return to active duty. *CSR/Alabama,* 193:504; Crawford, *Forney Forever,* 2, 22.

32. Richard Ingram, a native of Georgia, was a farmer living near Alexandria, Calhoun County, Alabama, in 1860 with real estate valued at $10,000 and a personal estate valued at $12,000. He was Amy Ingram Francis's younger brother. *Eighth Census/Alabama,* 2:652.

33. William Henry, a native of South Carolina, was listed in the 1860 census as a fifty-nine-year-old farmer living near Wehoga some twenty miles east-southeast of Jacksonville in present-day Cleburne County. He and Tom Francis made a trade that involved Alabama & Tennessee Rivers Railroad stock. Ibid., 544; Remington and Kallsen, *Historical Atlas of Alabama,* 1:74, 76.

34. Gabriel B. Douthit, a native of South Carolina, was the circuit clerk in Calhoun County, Alabama. *Eighth Census/Alabama,* 2:299; *Jacksonville Republican,* 2 August 1860.

35. Uria Dulaney, a native of South Carolina, was listed in the 1860 census as a sixty-year-old farmer living near Sulphur Springs some ten miles west-northwest of Jacksonville. *Eighth Census/Alabama,* 2:395, 690.

36. Isaac Frank and Elias Blun were merchants from Columbus, Georgia, who opened a new mercantile business in Jacksonville in September 1860. *Jacksonville Republican,* 20 September, 1 November 1860; *Eighth Census/Georgia,* 11:188, 192.

37. The Francis Mill was constructed on Cane Creek about two miles north of Tom Francis's postwar residence at Sulphur Springs in southwest Calhoun County. See Francis-Martin Family Papers; Calhoun County Tax Assessment, Calhoun County Courthouse, Anniston, Alabama, 1866:7, 1867:38, 52, 74, 1868:55, 83, 86.

38. John J. Woodward of Talladega was promoted to lieutenant colonel on 20 December 1861, and William H. Forney was promoted to major on 22 February 1862. *CSR/Alabama,* 193:505, 200:1935.

39. William F. Bush served as sutler to the 10th Alabama from November 1861 through September 1862 and continued to serve as commander of the Calhoun County Home Guards. Muster Roll, Calhoun Home Guards, Confederate Alabama Militia by Companies & Counties; *Jacksonville Republican,* 17 October, 11 November 1861.

40. Courtney James Clark returned to Jacksonville on a furlough prior to assuming his new assignment as chief surgeon of the Alabama hospitals in Richmond. *CSR/General & Staff,* 56; *Jacksonville Republican,* 30 January 1862; Griffith, "Mrs. Juliet Opie Hopkins and Alabama Military Hospitals," 119.

41. Richard Henderson Rivers, former president of Florence Wesleyan University, was the new president of Centenary Institute in Summerfield, Dallas County, Alabama, approximately ten miles north of Selma. McDonald, *Beginnings . . . of The University of North Alabama,* 37–38; Owen, *History of Alabama,* 1:215–16.

42. Miller Francis recorded 75 cases of diarrhea and 30 cases of dysentery in December 1861 and another 408 diarrhea cases and 76 dysentery cases in January 1862. These two intestinal disorders were the most prevalent of the army diseases. Miller W. Francis, Report of Sick and Wounded, Davis Ford, Virginia, 6th Alabama, December 1861 and January 1862, Confederate Regimental History Files; Cunningham, *Doctors in Gray,* 184–85.

43. Beauregard's furlough system was probably a victim of his running disputes with Jefferson Davis. The granting or refusing of furloughs was a major source of discontent between the Confederate soldier and his government. Williams, *Beauregard,* 96–112; Wiley, *The Life of Johnny Reb,* 135, 137, 139. .

44. Miller Francis was squarely in the pro-Beauregard camp and part of a growing anti-

Davis and anti-administration faction that emerged in the Confederate army following the first battle of Manassas. Francis-Martin Family Papers.

45. By early 1862, Vice President Alexander H. Stephens (1812–83) emerged as a member of the growing anti-Davis party and openly opposed the first Conscription Act passed in April 1862. Williams, *Beauregard,* 99, 112; Current, *Encyclopedia of the Confederacy,* 4:1539. See Alexander H. Stephens, *A Constitutional View of the War.*

46. Despite Miller Francis's comment, Robert T. Coles reported in his history of the 4th Alabama that nearly all of the regiment reenlisted during January 1862. Coles, *From Huntsville to Appomattox,* 36.

47. Dr. Samuel Preston Moore (1813–89), a native of Charleston, South Carolina, was appointed Confederate surgeon general on 30 July 1861 and served through the end of the war. Cunningham, *Doctors in Gray,* 27–29; Glenna R. Schroeder-Lein, *Confederate Hospitals on the Move: Samuel H. Stout and the Army of Tennessee,* 68–69, 192.

48. Beauregard left Virginia on 2 February 1862 but did not assume formal command of the Army of the Mississippi at Jackson, Tennessee, until 5 March. *OR,* 10, pt. 2:297; Williams, *Beauregard,* 115–22.

49. Gabe was one of several thousand Black Southerners, slave and free, who served in paramilitary positions with the Confederacy. Rollins, *Black Southerners in Gray,* 5–28, 37–50, 75–89. See also James H. Brewer, *The Confederate Negro: Virginia's Craftsmen and Military Laborers, 1861–1865* (Durham, N.C.: Duke University Press, 1969).

50. John Francis's furlough extension was signed by Dr. Courtney James Clark, Miller Francis's brother-in-law and longtime family friend. *CSR/General & Staff,* 56.

51. John T. Montgomery was the oldest son of James and Elizabeth Ingram Montgomery, Amy Ingram Francis's younger sister. He joined his younger brother, James Francis Montgomery, in Company I, 19th Alabama, when he enlisted as a private at Coloma, Alabama, on 27 April 1862. *CSR/Alabama,* 274:1342, 1343.

52. According to the 1860 census, John T. Montgomery, his parents, and his five siblings lived near Goshen, Cherokee County, Alabama, about three miles west of Spring Garden. *Eighth Census/Alabama,* 3: 281; Remington and Kallsen, *Historical Atlas of Alabama,* 1:47, 49, 51.

53. John Francis placed an announcement "To Arms! To Arms!!" in the *Jacksonville Republican* promising each private and noncommissioned officer a bounty of $50 when mustered into service. Muster Roll, Company B, 30th Alabama [List of soldiers who received $50 bounty for enlisting], Camp near Talladega, Ala., 26 April 1862, Confederate Muster Roll Collection; *Jacksonville Republican,* 20 February 1862.

54. Sarah "Sallie" McGehee Walker's letter to John C. Francis was printed in the *Jacksonville Republican.* She was the wife of lawyer/politician Thomas A. Walker, who was listed in the 1860 census with real estate valued at $120,000 and a personal estate valued at $160,000. *Jacksonville Republican,* 13 March 1862; *Eighth Census/Alabama,* 2:300; Owen, *History of Alabama,* 4:1719–20.

55. The Sallie Walker Boys were organized at Jacksonville on 5 March 1862 by Captain Charles M. Shelley, and John C. Francis was elected captain at age nineteen. Muster Roll of Captain John C. Francis Company Ala. Volunteers, 30th Regiment (P.A.), 29 March 1862, Confederate Regimental History Files.

56. A reference to the Alabama Allegheny front, the Sand Mountain–Lookout Mountain range, that stretches from Chattanooga to Birmingham. Thomas L. Connelly, *Discovering the Appalachians,* 77–78; Owen, *History of Alabama,* 1:650, 652.

57. Sallie Walker's donation of $500 to Captain John Francis for outfitting his company was a common practice, and many volunteer companies were named to honor some special benefactor or community leader. *Jacksonville Republican,* 17 October, 19 December 1861.

58. Camp Curry, near Talladega, was selected as the rendezvous and training center for the new companies that were mustered into Confederate service from Calhoun, Cherokee, Randolph, St. Clair, Shelby, and Talladega counties. *Jacksonville Republican,* 6 March 1862.

59. The Sallie Walker Boys arrived at Camp Curry on 13 March 1862 with 94 men: 15 officers, noncommissioned officers, and musicians and 79 privates. Muster Roll of Captain John C. Francis Company Ala. Volunteers, 30th Regiment (P.A.), Camp Curry near Talladega, Ala., 29 March 1862, Confederate Regimental History Files; *Jacksonville Republican,* 13 March 1862.

60. Manning K. Kimbrell, a thirty-eight-year-old wagon maker and Georgia native, enlisted as a private in the Sallie Walker Boys at Jacksonville on 5 March 1862. *CSR/Alabama,* 334:637; *Eighth Census/Alabama,* 2:299.

61. William Henry Forney returned to Virginia and the 10th Alabama in March 1862, and Charles Miller Shelley was appointed colonel on 31 January 1862 and assigned command of the 30th Alabama Volunteer Regiment. *CSR/Alabama,* 335:1030; *CSR/General & Staff,* 96; *Jacksonville Republican,* 20 February 1862; Owen, *History of Alabama,* 4:1542.

62. Daniel W. Beacham, a fifteen-year-old from Peeks Hill, Calhoun County, enlisted as a musician in the Sallie Walker Boys at Jacksonville on 5 March 1862. *CSR/Alabama,* 332:95.

63. John Chamness enlisted as a twenty-six-year-old private in the Sallie Walker Boys at Jacksonville on 5 March 1862. Ibid., 239.

64. In 1860 Henry Wolfe was a twenty-four-year-old farmer and South Carolina native who lived near Middleton, Calhoun County. He enlisted as a private in the Sallie Walker Boys on 5 March 1862. Ibid., 336:1275; *Eighth Census/Alabama,* 2:657.

65. Bradford Gober enlisted as a forty-two-year-old private in the Sallie Walker Boys at Jacksonville on 5 March 1862 "for the term of three years or the war." *CSR/Alabama,* 333:445.

66. Thomas S. Finch, a native of Spartanburg, South Carolina, enlisted as a twenty-three-year-old private in the Sallie Walker Boys at Jacksonville on 8 March 1862. He died at Bean's Station, Tennessee, on 17 July 1862. Ibid., 378; *Jacksonville Republican,* 4 September 1862.

67. Charles M. Shelley, a native of Tennessee, served as a lieutenant in a Talladega company at Fort Morgan and Mobile in 1861. He was elected captain of Company B, 5th Alabama Infantry Regiment, on 2 April 1861 and served in Virginia until he was appointed colonel in the 30th Alabama Volunteers. *CSR/Alabama,* 335: 1030; Owen, *History of Alabama,* 4:1542.

68. Euclid Johnson enlisted as a twenty-four-year-old private in the Sallie Walker Boys on 5 March 1862 at Jacksonville. He was appointed assistant quartermaster in the 30th Alabama by George W. Randolph, secretary of war, on 17 May 1862. *CSR/Alabama,* 334:607.

69. J. A. Storey, a thirty-nine-year-old private in Captain Thomas H. Patterson's Company I, 30th Alabama, enlisted at Talladega, Alabama, on 22 March 1862. He was appointed captain and assistant commissary for subsistence for the 30th Alabama on 27 May 1862. Ibid., 336:1120.

70. William C. Patterson, captain of Company A, 30th Alabama, declined the appointment as surgeon but served with the 30th Alabama until his resignation as lieutenant colonel on 28 January 1864. Ibid., 335:878; Samuel C. Kelly to Amie P. Kelly, Camp Curry, 29 March 1862, Kelly Letters.

71. C. H. Gorman, a Georgia native and physician, enlisted as a thirty-two-year-old private in Captain John Sawyer's Company F, 30th Alabama, at Talladega on 12 March 1862. He

was appointed assistant surgeon for the 30th Alabama and served until his resignation on 2 March 1864. *CSR/Alabama,* 333:453; *Eighth Census/Alabama,* 12:708.

72. The original letter from Dr. James C. Francis to William P. Chilton, Confederate congressman from the Montgomery district, is found in the service records of James C. Francis, Jr. *CSR/Alabama,* 122:579.

73. William P. Chilton (1810–71), a native of Kentucky, was elected to the Confederate Congress from Montgomery, Alabama, and was a member of the Quartermaster's and Commissary committees during the First Confederate Congress. *Clarke County Democrat,* 13 August 1863; Current, *Encyclopedia of the Confederacy,* 1:308–9; Owen, *History of Alabama,* 3:324.

74. A reference to letters written by John Foster to William P. Chilton on 10 March 1862 and by Thomas A. Walker and Abram J. Walker on 10 March 1862 to George W. Randolph, secretary of war, recommending Jim Francis. Chilton and Jabez L. M. Curry also forwarded letters to Randolph that were received on 10 April 1862. *CSR/Alabama,* 122:579.

75. Dr. James C. Francis played an active role on the home front raising funds and materials for the war effort. *Jacksonville Republican,* 22 November 1860, 24, 31 January 1861, 2 April, 17 October 1863; Francis-Martin Family Papers.

76. Wylie (Wilie) Carpenter was elected as a forty-six-year-old first lieutenant in the Sallie Walker Boys in March 1862. *CSR/Alabama,* 332:228

77. The 30th Alabama left Camp Curry near Talladega on 7 May 1862 and traveled to East Tennessee and not to Virginia. Samuel C. Kelly to Amie P. Camp, Montgomery, 8 May 1862, Kelly Letters.

78. Emma Francis's letter to her brother Hopkins Turney Francis in Selma was written on the back of John Francis's letter to their mother of the same date. See John's letter in Francis-Martin Family Papers.

79. The 6th Alabama was reorganized and its men reenlisted for the war at Yorktown, Virginia. However, Miller Francis, determined to join John Tyler Morgan's Partisan Rangers, submitted his resignation on 6 March 1862. *CSR/Alabama,* 158:789.

80. Tom Francis was ordered to Chattanooga on 12 February 1862 to act as assistant commissary for subsistence. *CSR/General & Staff,* 98.

81. The 30th Alabama traveled to Selma aboard eighteen boxcars of the Alabama & Tennessee Rivers Railroad on Wednesday, 7 May 1862. Samuel C. Kelly to Amie P. Kelly, Montgomery, 8 May 1862, Kelly Letters; Kelly, "A History of the Thirtieth Alabama Volunteers," 124.

82. At Selma the 30th Alabama crowded aboard the *Southern Republic* and a smaller boat for their fourteen-hour trip up the Alabama River to Montgomery. Samuel C. Kelly to Amie P. Kelly, Montgomery, 8 May 1862, Kelly Letters.

83. Taul Bradford, a native of Talladega County, was elected lieutenant colonel of the 30th Alabama at its organization on 26 March 1862. *CSR/Alabama,* 332:152; Kelly, "A History of the Thirtieth Alabama Volunteers," 123.

84. The Sallie Walker Boys and five other companies of the 30th Alabama traveled aboard the Montgomery & West Point Railroad to West Point, Georgia, and to Atlanta on the Atlanta & West Point Railroad. Black, *Railroads of the Confederacy,* 6, 9–10.

85. Danville Leadbetter, a native of Maine and a West Point graduate, became chief of the Confederate Engineer Bureau in August 1861. He was promoted to brigadier general on 27 February 1862 and given a field command near Chattanooga in North Alabama. Current, *Encyclopedia of the Confederacy,* 2:913–14.

86. William T. Alexander, J. W. Reaves, James H. Niman, Calvin M. Turner, and James M. White were privates in Company B, 30th Alabama, and they recovered from their camp diseases. *CSR/Alabama,* 332:37, 335:841, 968, 336:1193, 1243.

87. Daniel W. Beacham, a fifteen-year-old private drummer, and Thomas Warren, a twenty-year-old private, enlisted in the Sallie Walker Boys at Jacksonville on 5 March 1862. Ibid., 332:95, 336:1222.

88. Samuel Kelly reported to his wife Amie Kelly that the "Lincolnites" in Tennessee did not cheer "but stood and gazed." Samuel C. Kelly to Amie P. Kelly, Knoxville, 11 May 1862, Kelly Letters.

89. James [Olerum] was a clerk at a Chattanooga depot on the East Tennessee & Georgia Railroad and remained unidentified.

90. The Enfield rifle, manufactured by Enfield Armory in Great Britain, weighed nine pounds, three ounces with the bayonet, and had a bore diameter of .577 inches. Firing a bullet similar to the minié ball, it was very accurate at 800 yards and became the most popular gun in the Confederate army after 1862. William Bennett Edwards, *Civil War Guns: The Complete Story of Federal and Confederate Small Arms* (Harrisburg, Penn.: Stackpole, 1962), 82, 87, 246–47.

91. Joe Johnston evacuated Yorktown on the Virginia Peninsula and reached Williamsburg early on 4 May 1862. He withdrew westward toward Richmond on Monday, 5 May, when fighting broke out east of Williamsburg. *OR,* 11, pt. 1:568–70, 602–6, pt. 3:486, 488, 492; Craig L. Symonds, *Joseph E. Johnston: A Civil War Biography,* 152–57; Long, *The Civil War Day by Day,* 206–9.

92. Miller Francis made an official request to the Office of the Adjutant General to resign on 6 March 1862. *CSR/Alabama,* 158:789; *CSR/General & Staff,* 182.

93. Edmund Kirby Smith (1824–93) assumed command of the District of East Tennessee on 8 March 1862 at Knoxville. *OR,* 10, pt. 1:1, pt. 2:320–21; Parks, *General Edmund Kirby Smith,* 8, 36, 155–56.

94. Miller Francis failed to raise a company. However, the Calhoun Guards under Captain Daniel P. Forney and the Dudley Snow Rangers under Captain Robert W. Draper were mustered into Morgan's 51st Alabama Mounted Infantry at Oxford, Calhoun County, Alabama, on 11 August 1862. *Jacksonville Republican,* 1, 29 May, 24 July 1862; William C. Davis, ed., *Confederate Generals,* 4:190; Miller, *Wheeler's Favorites,* 35–39, 46–49, 74, 77.

95. The first Confederate Conscription Act became law on 16 April 1862 and provided for a draft for military service of all white males between the ages of eighteen and thirty-five for three years' service or until the war ended. Current, *Encyclopedia of the Confederacy,* 1:396.

96. Thomas R. Rowland (1834–62) enlisted in the Pope Walker Guards at Jacksonville on 4 June 1861 but died on 16 October 1862 from a wound inflicted while serving in John H. Morgan's cavalry in the battles of Augusta. *CSR/Alabama,* 198:1378; *Jacksonville Republican,* 9 July 1864.

97. William Henry Forney was wounded in the right shoulder at Williamsburg and captured on 5 May 1862 while in a hospital at William and Mary College. He was exchanged, promoted to colonel, and returned to lead the 10th Alabama in the Fredericksburg and Chancellorsville campaigns. *OR,* 11, pt. 1:592, 593; *CSR/Alabama,* 193:504, 505; *Jacksonville Republican,* 22 May 1862.

98. John H. Caldwell was promoted to lieutenant colonel in the 10th Alabama on 27 April 1862 and resigned on 10 June 1863 to resume his duties as solicitor for the 10th Judicial Circuit of Alabama. *CSR/Alabama,* 192:235; *Jacksonville Republican,* 2 January 1862.

99. Union losses at Williamsburg included 456 killed, 1,410 wounded, and 373 missing,

for a total of 2,239. Confederate losses numbered 1,570 killed and wounded and 133 missing, for a total of 1,703. *OR,* 11, pt. 1:568, 569, 587; Long, *The Civil War Day by Day,* 207.

100. George Taliaferro Ward (1810–62) was commissioned colonel of the 2nd Florida Infantry Regiment on 12 July 1861 and was killed at Fort Magruder, near Williamsburg, Virginia, on 5 May 1862. *OR,* 11, pt. 1:593, 605, 609; Wakelyn, *Biographical Dictionary of the Confederacy,* 428; Krick, *Lee's Colonels,* 387.

101. Christopher Haynes Mott (1826–62) was commissioned colonel of the 19th Mississippi on 11 June 1861. He was killed on 5 May 1862 at the battle of Williamsburg when the 9th Alabama and 19th Mississippi captured twelve guns of the 1st U.S. Artillery and the 6th New York Battery. *OR,* 11, pt. 1:567, 593, 598; *CSR/General & Staff,* 184; Krick, *Lee's Colonels,* 282.

102. Thomas Evans Irby (1823–62) was promoted to lieutenant colonel and commander of the 8th Alabama on 20 March 1862 just prior to his death at Williamsburg on 5 May. *OR,* 11, pt. 1:567, 586, 588; *CSR/Alabama,* 175:965; Krick, *Lee's Colonels,* 205; Owen, *History of Alabama,* 3:885; Brewer, *Alabama,* 600–602.

103. Jubal Anderson Early (1816–94) received a severe wound in the right shoulder at the battle of Williamsburg on 5 May 1862. His brigade at Williamsburg took heavy casualties. *OR,* 11, pt. 1:567, 603, 606; Current, *Encyclopedia of the Confederacy,* 2:501; Ralph White Gunn, *24th Virginia Infantry,* 17–19.

104. William Richard Terry (1827–97) was commander of the 24th Virginia Infantry at the battle of Williamsburg and received a shot in the face that left the right side of it paralyzed. *OR,* 11, pt. 1:604, 609, 611; Current, *Encyclopedia of the Confederacy,* 4:1582; Gunn, *24th Virginia Infantry,* 19.

105. Peter Hairston, Jr., (1835–1915) was commissioned lieutenant colonel of the 24th Virginia in May 1861 and recovered from his wounds suffered at the battle of Williamsburg on 5 May 1862. *OR,* 11, pt. 1:604, 609, 611; Krick, *Lee's Colonels,* 172; Gunn, *24th Virginia Infantry,* 19, 81.

106. Duncan Kirkland McRae (1820–88) was the commander of the 5th North Carolina Infantry Regiment in Early's brigade at the battle of Williamsburg. He retired from active duty on 3 June 1862. *OR,* 11, pt. 1:603, 604, 606, 608, 609, 962, 964; John H. Eicher and David J. Eicher, *Civil War High Commands* (Stanford: Stanford University Press, 2001), 510.

107. Captain Thomas J. Hardin was in command of Company I, 19th Mississippi, at Williamsburg. Despite McRae's criticism, Hardin was praised by Brigadier General Wilcox and others for gallantry on the field at Williamsburg. *OR,* 11, pt. 1:593, 600.

108. Fresh outbreaks of measles and mumps seemed to follow new military units to their first field camps. Samuel C. Kelly to Amie P. Kelly, Knoxville, Tenn., 14 May 1862, Kelly Letters; Cunningham, *Doctors in Gray,* 188–89, 215, 268.

109. James M. White was left behind to recover from the measles, and William T. Alexander and James H. Niman were left to recover from the mumps. *CSR/Alabama,* 332:32, 335:841, 336:1243.

110. William C. Patterson refused the appointment as surgeon of the 30th Alabama but received promotions to major and lieutenant colonel ahead of John Francis. Ibid., 335:878; Kelly, "A History of the Thirtieth Alabama Volunteers," 120, 168–69.

111. Leadbetter telegraphed Samuel Cooper (1798–1876), adjutant and inspector general of the Confederate Army, on 19 May 1862 requesting that Jim Francis be commissioned and appointed post commissary at Chattanooga. Leadbetter to Cooper, Chattanooga, 19 May 1862, Francis-Martin Family Papers.

112. John Horace Forney was appointed commander of the Department of Alabama and

West Florida at Mobile in April 1862 and requested Tom Francis's assignment to his staff as assistant commissary of subsistence. *CSR/General & Staff,* 98; *OR,* 6:663, 880–81, 886, 889; Bergeron, *Confederate Mobile,* 24–27.

113. Daniel W. Warlick enlisted as a twenty-four-year-old private in the Sallie Walker Boys at Jacksonville on 5 March 1862. He was paroled as a captain at Salisbury, North Carolina, on 2 May 1865. *CSR/Alabama,* 336:1221.

114. J. L. Mattison enlisted as a twenty-three-year-old private in the Sallie Walker Boys at Jacksonville on 5 March 1862 and was promoted to quartermaster sergeant. Ibid., 334:741.

115. Edward T. Clark enlisted as an eighteen-year-old private in the Sallie Walker Boys at Jacksonville on 5 March 1862. He was paroled at Salisbury, North Carolina, on 2 May 1865. Ibid., 332:247.

116. No compiled service records were found for Hop Francis. However, several miscellaneous files, official and family correspondence documented his service with the Confederate commissary bureau. Unfiled Papers & Slips, Roll 135, No. 5573; Francis-Martin Family Papers.

117. David R. Reaves and J. W. Reaves enlisted in the Sallie Walker Boys at Jacksonville on 5 March 1862. No service records were found for a third Reaves in the 30th Alabama. *CSR/Alabama,* 335:968–69.

118. Clinton, Tennessee, county seat for Anderson County, is located about 18 miles northwest of Knoxville. *Tennessee: A Guide to the State,* 336.

119. Big Creek Gap, Tennessee, was a small town located in Powell's Valley at the eastern base of the Cumberland Mountains some thirty-five miles southwest of Cumberland Gap. Connelly, *Army of the Heartland,* 14–15, 89, 189, 211; *Tennessee: A Guide,* 334–35.

120. Alexander Welch Reynolds (1817–76), a native of Virginia and an 1838 West Point graduate, was sent to support Edmund Kirby Smith in the Department of East Tennessee in the winter of 1862. *OR,* 16, pt. 2:682, 690–91, 699, 701, 712–13, 735–36; Connelly, *Army of the Heartland,* 187–88; Current, *Encyclopedia of the Confederacy,* 3:1322.

121. Campbell Wallace, a resident of Knoxville, Tennessee, was listed in the 1860 federal census as the president of the East Tennessee & Georgia Railroad. He owned real estate valued at $46,000 and a personal estate of $10,000. *Eighth Census/Tennessee,* 11:249; Black, *Railroads of the Confederacy,* 70, 106, 126.

122. Tom Francis was appointed to the rank of major and commissary for the Department of Alabama and West Florida at Mobile on 29 April 1862. *CSR/General & Staff,* 98.

123. Leadbetter formally ordered Tom Francis to report to Forney at Mobile on 13 June 1862. Ibid.

124. William Henry Forney remained a prisoner of war until paroled at Fort Monroe, Virginia, on 29 July 1862. *OR,* 11, pt. 1:592, 593; *CSR/General & Staff,* 96; *Jacksonville Republican,* 22 May 1862.

Chapter 4

1. Samuel C. Kelly to Amie P. Kelly, Camp near Readyville, Tenn., 18 December 1862, Kelly Letters.

2. Long, *The Civil War Day by Day,* 228; Parks, *General Edmund Kirby Smith,* 175, 188–90.

3. *Jacksonville Republican,* 14 August 1862.

4. *OR,* 16, pt. 2:677–79, 682–86, 693; Connelly, *Army of the Heartland,* 189–90; Kelly, "A History of the Thirtieth Alabama Volunteers," 128; Francis-Martin Family Papers.

5. *OR,* 16, pt. 2:730–31, 734; John Witherspoon DuBose, "The Thirtieth Alabama

Regiment," 1–4, Confederate Regimental History Files; Kelly, "A History of the Thirtieth Alabama Volunteers," 128–29.

6. *OR,* 16, pt. 2:323, 341, 747; Parks, *General Edmund Kirby Smith,* 200–202; *Tennesseans in the Civil War,* 1:179.

7. *CSR/Alabama,* 445:443.

8. Thomas Lawrence Connelly, *Autumn of Glory: The Army of Tennessee, 1862–1865,* 13; Miller, *Wheeler's Favorites,* 2–3.

9. *OR,* 16, pt. 2:741–49, 751–56, 777–78, 860, pt. 1:997–1002; Connelly, *Army of the Heartland,* 211–18; Parks, *General Edmund Kirby Smith,* 200–207.

10. Long, *The Civil War Day by Day,* 276; Connelly, *Army of the Heartland,* 256–70.

11. Samuel C. Kelly to Amie P. Kelly, Cumberland Gap, 23 October 1862, and [Tazewell, Tenn], 25 October 1862, Kelly Letters.

12. *OR,* 16, pt. 1:898, 935–36, 940–41; Connelly, *Army of the Heartland,* 266–70, 279–80; Long, *The Civil War Day by Day,* 277–81; Francis-Martin Family Papers.

13. *CSR/Alabama,* 158:789; Francis-Martin Family Papers.

14. *CSR/Alabama,* 445:443.

15. *OR,* 16, pt. 2:733, pt. 1:984; DuBose, "The Thirtieth Alabama Regiment," 13

16. *CSR/General & Staff,* 98; Unfiled Papers & Slips, 135:5573; Francis-Martin Family Papers; Bergeron, *Confederate Mobile,* 25–26.

17. Connelly, *Autumn of Glory,* 28–29; John A. Wyeth, *That Devil Forrest: Life of General Nathan Bedford Forrest,* 90–125; Francis-Martin Family Papers.

18. Connelly, *Autumn of Glory,* 26–28; Miller, *Wheeler's Favorites,* 3–5; Peter Cozzens, *No Better Place to Die: The Battle of Stones River,* 47, 51–52, 55, 231; James Lee McDonough, *Stones River: Bloody Winter in Tennessee,* 72, 254.

19. Connelly, *Autumn of Glory,* 40–41; Cozzens, *The Battle of Stones River,* 47; McDonough, *Stones River,* 33, 36–37; Miller, *Wheeler's Favorites,* 3–4; Samuel C. Kelly to Amie P. Kelly, Camp near Readyville, Tenn., 18 December 1862, Kelly Letters; Francis-Martin Family Papers.

20. *OR,* 20, pt. 2:464, 467, pt. 1:668, 688–91, 705–7, 711–12, 725, 734–35, 753–55, 763–66, 781–87, 793, 795, 797, 812–13, 844–53, 856–57, 917–22, 926–27, 944, 969; Connelly, *Autumn of Glory,* 44–66; McDonough, *Stones River,* 74–162, 170–201.

21. *OR,* 20, pt. 1:682–83, 691–92, 700–701; Connelly, *Autumn of Glory,* 66–69; Cozzens, *The Battle of Stones River,* 199–202; McDonough, *Stones River,* 213–17; Francis-Martin Family Papers.

22. Calvin C. Turner, James N. Bagley, James B. Moore, John A. Rutledge, and J. E. Seiber enlisted as privates in the Sallie Walker Boys at Jacksonville on 5 March 1862. H. H. Pitts and Namon V. Stephens enlisted as privates at Talladega on 24 March 1862. Muster Roll of Captain John C. Francis Company Ala. Volunteers, 30th Regiment (P.A.), Camp Curry near Talladega, Alabama, 29 March 1862, Confederate Muster Roll Collection.

23. John W. Carpenter, William J. Reynolds, T. J. Powers, Robert P. Alexander, James Marion Smith, William N. Champion, Daniel W. Beacham, Manning K. Kimbrell, J. S. Hollingsworth, and Wylie Carpenter enlisted in the Sallie Walker Boys at Jacksonville on 5 March 1862. Charles H. Woodruff, Thomas S. Finch, H. J. Page, Joseph C. Harmon, and W. F. R. Shurbutt enlisted as privates on 8 March and 8 May 1862 at Jacksonville or at Camp Curry. "Baird" was one of two brothers, E. B. Baird or W. W. Baird, who enlisted as privates at Jacksonville on 5 March 1862. *CSR/Alabama,* 332:36, 74, 76, 95, 226, 228, 245, 333:378, 567, 508, 334:637, 335:866, 937, 972, 1036, 1069, 336:1069, 1208, 1280.

24. Thomas E. Poss, John Milner, David L. Roberts, and Thomas Warren enlisted as pri-

vates in the Sallie Walker Boys at Jacksonville on 5 March 1862. Benjamin F. Garvin enlisted as a private at Talladega on 24 March 1862, and William T. Clem, a farrier by trade, enlisted as a private in Company B at a later date. "Dowdle" was one of two brothers, James W. Dowdle or John F. Dowdle, who enrolled as privates at Jacksonville on 5 March 1862. Ibid., 332:249, 333:311, 431, 334:813, 335:935, 987, 336:1222.

25. Mumps and measles reduced the 30th Alabama from approximately 900 soldiers to 400 by 3 June 1862. Samuel C. Kelly to Amie P. Kelly, Cumberland Gap, Tenn., 3 June 1862, Kelly Letters.

26. William B. Redman, a thirty-two-year-old private, enlisted in the Sallie Walker Boys at Jacksonville on 5 March 1862; he was left at Camp Curry because of sickness and given a furlough home to recover. *CSR/Alabama,* 335:965.

27. Carter Littlepage Stevenson (1817–88), a native of Virginia and an 1838 West Point graduate, was commander of the Second Brigade in the Department of East Tennessee. *OR,* 10, pt. 2:573; Current, *Encyclopedia of the Confederacy,* 4:1545; DuBose, "The Thirtieth Alabama Regiment," 1–3.

28. On 10 June 1862 the Second Brigade strength was reported to be 3,725 present for duty and 5,275 as an aggregate present and absent. *OR,* 16: pt. 2:715.

29. Bill was a free Black servant hired by John Francis to assist with camp duties. His monthly pay of $10 was a dollar less than a private earned per month in the Confederate army. Rollins, *Black Southerners in Gray,* 10–11. See also Robert E. Greene, *Black Defenders of America, 1775–1973* (Chicago: Johnson Publishing Company, Inc., 1977), 53–102.

30. "Miss No. 1" was apparently a reference to John's horse.

31. John W. Carpenter recovered and was captured at the battle of Baker's Creek on 16 May 1863 and exchanged on 4 July 1863. *CSR/Alabama,* 332:226.

32. Wylie Carpenter submitted his resignation on 22 June 1862. C. H. Gorman, assistant surgeon for the 30th Alabama, certified that Carpenter was incapable of performing his duties. Ibid., 228.

33. James Marion Smith received a certificate of disability for discharge on 11 August 1862. He recovered and served with the 30th Alabama until his capture at the battle of Baker's Creek on 16 May 1863. Ibid., 336:1069.

34. T. J. Powers and William J. Reynolds recovered and continued their service with the 30th Alabama. Ibid., 335:937, 972.

35. Robert P. Alexander recovered and continued to serve as a wagon master for the regiment. Ibid., 332:36.

36. Charles H. Woodruff and William H. Walker recovered from their illnesses and served with the 30th Alabama through the Vicksburg campaign in 1863. Ibid., 336:1279.

37. The 4-foot 9-inch William N. Champion received a certificate of disability for discharge on 18 November 1862 because of his "youth & feebleness." Ibid., 332:245.

38. John W. Glover recovered and served in Company B, 30th Alabama, until he completed a "form for a retiring soldier" at Smithfield, North Carolina, on 3 April 1865. Ibid., 333:444.

39. John Milner and David Roberts recovered from the mumps at Clinton, Tennessee, but they were discharged for disability within the next three months. Ibid., 334:813, 335:987.

40. James N. Bagley was left at Big Creek Gap, Tennessee, and recovered to serve Company B, 30th Alabama until wounded and captured at the battle of Baker's Creek on 16 May 1863. He was exchanged on 17 July 1863 and paroled at Meridian, Mississippi, on 10 May 1865. Ibid., 332:69

41. Robert F. Allen survived his illness at Cumberland Gap but died at Grant Hospital in Atlanta, Georgia, on 1 February 1863. Ibid., 41.

42. John Whaley (Whatley), a twenty-two-year-old private in the Sallie Walker Boys, recovered to serve the 30th Alabama beyond East Tennessee. Ibid., 336:1238.

43. N. D. S. Culbreath recovered, but he was wounded and captured at the battle of Baker's Creek on 16 May 1863. Ibid., 332:283.

44. Thomas Jefferson Downing survived the mumps at Cumberland Gap and the surrender at Vicksburg on 4 July 1863. Ibid., 333:313.

45. While they survived the mumps and returned to duty, Thomas E. Poss died in Kentucky on 4 November 1862; W. H. Gennings died at Vicksburg on 7 February 1863; Joseph C. Harmon "died on or about" 31 March 1863 at Vicksburg; and L. D. Moses died at Vicksburg on 1 June 1863. Ibid., 433, 508, 334:822, 335:935.

46. Johnson R. Kirby, W. T. Hutchinson, R. J. Copeland, and William J. Clem recovered from their illnesses and served with Company B, 30th Alabama, through several campaigns, including Vicksburg, Atlanta, and Nashville. Ibid., 332:249, 266, 333:598, 334:643.

47. Union troops from the Third Division, Army of the Ohio, shelled Chattanooga from north of the Tennessee River on the afternoon of 7 June 1862 and for about three hours on the morning of 8 June. *OR,* 10, pt. 1:919–21, pt. 2:633, 634; Parks, *General Edmund Kirby Smith,* 181–82; Long, *The Civil War Day by Day,* 223.

48. While one Union report claimed 100 Confederates killed and wounded and 18 prisoners, Edmund Kirby Smith reported, "Our loss 3 wounded" and Union losses at 8 killed and the abandonment of one 4-inch rifle brass cannon. *OR,* 10, pt. 1:920–22.

49. There were two skirmishes near Wilson's Gap, Tennessee, on 10 and 18 June 1862, but Company B was not involved. Ibid., 53, 77; Long, *The Civil War Day by Day,* 225, 228.

50. Stevenson's division concentrated near Morristown, Tennessee, about 42 miles northeast of Knoxville on the East Tennessee & Virginia Railroad, under orders to make a stand near Bean's Station and Clinch Mountain. *OR,* 10, pt. 1:692–94, 697–98, 700–701; Parks, *General Edmund Kirby Smith,* 189–90.

51. Edmund Kirby Smith ordered the evacuation of Cumberland Gap, which was accomplished by Carter L. Stevenson on 18 June 1862. Kirby Smith was determined to prevent a Union advance on Chattanooga. *OR,* 16, pt. 1:680–81.

52. J. N. Baugh, John W. Gidley, and William N. Champion were sent to Morristown, Tennessee, on 21 June 1862 to recover from their illnesses. *CSR/Alabama,* 332:88, 245, 333:434.

53. William B. Redman was listed as a patient at Fair Grounds Hospital at Knoxville on 22 November 1862. Ibid., 335:965.

54. S. V. Putman died of an unspecified disease on 1 January 1863. Ibid., 947.

55. John Whaley (Whatley), a twenty-two-year-old private, recovered from his broken arm but was killed during the siege of Vicksburg on 5 June 1863. Ibid., 336:1238.

56. Tazewell, county seat of Claiborne County, was the center of a pro-Union county with few slaves and had voted 1,242 to 250 against secession. *OR,* 10, pt. 2:389–90; Groce, *Mountain Rebels,* 36–37.

57. Morristown, county seat of Hamblen County, is located in a valley enclosed by the Clinch Mountains. *Tennessee: A Guide,* 301.

58. William L. Blackford was listed as the surgeon in the compiled service records for the 30th Alabama. *CSR/Alabama,* 332.

59. The two batteries in Stevenson's second brigade were the Eufaula (Alabama) Light Artillery, commanded by Lieutenant W. A. McTyer, and the Cherokee Artillery from Rome, Georgia, commanded by Captain J. G. Yeiser. *OR,* 16, pt. 2:697–98, 715, 719, 984.

60. Robert P. Alexander enlisted as a thirty-five-year-old private in the Sallie Walker Boys at Jacksonville on 5 March 1862 for the war. *CSR/Alabama,* 332:32.

61. Thomas J. Powers enlisted as a twenty-four-year-old private in the Sallie Walker Boys at Jacksonville on 5 March 1862. His brother, J. A. Powers, was also a private in Company B and was paroled at Salisbury, North Carolina, on 2 May 1865. Ibid., 335:936–37.

62. George W. Morgan, commander of Union forces at Cumberland Gap, sent greetings to Edmund Kirby Smith, his old West Point friend, and later a personal note and two bottles of wine. Parks, *General Edmund Kirby Smith,* 190–91.

63. George W. Vansant enlisted in the Sallie Walker Boys at Jacksonville on 5 March 1862 and was elected second lieutenant. He cited physical disability in his letter of resignation on 25 June 1862 but apparently personal differences prompted his resignation. *CSR/Alabama,* 336:1198.

64. Taul Bradford, a native of Talladega, was second in command to Colonel Charles M. Shelley of the 30th Alabama. There was some personal animosity between Bradford and the Calhoun County officers in the 30th Alabama. Ibid., 332:152.

65. In 1862, Rutledge, Tennessee, was a small village in the shadows of the Clinch Mountains and county seat of Grainger County some forty miles northeast of Knoxville. *Tennessee: A Guide,* 312, 314.

66. James E. Rains (1833–62), colonel of the 11th Tennessee, served as brigade commander under Carter L. Stevenson at Cumberland Gap. *CSR/Tennessee,* 162:1422; *OR,* 10, pt. 1:44–45, pt. 2:356–57.

67. Seth Maxwell Barton (1829–1900), a Virginia native and an 1849 West Point graduate, was commander of the Third Brigade in Carter L. Stevenson's First Division, Army of East Tennessee. *OR,* 10, pt. 1:58, 60–61, 593; Current, *Encyclopedia of the Confederacy,* 1:136.

68. On 5–6 August 1862, several regiments from Barton's brigade and Colonel Thomas H. Taylor's brigade intercepted Colonel John F. DeCourcy's Union force with 200 wagon loads of forage near Tazewell. *OR,* 16, pt. 1:694, 835–36, pt. 2:7, 323, 341; *Tennesseans in the Civil War,* 1:179.

69. William Warren was listed in the 1860 census as a forty-eight-year-old farmer, and his son, Thomas Warren, was a twenty-year-old private in Company B, 30th Alabama. *1860 Federal Census/Alabama,* 2:372; *CSR/Alabama,* 336:1222.

70. William Wallace Gordon was commander of the 11th Tennessee cavalry battalion, composed of six companies, which was officially organized on 8 January 1862. *CSR/Tennessee,* 46:200; *Tennesseans in the Civil War,* 1:32–33; *OR,* 16, pt. 1:836, pt. 2:715, 984.

71. Thomas Hart Taylor (1825–1901), a native of Kentucky, commanded a brigade in Stevenson's division. *OR,* 16, pt. 2:685–86, 735, 715, 719, 984; Current, *Encyclopedia of the Confederacy,* 4:1572; *Tennesseans in the Civil War,* 1:179.

72. While the telegraph came into general use during the Civil War, the Union military telegraph service was more extensive than the Confederate service, some 15,000 miles compared to 1,000 miles established by Confederate forces. Current, *Encyclopedia of the Confederacy,* 4:1573.

73. Lucius C. Mitchell returned to the sutler trade with the 30th Alabama after his brief service in the 10th Alabama. *CSR/Alabama,* 196:1496, 197:1089; *Jacksonville Republican,* 14 November 1861.

74. Confederate forces invested the Cumberland Gap area on the Tennessee side on 12–13 August 1862 and began to threaten Union General Morgan's position at Cumberland Gap. *OR,* 16, pt. 1:937–39, 993, 999, 1001, pt. 2:747–49, 767, 751–56, 777–78.

75. The large smoke reported by John Francis was the extra supplies and equipment

burned by Union forces at Cumberland Gap in preparation for their retreat. Ibid., pt. 1:860–61, 992–96, 999, 1001.

76. Confederate forces under Robert E. Lee defeated the Union Army of Virginia under John Pope (1822–92) in the battle of Second Manassas on 29–30 August 1862. *OR,* 12, pt. 2:20–50, 551–60, 563–68; Long, *The Civil War Day by Day,* 257–58.

77. Confederate cavalry under John S. Scott entered the state capital, Frankfort, Kentucky, on 3 September 1862 and raised the flag of the 1st Louisiana cavalry over the capitol. *OR,* 16, pt. 1:938, pt. 2:766–67, 769, 777–78, 796; Parks, *General Edmund Kirby Smith,* 206–17; Long, *The Civil War Day by Day,* 254–61.

78. David L. Roberts enlisted in the Sallie Walker Boys at Jacksonville on 5 March 1862, and on 10 July 1862 John Francis signed his application for discharge and certificate of disability at a camp near Rutledge, Tennessee. *CSR/Alabama,* 335:987.

79. Jesse Harris, a twenty-year-old private in Company G, 10th Alabama, was killed at Second Manassas on 30 August 1862. Ibid., 194:670; *Jacksonville Republican,* 18 September, 13 November 1862.

80. Cornelius "Neel" Littlejohn, a nineteen-year-old private in Company G, 10th Alabama, was killed at Second Manassas "on or about" 31 August 1862. *CSR/Alabama,* 196:925; *Jacksonville Republican,* 18 September, 13 November 1862.

81. Moses Lee raised a volunteer company, Moore Rifles, 48th Alabama, and was killed at the battle of Second Manassas on 30 August 1862. *CSR/Alabama,* 170:580; *OR,* 12, pt. 2:816; *Jacksonville Republican,* 26 June, 18 September 1862.

82. Judge Alexander Woods routinely filed claims to recover unpaid salaries and other benefits due to the families of deceased soldiers from Calhoun County. See *Jacksonville Republican* (1861–65) and enclosures in Woods to John C. Francis, 15 September 1863, Francis-Martin Family Papers.

83. With no bread for his men and no forage for his animals, George W. Morgan ordered the evacuation of Cumberland Gap on 16 September 1862. *OR,* 16, pt. 1:992–96, 999.

84. James H. Finch served with the 30th Alabama until his death near Jonesborough, Georgia, on 31 August 1864. "Last Words of Lieut. J. H. Finch," 30th Alabama, Confederate Regimental History Files; *CSR/Alabama,* 333:377.

85. Green B. Skelton enlisted in the Sallie Walker Boys at Jacksonville on 5 March 1862. He was severely wounded on 26 May 1864 and resigned as second lieutenant in Company B, 30th Alabama, on 14 December 1864. Ibid., 335:1053; *Jacksonville Republican,* 20 August 1864.

86. David M. Anderson recruited the Isbell Guards mustered in as Company C, 30th Alabama, at Camp Curry. He was shot through the left lung at the battle of Baker's Creek, Mississippi, on 16 May 1863 and died 17 May at Roberts' Hospital, fifteen miles west of Clinton, Mississippi. *CSR/Alabama,* 332:45; *Jacksonville Republican,* 4 July 1863.

87. The Union retreat from Cumberland Gap was completed under the cover of darkness on 17 September 1862 and was announced to the nearby Confederate forces when Lieutenant Colonel George W. Gallup destroyed the remaining buildings and blew up the principal magazine. *OR,* 16, pt. 1:992–96, pt. 2:844–47, 850–53.

88. C. D. Phillips, 52nd Georgia, Barton's brigade in Stevenson's division, became commander of the 52nd Georgia at Vicksburg. Ibid., 16, pt. 2:715, 719, 984; 17, pt. 1:668, 678, 697, pt. 2:824.

89. Robert F. Allen and Hamilton Allen were brothers from Jacksonville, but their service records do not document a promotion to corporal for either brother. *CSR/Alabama,* 332:39, 41.

90. Namon V. Stephens (Stevens) enlisted as a seventeen-year-old private in Company B, 30th Alabama, at Talladega on 24 March 1862. Ibid., 336:1108.

91. Stevenson's division marched into Kentucky a few days after occupying Cumberland Gap in pursuit of George W. Morgan's retreating Union forces. *OR,* 16, pt. 2:719, 920, 922–23, 925–28.

92. Fielding Snow operated a tan yard in Jacksonville and was listed in the 1860 census as a fifty-three-year-old farmer with real estate valued at $5,000 and a personal estate valued at $10,000. *Eighth Census/Alabama,* 2:293.

93. Mobile Bay was captured by Admiral David Farragut's fleet on 5 August 1864, but Mobile was not occupied until 13 April 1865 by Union forces under General Edward R. S. Canby (1817–73). McMillan, *The Alabama Confederate Reader,* 297–99, 432–33.

94. Unfortunately none of John Francis's Kentucky letters survived. Francis-Martin Family Papers.

95. Camp Dick Robinson was located south of Lexington, Kentucky, and was used by pro-Unionist Kentuckians for training and arming pro-Union forces. Connelly, *Army of the Heartland,* 44, 87.

96. Sam White and J. R. McElreath recovered and returned to active duty. *CSR/Alabama,* 334:773, 336:1244.

97. Thomas E. Poss enlisted as a thirty-year-old private in the Sallie Walker Boys at Jacksonville on 5 March 1862 and died in Kentucky on 4 November 1862. Ibid., 335:935.

98. William N. Champion was one of several Confederate soldiers captured by Union forces in Kentucky and was declared exchanged on 11 January 1863. Ibid., 332:245.

99. J. N. Baugh placed a "Notice" in the *Jacksonville Republican* on 30 October 1862 requesting that clothing be delivered no later than 15 November 1862. *CSR/Alabama,* 332:88.

100. John Francis's request for blankets and clothing from home became commonplace after the first year of the war. Francis-Martin Family Papers; Wiley, *The Life of Johnny Reb,* 113–14.

101. The Kentucky campaign ended at the battle of Perryville on 8 October 1862, and Bragg's and Kirby Smith's forces withdrew southeast through Cumberland Gap. *OR,* 16, pt. 1:898, pt. 2:927–28, 935–37, 939–45, 949–51, 958–60, 963–77; Connelly, *Army of the Heartland,* 266–70, 279–80; Long, *The Civil War Day by Day,* 273–81.

102. Bragg began planning his Middle Tennessee campaign within days after retreating from Kentucky. His plans were approved and confirmed by Adjutant General Samuel Cooper in Richmond on 1 November 1862. Connelly, *Autumn of Glory,* 13–15; *OR,* 30, pt. 2:384–86.

103. Jim Francis apparently purchased a pony for his youngest brother, nine-year-old Charles Henry Francis, whose birthday was 9 October 1862. Major Brooks remains unidentified. Francis-Martin Family Papers.

104. Joseph Hugh Francis enlisted as a private in Company A, 51st Alabama Mounted Infantry, at Jacksonville on 11 August 1862. His service records indicate that he was detailed to the commissary department at Chattanooga. *CSR/Alabama,* 445:443.

105. Jim Francis's postscript to his father was the first of several conversations regarding Mary Emma Francis attending Centenary Institute. Francis-Martin Family Papers.

106. During the third quarter of 1862, 1 July–6 September 1862, Hop Francis was listed as a storekeeper and continued on special detail to the commissary bureau under his brother Major Tom Francis at Mobile. Unfiled Papers & Slips, 135:5573.

107. Lenoir's Station, present-day Lenoir City, Tennessee, was located on the East Tennessee & Georgia Railroad some 25 miles south of Knoxville. *Tennessee: A Guide,* 305.

108. William M. Weir enlisted as a forty-four-year-old private in the Sallie Walker Boys at Jacksonville on 5 March 1862 and was detailed to the quartermaster service under Captain Euclid Johnson. *CSR/Alabama,* 334:607, 336:1234.

109. William A. Jarrel enlisted as a thirty-two-year-old private in Company B, 30th Alabama, at Camp Curry near Talladega on 26 March 1862. He was listed in the 1860 census as a farm laborer with a personal estate of $100, a wife, Loucinda, and six children under the age of ten. Ibid., 334:601; *Eighth Census/Alabama,* 2:446.

110. James Marion Smith was issued a certificate of disability for discharge at Tazewell, Tennessee, on 11 August 1862. *CSR/Alabama,* 336:1069.

111. David L. Roberts received a discharge for disability on 10 July 1862. Judge Woods provided John Francis with a power of attorney to collect Roberts's unpaid salary and other benefits. Ibid., 335:987.

112. Because of its location, Centenary Institute was considered a safe refuge for young southern ladies who lived in the more exposed areas of Alabama and surrounding states. McDonald, *Beginnings . . . of the University of North Alabama,* 38.

113. John Francis was vaccinated for smallpox. Samuel Preston Moore, surgeon general, directed that all hospital patients be vaccinated for smallpox on 6 February 1862. Three months later he issued instructions for the vaccination of all soldiers. Cunningham, *Doctors in Gray,* 197.

114. William T. Wood raised Company G, 30th Alabama, in Randolph County, and was mustered in at Camp Curry near Talladega on 31 March 1862. Muster Roll of Captain William T. Wood Company Ala. Volunteers, 30th Regiment (P.A.), Camp Curry near Talladega, Ala., 31 March 1862, Confederate Muster Roll Collection; *CSR/Alabama,* 336:1278.

115. The receipt for the money sent by William Wood in November 1862 was lost, but other receipts for money delivered to family members in Jacksonville and Calhoun County can be found in the Francis-Martin Family Papers.

116. Camp Stewart's Creek was located south of Lavergne, Tennessee, on the Murfreesboro and Nashville pike about ten miles northwest of Murfreesboro. Stewart's Creek was one of several small streams that intersected the Murfreesboro turnpike and served as a defensive line for the Confederates until 26 December 1862. *OR,* 20, pt. 1:183–84, 958; Esposito, *West Point Atlas,* 1:77.

117. John Hunt Morgan (1825–64), a native of Lexington, Kentucky, was the commander of one of five cavalry brigades created by Bragg. *OR,* 20, pt. 1:132–58; Connelly, *Autumn of Glory,* 27–29.

118. Miller Francis purchased a lot from Richard G. Earle, a Jacksonville attorney, prior to his enlistment in 1861. *Eighth Census/Alabama,* 2:290; *Jacksonville Republican,* 1 November 1860.

119. Wartrace, Tennessee, was located on the Nashville and Chattanooga Railroad between Tullahoma and Murfreesboro. Connelly, *Autumn of Glory,* 113.

120. William "Jack" Roberts enlisted as a private in Company A, 51st Alabama, at Fort Pillow, Tennessee, on 22 March 1862. He was wounded at Lavergne, Tennessee, returned to active duty, and served until his parole at Talladega, Alabama, on 26 May 1865. *CSR/Alabama,* 447:1168.

121. Forrest and John Hunt Morgan under Bragg's cavalry reorganization were assigned to partisan service operating behind Union lines, raiding and disrupting communications and supplies. *OR,* 20, pt. 1:132–58, 657, 663, 672–73; Connelly, *Autumn of Glory,* 27.

122. James Montgomery was married to Elizabeth Jane Ingram, a younger sister to Amy

Ingram Francis. He was listed in the 1860 census as a forty-eight-year-old merchant living at Goshen, Cherokee County, Alabama, with real estate valued at $5,000 and a personal estate valued at $48,000. *Eighth Census/Alabama,* 3:281; Francis-Martin Genealogy Collection.

123. Pork was the primary meat supplied to Confederate soldiers. Shortages of pork and salt were common throughout the Confederate states by fall 1862. *Jacksonville Republican,* 30 May 1863, 2 March 1864; Massey, *Ersatz in the Confederacy,* 61.

124. David B. Stewart was listed in the 1860 census as a forty-one-year-old farmer living near Jacksonville. His son, Clark B. Stewart, was a private in Company A, 51st Alabama. *Eighth Census/Alabama,* 2:319; *CSR/Alabama,* 447:1342.

125. Elements of Joe Wheeler's (1836–1906) cavalry brigade, including the 1st Alabama, 3rd Alabama, and 51st Alabama, were involved in a skirmish with Union forces between Mill Creek and Lavergne, Tennessee. Union losses were 29 killed and wounded, and Confederate losses were 8 killed and wounded. *OR,* 20, pt. 1:15–19, 22–23, 16, pt. 2:613, 619, 938; Evans, *Confederate Military History: Alabama,* 8:351.

126. The 1st Alabama Cavalry was organized at Montgomery, Alabama, on 12 November 1861, with companies from Autauga, Butler, Calhoun, Dale, Mobile, Montgomery, Monroe, Morgan, Pike, and Tallapoosa counties. *OR,* 26, pt. 1:834, pt. 2:131, 157, 275, 402, 511; Brewer, *Alabama,* 677–78.

127. Charles H. Carter, a private in Company H, 51st Alabama, died on 7 November 1862. *CSR/Alabama,* 445:217.

128. John L. Meadows, a private in Company F, 51st Alabama, was the other soldier killed in November 1862. Ibid., 446:894.

129. Despite Miller Francis's comments, service records indicated William "Jack" Roberts recovered and served until paroled at Talladega, Alabama, on 26 May 1865. Ibid., 447:1168.

130. Camp Selby was located near Readyville, Tennessee, a small village 12 miles east of Murfreesboro. *Tennessee: A Guide,* 470; Esposito, *West Point Atlas,* 1:77.

131. "Mr. Nunnelley" was one of two brothers, Benjamin F. Nunnelly or Joseph Nunnelly, who were privates in Company B, 30th Alabama. *CSR/Alabama,* 335:854, 857.

132. William R. Rutledge enlisted as a forty-two-year-old private in the Sallie Walker Boys at Jacksonville on 5 March 1862. His service records were silent about his illness and absence, but he served until paroled at Talladega on 22 May 1865. Ibid., 1000.

133. Henry McBee raised the Ryan Guards, Company E, 30th Alabama, in March 1862 and was elected captain. He resigned on 2 September 1862 and was replaced by Captain Samuel C. Kelly. Ibid., 747; *Jacksonville Republican,* 27 February, 3 April 1862; Kelly, "A History of the Thirtieth Alabama Volunteers," 121, 123.

134. R. J. Martin, a tailor by occupation, enlisted as a forty-six-year-old private in the Sallie Walker Boys at Jacksonville on 5 March 1862. He was issued a certificate of disability and discharged for "chronic rheumatism" on 26 August 1862. *CSR/Alabama,* 334:726; *Jacksonville Republican,* 6 June 1861.

135. John Hays was listed in the 1860 census as an eighteen-year-old laborer living at Mount Polk, Calhoun County. No service records exist for John Hays in the 30th Alabama. *Eighth Census/Alabama,* 2:586; *CSR/Alabama,* 333:525–27.

136. Bridgeport, Jackson County, Alabama, was an important Confederate supply depot located west of Raccoon Mountain on the Tennessee River and on the Nashville & Chattanooga Railroad. Connelly, *Autumn of Glory,* 254–55; Esposito, *West Point Atlas,* 1:77 Owen, *History of Alabama,* 1:169.

137. Franklin Woodruff raised the Alexandria Rifles in May 1861 but resigned on 14 July

1862 at Richmond, Virginia, because of his age and illness. *CSR/Alabama,* 200:1726; *Jacksonville Republican,* 23 May 1861.

138. A rood is a British unit equal to seven or eight yards. Osnaburg, a coarse durable cotton fabric, was used for clothing, upholstery, or curtains. Brown drilling, a fairly heavy twilled cotton fabric, was probably used by the Francis women to make work clothes, uniforms, and ticking. *The Butterick Fabric Handbook: A Consumer's Guide to Fabrics for Clothing and Home Furnishings,* ed, Irene Cummings Kleeburg (New York: Buttrick Publishing, 1975), 96; Norma Hollen and Jane Sadler, *Textiles* (2d ed., 1955; New York: Macmillan Company, 1964), 146.

139. Spartan Allen, a Jacksonville resident, had two sons, Hamilton and Robert F. Allen, serving with the 30th Alabama. *Eighth Census/Alabama,* 2:411; *CSR/Alabama,* 332:39, 41.

140. Thomas C. Brown enlisted as a twenty-five-year-old private in Company I, 51st Alabama, at Selma, Alabama, on 8 June 1862. He received a discharge for disability on 9 January 1863. *CSR/Alabama,* 445:170.

141. The 51st Alabama was involved in skirmishes at Kimbrough's Mill, Carter's Farm, Dobbin's Ferry, and on the Nolensville Pike near Lavergne on 6–11 December 1862. *OR,* 20, pt. 1:2, 34–40, 73.

142. Hugh Francis was Dr. James C. Francis's younger brother, and Captain Miller "Tobe" Turney, Miller Francis's first cousin, was an assistant quartermaster with the 23rd Tennessee Infantry Battalion at Tullahoma, Tennessee. *Eighth Census/Tennessee,* 6:74, 80; *CSR/General & Staff,* 252; *CSR/Tennessee,* 111:1573.

143. On 26 December 1862, the Union army under William Starke Rosecrans (1819–98) moved out of Nashville and engaged pickets and elements of Bragg's forces along the roads between Nashville and Murfreesboro. *OR,* 20, pt. 1:184, 446, 448, 457–58, 464–66, 958, 961–62; Connelly, *Autumn of Glory,* 45.

144. John Tyler Morgan's 51st Alabama was in Wheeler's cavalry division under the command of Joe Wheeler, who was also Bragg's chief of cavalry. *OR,* 20, pt. 1:466; Connelly, *Autumn of Glory,* 27; Davis, *Confederate Generals,* 4:190; Cozzens. *No Better Place to Die,* 231.

Chapter 5

1. *OR,* 17, pt. 2:821–31; Samuel Carter III, *The Final Fortress: The Campaign for Vicksburg, 1862–1863,* 99–104.

2. Samuel C. Kelly to Amie P. Kelly, Four miles south of Vicksburg, on R.R., 5 January 1863, Kelly Letters.

3. Ibid.; *OR,* 17, pt. 2:826.

4. Samuel C. Kelly to Amie P. Kelly, In detached camps, at Four Mile Bridge, Vicksburg, 15 February 1863, Kelly Letters; ibid., 28 February 1863; *CSR/General & Staff,* 60; Kelly, "A History of the Thirtieth Alabama Volunteers," 133–34.

5. *CSR/Tennessee,* 339:1466.

6. Ibid., 340:526; *CSR/Mississippi,* 296:979; McDonald, *Beginnings . . . of the University of North Alabama,* 77–78.

7. McDonald, *Beginnings . . . of the University of North Alabama,* 11–12, 15, 19, 37–38, 72; Owen, *History of Alabama,* 1:215–16.

8. Owing to his continuing poor health, Forney was relieved as commander at Mobile by Bragg on 8 December 1862. *OR,* 20, pt. 2:403, 423; ibid., 15:899; *CSR/General & Staff,* 96.

9. *CSR/Alabama,* 158:789; *CSR/General & Staff,* 98.

10. *CSR/General & Staff,* 98.

11. *Eighth Census/Tennessee,* 6:74, 78; *Jacksonville Republican,* 9 July 1864; Francis-Martin Genealogy Collection.

12. *Jacksonville Republican,* 24 January, 16 May 1861, 11, 28 August 1862, 15 January, 5, 12 February 1863, 20 August 1864.

13. *OR,* 24, pt. 2:663, 678; Samuel C. Kelly to Amie P. Kelly, Near Port Gibson, 2 May 1863, Kelly Letters; Edwin Cole Bearss, *The Campaign for Vicksburg,* 2:253–59, 305–16, 348, 402–5.

14. *OR,* 24, pt. 2:678–82; Samuel C. Kelly to Amie P. Kelly, Near Port Gibson, 2 May 1863, Kelly Letters; Carter, *The Final Fortress,* 182–83; Bearss, *The Campaign for Vicksburg,* 2:402–7.

15. *OR,* 24, pt. 1:663, 672, 678–82; Samuel C. Kelly to Amie P. Kelly, Near Vicksburg, 6 May 1863, Kelly Letters; Bearss, *The Campaign for Vicksburg,* 2:348–49, 358–71; Kelly, "A History of the Thirtieth Alabama Volunteers," 135–39.

16. *OR,* 23, pt. 1:285–93; Wyeth, *That Devil Forrest,* 170–93; Long, *The Civil War Day by Day,* 337, 342, 344–45, 347; McMillan, *The Alabama Confederate Reader,* 186–89.

17. *OR,* 23, pt. 2:293; *Jacksonville Republican,* 9 May 1863; Wyeth, *That Devil Forrest,* 193–98; McMillan, *The Alabama Confederate Reader,* 199–200.

18. *Jacksonville Republican,* 9 May 1863.

19. *OR,* 24, pt. 1:261–65, pt. 2:93–8,101–6; Bearss, *The Campaign for Vicksburg,* 2:586–651.

20. *OR,* 24, pt. 2:148–58; Joseph Dill Alison, "War Diary of Dr. Joseph Dill Alison," 395, 398.

21. *OR,* 24, pt. 2:103.

22. Ibid., pt. 1:281–86, 330–31, pt. 2:326–28, pt. 3:423–24, 460, 478–95; *CSR/Alabama,* 333:401; Bearss, *The Campaign for Vicksburg,* 3:1279–94.

23. *OR,* 24, pt. 3:478–95; *CSR/Alabama,* 333:401; Bearss, *The Campaign for Vicksburg,* 3:1301–4.

24. *OR,* 24, pt. 3:1001–2, 1025; *CSR/Alabama,* 333:401; Bearss, *The Campaign for Vicksburg,* 3:1305–9; Black, *Railroads of the Confederacy,* 141.

25. Internal evidence indicates that this letter was written between 3 January and 6 January 1863, and a closing page is missing. Francis-Martin Family Papers.

26. Bragg lost one-fourth of his infantry on 15 December 1862 when President Davis ordered the transfer of Carter L. Stevenson's division to reinforce the Army of Vicksburg under John C. Pemberton (1814–81). *OR,* 17, pt. 2:800, 825; Connelly, *Autumn of Glory,* 40–41.

27. The 30th Alabama began leaving Middle Tennessee on 18 December 1862 for the three-week trip to Vicksburg, Mississippi. *OR,* 17, pt. 2:800, 825; Samuel C. Kelly to Amie P. Kelly, Camp near Readyville, Tenn., 18 December 1862, Kelly Letters.

28. Demopolis, Marengo County, Alabama, is located on the east bank of the Tombigbee River at its confluence with the Black Warrior River. Black, *Railroads of the Confederacy,* 74–75, 153–58.

29. John H. Forney was relieved as commander of the District of the Gulf on 8 December 1862 owing to his health problems and placed on leave to restore his physical condition. *CSR/General & Staff,* 96; *Jacksonville Republican,* 1 January 1863; *OR,* 15:899; *OR,* 20, pt. 2:403, 423; Bergeron, *Confederate Mobile,* 26–27.

30. John C. Pemberton, a native of Philadelphia and a West Point graduate, was appointed commander at Vicksburg by President Davis and assumed command of the Department of

Mississippi and East Louisiana on 14 October 1862. Current, *Encyclopedia of the Confederacy,* 3:1188–89.

31. Five companies of the 30th Alabama under command of John Francis arrived at Vicksburg on Sunday, 28 December 1862. Samuel C. Kelly to Amie P. Kelly, Four miles south of Vicksburg, on R.R., 5 January 1863, Kelly Letters.

32. Sherman's forces launched their assault near Snyder's Mill on Saturday, 27 December 1862, some ten miles northeast of Vicksburg on the Yazoo River. *OR,* 17, pt. 1:605–11, 625, 647–674; Long, *The Civil War Day by Day,* 300–307; Carter, *The Final Fortress,* 99–104.

33. Seth M. Barton was commander of the First Brigade, which included the 40th Georgia, 42nd Georgia, 43rd Georgia, and 52nd Georgia regiments and Capt. Joseph W. Anderson's artillery battery. *OR,* 17, pt. 1:676–77, pt. 2:806, 821, 824–25, 831; Current, *Encyclopedia of the Confederacy,* 4:1605.

34. The major Union assault came on Monday, 29 December 1862, at the Devil's Triangle on Chickasaw Bayou. *OR,* 17, pt. 1:667, 669, 682–83, 686, 689; Samuel C. Kelly to Amie P. Kelly, Four miles south of Vicksburg, on R.R., 5 January 1863, Kelly Letters.

35. On 4 January 1863, Sherman's forces came under the command of John Alexander McClernand, who launched an expedition against Fort Hindman, fifty miles up the Arkansas River. *OR,* 17, pt. 1:698–715, 721–41, 745–49, 754–63, 780–86.

36. Sherman's losses in the battle of Chickasaw Bayou included 208 killed, 1,005 wounded, and 563 missing out of approximately 31,000. Confederate losses included 63 killed, 134 wounded, and 10 missing out of a force of 14,000 engaged. Long, *The Civil War Day by Day,* 301.

37. George W. Morgan led the Third Division at the battle of Chickasaw Bayou, and one brigade under Colonel John F. De Courcey lost 355 killed, wounded, and missing. *OR,* 17, pt. 1:637–40, 651–60; Bearss, *The Campaign for Vicksburg,* 1:159–66, 179–204, 228.

38. Charles M. Shelley met Samuel C. Kelly's Company E and a second company at Meridian, Mississippi, and traveled by boxcars to Jackson, Mississippi. Samuel C. Kelly to Amie P. Kelly, Four miles south of Vicksburg, on R.R., 5 January 1863, Kelly Letters.

39. Mary Theresa Francis Turney (1809–79) was Dr. James C. Francis's sister and the widow of Hopkins Lacy Turney. She moved her three youngest children and her daughter-in-law from Winchester, Tennessee, to Jacksonville. Francis-Martin Genealogy Collection; *Eighth Census/Tennessee,* 6:78.

40. Decherd, Tennessee, a small depot on the Nashville & Chattanooga Railroad, was located at the intersection with the Winchester & Alabama Railroad. See 1861–65 map of Tennessee in *Atlas to Accompany the Official Records of the Union and Confederate Armies.*

41. Robert F. Allen was admitted to Grant Hospital in Atlanta, Georgia, on 20 January 1863 and died on 1 February. *CSR/Alabama,* 332:41.

42. Port Hudson, Louisiana, north of Baton Rouge and about 240 river miles south of Vicksburg, was considered the next most critical defensive position on the Mississippi River. *OR,* 24, pt. 1:41, 91, 201, 242–43, 246, pt. 2:439, 499, 501, 998; Carter, *The Final Fortress,* 83.

43. The 30th Alabama was in camps on the Southern Railroad of Mississippi, which connected west from Meridian through Jackson to Vicksburg. Black, *Railroads of the Confederacy,* 154.

44. Daniel Beacham, John M. Smith, and James N. Bagley recovered from their sickness, but John A. Rutledge died on 23 January 1863. *CSR/Alabama,* 332:69, 95, 335:1002, 336:1069.

45. Vicksburg was a prosperous river port with a population of 5,000 built on a series of

bluffs and rolling hills. Known locally as the "City of a Hundred Hills," Jefferson Davis referred to it as the "Gibralter of the West." Carter, *The Final Fortress,* 12, 18–20.

46. "Aunt Finney & family" are unidentified Francis kinsmen from Tennessee who sought refuge in Jacksonville.

47. Thirteen Union gunboats and 50 transports under Rear Admiral David Dixon Porter steamed up the Arkansas River to support John A. McClernand's successful expedition against Fort Hindman on 5–12 January 1863. *OR,* 17, pt. 1:612–13, 699, 706, 726, 754–56, 764, 779; Boatner, *The Civil War Dictionary,* 24–25.

48. Alexander Woods advertised "A Beautiful Residence and Town Lot For Sale" in the *Jacksonville Republican* in June 1860 and for next three years. *Jacksonville Republican,* 5 December 1861.

49. Jim Francis was referring to the Richard G. Earle lot and a property that Miller Francis was also interested in purchasing. Francis-Martin Family Papers.

50. D. F. Smith was listed in the 1860 census as thirty-one-year-old minister living in Jacksonville. Jim Crook remains unidentified. *Eighth Census/Alabama,* 2:296, 299.

51. George was one of six male slaves owned by Dr. James C. Francis listed in the 1860 federal slave schedule. Francis-Martin Family Papers; *Eighth Census/Alabama, Slave Schedule,* 1:265.

52. Samuel Hollingsworth Stout became post surgeon at Chattanooga on 22 March 1862 and medical director for the Army of Tennessee hospitals on 22 August 1862. Schroeder-Lein, *Confederate Hospitals on the Move,* 17, 26–27, 30–34, 41, 50–56, 60–61.

53. S. V. Putman enlisted as a private in Company B, 30th Alabama, at Camp Curry on 15 April 1862. His service records indicate that he died "of disease" on 1 January 1863. *CSR/Alabama,* 335:947.

54. Adam Ferdinand Naff, a native of Greene County, Tennessee, was a classmate of John Francis at Florence Wesleyan University during the 1860–61 academic year. *Eighth Census/Tennessee,* 8:337.

55. Adam Naff enlisted as a private in Company I, 60th Tennessee Mounted Infantry, at Newport, Tennessee, on 1 October 1862. He was detailed as a clerk in the commissary department of John C. Vaughn's brigade on 31 December 1862. *CSR/Tennessee,* 339:1466.

56. Henry C. Edington was listed in the junior class at Florence Wesleyan University for 1859–60. He enlisted as a private in Company I, 61st Tennessee Mounted Infantry, at Warrensburg, Tennessee, on 4 October 1862. Ibid., 340:526; McDonald, *Beginnings . . . of the University of North Alabama,* 77.

57. John Francis's letter to James Freeman Grant, editor and publisher of the *Jacksonville Republican,* appeared in the paper's 19 March 1863 issue.

58. The eight men lost to smallpox at the quarantine camp were John Rutledge, W. F. R. Shurbutt, James B. Moore, H. J. Page, Calvin C. Turner, William H. Gennings, John Willingham, and Thomas J. Proer. Their obituaries written by John Francis appeared in the *Jacksonville Republican* on 19 February and 19 March 1863.

59. Julia Clark Francis was visiting her elderly parents, John and Susan Clark, who lived near Monticello, Jasper County, Georgia. *Eighth Census/Georgia,* 9:252.

60. Dr. Courtney James Clark, Julia Francis's brother, was returning to his assignment as chief surgeon of the Third Alabama Hospital in Richmond, Virginia. *CSR/General & Staff,* 56.

61. According to the 1860 federal slave schedule, Miller Francis owned one slave house and

three other slaves, a seventeen-year-old female, a fourteen-year-old male, and an eleven-year-old female. *Eighth Census/Alabama, Slave Schedule,* 1:265.

62. Mary Miller "Minnie" Francis was fifteen months old, the third child and only daughter of Julia and Miller Francis. Francis-Martin Genealogy Collection.

63. Miller Francis remained on duty with the 51st Alabama in Wheeler's cavalry with Bragg's army in Middle Tennessee. *CSR/Alabama,* 158:789; Miller, *Wheeler's Favorites,* 6.

64. Henry A. Earns served as a private in Company G, 10th Alabama, until he was appointed collector of the tax-in-kind in Calhoun County, Alabama, in 1863. *CSR/Alabama,* 193:490; Richard D. Goff, *Confederate Supply,* 85–87.

65. Mary Francis was the thirteen-year-old daughter of Hugh Francis, who moved his family from Winchester, Tennessee, to Jacksonville as a refuge from the war. Harriet was apparently one of the Turney cousins who also sought refuge in Jacksonville. *Eighth Census/Tennessee,* 6:74.

66. Antoinette M. Milton was the wife of W. B. Milton, a twenty-nine-year-old merchant, in Selma, Alabama. *Eighth Census/Dallas County,* 4:840.

67. Dr. Richard Henderson Rivers, president of Centenary Institute, taught John Francis moral philosophy and belles lettres at FWU. McDonald, *Beginnings . . . of the University of North Alabama,* 15, 37–38, 72.

68. The Sallie Walker Boys were hit hard by smallpox. The eight deaths attributed to smallpox occurred between 23 January and 24 February 1863. Samuel C. Kelly to Amie P. Kelly, In detached camps, at Four Mile Bridge, Southern R.R., Vicksburg, 15 February 1863, Kelly Letters; *Jacksonville Republican,* 19 February, 19 March 1863.

69. David M. Anderson was commander of the Isbell Guards, Company C, 30th Alabama. *CSR/Alabama,* 332:45.

70. Jasper L. Hoke served in Company B, 30th Alabama, but there were no service records for Joe Hoke. *CSR/Alabama,* 333:564.

71. After John H. Forney was relieved at Mobile, Tom Francis requested a transfer for temporary duty with Major Theodore Johnston, chief of subsistence for Mississippi and East Louisiana. *CSR/General & Staff,* 98; Bergeron, *Confederate Mobile,* 27.

72. Daniel W. Warlick's bad eye was caused by smallpox pustules that formed either on his eyelids or the eye itself. He recovered without deep scarring or loss of sight. He was promoted to captain and paroled at Salisbury, North Carolina, on 2 May 1865. *CSR/Alabama,* 336:1221; G. C. Cook, *Manson's Tropical Diseases* (London: W. B. Saunders Company, Ltd., 1997), 274; Kurt J. Isselbacher et al. *Harrison's Principles of Internal Medicine* (New York: McGraw-Hill, Inc., 1994), 797.

73. The *Queen of the West* was sunk by Confederate gunners on the Red River near Fort DeRussy, Louisiana, on 14 February 1863. The *Indianola* was captured on 24 February near Palmyra Island below Vicksburg. *OR,* 24, pt. 1:18–9, 341–48, 361–70; Carter, *The Final Fortress,* 123–28.

74. John L. Irwin, a private in Company I, 21st Mississippi Infantry Regiment, was a former classmate at Florence Wesleyan University during the 1860–61 academic year. McDonald, *Beginnings . . . of the University of North Alabama,* 77–78.

75. Mary Abernathy was the fifteen-year-old daughter of Miles and Anna Abernathy and younger sister of Fannie Francis, Tom's wife. *Eighth Census/Alabama,* 2:297.

76. Anna Clark was the sixteen-year-old daughter of John R. Clark. Ibid., 292.

77. Elizabeth J. Montgomery was the daughter of Hezekiah and Amy Bussy Ingram and

Hezekiah Ingram, younger brother of Amy Ingram Francis. Francis-Martin Genealogy Collection.

78. In 1863, Spring Garden, Alabama, was a small community located between Jacksonville and Rome, Georgia. Remington and Kallsen, *Historical Atlas of Alabama,* 1:47.

79. Tullahoma, Tennessee, became the supply base and headquarters for Bragg's Army of Tennessee following its defeat at Murfreesboro. *OR,* 23, pt. 2:697–99, 760, 781–84; Connelly, *Autumn of Glory,* 68–69, 112–13.

80. The deserters reported by Jo Francis received a mild punishment. It was not uncommon for deserters to be executed in view of thousands of their former comrades. See Samuel C. Kelly to Amie P. Kelly, In camp with the brigade, one mile from Vicksburg, 7 March 1863, Kelly Letters.

81. Because of his position, Tom Francis provided his brother John Francis with foodstuffs and other items not readily available to Confederate forces at Vicksburg. Francis-Martin Family Papers.

82. Nathaniel P. Banks lead an expedition against Port Hudson, Louisiana, on 13–14 March 1863 to support Rear Admiral David G. Farragut's attempt to run the batteries at Port Hudson. *OR,* 24, pt. 3:104, 125, 668–69, 695; Long, *The Civil War Day by Day,* 326–28.

83. Farragut successfully ran the batteries at Port Hudson with his flagship sloop *Hartford* and the gunboat *Monongahela* on 14 March 1863. However, the *Richmond* was badly damaged and the *Mississippi* destroyed by fire. *OR,* 24, pt. 3:668–69, 672–73.

84. Despite his failure in March 1863, Port Hudson surrendered to Banks on 9 July 1863 following a six-week siege. *OR,* 24, pt. 1:201, 246, pt. 3:499, 501.

85. Ulysses S. Grant chose to move south of Vicksburg, drove through the Big Black River Valley via Port Gibson to Raymond and Jackson, and turned west to lay siege to Vicksburg. *OR,* 24, pt. 1:571–787; Bearss, *The Campaign for Vicksburg,* 2:317–559.

86. Grant attempted to construct a mile-long canal across De Soto Point opposite Vicksburg. However, Confederate cannon fire forced the Union to abandon the "Grant Canal" by late April 1863. *OR,* 24, pt. 1:70–5, 78; Bearss, *The Campaign for Vicksburg,* 1:436–49.

87. Henry M. Compton was chief surgeon of the Second District, Department of Mississippi and East Tennessee, at Vicksburg. *CSR/General & Staff,* 60; *CSR/Tennessee,* 257:362; *Tennesseans in the Civil War,* 1:246–47.

88. The sore eyes of Daniel W. Warlick and Thomas Littlejohn were caused by smallpox pustules on their eyelids. They recovered and served until paroled at Salisbury, North Carolina, on 2 May 1865. *CSR/Alabama,* 334:676, 336:1221.

89. Joseph C. Harmon enlisted in Company B on 6 May 1862 at Talladega. He died at Vicksburg "on or about" 31 March 1863. Ibid., 333:508.

90. W. R. Moore was captured at Vicksburg on 4 July 1863 and exchanged with other sick and wounded Confederate officers and soldiers at Fort Morgan on 22 July 1863. He was paroled at Talladega on 23 May 1865 by Brigadier General Morgan Henry Chrysler. Ibid., 334:811.

91. William J. Reynolds enlisted as a thirty-two-year-old private in the Sallie Walker Boys at Jacksonville on 5 March 1862. Ibid., 335:972.

92. Erysipelas was a common diagnosis during the Civil War. The term was used to describe both the primary skin disease and the inflammation that developed around wounds. It is an infectious skin disease characterized "by redness, swelling, vesicles, bullae, fever, pain, and lymphadenopathy." Kenneth N. Anderson et al., *Mosby's Medical, Nursing, and Allied Health Dictionary.* (St. Louis: Mosby, 1998), 583; Steiner, *Disease in the Civil War,* 222.

93. Confederate forces established two batteries, each with four guns, on the bluffs at Warrenton six miles below Vicksburg. The batteries shelled Union gunboats and transports through late April 1863. *OR,* 24, pt. 1:336–38, 480, 517, 565–66, 568–70; Bearss, *The Campaign for Vicksburg,* 1:623, 2:72, 78–9.

94. Four Union ironclads, *Carondelet, Cincinnati, Mound City,* and *Pittsburg,* under Rear Admiral David Dixon Porter were temporarily trapped by Confederate forces on Deer Creek on Sunday, 22 March 1863. *OR,* 24, pt. 1:67–68, 431–67; Bearss, *The Campaign for Vicksburg,* 1:531–89.

95. Despite his military duties, Jim Francis continued his partnership with William P. Becker and his wartime speculation in tobacco, cotton, and slaves. Francis-Martin Family Papers.

96. J. M. Clay was listed in the 1860 federal census as a twenty-eight-year-old merchant with real estate valued at $2,500 and a personal estate valued at $17,500. *Eighth Census/ Alabama,* 4:849.

97. Miller Francis and the 51st Alabama were stationed near Shelbyville, Tennessee, headquarters for Lt. Gen. Leonidas Polk's corps in Bragg's Army of Tennessee. *OR,* 23, pt. 2:714, 717–20, 722–23, 725, 733–35; Connelly, *Autumn of Glory,* 116–17.

98. James D. Porter was married to Susan Francis, one of Dr. James C. Francis's sisters. Francis-Martin Genealogy Collection.

99. Robert Wells enlisted in Company H, 30th Alabama, in St. Clair County, Alabama, on 20 March 1862. He was killed at the battle of Chickamauga on 22 September 1863. *CSR/ Alabama,* 336:1235.

100. Two Union batteries were located on De Soto Point within 3,000 yards of Vicksburg. Their 30-pounder Parrott rifles could hurl their conical-shaped shells into the city. *Vicksburg Whig,* 21 April 1863; *OR,* 24, pt. 1:70, 75, 125; Bearss, *The Campaign for Vicksburg,* 2:59.

101. Euclid Johnson, assistant quartermaster for the 30th Alabama, was on a special patrol with Lt. Col. Edmund Winston Pettus (1821–1907) up the Sunflower River. They returned with about 5,000 bushels of corn, 8,000 pounds of bacon, and a small number of cattle and hogs. *OR,* 24, pt. 1:725–26, 763; Bearss, *The Campaign for Vicksburg,* 2:101–2, 114, 117–20.

102. Maj. Gen. Dabney H. Maury (1822–1900) left Vicksburg on 17 April 1863 to become commander of the Department of East Tennessee. Current, *Encyclopedia of the Confederacy,* 3:1017; Bearss, *The Campaign for Vicksburg,* 2:104, 3:779.

103. Miller Francis made his trip to Atlanta, Georgia, on 9–12 April 1863 and visited his wife, Julia, and their children near Monticello, Georgia. Francis-Martin Family Papers.

104. William Henry Fowler (1826–67) helped raise a volunteer company, the Warrior Guards, Company H, 5th Alabama Volunteer Regiment. After a year of service, he transferred to the artillery service, raised a battery, and was commissioned colonel and assigned to Mobile. *CSR/Alabama,* 140:731; Brewer, *Alabama,* 269, 597; Owen, *History of Alabama,* 3:607–8.

105. Hop Francis was not captured, and there are no records to indicate why Tom Francis thought his brother had become a prisoner of war. Francis-Martin Family Papers.

106. The river bluffs at Warrenton, Mississippi, contained the most southern batteries that threatened the passage of Union gunboats and transports. Bearss, *The Campaign for Vicksburg,* 1:441, 443, 455, 623–24.

107. L. D. Moses enrolled as a twenty-five-year-old private in the Sallie Walker Boys at Jacksonville on 5 March 1862. He was listed on a register of deceased soldiers at Vicksburg on 1 June 1863. *CSR/Alabama,* 334:822.

108. Robert W. Memminger served as assistant adjutant general on Pemberton's staff in

South Carolina. He was transferred to Pemberton's Army of Mississippi at Vicksburg and promoted to major on 29 December 1862. *CSR/General & Staff,* 176; *OR,* 24, pt. 1:93, pt. 3:729, 809.

109. Theodore Johnston was appointed commissary of subsistence for the Department of Mississippi and Eastern Louisiana on 16 December 1862. *CSR/General & Staff,* 141; OR, 24, pt. 3:595–98, 614–16, 651–52.

110. John H. Forney received an order from John C. Pemberton on 17 April 1863 to replace Dabney H. Maury as division commander at Vicksburg. *OR,* 24, pt. 3:756, 761, 758; *CSR/General & Staff,* 96; *CSR/Alabama,* 193:504.

111. The original copy of Tom Francis's letter to Robert W. Memminger was found in Francis's service records. *CSR/General & Staff,* 98.

112. John M. Wyly was an aide-de-camp to John H. Forney at Vicksburg and Enterprise, Mississippi, and in the Trans-Mississippi Department. *CSR/Alabama,* 200:1758; *CSR/General & Staff,* 66.

113. Julia F. Scales, the fourteen-year-old daughter of Robert and Ann Scales, died from the complications of erysipelas on 9 May 1863. *Eighth Census/Alabama,* 2:389; *Jacksonville Republican,* 16 May 1863.

114. Colonel Abel D. Streight led a Union force of approximately 1,700 on a raid on 26 April 1863 across North Alabama from Tuscumbia, Alabama, to Rome, Georgia. *Jacksonville Republican,* 9 May 1863; *OR,* 23, pt. 1:280–93; McMillan, *The Alabama Confederate Reader,* 186–88, 192–99.

115. Streight's raiders destroyed the Round Mountain Iron Works located at Centre, Cherokee County, Alabama, on 2 May 1863. *Jacksonville Republican,* 9 May 1863; McMillan, *The Alabama Confederate Reader,* 188.

116. Streight's brigade included his own 51st Indiana regiment, 73rd Indiana, 3rd Ohio, 80th Illinois, and two companies of the 1st Middle Tennessee Cavalry, Alabama unionists. *OR,* 23, pt. 1:281, 285–93; McMillan, *The Alabama Confederate Reader,* 187.

117. Forrest with 600 cavalry pursued Streight's raiders across North Alabama and fought several skirmishes from 30 April through 2 May 1863. *OR,* 23, pt. 1:288–92; *Jacksonville Republican,* 9 May 1863.

118. Grant's 47-day siege of Vicksburg began on 18 May 1863 and continued until Pemberton agreed to surrender the city on 4 July 1863. *OR,* 24, pt. 3:466–67, 469–72; Alison, "War Diary of Dr. Joseph Dill Alison," 394–98.

119. John H. Wisdom, a rural mailman, rode the 67 miles from Gadsden to Rome, Georgia, to warn of Streight's raiders. McMillan, *The Confederate Alabama Reader,* 188.

120. Elijiah Woolum, a stage driver and Jacksonville resident, drove his buggy to Rome, Georgia, and used his express business as a ploy to learn about the location of the Union raiders. *Jacksonville Republican,* 9 May 1863; *Eighth Census/Alabama,* 2:294.

121. Thomas A. Walker, a state senator, Joseph B. Forney, a Jacksonville merchant, and Dr. John Z. Nisbet, a Jacksonville physician, joined the Calhoun Home Guards and others who hit the road for Rome, Georgia. *Jacksonville Republican,* 9 May 1863; *Eighth Census/Alabama,* 2:293, 295, 299.

122. Martha B. Francis, the wife of John W. Francis, taught piano in her Jacksonville home. Francis-Martin Genealogy Collection.

123. Streight surrendered his Union forces to Forrest on 3 May 1863 near Lawrence, Cherokee County, Alabama. *Jacksonville Republican,* 9 May 1863; *OR,* 23, pt. 1:293; McMillan, *The Alabama Confederate Reader,* 188.

124. William S. McGee enlisted in Company I, 30th Alabama, at Camp Curry near Talladega on 22 March 1862. *CSR/Alabama,* 334:776.

125. On 29 April 1863, Edward D. Tracy's Alabama brigade marched 40 miles from Warrenton to the vicinity of Port Gibson, Mississippi. *OR,* 24, pt. 1:663, 678, pt. 3:240–42, 801–2, 805–6, 808–9; Bearss, *The Campaign for Vicksburg,* 2:253–59, 305–16, 348, 402–5.

126. Tracy's brigade joined brigades under the command of Martin E. Green (1825–63) and William E. Baldwin (1827–64) in the early morning hours of 1 May 1863. *OR,* 24, pt. 1:672–82; Samuel C. Kelly to Amie P. Kelly, Near Port Gibson, 2 May 1863, Kelly Letters.

127. J. W. Johnston's Botetourt Virginia artillery was located on a ridge in the center of the Confederate line with the 30th Alabama posted on either side. *OR,* 24, pt. 1:679, 681, pt. 3:703; Bearss, *The Campaign for Vicksburg,* 3:348, 358, 364–65, 379–81, 406.

128. Company B, 30th Alabama, took up a defensive position in the "yard of a Negro cabin" near the Andrews plantation on the Bruinsburg road. *OR,* 24, pt. 1:663, 672–73, 678–81; James D. Arnold to Thomas M. Owen, Jacksonville, Ala., 4 Feb. 1911, Confederate Regimental History Files.

129. Edward D. Tracy was shot by a sniper, collapsed in the arms of Charles M. Shelley and Samuel C. Kelly, and died before they reached safety. *OR,* 24, pt. 1:258, 659, 667; Samuel C. Kelly to Amie P. Kelly, Near Port Gibson, 2 May 1863, Kelly Letters.

130. Benjamin F. Garvin was detailed for hospital duty on 12 March 1864 and listed in the "invalid corps PACS" with a retirement date of 9 November 1864. *CSR/Alabama,* 333:431.

131. George W. Stephens's service records were incomplete and only confirmed his rank as a private in Company B, 30th Alabama. Ibid., 336:1102.

132. James M. Karr (Kerr) was captured at Snyder's Bluff near Vicksburg on 26 May 1863. He was sent as a prisoner of war to Alton, Illinois, and exchanged at City Point, Virginia, on 12 June 1863. Ibid., 334:623.

133. Luke R. Roberts enlisted as a thirty-three-year-old private in the Sallie Walker Boys at Jacksonville on 5 March 1862. Ibid., 335:988.

134. Oliver E. Langley enlisted as a twenty-year-old private in the Sallie Walker Boys at Jacksonville on 5 March 1862. Ibid., 334:655.

135. Namon V. Stephens died of his wounds at Demopolis, Alabama, on 25 June 1863. Ibid., 336:1108.

136. John Ford was captured on 1 May 1863 at Port Gibson and died of typhoid fever on 10 June 1863 as a prisoner of war at Alton, Illinois. Ibid., 333:391.

137. John W. Gidley was captured at Port Gibson, sent as a prisoner of war to Alton, Illinois, and exchanged at City Point, Virginia, on 12 June 1863. Ibid., 434.

138. William Hughes Newton was captured at Port Gibson on 1 May 1863, sent as a prisoner of war to Alton, Illinois, and died of smallpox on 25 June 1863 at Camp Morton, Indianapolis, Indiana. Ibid., 335:838.

139. Benjamin F. Nunnelly was captured at Port Gibson, sent as a prisoner of war to Alton, Illinois, and exchanged at City Point, Virginia, on 21 June 1863. He died of smallpox at the 3rd Division Hospital, Howard's Grove, Richmond, Virginia, on 1 August 1863. Ibid., 854.

140. The aggregate losses for Tracy's brigade were 18 killed, 112 wounded, and 142 missing. Samuel C. Kelly to Amie P. Kelly, Near Port Gibson, 2 May 1863, Kelly Letters; Bearss, *The Campaign for Vicksburg,* 2:406.

141. Thomas H. Patterson was shot through the thigh, became a prisoner of war, and was exchanged. He was promoted to major on 28 January 1864 and lieutenant colonel on 12 May

1864 and died at Atlanta on 30 July 1864. *CSR/Alabama,* 335:877; James D. Arnold to Thomas M. Owen, Jacksonville, Ala., 4 Feb. 1911, Confederate Regimental History Files.

142. Edmund W. Pettus and a number of men of the 20th Alabama were captured on the Confederate right near Bayou Pierre about 2:30 P.M. on 1 May 1863. *CSR/Alabama,* 282:1489; *OR,* 24, pt. 1:681–82, pt. 3:841; Samuel C. Kelly to Amie P. Kelly, [Vicksburg], 6 May 1863, Kelly Letters.

143. Confederate losses numbered 60 killed, 340 wounded, and 387 missing. Union losses were 131 killed, 719 wounded, and 25 missing. Bearss, *The Campaign for Vicksburg,* 2:405, 407.

144. R. V. Bowman (Bonneau) served as assistant commissary for subsistence at the commissary depot at Selma, Alabama, from February 1864 through May 1865. *CSR/General & Staff,* 28; *Jacksonville Republican,* 2 April 1864.

145. Carter L. Stevenson's division was held in reserve at the battle of the Big Black River on 17 May 1863. *OR,* 24, pt. 3:321–22, 344, 887–89, 891–92; Bearss, *The Campaign for Vicksburg,* 3:53–89.

146. The Southern Telegraph Company of Richmond, Virginia, a private company, was the largest telegraph company in the Confederacy. Current, *Encyclopedia of the Confederacy,* 4:1573, 1685.

147. Stephen D. Lee became commander of Tracy's Alabama brigade after his death at the battle of Port Gibson on 1 May 1863. *OR,* 24, pt. 2:103.

148. Thomas R. Beavers enlisted in Edward P. Woodward's company at Mt. Pisgah Church, St. Clair County, Alabama, on 12 March 1862. He was not promoted to captain and resigned as a first lieutenant on 3 September 1864. *CSR/Alabama,* 332:107; Thomas R. Beavers to Thomas M. Owen, Jacksonville, Ala., 12 March 1912, Confederate Regimental History Files.

149. J. C. M. Spruill enlisted as a twenty-two-year-old corporal in Edward P. Woodward's company, Company H, 30th Alabama, in St. Clair County on 20 March 1862. He was paroled at Vicksburg on 8 July 1863 as a first lieutenant. *CSR/Alabama,* 336:1093.

150. F. A. Turner enlisted as a thirty-three-year-old sergeant in Company C, 30th Alabama, at Talladega, Alabama, on 5 March 1862. He was paroled at Vicksburg as a first lieutenant. Ibid., 1198.

151. William T. Green enlisted in the Isbell Guards and was elected second lieutenant when the company mustered in at Camp Curry as Company C, 30th Alabama. His service records do not indicate when he was killed. Ibid., 333:468.

152. J. L. Butler enlisted as a private in Company K, 30th Alabama, after it was mustered in at Camp Curry on 29 March 1862. He was captured at Vicksburg on 4 July 1863 and paroled on 15 July. Ibid., 332:201.

153. John Bass Smith, Company K, 30th Alabama, died at Vicksburg on 14 July 1863. Ibid., 336:1068.

154. Joe Johnston advanced toward Vicksburg with about 31,000 troops on 28 June to relieve Pemberton. He countermarched back to Jackson when he learned of Pemberton's surrender to Grant on 4 July 1863. *OR,* 24, pt. 1:244–45, pt. 3:985, 987; Bearss, *The Campaign for Vicksburg,* 3:1149–52.

155. Ada Barnett was listed in the 1860 census as the eighteen-year-old daughter of fifty-one-year-old R. Barnett, a lawyer, and his wife, Julia. She and John Francis apparently met at some of the socials in Vicksburg before the Union siege. *Eighth Census/Mississippi,* 8:922.

156. John Francis was in command of the 30th Alabama at the time of paroling. Parole

certificates were signed by all Confederate officers and soldiers following the formal surrender of Vicksburg on 4 July 1863. *OR,* 24, pt. 3:478–79, 481, 483–85, 487–91, 493–96.

157. John Francis arrived at Brandon, Mississippi, on 13 July 1863. Ibid., 481, 493–94, 1000–2, 1005–7; Bearss, *The Campaign for Vicksburg,* 3:1304–6.

Chapter 6

1. Long, *The Civil War Day by Day,* 384–86.

2. McMillan, *The Alabama Confederate Reader,* 233–36; Rogers et al., *Alabama,* 213–14.

3. Samuel C. Kelly to Amie P. Kelly, Paroled Camps, Three miles below Talladega, Ala., 29 August 1863, Kelly Letters; *CSR/Alabama,* 333:401; Kelly, "A History of the Thirtieth Alabama Volunteers," 144–45; Bearss, *The Campaign for Vicksburg,* 3:1310–11.

4. Samuel C. Kelly to Amie P. Kelly, Demopolis, Ala., 25 September 1863, Kelly Letters; Kelly, "A History of the Thirtieth Alabama Volunteers," 146.

5. Samuel C. Kelly to Amie P. Kelly, Demopolis, Ala., 17, 18 October 1863, Kelly Letters; Kelly, "A History of the Thirtieth Alabama Volunteers," 146.

6. Samuel C. Kelly to Amie P. Kelly, Demopolis, Ala., 19 October 1863, Kelly Letters; *CSR/Alabama,* 333:401; Francis-Martin Family Papers.

7. Samuel C. Kelly to Amie P. Kelly, Lookout Mountain, 8, 15 November 1863, Kelly Letters; Kelly, "A History of the Thirtieth Alabama Volunteers," 147–48; James Lee McDonough, *Chattanooga: A Death Grip on the Confederacy,* 133–34; *OR,* 31, pt. 2:658, 695, 704–5, 731–32, pt. 3:695, 709.

8. *OR,* 31, pt. 2:693–96, 698–99, 704–5, 731–32; John C. Brown, "Lookout Mountain: Report of Brigadier-General J. C. Brown, Headquarters Brown's Brigade, November 30, 1863," 182–83; McDonough, *Chattanooga,* 134–35.

9. *OR,* 31, pt. 2:731–32; Kelly, "A History of the Thirtieth Alabama Volunteers," 149; McDonough, *Chattanooga,* 137–38.

10. *OR,* 31, pt. 2:393, 395, 695–96, 705, 731–33; Samuel C. Kelly to Amie P. Kelly, Near Dalton, Ga., 1 December 1863, Kelly Letters; R. J. Cunningham to Thomas M. Owen, Talladega., 18 July 1913, 30th Alabama Infantry Regiment, Confederate Regimental History Files.

11. Samuel C. Kelly to Amie P. Kelly, Near Dalton, Ga., 1 December 1863, Kelly Letters; Esposito, *West Point Atlas,* 1:116; McDonough, *Chattanooga,* 143–44, 159, 164, 174.

12. *OR,* 31, pt. 2:631, 633, 636, 652–53, 656, 735–36, 748–51; McDonough, *Chattanooga,* 164–74, 184–85.

13. *OR,* 31, pt. 2:305, 464–68, 471–77, 509, 520–28, 535–38, 546, 740–42; William T. Sherman, *Memoirs of General William T. Sherman* (1875; reprint, 2 vols. in 1, with a foreword by B. H. Liddell Hart, Bloomington: Indiana University Press, 1957), 362–64; McDonough, *Chattanooga,* 143–59, 166–69, 171–80, 182–94, 200–202; Kelly, "A History of the Thirtieth Alabama Volunteers," 149–51.

14. *OR,* 32, pt. 2:321, 403–4, 604, 754–57; Samuel C. Kelly to Amie P. Kelly, Near Dalton, Ga., 1 December 1863, Kelly Letters; Connelly, *Autumn of Glory,* 276; McDonough, *Chattanooga,* 220–25.

15. *OR,* 31, pt. 2:740–41; Connelly, *Autumn of Glory,* 275–76; McDonough, *Chattanooga,* 181–86, 194, 200–202.

16. Samuel C. Kelly to Amie P. Kelly, [Dalton], 13 December 1863, Kelly Letters; Connelly, *Autumn of Glory,* 277; George E. Brewer, "The Thirtieth Alabama Regiment," Confederate Regimental History Files, 17.

17. *CSR/Tennessee,* 214:264, 266; *Jacksonville Republican,* 2 April 1863; Francis-Martin Genealogy Collection.

18. *CSR/Alabama,* 274:1342, 1343; Francis-Martin Genealogy Collection.

19. *CSR/Tennessee,* 111:1573; Francis-Martin Genealogy Collection.

20. *OR,* 31, pt. 3:835–36; Symonds, *Joseph E. Johnston,* 248–50; Kelly, "A History of the Thirtieth Alabama Volunteers," 151; Brewer, "The Thirtieth Alabama Regiment," 17.

21. Rowland Journals, 26.

22. *CSR/Alabama,* 333:401; Brewer, "The Thirtieth Alabama Regiment," 17; Francis-Martin Family Papers.

23. Tom Francis's correspondence regarding land purchases in Calhoun County, Alabama were never found. Francis-Martin Family Papers.

24. Pemberton and his officers and soldiers from Vicksburg stopped at Brandon, Mississippi, in mid-July before moving to the headquarters for paroled prisoners at Enterprise, Mississippi, on 20 July 1863. *OR,* 24, pt. 3:1001–2, 1005–7, 1010–11, 1014–15, 1018–19, 1021.

25. James Crow was listed as a fifty-three-year-old farmer in the 1860 census with real estate valued at $20,000 and a personal estate valued at $39,000. *Eighth Census/Alabama,* 2:295.

26. M. J. A. Keith was a successful businessman and banker in Selma, Alabama. Ibid., 4:797; *CSA/Alabama,* 122:579.

27. Companies A and D in the 51st Alabama were originally composed of men from Calhoun County. Company A was reorganized as a cavalry unit from the 2nd Alabama Infantry Regiment at Fort Pillow, Tennessee, on 22 May 1862. The Dudley Snow Rangers were organized as Company D at Oxford, Alabama, on 11 August 1862 under Captain Robert D. Draper. Miller, *Wheeler's Favorites,* 35, 46. See also *Jacksonville Republican,* 1 May–24 July 1862.

28. William T. Fain, first lieutenant in Company A, 51st Alabama, was captured at Shelbyville, Tennessee, on 27 June 1863. He was exchanged on 20 February 1865 and paroled at Charlotte, North Carolina, on 3 May 1863. Miller, *Wheeler's Favorites,* 8, 9, 147.

29. James D. Webb was wounded in a skirmish near Elk River, Tennessee, and died on 19 July 1863. *CSR/Alabama,* 447:1474.

30. Stephen A. McCraw, assistant adjutant general in the 51st Alabama, was wounded and captured at Shelbyville, Tennessee, on 27 June 1863. He was exchanged in 1864 and paroled at Selma on 25 May 1865. Miller, *Wheeler's Favorites,* 182.

31. In the skirmish at Shelbyville, Tennessee, on 27 June 1863, Wheeler, his escort, and others jumped into the flooded Duck River to escape the Union cavalry and lost 104 men captured. Ibid., 8–9.

32. William D. Burton, first lieutenant in Company D, Sydenham W. Cowling, captain in Company H, William Pelham, second lieutenant in Company A, James T. Dye, major in Company C, and C. F. Force, captain in Company E, were captured at Shelbyville, Tennessee, on 27 June 1863. *CSR/Alabama,* 445:192; Miller, *Wheeler's Favorites,* 13–14, 135, 144, 148–49.

33. William D. Bush, a sergeant in Company A, 51st Alabama, was captured at Shelbyville, Tennessee, on 27 June 1863. He was released as a POW on 14 June 1865. Miller, *Wheeler's Favorites,* 125.

34. William D. White was a captain in Company D, 51st Alabama. Frank was appar-

ently Miller's seventeen-year-old slave. *CSR/Alabama,* 447:1574; *Eighth Census/Alabama, Slave Schedule,* 1:265.

35. The Confederate Congress enacted the Impressment Act on 26 March 1863 in an effort to obtain supplies for the war effort. Individuals whose property was impressed were paid in Confederate scrip or issued a certificate entitling them to payment later. Goff, *Confederate Supply,* 99–102; Current, *Encyclopedia of the Confederacy,* 3:809–10, 4:1560.

36. Elijah Woolum was listed as a thirty-seven-year-old stage driver in the 1860 census; he operated a stage and express line between Jacksonville and Rome, Georgia. *Eighth Census/Alabama,* 2:294.

37. On Friday, 21 August 1863, after four consecutive days of Union bombardment, Major General Quincey Adams Gillmore (1825–88) demanded the surrender of Fort Sumter and evacuation of Morris Island and threatened to bombard Charleston if his demands were not met. *OR,* 28, pt. 1:596–600; Long, *The Civil War Day by Day,* 398–400.

38. The Union campaign against Chattanooga started on 16 August 1863, when William S. Rosecrans (1819–98) moved the Army of the Cumberland south from Tullahoma toward the Tennessee River and Chattanooga. The city was hit by several shells on 21 August. *OR,* 28, pt. 1:682–86, 30, pt. 1:50–51, 445–49; Long, *The Civil War Day by Day,* 397, 399–400.

39. Blue Mountain, present-day Anniston, Calhoun County, Alabama, was the end of the line for the Alabama & Tennessee Rivers Railroad. Black, *Railroads of the Confederacy,* 158.

40. Lark Francis was a family servant and one of thirteen slaves listed in the 1860 federal slave schedule as owned by Dr. James C. Francis. *Eighth Census/Alabama, Slave Schedule,* 265; *Ninth Census/Alabama,* 3:532.

41. Miles W. Abernathy was a partner with Daniel Warlick, Gabriel B. Douthit, and G. W. Mathews in a tan yard at Jacksonville. Fielding Snow of Jacksonville was the owner of Snow's tan yard. *Eighth Census/Alabama,* 2:293, 297; *Jacksonville Republican,* 4 October 1860.

42. Over a period of fifteen months, the 30th Alabama was reduced from approximately 1,099 men in May 1862 to about 200 men at the Talladega reception center in August 1863. Kelly, "A History of the Thirtieth Alabama Volunteers," 144.

43. Edward T. Clark was the second oldest son of John R. Clark of Jacksonville. He enlisted in the Sallie Walker Boys at Jacksonville on 5 March 1862 and was paroled at Salisbury, North Carolina, on 2 May 1865. *CSR/Alabama,* 332:247; *Eighth Census/Alabama,* 2:292.

44. The 31st Alabama was brigaded with the 20th, 23rd, 30th, and 46th Alabama regiments at Demopolis under the command of Brigadier General Edmund W. Pettus. *CSR/Alabama,* 282:1489; Brewer, *Alabama,* 638–39.

45. The young handicapped Scott apparently worked briefly as an overseer for Tom Francis on his land in Calhoun County. Francis-Martin Family Papers.

46. By 1862 sugar and salt were in short supply and had virtually disappeared in parts of the Confederate states. Both were hoarded by speculators and became extremely scarce throughout the war. Current, *Encyclopedia of the Confederacy,* 2:595–96, 3:1244, 4:1559–60; Massey, *Ersatz in the Confederacy,* 20–21, 28, 63–67.

47. John B. Abernathy, a Jacksonville resident, was listed in the 1860 census as a fifty-year-old farmer with real estate valued at $3,000 and a personal estate of $13,000. *Eighth Census/Alabama,* 2:309.

48. Enterprise, Mississippi, was the official parole camp for the Vicksburg and Port Hudson garrisons. *OR,* 24, pt. 3:1002, 1014–15, 1018, 52, pt. 2:516; Bearss, *The Campaign for Vicksburg,* 3:1307–10.

49. Robert Ould (1820–82), Confederate agent for prisoner exchange, declared the officers and men of Stevenson's division, Bowen's division, Moore's brigade, and Waul's Texas legion exchanged on 12 September 1863. Bearss, *The Campaign for Vicksburg,* 3:1310–11; Current, *Encyclopedia of the Confederacy,* 3:1256–57; Wakelyn, *Biographical Dictionary of the Confederacy,* 336.

50. Joe Johnston remained the department commander of Confederate forces in Mississippi and East Louisiana, which included the paroled and exchanged Alabama troops from the Vicksburg garrison. *OR,* 24, pt. 3:1048–49, 1051, 1058, 1065, 1070; Connelly, *Autumn of Glory,* 146–49, 157.

51. After Braxton Bragg abandoned Chattanooga on 9 September 1863, there were numerous skirmishes between Union and Confederate forces on 9–14 September 1863 south of Chattanooga in and about Lookout Mountain, Blue Bird Gap, Davis' Cross Roads, Lee and Gordon's Mills, Rome, La Fayette, Rossville, Ringgold, and Summerville, Georgia. *OR,* 30, pt. 1:27, 53–54, 185–86, 270–74, 284–85, 326–28, 372, 446–47, 450–51, 689–90, 910; Connelly, *Autumn of Glory,* 172–200.

52. With more men entering the Confederate service, land management for absentee landowners like Tom Francis became increasingly difficult and led to decreased productivity. Francis-Martin Family Papers.

53. John Rowland, a successful Jacksonville merchant, suffered the loss of a servant as a runaway. *Eighth Census/Alabama,* 2:296.

54. The 30th Alabama left the reception center near Talladega on Wednesday, 23 September 1863, and traveled in open boxcars via Selma to Demopolis on the Tombigbee River the following day. Samuel C. Kelly to Amie P. Kelly, Demopolis, Ala., 25 September 1863, Kelly Letters.

55. William C. Denman, a Jacksonville resident, enlisted as a twenty-five-year-old private in the Sallie Walker Boys on 5 March 1862. He was transferred to Wheeler's escort in the Army of Tennessee on 23 January 1864. *CSR/Alabama,* 333:300.

56. William C. Patterson was seriously wounded and captured at the battle of Baker's Creek, Mississippi, on 16 May 1863. His health was compromised, and his resignation as lieutenant colonel was accepted on 28 January 1864. Ibid., 335:878.

57. Tom Francis expressed the frustrations of all wartime absentee landowners and farmers who worried about their lands and crops. Francis-Martin Family Papers.

58. Archibald Downing, a native of South Carolina, was listed in the 1860 census as a fifty-two-year-old farmer living near Morrisville in southwestern Calhoun County. *Eighth Census/Alabama,* 2:666.

59. The 51st Alabama, Wheeler's cavalry corps, went into camp on 9 October 1863 near Courtland, Lawrence County, Alabama, and remained until 26 October when Bragg ordered Wheeler back to Chattanooga. *OR,* 31, pt. 1:25–28, 798, 30, pt. 1:210–11, pt. 2:668–70, 686–90, 717–19, 722–25; Connelly, *Autumn of Glory,* 270.

60. The 30th Alabama, Pettus's brigade, received orders on 27 October 1863 to report to Bragg's Army of Tennessee near Chattanooga and arrived at Newnan, Georgia, on 31 October. Samuel C. Kelly to Amie P. Kelly, Demopolis, 28 October 1863, and Newnan, Ga., 31 October 1863, Kelly Letters.

61. Jim Francis received a transfer to Augusta, Georgia, and was placed in charge of the office of purchasing commissary. *CSR/General & Staff,* 98.

62. William D. White enlisted in Company D, 51st Alabama, at Oxford, Alabama, on

27 May 1862. He was captured on 7 October 1863 in a skirmish at Farmington, Tennessee. *CSR/Alabama,* 447:1504; Miller, *Wheeler's Favorites,* 16–17, 22, 229.

63. Jane Tulley, a thirty-six-year-old native of Ireland, was listed in the 1860 census and operated a millinery store in Selma, Dallas County, Alabama. *Eighth Census/Alabama,* 4:808.

64. The Francis plantation was located at Ohatchee, near the confluence of Ohatchee Creek and Tallasseehatchee Creek, approximately 18 miles west and southwest of Jacksonville. Francis-Martin Family Papers; Remington and Kallsen, *Historical Atlas of Alabama,* 1:35, 39.

65. Thomas Hill Watts (1819–92), a native of Butler County, Alabama, was elected governor of Alabama in August 1863. An old Whig and Unionist, he carried every county, including Calhoun County, except Jackson, Madison, Marion, and St. Clair. McMillan, *Disintegration of a Confederate State,* 73–75, 82–83; Owen, *History of Alabama,* 4:1732.

66. William H. T. Walker (1816–64), a native of Georgia and an 1837 West Point graduate, was in charge of all Confederate troops west of Chattanooga Creek until he took a leave on 12 November 1863. *OR,* 30, pt. 1:229–30, pt. 2:239–47, 31, pt. 1:221–22, 717–18; Current, *Encyclopedia of the Confederacy,* 4:1680–81.

67. James B. Martin, Jr., served as a second lieutenant and assistant adjutant general in the 10th Alabama and was later promoted to captain and transferred to the commissary service. *CSR/Alabama,* 196:974.

68. John W. Francis, Company G, 10th Alabama, received an extended furlough and sick leave after suffering a severe wound at the battle of Salem Church, Virginia, on 3 May 1863. Ibid., 193:513.

69. The 30th Alabama moved from Chickamauga Station on the Western & Atlantic Railroad about three miles east of Chattanooga and swung south and west to Lookout Mountain. Esposito, *West Point Atlas,* 1:115; Connelly, *Discovering the Appalachians,* 76.

70. Raccoon Mountain, located on the south shore of the Tennessee River, straddles the state line in northeast Alabama and northwest Georgia, west of Lookout Mountain and west and southwest of Chattanooga. *OR,* 31, pt. 1:82–87, 224–25; McDonough, *Chattanooga,* 47, 55, 62, 81.

71. To move supplies to Chattanooga, Grant's forces used the Nashville & Chattanooga Railroad to Stevenson, Alabama, where it intersected the Memphis & Charleston Railroad, *OR,* 31, pt. 1:16–30; Black, *Railroads of the Confederacy,* 6; Esposito, *West Point Atlas,* 1:115.

72. John D. Adrian (Adrine) enlisted as a private in Company A, 4th Alabama, at Selma, Alabama, on 26 April 1861. *CSR/Alabama,* 118:28.

73. Thomas Beasley was listed in the 1860 census as a forty-one-year-old farmer living near Palestine, Calhoun County, Alabama. *Eighth Census/Alabama,* 2:480.

74. Sherman arrived with four divisions at Bridgeport, Alabama, west of Chattanooga, on 15 November 1863. He crossed the Tennessee River near South Chickamauga Creek the night of 23 November to position his troops opposite the Confederate right flank. *OR,* 31, pt. 3:119, 139–40, 152–53, 223, 232, 237; Esposito, *West Point Atlas,* 1:116; Long, *The Civil War Day by Day,* 433, 435–36.

75. On 4 November 1863, James Longstreet was ordered by Bragg to march into East Tennessee to oppose the Union Army of the Ohio under Ambrose E. Burnside (1824–81) at Knoxville. *OR,* 31, pt. 3:634–38, 644; Connelly, *Autumn of Glory,* 262–65; Esposito, *West Point Atlas,* 1:116.

76. Colonel Thomas C. Lanier (1824–91) from Pickens County was in command of the 42nd Alabama at Lookout Mountain in November 1863. The 42nd Alabama was organized

at Columbus, Mississippi, in May 1862 with companies from Conecuh, Fayette, Marion, Mobile, Monroe, Pickens, Talladega, and Wilcox counties. *OR,* 31, pt. 2:658, 685–90, 704–6; Brewer, *Alabama,* 502, 652; Krick, *Lee's Colonels,* 456.

77. Company H, commanded by Captain William H. Burr, was the only company from St. Clair County in the 30th Alabama. Samuel C. Kelly to Amie P. Kelly, Lookout Mt., 11 November 1863, Kelly Letters.

78. William P. Becker, Jim Francis's business partner, enlisted as a sergeant in Company G, 44th Alabama, on 18 April 1862. He was promoted and served as captain and assistant adjutant general in Law's brigade. *CSR/Alabama,* 407:132.

79. Samuel M. Thomas (Thames) mustered in as a twenty-seven-year-old private in Company D, 30th Alabama, at Talladega, Alabama, on 31 March 1862. His resignation was approved on 27 October 1863. Ibid., 336:1168.

80. Carnes's, Corput's, and Rowan's batteries and the 20th Alabama Battalion began shelling Union forces across Lookout Creek at daybreak on 17 November 1863. *OR,* 31, pt. 2:662; Samuel C. Kelly to Amie P. Kelly, [Lookout Mountain], 17 November 1863, Kelly Letters.

81. The 30th Alabama moved to the east side of Lookout Mountain about 16 November 1863 as Carter L. Stevenson was given command on top of the mountain. *OR,* 31, pt. 2:662, 678, 723, 733, pt. 3:695; Samuel C. Kelly to Amie P. Kelly, [Lookout Mountain], 17 November 1863, Kelly Letters.

82. W. Coleman Land was listed in the 1860 census as a forty-six-year-old watchmaker with a personal estate valued at $4,000. *Eighth Census/Alabama,* 2:286; *Jacksonville Republican,* 2 January 1862.

83. Major John Francis purchased or collected blankets and quilts for the 30th Alabama in Calhoun and Talladega counties during a visit on 24–31 October 1863. Francis-Martin Family Papers; *Jacksonville Republican,* 31 October 1863.

84. Major General Joseph Hooker opened the battle of Lookout Mountain, "the battle above the clouds," when his 12,000 Union troops began crossing Lookout Creek about 8:00 A.M. on 24 November 1863 and struck Confederate forces under Carter L. Stevenson. *OR,* 31, pt. 2:314–17, 718–22; Brown, "Lookout Mountain," 182–83.

85. Edward Cary Walthall (1831–98) commanded a brigade that numbered approximately 1,500 and occupied the Confederate right flank to the vicinity of the Craven's house on 24 November 1863. *OR,* 31, pt. 2:692–96, 698–99, 704–5, 731–32; McDonough, *Chattanooga,* 134–40.

86. The Craven's house was located on a bench or plateau of fairly level land halfway up the north face of Lookout Mountain and overlooked Moccasin Bend of the Tennessee River. *OR,* 31, pt. 2:315–17, 677, 718–22, 731; McDonough, *Chattanooga,* 131, 134, 137–38.

87. With the 31st Alabama, a reserve force, the 20th Alabama under Captain John W. Davis, reinforced the Confederate left flank, drove the Union forces back, and held the higher ground for the remainder of the battle. *OR,* 31, pt. 2:662, 726, 732–33; McDonough, *Chattanooga,* 139.

88. Four companies of the 30th Alabama, including Company B, were deployed as skirmishers on Smith's Trail on top of Lookout Mountain. *OR,* 31, pt. 2:733; Kelly, "A History of the Thirtieth Alabama Volunteers," 149.

89. Major John Francis withdrew his men about 7:00 P.M. on 24 November, followed John C. Brown's brigade down the mountain, and bivouacked on the east side of Chattanooga Creek. *OR,* 31, pt. 2:733; Brown, "Lookout Mountain," 182–83.

90. M. T. Sewell enlisted as a private in the Ryan Guards, Company E, 30th Alabama, on 6 March 1862. *CSR/Alabama,* 335:1023; *Jacksonville Republican,* 27 February 1862.

91. The 30th Alabama was located on the Confederate right on the north end of Missionary Ridge near Tunnel Hill, where Sherman launched the first general assault about 11:00 A.M. on 25 November. *OR,* 31, pt. 2:746–53; Connelly, *Autumn of Glory,* 273–75; Samuel C. Kelly to Amie P. Kelly, Near Dalton, Ga., 1 December 1863, Kelly Letters.

92. Brigadier General Zachariah Cantey Deas (1819–82) commanded an all-Alabama brigade, and Brigadier General Alfred Jefferson Vaughan commanded an all-Tennessee brigade at Missionary Ridge. *OR,* 31, pt. 2:659, 741; Current, *Encyclopedia of the Confederacy,* 2:459, 4:1652–53; Wakelyn, *Biographical Dictionary of the Confederacy,* 73–74, 166.

93. In the early hours of 26 November 1863, Bragg's Army of Tennessee retreated through Ringgold Gap, about twenty miles southeast of Chattanooga, and reached Dalton, Georgia, on 28 November. *OR,* 31, pt. 2:321–23, 402–4, 606, 753–58; Connelly, *Autumn of Glory,* 276; McDonough, *Chattanooga,* 220–25; Samuel C. Kelly to Amie P. Kelly, Near Dalton, Ga., 1 December 1863, Kelly Letters.

94. Joseph S. Hollingsworth recovered from his wound at Lookout Mountain and served until paroled at Salisbury, North Carolina, on 2 May 1865. *CSR/Alabama,* 333:567.

95. John K. Landers recovered from his wound at Missionary Ridge and was sent to Rock Island, Illinois, as a prisoner of war. He was discharged on 17 January 1864. Ibid., 334:649.

96. M. Thomas Durham recovered from his wound at Missionary Ridge and served until paroled at Salisbury, North Carolina, on 2 May 1865. Ibid., 333:331.

97. John P. Cook recovered from his wound at Missionary Ridge and served until paroled at Salisbury, North Carolina, on 2 May 1865. Ibid., 332:264.

98. Barney Baxter's service records were silent about his service after Missionary Ridge. Ibid., 90.

99. Daniel W. Warlick served as commander of Company B, 30th Alabama, during the Chattanooga campaign, and Major John Francis performed regimental duties. Ibid., 336:1221.

100. John W. Glover recovered from his wound and served until his retirement at Smithfield, North Carolina, on 3 April 1865. Ibid., 333:444.

101. Catherine Buchanan Francis was married to Hugh Francis, Dr. James C. Francis's younger brother. Their son, Joseph Hugh Francis, was a private in Company D, 23rd Tennessee Infantry Battalion, at the battles of Lookout Mountain and Missionary Ridge. *CSR/Tennessee,* 214:264; *Eighth Census/Tennessee,* 6:74; Francis-Martin Genealogy Collection.

102. Dalton, Georgia, was located on the Western & Atlantic Railroad 38 miles southeast of Chattanooga and approximately 80 miles north of Atlanta. *OR,* 31, pt. 3:547; Lee Kennett, *Marching Through Georgia: The Story of Soldiers & Civilians During Sherman's Campaign* (New York: HarperCollins Publishers, 1995), 10.

103. While the 30th Alabama losses were small, the Confederate losses at Missionary Ridge were 361 killed, 2,160 wounded, and 4,146 missing, many as prisoners of war, for a total of 6,667. Samuel C. Kelly to Amie P. Kelly, Near Dalton, Ga., 1 December 1863, Kelly Letters; Long, *The Civil War Day by Day,* 438.

104. Emma Francis wrote a tearful letter to her brother Jim Francis on 24 November 1863, expressing the loneliness and isolation felt through the centuries by students living away from their families. Francis-Martin Family Papers.

105. Sarah "Sadie" Galphin Whitehead was the daughter of Amos Grattan and Elizabeth McKinne Whitehead of Ivanhoe, Burke County, Georgia. *Eighth Census/Georgia,* 1:912; Rowland Journals, iii.

106. Jim Francis stayed busy in the fall quarter purchasing and shipping supplies to support Lee's Army of Northern Virginia. His records for December 1863 report multiple ship-

ments of corn. E. M. Love to L. B. Northrup, Bureau of Subsistence, Richmond, 12 January 1864, in Lucius Bellinger Northrup, "Resources of the Confederacy in February, 1865: Report of Commissary General Northrup," 100; *CSR/General & Staff,* 98.

107. Amos Grattan Whitehead was a prominent slaveowner and landowner. He was listed in the 1860 census as a forty-two-year-old planter with real estate valued at $21,200 and a personal estate valued at $81,975. *Eighth Census/Georgia,* 1:912.

108. Jo Francis remained on special detail to the commissary department as authorized by Brigadier General Nathan B. Forrest for 31 October–31 December 1863. *CSR/Alabama,* 445:443.

109. Wyly (Wiley) Wright enlisted as a twenty-year-old private in the Sallie Walker Boys at Jacksonville on 5 March 1862. He was paroled at Salisbury, North Carolina, on 2 May 1865. Ibid., 336:1285.

110. Following the defeat at Missionary Ridge, morale in the Army of Tennessee was extremely low, and thousands wandered off as the army retreated to Dalton. Bragg's army was reduced from about 64,000 in late October 1863 to approximately 30,000 at Dalton. Connelly, *Autumn of Glory,* 277; Samuel C. Kelly to Amie P. Kelly, [Dalton], 13 December 1863, Kelly Letters.

111. The winter quarters of both armies were populated by Black servants who performed a number of chores and paramilitary duties. Wiley, *The Life of Johnny Reb,* 103, 117, 327–28; Rollins, *Black Southerners in Gray,* 75–89.

112. Thomas H. Patterson, Company I, 30th Alabama, submitted a second resignation letter for William C. Patterson dated at Talladega, Alabama, on 27 December 1863. *CSR/Alabama,* 335:877, 878.

113. John Rowland was a young Jacksonville merchant. No service records were found to connect him to the 51st Alabama. *Eighth Census/Alabama,* 2:296.

114. Captain William P. Howell reported that a number of masonic lodges were organized in the winter camps at Dalton, including the John C. Reid Lodge in the 28th Alabama and a second known as the Zach Deas Lodge. William P. Howell, "History of the 25th Alabama Infantry Regiment," Confederate Regimental History Files.

115. Hugh Francis was working as an agent for Confederate postal service and visiting his son, Joseph H. Francis, a private in Company D, 23rd Tennessee. Francis-Martin Genealogy Collection; *Eighth Census/Tennessee,* 6:74; *CSR/Tennessee,* 214:264; *Jacksonville Republican,* 2 April 1863.

116. Benjamin Jefferson Hill (1825–80) was commander of the 35th Tennessee at Dalton. He also served as provost marshal general of the Army of Tennessee under Joe Johnston from late 1863 through 30 November 1864. *CSR/Tennessee,* 262:934; Krick, *Lee's Colonels,* 448.

117. Alfred Y. Glover served as assistant commissary for subsistence at Dalton, Georgia, in December 1863. *CSR/Alabama,* 403:451.

118. Despite his efforts to get a permanent assignment to the commissary department, Jo Francis remained in the 51st Alabama until his parole at Charlotte, North Carolina, on 3 May 1865. Ibid., 445:443.

119. Tom and Fannie Francis did not attend the wedding of Jim Francis and Sadie Whitehead on Wednesday, 17 February 1864. Rowland Journal, 50.

120. Tom Francis was obviously concerned about getting his hogs slaughtered and securing the meat. Shortages of bacon were widespread by late 1863, and commissary officers advertised in local papers offering to buy bacon for the army. *Jacksonville Republican,* 30 May 1863, 2 April 1864.

121. The real purpose for writing his mother was made clear when Tom Francis, absentee farmer and landowner, confessed his frustration at not hearing from his father and not knowing the status of his fields and lands in Calhoun County. Francis-Martin Family Papers.

122. Another example of the use and trust placed in body servants by Confederate soldiers. *CSR/Alabama,* 332:247; Rollins, *Black Southerners in Gray,* 9–16, 75–87.

123. Jim Montgomery (1844–64), John Francis's first cousin, volunteered as a seventeen-year-old private in Company I, 19th Alabama Infantry Regiment, at Coloma, Alabama, on 10 August 1861. Francis-Martin Genealogy Collection; *CSR/Alabama,* 274:1342.

124. Joseph H. Francis, son of Hugh Francis, was a member of the 23rd Tennessee stationed near Dalton, Georgia. *CSR/Tennessee,* 214:264.

125. The 51st Alabama was near Knoxville, Tennessee, on 31 December 1863 in Colonel Alfred A. Russell's brigade, and Morgan's division in Will Martin's cavalry corps with James Longstreet's army. *OR,* 31, pt. 3:891.

126. Robert J. Clark, oldest son of John R. Clark, was listed in the 1860 census as a nineteen-year-old dry goods clerk, but he does not appear on service records for the 30th Alabama. His younger brother Edward T. Clark was in Company B, 30th Alabama. *Eighth Census/Alabama,* 2:292.

127. Major John Francis prepared and submitted a "Report of furloughs entitled to under gen'l. order 227" on 24 December 1863 for the ten companies in the 30th Alabama. Francis-Martin Family Papers.

128. Dr. James C. Francis apparently did not make a visit to the winter quarters of the Army of Tennessee. Ibid.

129. Annie Clark (c. sixteen years old) was enrolled in school at Centenary Institute at Summerfield, Alabama, with Emma Francis. Her brothers were Robert J. and Edward T. Clark, the latter a private in Company B, 30th Alabama. *Eighth Census/Alabama,* 2:292; *CSR/Alabama,* 332:247.

Chapter 7

1. Connelly, *Autumn of Glory,* 281–86; Symonds, *Joseph E. Johnston,* 248; Richard E. Beringer et al., *Why the South Lost the Civil War,* 286–92.

2. Ulysses S. Grant, *Personal Memoirs of Ulysses S. Grant* (1885; reprint, 2 vols. in 1, New York: The Great Commanders, 1994), 337–42; Sherman, *Memoirs,* 25–30; Esposito, *West Point Atlas,* 1:120–47; David Herbert Donald, *Lincoln* (New York: Simon & Shuster, 1995), 488–92, 498–501.

3. Sam Watkins, *"Company Aytch" or A Side Show of the Big Show and Other Sketches,* 102–5; Symonds, *Joseph E. Johnston,* 249–50.

4. *CSR/Alabama,* 333:401, 335:878; Francis-Martin Family Papers.

5. Rowland Journal, 50; Francis-Martin Family Papers.

6. *CSR/General & Staff,* 164; *OR,* 32, 3:684, 767; *Jacksonville Republican,* 9, 23 April 1863; Miller, *Wheeler's Favorites,* 19.

7. *CSR/General & Staff,* 96; *OR,* 32, pt. 2:589; Connelly, *Autumn of Glory,* 251, 253, 313; Current, *Encyclopedia of the Confederacy,* 2:776–77; Boatner, *Civil War Dictionary,* 402, 407–8.

8. Francis-Martin Family Papers.

9. Charles Alden Rowland (1833–1902) served as a quartermaster sergeant in the 43rd Georgia Infantry Regiment in Stovall's brigade. Rowland Journal, iv, 86–87; *OR,* 32, pt. 2:589.

10. *CSR/General & Staff,* 98; Francis-Martin Family Papers.

11. Grant, *Personal Memoirs,* 362–63, 383–90; Sherman, *Memoirs,* 29–34; Albert Castel, *Decision in the West: The Atlanta Campaign of 1864,* 111–19, 135–39.

12. Reynolds's brigade included the 58th and 60th North Carolina and 54th and 63rd Virginia infantry regiments. *OR,* 32, pt. 2:587.

13. *CSR/Alabama,* 333:401; *Jacksonville Republican,* 21 May 1864, 20 January 1866; Francis-Martin Family Papers.

14. *Jacksonville Republican,* 20 January 1866; Francis-Martin Family Papers.

15. *CSR/Alabama,* 445:443; List of Detailed Men–Present and Absent [since 1 April 1864], 51st Alabama Cavalry, Confederate Muster Roll Collection; Francis-Martin Family Papers.

16. Gabe chose to escape to freedom while the 51st Alabama was in Longstreet's corps near Knoxville. *Eighth Census/Alabama, Slave Schedule,* 1:265.

17. The number of fugitive slaves escaping to the Union lines grew as more areas of the Confederacy came under Union control. James M. McPherson, *The Negro's Civil War: How American Negroes Felt and Acted During the War for the Union* (New York: Pantheon Books, 1965), 25–28, 59–63.

18. Pork and bacon supplies in the Confederacy had been significantly reduced by January 1864 by the ravages of war and disease. Gates, *Agriculture and the Civil War,* 89–93; Massey, *Ersatz in the Confederacy,* 60–62; *Jacksonville Republican,* 2 April 1864.

19. By January 1864, corn had become an important food for both civilian and military populations in the Confederate states. The Alabama legislature attempted to limit the sale of corn to the county where it was produced. Gates, *Agriculture and the Civil War,* 101.

20. It is difficult to estimate the true value of Tom Francis's $10,000 in Confederate money and bonds in January 1864. However, at the beginning of 1864, one dollar in gold in Richmond was worth about $20 to $20.50 in Confederate treasury notes. Long, *The Civil War Day by Day,* 727–28.

21. Richard (Dick) Avery Ingram and Hezekiah Ingram, younger brothers of Amy Ingram Francis, lived near Alexandria, 12 miles southwest of Jacksonville. Francis-Martin Genealogy Collection; *Eighth Census/Alabama,* 2:652, 667.

22. Apparently a reference to his uncle James Montgomery, whose wife, Elizabeth Jane Ingram, was a younger sister to Amy Ingram Francis. *Eighth Census/Alabama,* 3:281; Francis-Martin Genealogy Collection.

23. There was a serious shortage of horses and mules east of the Mississippi, but the Francis family apparently needed to reduce their stock. Goff, *Confederate Supply,* 72–73, 212–13. See also Charles W. Ramsdell, "General Robert E. Lee's Horse Supply, 1862–1865," *American Historical Review* 35 (July 1930):758–77.

24. Jim and Kit, slaves owned by Tom Francis, lived on his land in Calhoun County under Dr. James C. Francis's supervision. Francis-Martin Family Papers.

25. John H. Forney remained with his post at Enterprise, Mississippi, until July 1864, when he was transferred to command a Texas infantry division in the Trans-Mississippi Department. *CSR/General & Staff,* 96; Annie Forney Daugette, "The Life of Major General John H. Forney," 375–77.

26. Martin's cavalry division reported at Dalton on 30 April 1864 with two brigades commanded by Brigadier Generals John Tyler Morgan and Alfred Iverson. *OR,* 32, pt. 3:684, 720, 739, 748, 767–68, 801, 866, 870; Miller, *Wheeler's Favorites,* 18–19, 78, 80.

27. William C. Patterson's resignation became effective on 28 January 1864. *CSR/Alabama,* 335:878.

28. Charles M. Shelley left camp on 14 January 1864, leaving Major John Francis in command of the 30th Alabama. Samuel C. Kelly to Amie P. Kelly, Stump House, 14 Jan. 1863, Kelly Letters.

29. B. O. Ramey served as commander of the Home Reserves in Calhoun County. *Jacksonville Republican,* 31 October, 19 December 1863.

30. Samuel Rush Watkins, Company H, 1st Tennessee, provided a different perspective on the weather and described spending time in winter quarters at Dalton "during the cold, bad winter of 1863–64." Watkins, *"Company Aytch,"* 102.

31. Joe Johnston provided regular rations, tobacco and whiskey twice a week, and clothes, shoes, and hats as needed, and he granted furloughs to one-third of the army at a time. Ibid., 102–5; Symonds, *Joseph E. Johnston,* 249–50.

32. Elizabeth McKinne Wilde (1857–64), daughter of Anne McKinne Whitehead (1836–1909) and John Richard Wilde (1835–98), died of typhoid fever on 1 February 1864. Rowland Journals, 37–39, 41–43.

33. Augusta, Georgia, was an important manufacturing and transportation center on the upper Savannah River. It suffered little damage from Sherman's Georgia campaign and remained in Confederate hands until April 1865. Black, *Railroads of the Confederacy,* 6, 9, 73, 161–62, 259; Michael Golay, *A Ruined Land: The End of the Civil War* (New York: John Wiley & Sons, Inc., 1999), 95, 189–91; Beringer, *Why the South Lost the Civil War,* 217.

34. Sadie Whitehead turned nineteen on 26 January 1864 and married James Carrington Francis, Jr., on 17 February 1864. Rowland Journals, 40, 50.

35. Ever the dutiful and loyal son, John Francis gave his father his travel itinerary to attend Jim Francis's wedding. Francis-Martin Family Papers.

36. William E. Wailes, Company F, 3rd Alabama cavalry, was detached as aide-de-camp to Joe Wheeler on 18 November 1862. He remained with Wheeler's staff as assistant adjutant general until paroled in 1865. *CSR/Alabama,* 12:1499.

37. Joe Wheeler was commander of the cavalry corps of the Army of Tennessee from 16 March 1863 through the fall of 1864. *OR,* 32, pt. 2:605, 708, 798–99, 820, pt. 3:510, 592, 658, 674, 795, 810–11, 870; Castel, *Decision in the West,* 111, 127–28.

38. Union and Confederate forces were involved in several skirmishes along Rocky Face Ridge on 23–27 February 1864. *OR,* 32, pt. 1:417–84; Castel, *Decision in the West,* 54; Long, *Civil War Day by Day,* 468–69.

39. John Francis was one of twenty attendants at the wedding of Jim Francis and Sadie Whitehead on 17 February 1864. Rowland Journals, 50.

40. Frank Ward remained unidentified.

41. Major Tom Francis and Hop Francis were temporarily assigned to the Demopolis commissary post with John H. Forney. *CSR/General & Staff,* 96, 98.

42. Miller "Tobe" Francis Turney was a captain and assistant quartermaster with the 23rd Tennessee Battalion in Brown's brigade, Stevenson's division. His mother, Mary Theresa Francis Turney, was Dr. James C. Francis's older sister. *CSR/General & Staff,* 252; *Eighth Census/Tennessee,* 6:80.

43. Dr. Wallace Estill and his wife were prewar residents of Winchester, Franklin County, Tennessee. He served as surgeon in Peter Turney's 1st Tennessee Infantry Regiment. *Tennesseans in the Civil War,* 1:255; *CSR/General & Staff,* 87.

44. Captain Euclid Johnson was assistant quartermaster in the 30th Alabama. *CSR/Alabama,* 334:607.

45. John H. Forney met with Joe Johnston at Dalton and traveled to Richmond in May

1864 to request orders and an assignment to command. *CSR/General & Staff,* 96; Daugette, "The Life of Major General John H. Forney," 375.

46. Thomas Carmichael Hindman was replaced as commander of the Second Corps in Johnston's Army of Tennessee by Lieutenant General John Bell Hood on 28 February 1864. *OR,* 31, pt. 2:684, pt. 3:824–25, 833, 850, 32, pt. 2:812; Connelly, *Autumn of Glory,* 251, 253, 313.

47. Will Martin's cavalry division, including the 51st Alabama, arrived at Dalton in late March 1864. *OR,* 32, pt. 3:615, 654, 681, 684, 767; Miller, *Wheeler's Favorites,* 19.

48. John M. Wyly served on John H. Forney's staff (1861–65) and traveled to Dalton with Forney, who was looking for a new command. *CSR/Alabama,* 200:1758.

49. John H. Forney apparently came to visit Joe Johnston at Dalton to discuss a transfer to the Army of Tennessee. He was transferred to the Trans-Mississippi Department in July 1864 to command a Texas infantry division. *CSR/General & Staff,* 96; *OR,* 32, pt. 3:608; Crawford, *Forney Forever,* 19, 21, 23; Daugette, "The Life of Major General John H. Forney," 375.

50. Thomas C. Hindman submitted a letter of resignation after Hood replaced him as commander of the Second Corps on 28 February 1864, but President Davis refused to accept his resignation. *OR,* 32, pt. 2:812, 820; Richard M. McMurry, *John Bell Hood and the War for Southern Independence* (Lexington: University Press of Kentucky, 1982), 85–86, 88–89, 98.

51. Emma and Willie Francis were enrolled for the winter quarter at Centenary Institute in Summerfield, Alabama. Francis-Martin Family Papers.

52. The new $500 treasury notes with the portrait of General Thomas J. "Stonewall" Jackson (1824–63) were issued by the Confederate government by an act of 17 February 1864. Current, *Encyclopedia of the Southern Confederacy,* 1:433–34, 438; Schwab, *Confederate States of America,* 165–66.

53. Jo Francis was on furlough in Jacksonville and was ordered to return to active duty with the 51st Alabama. *CSR/Alabama,* 445:443.

54. Hop Francis was also on a furlough from his temporary commissary post at Demopolis, Alabama. Francis-Martin Family Papers.

55. Dr. James C. Francis was exchanging old treasury notes for a new $1,000 Confederate treasury certificate under the Funding Act of 17 February 1864. Schwab, *Confederate States of America,* 64, 117.

56. Tom Francis also attempted to exchange old treasury notes for his brother Miller Francis and Archibald Downing. Ibid.; *CSR/Alabama,* 193:452.

57. Counterfeit bank notes and treasury notes had appeared in large numbers throughout the Confederacy by 1862, and counterfeit currency was circulated by the invading Union armies. Schwab, *Confederate States of America,* 159–61.

58. M. J. A. Keith was a successful businessman and banker in Selma and was well known to both Tom and Jim Francis. *Eighth Census/Alabama,* 4:797.

59. The Union army near Chattanooga and in northern Georgia numbered approximately 82,000 present for duty in March 1862 and increased to 100,000 before the fighting began in May 1864. Symonds, *Joseph E. Johnston,* 266–67; Castel, *Decision in the West,* 78, 91; Kennett, *Marching Through Georgia,* 39.

60. Martin's cavalry division, including the 51st Alabama, was in camps near Oxford and Blue Mountain, Calhoun County, Alabama, from late March through late April 1864. *CSR/General & Staff,* 164; *Jacksonville Republican,* 9, 23 April 1864.

61. Miller Francis returned home 28 March 1864 with the 51st Alabama when it estab-

lished camps at Blue Mountain, Calhoun County, Alabama, before moving to Rome, Georgia, in April 1864. *OR,* 32, pt. 3:684, 767; *Jacksonville Republican,* 9 April 1864; Miller, *Wheeler's Favorites,* 19.

62. John W. Francis returned to Virginia after an extended furlough and delivered Jim Francis's slaves to Augusta on his return to the 10th Alabama. *CSR/Alabama,* 195:513; Francis-Martin Family Papers.

63. Elizabeth Estill Turney was the wife of Hopkins Lacey Turney, Jr., a first cousin to the Francis siblings. She sought refuge in Jacksonville with her mother-in-law, Mary Theresa Francis Turney. *Eighth Census/Tennessee,* 6:78; Francis-Martin Genealogy Collection.

64. Amy Francis raised an important issue with her question about Dr. Rivers's willingness "to take the money." The money was probably old issue currency and circulated at an inflated rate. See Schwab, *The Confederate States of America,* and Eugene M. Lerner, *Money, Prices, and Wages in the Confederacy, 1861–1865* (Chicago: University of Chicago Press, 1954).

65. John M. Smith enlisted in the Sallie Walker Boys at Jacksonville on 5 March 1862 and was elected second sergeant in Company B, 30th Alabama, at Camp Curry. *CSR/Alabama,* 335:1070.

66. When Jabez L. M. Curry ran for reelection to the Confederate Congress in November 1863, he was defeated by Marcus Henderson Cruikshank. He served on Joe Johnston's staff, March to July 1864, and for two months was a special aide to Joe Wheeler. McMillan, *The Alabama Confederate Reader,* 235–38; Current, *Encyclopedia of the Confederacy,* 1:439–40.

67. William M. Weir enlisted as a private in the Sallie Walker Boys at Jacksonville on 5 March 1862, and his service records listed no promotions. *CSR/Alabama,* 336:1234; *Jacksonville Republican,* 27 November 1862.

68. William W. Loring led his division in Mississippi by rail to Blue Mountain and overland through Calhoun County on 4–9 May 1864 to Rome, Georgia, en route to join Joe Johnston's Army of Tennessee. *OR,* 32, pt. 3:862, 38, pt. 4:97, 660–61, 670, 674–75, 680, 684–85; *CSR/General & Staff,* 159.

69. John Francis failed to mention the grand review of the army held by Joe Johnston on 19 April 1864. Rowland Journals, 86–87; Symonds, *Joseph E. Johnston,* 267–68; Castel, *Decision in the West,* 119.

70. Catharine Barnes Rowland (1838–1917) was Jim Francis's sister-in-law, and her husband, Charles Alden Rowland (1833–1902), was quartermaster sergeant in the 43rd Georgia Volunteer regiment. Rowland Journals, iii–iv; Lillian Henderson, *Roster of the Confederate Soldiers of Georgia, 1861–1865,* 4:701, 709.

71. Nicholas Airhart (Airheart) enlisted in the Ryan Guards, Company E, 30th Alabama, in Calhoun County, Alabama, on 6 March 1862. He submitted his letter of resignation as second lieutenant on 12 April 1864. *CSR/Alabama,* 332:32.

72. The Cleveland road ran north from Dalton through Crow Valley to Cleveland, Tennessee. It was located on the right wing of Johnston's army. *OR,* 31, pt. 3:866, 869; Symonds, *Joseph E. Johnston,* 273.

73. Nathaniel P. Banks's Red River Campaign, designed to capture Shreveport, Louisiana, suffered a series of defeats and setbacks between 12 March and 21 April 1864. Boatner, *The Civil War Dictionary,* 42, 118, 685–89; Long, *The Civil War Day by Day,* 474–506.

74. In mid-April 1864, Grant was preparing for a major campaign against Lee's Army of Northern Virginia. Grant, *Personal Memoirs,* 361–62, 372–83; Long, *The Civil War Day by Day,* 480–81, 483, 486, 490–92.

75. By late April 1864 Sherman's forces numbered approximately 100,000, nearly twice the size of Johnston's army, with 254 artillery pieces to 144 in the Confederate army. Long, *The Civil War Day by Day,* 483, 490–92; Castel, *Decision in the West,* 111–19.

76. Despite entreaties and invitations, Jim and Sadie Francis received no visits from Dr. Francis, Jim's mother, Amy, or his younger siblings. Francis-Martin Family Papers.

77. On Friday, 29 April 1864, two Union cavalry detachments clashed with Confederate pickets and cavalry near Tunnel Hill. *OR,* 32, pt. 1:688–92; Long, *The Civil War Day by Day,* 490–91.

78. Edward T. Clark recovered from dysentery and a painful arm wound received near Atlanta on 30 July 1864. He was paroled at Salisbury, North Carolina, on 2 May 1865. *CSR/Alabama,* 332:247; *Jacksonville Republican,* 20 August 1864.

79. J. L. Mattison enlisted as a twenty-three-year-old private in the Sallie Walker Boys at Jacksonville on 5 March 1862 and was later promoted to quartermaster sergeant. His service records were silent about his service after July 1863. *CSR/Alabama,* 334:741.

80. On 30 April 1864, Alexander W. Reynolds's brigade in Stevenson's division included four regiments, 58th North Carolina, 60th North Carolina, 54th Virginia, and 63rd Virginia. *OR,* 38, pt. 1:483, pt. 3:617, 869.

81. Nathan Shelley, a former Alabama legislator from Talladega, was elected attorney general in Texas and commissioned a brigadier general in the Texas state troops. Owen, *History of Alabama,* 4:1542.

82. Cartersville, Georgia, was located on the Western & Atlantic Railroad, which connected Dalton to Atlanta. Henry Woodhead, ed., *Echoes of Glory: Illustrated Atlas of the Civil War,* 249.

83. Martha Grant Francis was the wife of John W. Francis, and her newborn baby boy was their second child, joining his older sister, Nora (c. five years old). *Eighth Census/Alabama,* 2:286.

84. Calhoun, Georgia, was located on the Western & Atlantic Railroad about twenty-five miles northeast of Rome and twenty miles south of Dalton. Black, *Railroads of the Confederacy,* 6, 248–49, 259; Woodhead, *Echoes of Glory,* 249.

85. Rome, Georgia, located on the Etowah River, was on the Rome Railroad, which connected to the Western & Atlantic Railroad at Kingston. Black, *Railroads of the Confederacy,* 158; Woodhead, *Echoes of Glory,* 249.

86. John T. Morgan's brigade included the 1st Alabama Cavalry, 3rd Alabama Cavalry, 4th Alabama Cavalry, 7th Alabama Cavalry, 51st Alabama, and the 12th Alabama Battalion. It was assigned picket and courier duty on the Confederate left. *OR,* 38, pt. 3:642, pt. 4:711, 720, 722; Miller, *Wheeler's Favorites,* 24.

87. James B. McPherson's Army of the Tennessee struck the 66th Georgia in Steven's brigade on Johnston's left flank at Resaca about midafternoon on 9 May 1864. *OR,* 38, pt. 4:54–116; Castel, *Decision in the West,* 135–39.

88. On 11 May 1864, near Rocky Face Ridge, John Francis was wounded at about 9:00 A.M. while talking with Brigadier General Edmund W. Pettus. Family tradition holds that he was shot by a Yankee sharpshooter. *OR,* pt. 3:814; *CSR/Alabama,* 333:401; *Jacksonville Republican,* 21 May 1864.

89. Family tradition assumes this letter was written by John Francis's younger brother Jo Francis. However, Joe H. Francis, oldest son of John's uncle Hugh Francis, wrote this brief note to Dr. Francis. Jo Francis was in camp with the 51st Alabama at Calhoun, Georgia, on 10 May 1864. *CSR/Tennessee,* 214:264, 266.

90. Captain William F. "Tobe" Turney sent Jim Francis a telegram early on 12 May 1864 reporting his cousin John Francis's death. Ibid., 111:1573.

91. Elizabeth Rebecca Francis was born on 26 October 1835 and died on 2 May 1837. Francis-Martin Genealogy Collection.

92. Sadie Whitehead Francis met John Francis when he participated in her wedding in February 1864. Rowland Journals, 50–51, 69.

93. William Dowse Whitehead (1841–62) enlisted as a corporal in the Burke Sharpshooters, Company D, 2nd Georgia Volunteer Infantry, on 19 April 1861 in Burke County, Georgia. He was killed at the battle of Malvern Hill on 1 July 1862 and buried at Hollywood Cemetery, Richmond, Virginia. Ibid., iv; Henderson, *Roster of the Confederate Soldiers of Georgia,* 1:394.

94. Despite Euclid Johnson's telegraph, Jim Francis arrived after John Francis was buried near Kingston, Georgia. His remains were reinterred in the Jacksonville cemetery on Tuesday, 16 January 1866. *Jacksonville Republican,* 20 January 1866.

95. The 51st Alabama left Oxford and Blue Mountain in late April 1864 and established camps near Calhoun, Georgia, in early May 1864. *OR,* 32, pt. 3:514, 684, 739, 767, 870; *Jacksonville Republican,* 9 April 1864.

96. Morgan's brigade, including the 51st Alabama under the command of Colonel Milton L. Kirkpatrick, was stretched from Rome to Calhoun, Georgia, along the Oostanaula River. *OR,* 38, pt. 3:642, 801, 870, 899, 963; Krick, *Lee's Colonels,* 456; Woodhead, *Echoes of Glory,* 249.

97. Sherman's army made contact with Johnston's army in their new defensive positions at Resaca, about 90 miles from Atlanta, on the afternoon of 13 May. *OR,* 38, pt. 3:722, 874–75, pt. 4:698–703; Castel, *Decision in the West,* 149–54.

98. There was no glorious victory at Resaca. Johnston's army retreated across the Oostanaula around midnight on 15 May and reached Calhoun about 3:30 A.M. on 16 May 1864. *OR,* 38, pt. 4:170–203, 712–13, 716–17; Castel, *Decision in the West,* 150–81.

99. Cartersville was located on the Western & Atlantic Railroad southeast of Cassville and north of the Etowah River. Esposito, *West Point Atlas,* 1:145.

100. Morgan's brigade was involved in several skirmishes and engagements from 13 May through 15 May at Resaca, at Adamsville on 17 May, and on the Kingston road on 19 May. *OR,* 38, pt. 4:700–701, 709, 711–13, 715, 720–22; Castel, *Decision in the West,* 153, 168, 172–73, 190.

101. Jo Francis was on a special detail with Johnston's wagon train, which retreated to Cartersville on 17–19 May 1864. *CSR/Alabama,* 445:443; *OR,* 38, pt. 4:717, 722, 724–25; Castel, *Decision in the West,* 192–98.

102. Johnston's army retreated to Adairsville in the early morning of 17 May 1864 and that evening retreated southeastward below Cassville. *OR,* 38, pt. 4:232–69, 720–23, 726, 728; Castel, *Decision in the West,* 192–94.

103. By 20 May 1864, Joe Johnston's army was forced to retreat ever closer to Atlanta by Sherman's flanking efforts and superior numbers. *OR,* 38, pt. 4:267–69, 730–31; Castel, *Decision in the West,* 128–209.

104. On the night of 24 May 1864, Joe Wheeler led a raid from Cartersville to Cass Station; he captured 80 wagons and took 158 prisoners. *OR,* 38, pt. 4:742; Castel, *Decision in the West,* 219–20.

105. Jo Francis's poetry to his mother was an adaptation of an old Primitive Baptist hymn "Sister Thou Wast Mild and Lovely." Ginny Hawker and Kay Justice, *Pathway to West Virginia* (Cox's Mill, W. Va: Pathway Productions, 1988).

106. Marietta, Georgia, was located on the Western & Atlantic Railroad southeast of Allatoona, east of Kennesaw Mountain, and about 12 miles north of Atlanta. *OR,* 38, pt. 4:551–52, 783–84; Castel, *Decision in the West,* 289–90; Esposito, *West Point Atlas,* 1:145.

Chapter 8

1. *OR,* 38, pt. 2:515–16, 571, 646–47, 684–85, pt. 3:612–21, pt. 5:92–93, 99–100, 865, 868–71; Watkins, *"Company Aytch,"* 143; Castel, *Decision in the West,* 329–41, 360–63.

2. *CSR/General & Staff,* 98; Francis-Martin Family Papers.

3. *OR,* 38, pt. 2:904–11; *Jacksonville Republican,* 23 July 1864; McMillan, *The Alabama Confederate Reader,* 255–71; Moore, *A Calhoun County, Alabama, Boy,* 17.

4. Francis-Martin Family Papers.

5. Connelly, *Autumn of Glory,* 512; Joseph T. Glatthaar, *The March to the Sea and Beyond: Sherman's Troops in the Savannah and Carolinas Campaigns,* 9–10; Long, *The Civil War Day by Day,* 604–16.

6. *CSR/General & Staff,* 98; *CSR/Alabama,* 445:443, 158:789; Rowland Journals, 242–46.

7. Samuel J. Martin, *Kill-Cavalry: The Life of Union General Hugh Judson Kilpatrick,* 205–13; Long, *The Civil War Day by Day,* 627–36; Miller, *Wheeler's Favorites,* 28–29.

8. *OR,* 47, pt. 2:450; John G. Barrett, *Sherman's March Through the Carolinas,* 50, 56–57; Martin, *Kill-Cavalry,* 212–14; Long, *The Civil War Day by Day,* 636.

9. *OR,* 44:411–12; Barrett, *Sherman's March Through the Carolinas,* 52–54, 58–60, 80–89, 96–97, 102, 106, 110; Glatthaar, *March to the Sea and Beyond,* 142–46; McMillan, *The Alabama Confederate Reader,* 273–76; Miller, *Wheeler's Favorites,* 28–29.

10. Rowland Journals, 281; Francis-Martin Genealogy Collection; Francis-Martin Family Papers.

11. Grant, *Personal Memoirs,* 541–51; Francis-Martin Family Papers.

12. *OR,* 47, pt. 1:1061; Symonds, *Joseph E. Johnston,* 355–57.

13. J. D. Arnold to T. M. Owen, Jacksonville, Ala., 4 February 1911, 30th Alabama Infantry Regiment, Confederate Regimental History Files; George Brewer, "From Manuscript by Geo. Brewer," 30th Alabama Infantry Regiment, ibid.; Kelly, "A History of the Thirtieth Alabama Volunteers," 167.

14. On 2 June 1864 the Confederate and Union armies faced each other in the Dallas–New Hope Church area northwest of Atlanta with scattered skirmishing and sniping. *OR,* 38, pt. 4:385–86, 389–90, 392–93, 752–54, 756; Castel, *Decision in the West,* 256–57; Esposito, *West Point Atlas,* 1:145; Long, *The Civil War Day by Day,* 513–14.

15. Major Miller Francis remained with the 51st Alabama near Atlanta. *CSR/Alabama,* 158:789.

16. Hop Francis continued to serve on special detail as a storekeeper with the commissary depot in Montgomery, Alabama. Unfiled Papers & Slips, 135:5385, 5573.

17. Captain Jim Francis received a transfer from the commissary purchasing office in Augusta to the commissary depot in Athens, Georgia. *CSR/General & Staff,* 98.

18. John T. Montgomery, a first cousin, was seriously wounded during the Atlanta campaign and attached as a nurse to Lee Hospital at Columbus, Georgia, in October 1864. *CSR/Alabama,* 274:1343.

19. The right flank of Johnston's army fought a series of skirmishes at Pine Mountain and

Acworth on 5 June, at Big Shanty and Raccoon Creek on 6 June, and at Lost Mountain on 8 June. *OR,* 38, pt. 4:422–24, 428, 435–37, 758–61, 764–65; Castel, *Decision in the West,* 259–67.

20. By June 1864, Major Daniel Peter Forney had served in three Alabama units: 2nd Alabama Volunteers, Morgan's 51st Alabama, and 3rd Alabama Cavalry. His service records are silent on his assignment in the Trans-Mississippi with his brother John H. Forney. *CSR/Alabama,* 445:442; *CSR/General & Staff,* 96; Miller, *Wheeler's Favorites,* 35–36.

21. Captain Jim Francis moved to his new assignment in Athens, Georgia, in late July 1864. *CSR/General & Staff,* 98.

22. Union forces controlled Huntsville and much of North Alabama, but there were no reports of a Union raid near Blue Mountain in late May or early June 1864. *OR,* 38, pt. 4:379, 382–85, 391, 733, 754, 760; McMillan, *The Alabama Confederate Reader,* 127, 262.

23. J. J. D. Renfroe, a Baptist minister from Talladega, Alabama, served as chaplain to the 10th Alabama Infantry Regiment. He resigned on 29 October 1864 at Petersburg, Virginia. *CSR/Alabama,* 198:1320; *Eighth Census/Alabama,* 12:629; McMillan, *The Alabama Confederate Reader,* 95.

24. The new $5 bills were redesigned and lithographed in Scotland by Edward Keatinge with the note backs in blue. They were referred to as "blue backs" and also featured a red tint on the face of each note. Schwab, *Confederate States of America,* 64–65; Current, *Encyclopedia of the Confederacy,* 1:433, 437–38.

25. Joseph H. Francis was the eldest son of Hugh and Catherine Buchanan Francis. His service records do not provide details regarding his wound received in June 1864 during the Atlanta campaign. *CSR/Tennessee,* 214:264.

26. Hopkins Turney Francis (1846–64) enlisted in the 23rd Tennessee at Dalton, Georgia, on 20 January 1864, eleven days before his eighteenth birthday. He was killed on 22 June 1864 in action near Marietta, Georgia. Ibid., 214:266.

27. Sherman launched an artillery bombardment of Joe Johnston's forces entrenched on Kennesaw Mountain at 8:00 A.M. on Monday, 27 June 1864. He followed with a general attack that faltered, suffering nearly 3,000 casualties and failing to dislodge the Confederates. *OR,* 38, pt. 1:335–36, 632–39, 685–98, 703–11, 887–88, pt. 3:98–99, 178–88, 221–22, 317–18, 900–901, 913–15; Castel, *Decision in the West,* 305–21.

28. George W. Harrison enlisted in Company D, 51st Alabama, at Oxford, Alabama, on 11 August. His service records are silent on the date and place of his death. *CSR/Alabama,* 446:571.

29. John B. Prater enlisted as a private in Company A, 51st Alabama, on 22 March 1862, at Fort Pillow, Tennessee. His service records are silent on his service in the Atlanta campaign. Ibid., 447:1090.

30. Burr Nabors enlisted in Company A, 51st Alabama, at Fort Pillow, Tennessee, on 22 March 1862. His service records provide no information after 31 December 1863. Ibid., 971.

31. John T. Morgan was accused of drunkenness and placed under arrest at Atlanta. Hood dismissed the charges against him as unfounded, but Morgan was not restored to command of his cavalry brigade. *CSR/General & Staff,* 182; Current, *Encyclopedia of the Confederacy,* 4:1746; Davis, ed., *Confederate Generals,* 4:191.

32. William Wirt Allen (1835–94) replaced Morgan as brigade commander in Martin's division, Wheeler's cavalry corps. *CSR/Alabama,* 1:35; Current, *Encyclopedia of the Confederacy,* 4:27.

33. On 5 August 1864, Morgan was released from arrest and assigned to organize stragglers from the cavalry corps into a unit. Davis, *Confederate Generals,* 4:191.

34. William D. White enlisted in the Dudley Snow Rangers, Company D, 51st Alabama Mounted Infantry, at Oxford, Alabama, on 27 May 1862. He was elected captain on 7 May following the resignation of Captain Robert W. Draper on 20 April 1863. *CSR/Alabama,* 447:1504; *Jacksonville Republican,* 24 July 1862; Miller, *Wheeler's Favorites,* 46, 229.

35. The Board of Domestic Missions of the Southern Baptist Convention, the Presbyterian Church's Committee on Domestic Missions, and the Methodist Episcopal Church (South) played leading roles in ministering to Confederate soldiers and supplying Bibles, testaments, and religious tracts. Gardiner H. Shattuck, Jr., *A Shield and Hiding Place: The Religious Life of the Civil War Armies* (Macon, Ga.: Mercer University Press, 1987), 46–49.

36. Joseph H. Francis and Hopkins Turney Francis were sons of Hugh and Catherine Buchanan Francis. Turney Francis was killed near Atlanta on 22 June and buried at Jacksonville on 26 June 1864. *CSR/Tennessee,* 214:266; *Jacksonville Republican,* 9 July 1864.

37. Alexander Woods, probate court judge of Calhoun County, and J. J. D. Renfroe, a Baptist minister from Talladega, met the boat carrying the remains of Turney Francis on Saturday, 25 June 1864, at Montgomery, Alabama. *Eighth Census/Alabama,* 2:285, 12:629.

38. Hop Francis's cousin Joseph H. Francis was in the Montgomery area and claimed his brother Turney Francis's body. *Jacksonville Republican,* 9 July 1864; Francis-Martin Genealogy Collection.

39. Late on the evening of 2 July 1864, Johnston's army withdrew from its defensive positions on Kennesaw Mountain and established temporary entrenchments eight miles south of Marietta at Smyrna Station. Connelly, *Autumn of Glory,* 391–92; Castel, *Decision in the West,* 327–30.

40. John R. Castleberry enlisted in Company F, 51st Alabama Mounted Infantry, at Talladega on 29 May 1862. He was elected second lieutenant on 2 September 1862 and assigned to Morgan's wagon train in December 1863. *CSR/Alabama,* 445:219; Miller, *Wheeler's Favorites,* 53, 128.

41. J. H. Payne enlisted as a private in Company I, 51st Alabama Mounted Infantry, at Selma, Alabama, on 29 July 1862. He was wounded slightly at Murfreesboro on 31 December 1862 and was detailed as a wagon driver by John T. Morgan in December 1863. *CSR/Alabama,* 447:1029; Miller, *Wheeler's Favorites,* 65, 197.

42. During the morning hours, Union bands played and troops celebrated Independence Day. On the evening of the fourth, there was heavy fighting along the center of the Confederate line east of the Western & Atlantic Railroad. Castel, *Decision in the West,* 331–32.

43. The 3rd Alabama Cavalry Regiment was made up of companies from Autauga, Calhoun, Choctaw, Dallas, Mobile, Monroe, and Perry counties. Brewer, *Alabama,* 679–80; Miller, *Wheeler's Favorites,* 81.

44. The Union forces celebrated the fourth with bands playing and cheering and drinking by the troops, especially by Oliver O. Howard's corps in George H. Thomas's Army of the Tennessee. Castel, *Decision in the West,* 331–32.

45. Prior to the war, Eufaula, Barbour County, Alabama, was a prosperous community on the west bank of the Chattahoochee River and home to many successful slave-owning planters. David Williams, *Rich Man's War: Class, Caste, and Confederate Defeat in the Lower Chattahoochee Valley* (Athens: University of Georgia Press, 1998), 10, 13–18.

46. The deteriorating status of the Francis brothers' horses paralleled the condition of

horses and draft animals in the Confederate armies. Their animals were malnourished and weak from the lack of adequate supplies of corn and forage. Goff, *Confederate Supply,* 212–13, 237–39.

47. On 10–19 July 1864, Major General Lovell H. Rousseau led a successful Union cavalry raid through east Alabama to destroy the West Point & Montgomery Railroad from Tuskegee to Opelika, Alabama. *OR,* 38, pt. 2:904–9; McMillan, *The Alabama Confederate Reader,* 259–73.

48. After delays caused by Union raids in north Georgia, Jim and Sadie Francis moved from Augusta to Athens after 26 July 1864. Rowland Journals, 147, 150–52, 154–55.

49. Sadie Whitehead Francis's father, Amos Grattan Whitehead, and her two brothers, John Philpot Whitehead II and William Dowse Whitehead, attended the University of Georgia at Athens. Ibid., iv, 23.

50. Leiper and his family were acquaintances of Jim Francis's Whitehead and Rowland in-laws. Ibid., 105, 124–29, 145, 166–67, 181.

51. Apparently a reference to Daniel Peter Forney of the 3rd Alabama Cavalry, Morgan's brigade, Martin's division. *CSR/Alabama,* 445:442; *CSR/General & Staff,* 96; Krick, *Lee's Colonels,* 439.

52. John W. Francis, a first lieutenant in Company G, 10th Alabama, was killed on 30 July 1864 during the Union siege of Petersburg, Virginia. He was survived by his wife, Martha, a daughter, Nora L. Francis, and a young son. *CSR/Alabama,* 193:513; *Eighth Census/Alabama,* 2:286; *Jacksonville Republican,* 20 August 1864.

53. Sadie Whitehead Francis was approximately three months pregnant with her first child, Elizabeth McKinne Francis, born in Athens, Georgia, on 23 February 1865. Francis-Martin Genealogy Collection; Francis-Martin Family Papers.

54. The only Union raids actually to come close to Athens, Georgia, occurred on Tuesday, 2 August 1864. Athens remained free of Union troops until the surrender of Johnston's Army of Tennessee on 28 April 1865. Kenneth Coleman, *Confederate Athens* (Athens: University of Georgia Press, 1967), 170–72.

55. The Francis family lost four kinsmen within ninety days between 12 May and 30 July 1864: John C. Francis, Hopkins Turney Francis, John W. Francis, and James Montgomery. Their obituaries appeared in the *Jacksonville Republican* on 21 May, 9 July, 20 August, 1 September 1864.

56. W. Coleman Land was a jeweler and watchmaker in Jacksonville. *Eighth Census/Alabama,* 2:286; *Jacksonville Republican,* 2 January 1862.

57. Tom Crow was listed in the 1860 census as the eighteen-year-old son of Daniel Crow living with his parents at Alexandria, Calhoun County, Alabama. *Eighth Census/Alabama,* 2:679.

58. Daniel Weisiger Adams (1821–72) commanded a cavalry brigade in North Alabama and Mississippi in 1864 and assumed command of the District of Central Alabama on 24 September 1864. Current, *Encyclopedia of the Confederacy,* 1:1; Wakelyn, *Biographical Dictionary of the Confederacy,* 67.

59. Fred was a servant employed by Tom Francis in the Confederate commissary service. He traveled from Blue Mountain to Selma by the Tennessee & Alabama Rivers Railroad and to Meridian, Mississippi, over the Alabama & Mississippi Rivers Railroad. See Richard Rollins, "Servants and Soldiers: Tennessee's Black Southerners in Gray" in Rollins, ed., *Black Southerners in Gray: Essays on Afro-Americans in Confederate Armies,* 75–93.

60. William McMinn served as an assistant quartermaster with the 10th Alabama in Virginia. He was promoted to major and transferred to the commissary bureau in Alabama after 1862. *CSR/Alabama,* 195:1052.

61. Fort Browder was located approximately 12 miles northwest of Eufaula, Alabama, near the source of Chewalla Creek. Remington and Kallsen, *Historical Atlas of Alabama,* 1:12, 14.

62. Gabriel B. Douthit was the circuit clerk of Calhoun County, Alabama. *Eighth Census/Alabama,* 2:299; *Jacksonville Republican,* 23 July 1864.

63. Captain William D. White, Company D, 51st Alabama, was apparently in command of a small detachment of Allen's cavalry brigade at Fort Browder. *CSR/Alabama,* 447:1504.

64. Glenville, Alabama, was located about fifteen miles north of Fort Bowder and three miles east of the North Fork Cowikee Creek. Owen, *History of Alabama,* 2:1213; Anne Kendrick Walker, *Backtracking in Barbour County; A Narrative of the Last Alabama Frontier* (Richmond, Va.: The Dietz Press, 1941), 152.

65. Edward L. Woodward, Jo Francis's first cousin, enlisted as a private in Company D, 51st Alabama Mounted Infantry, at Fosterville, Tennessee, in May 1863. His mother was Malinda Jane Francis, Dr. James C. Francis's younger sister, and his father was Edward Levy Woodward. Francis-Martin Genealogy Collection; *CSR/Alabama,* 447:1558.

66. William A. Driskill was listed in the 1860 census as a thirty-one-year-old grocer. He lived in Jacksonville in close proximity to Dr. James C. Francis's family and Miller and Julia Francis. *Eighth Census/Alabama,* 2:285.

67. A reference to the death of Jim Montgomery (1844–64), a first cousin and son of James and Elizabeth Montgomery, whose obituary appeared in the *Jacksonville Republican* on 1 September 1864. Francis-Martin Genealogy Collection; *Jacksonville Republican,* 1 September 1864.

68. Jim Francis was engaged in purchasing cattle and other supplies sent to support Robert E. Lee's Army of Northern Virginia. *CSR/General & Staff,* 98.

69. Wilson Michael Bates was a prominent planter and slave owner in Barbour County, Alabama, with real estate valued at $22,000 and a personal estate valued at $131,000 in 1860. His Batesville Plantation was located about three miles north of Fort Browder along the South Fork Cowikee Creek. *Eighth Census/Alabama,* 1:389; Walker, *Backtracking in Barbour County,* 327–30.

70. Religious revivals, prayer meetings, and conversions were widespread in Confederate forces. Shattuck, *A Shield and Hiding Place,* 102–04. See also Michael Barton, *Goodmen: The Character of Civil War Soldiers* (University Park: Pennsylvania State University Press, 1981), 24–33.

71. The Cowikee Church was apparently close to Fort Browder.

72. Unlike the wild turkey, the opossum was never valued for its meat, but it has been the target of hunters for over three hundred years for sport and its fur. See South Carolina Wildlife Magazine, *Southeastern Wildlife Cookbook: A Collection of Recipes for Sea and Freshwater Food, Large and Small game, and Savory Oddities from the Wild,* rev. ed. (Columbia: University of South Carolina Press, 1989), 49–50.

73. Wheeler's cavalry corps, including the 51st Alabama, harassed Union cavalry units from Dalton, Georgia, north, to Gadsden, Alabama, on the west, and eastward to Augusta, Georgia, from mid-October through November 1864. Miller, *Wheeler's Favorites* 26–27.

74. While Jo Francis was reading Charles Dickens's *David Copperfield* at Fort Browder, Catharine Barnes Whitehead Rowland, Jim Francis's sister-in-law, also found the novel to be delightful reading and declared it Dickens's best. Rowland Journals, 259.

75. Emma and Willie Francis returned to their studies at Centenary Institute in October 1864. Francis-Martin Family Papers.

76. Jo Francis's Miss Cade remains elusive and unidentified.

77. Joseph H. Francis, "Cousin Jo" and eldest son of Hugh and Catherine Buchanan Francis, was apparently on furlough from the 23rd Tennessee Battalion and passing through on his way to visit his uncle James D. Porter. Porter was married to Susan M. Francis, an older sister of Dr. James C. Francis. Francis-Martin Genealogy Collection; *CSR/Tennessee,* 214:264.

78. Jo Francis's letter was written in ink over a letter from his sister Emma that was written in pencil. Francis-Martin Family Papers.

79. In 1864, Wilsonville, Alabama, was located on the Alabama & Tennessee Rivers Railroad in eastern Shelby County about one mile from the Coosa River. Remington and Kallsen, *Historical Atlas of Alabama,* 1:288, 293; Owen, *History of Alabama,* 2:1407.

80. Jo Francis was on detail with a wagon train in support of William Wirt Allen's division, Wheeler's cavalry corps. Allen replaced Will Martin as commander of the division in August 1864. *CSR/Alabama,* 1:35; Current, *Encyclopedia of the Confederacy,* 1:27.

81. Wheeler's cavalry corps traveled eastward through Milledgeville on the Oconee River to Waynesboro. They fought Union cavalry commanded by Brigadier General Hugh Judson Kilpatrick (1836–81) for two days before arriving at Augusta on the Savannah River. *OR,* 44:362–65, 406–10, 647, 917, 988; Long, *The Civil War Day by Day,* 600–601; Glatthaar, *The March to the Sea and Beyond,* 160.

82. Jo Francis arrived at Amos Grattan Whitehead's home, Ivanhoe, Burke County, Georgia, on 14 December 1864. Whitehead's plantation suffered extensive damage from Kilpatrick's Union cavalry forces on 27 November 1864. *OR,* 44:917; Rowland Journals, 222–24, 236.

83. John Richard Wilde married Anne McKinne Whitehead, oldest daughter of Elizabeth McKinne (1816–90) and Amos Grattan Whitehead, on 29 April 1856, and they lived in Augusta. Rowland Journal, iv, 12–13, 21, 50–51, 164–65, 236–37.

84. Barnwell County, South Carolina, is part of the coastal plain and remained very rural, agricultural, and sparsely populated well into the late twentieth century. Charles F. Kovack and John J. Winberry, *South Carolina: A Geography* (Boulder, Co.: Westview Press, 1987), 144, 149, 174.

85. Sherman's Georgia campaign reached Savannah on Saturday, 10 December 1864, and seven days later he demanded that Lieutenant General William Joseph Hardee surrender the city. Hardee evacuated his 10,000 men on 20 December 1864 by slipping across the Savannah River into South Carolina. *OR,* 44:743, 761, 772–73, 786, 968, 974; Glatthaar, *The March to the Sea and Beyond,* 9–10.

86. Sherman's army wrecked four railroad lines in South Carolina, including the South Carolina Railroad at Branchville. Glatthaar, *The March to the Sea and Beyond,* 137.

87. Jo Francis's request to his sister Willie to commit his letter to the "flames" was not an uncommon request from a Civil War soldier. Whenever they expressed their most personal doubts, they often asked their correspondent to destroy their letters. Francis-Martin Family Papers.

88. Mary Grant (c. nineteen years old) was the daughter of Elizabeth L. and James Freeman Grant, editor and publisher of the *Jacksonville Republican. Eighth Census/Alabama,* 2:291; Moore, *A Calhoun County Boy,* 19.

89. Jim and Sadie Francis spent the Christmas holidays with her sisters, Catharine Barnes Whitehead Rowland and Anne McKinne Wilde, and her parents in Augusta and Ivanhoe, Georgia. Rowland Journals, 242–46.

90. Miller Francis made a brief visit to Ivanhoe, Burke County, Georgia, on 1 December 1864, where he met Jim Francis's in-laws, Amos and Elizabeth Whitehead, and their daughter Catharine Barnes Whitehead Rowland and her family. Ibid., 227.

91. Mary Turney, daughter of Mary Theresa Francis and the late Hopkins Lacey Turney, married Gideon C. Ellis on 12 January 1865. He was an attorney in Jacksonville and had served as a private in Company A, 51st Alabama. *Eighth Census/Tennessee,* 6:78; *Eighth Census/ Alabama,* 2:286; *CSR/Alabama,* 445:399.

92. Candles had grown increasingly scarce in the Confederacy since 1861. Massey, *Ersatz in the Confederacy,* 106.

93. Another reference to Mary Grant, who was returning to school at Summerfield. *Eighth Census/Alabama,* 2:291.

94. The $300 payment to Richard Henderson Rivers, president of Centenary Institute, was apparently for tuition and fees for the winter term for Emma and Willie. McDonald, *Beginnings . . . of the University of North Alabama,* 37–38.

95. The $200 payment to Greene B. Garrett was for room and board for Emma and Willie. He was listed in the 1860 census as a fifty-nine-year-old Methodist Episcopal minister living at Summerfield, Alabama. *Eighth Census/Alabama,* 4:864.

96. Branchville, South Carolina, was a rail junction between Augusta and Charleston for the South Carolina Railroad and the Charlotte & South Carolina Railroad. Black, *Railroads of the Confederacy,* 272–73; Glatthaar, *The March to the Sea and Beyond,* 137; Golay, *A Ruined Land,* 100.

97. Lou Grant, Mary Grant's brother, was apparently on furlough from the 10th Alabama. He was paroled as a first lieutenant and adjutant of the 10th Alabama at Talladega, Alabama, on 23 May 1865. *CSR/Alabama,* 194:549; 10th Alabama Infantry Regiment, Confederate Regimental History Files.

98. Martha Bolling Jones Rivers was the wife of Dr. Richard Henderson Rivers and the mother of nine children. One writer noted that she became paralyzed in 1852 but does not indicate how it impacted her health. McDonald, *Beginnings . . . of the University of North Alabama,* 38, 40.

99. Apparently Mary Theresa Francis Turney, a wartime refugee in Jacksonville, had considered moving to Florida. Her eldest son, Colonel Peter Turney, was assigned to command a subdistrict of the Department of South Carolina, Georgia, and Florida on 18 August 1864 and later surrendered at Lake City, Florida, on 18 May 1865. *Eighth Census/Tennessee,* 6:78; *CSR/ Tennessee,* 111:1574.

100. The newlyweds, Gideon C. and Mary Turney Ellis, were now boarders with her first cousin Mary Eliza Woodward Forney, the wife of William H. Forney and the daughter of Edward Levy and Malinda Jane Francis Woodward. Francis-Martin Genealogy Collection; Crawford, *Forney Forever,* 2.

101. Apparently Miller Francis owned a small farm at Bitnose, a small community in Calhoun County, and his wife, Julia Abernathy Francis, decided not to leave Jacksonville. Francis-Martin Family Papers.

102. Tom Francis's service records provide no information about his 40-day furlough or why he was considered not fit for field duty. *CSR/General & Staff,* 98.

103. W. W. Griffith was married to Dr. James C. Francis's youngest sister, Elizabeth Francis. Francis-Martin Genealogy Collection.

104. Edward Levy Woodward was a successful Jacksonville businessman and partner in several businesses. He was listed in the 1860 census as a fifty-three-year-old merchant with real estate valued at $12,000 and a personal estate valued at $60,000. Francis-Martin Gene-

alogy Collection; *1860 Federal Census/Alabama,* 2:287; *Jacksonville Republican,* 1 November 1860, 26 January, 24 October 1861.

105. J. M. Carroll was operating a dry goods business "at the Drug Store on the east side of the Public Square" in January 1866. He was not listed in the 1860 census for Calhoun County, Alabama. *Jacksonville Republican,* 27 January 1866.

106. Sadie Francis was approximately eight months pregnant with her first child. Francis-Martin Genealogy Collection.

107. A reference to her brother William Dowse Whitehead, killed at the battle of Malvern Hill, Virginia, on 1 July 1862, and to her brother-in-law and Emma Francis's brother, John Clark Francis, who was mortally wounded at Rocky Face Ridge on 11 May 1864. Henderson, *Roster of the Confederate Soldiers of Georgia,* 1:394; *CSR/Alabama,* 333:401.

108. Union cavalry forces under the command of Brigadier General Hugh Judson Kilpatrick ransacked the Whitehead's Ivanhoe plantation on Sunday, 27 November 1864. Rowland Journals, 222–24; Martin, *Kill-Cavalry,* 198–200.

109. Miller and Jo Francis visited Sadie Francis's family in December 1864 at Ivanhoe, Burke County, Georgia, and they apparently visited Jim and Sadie Francis in Athens, Georgia, on 3 January 1865, after their return. Rowland Journal, 227, 236, 246.

110. Jo Francis remained on special detail assigned to the brigade surgeon, his brother Miller Francis. *CSR/Alabama,* 445:443; List of Detailed Men, 51st Alabama Cavalry, January 1865, Confederate Regimental History Files; *OR,* 44:406–12, 47, pt. 2:1071.

111. Elements of Wheeler's cavalry were routed in a skirmish on Tuesday, 7 February 1865, at Blackville, South Carolina, by Union forces that included a detachment of Kilpatrick's cavalry. *OR,* 47, pt. 2:351–52; Barrett, *Sherman's March Through the Carolinas,* 50; Martin, *Kill-Cavalry,* 212; Long, *The Civil War Day by Day,* 636.

112. On 11 February 1865, Kilpatrick's Union cavalry brigade was struck on both flanks by Wheeler's cavalry at Aiken, South Carolina. The fight ended with a hasty Union retreat. *OR,* 47, pt. 2:449–50, 1295; Barrett, *Sherman's March Through the Carolinas,* 56–57; Martin, *Kill-Cavalry,* 213–14.

113. Aiken, Aiken County, South Carolina, was seventeen miles from Augusta, Georgia, on the South Carolina Railroad. Sherman ordered Kilpatrick in February 1865 to destroy numerous mills near Aiken that produced equipment for the Confederate army. Black, *Railroads of the Confederacy,* 5, 272–73, 287; Alice Hamilton Cromie, *A Tour Guide to the Civil War* (2nd ed., New York: E. P. Dutton, 1975), 265.

114. On 2 October 1864, President Davis appointed Beauregard commander of the Military Division of the West, which extended from Georgia to the Mississippi River and later east to the Atlantic Ocean. By 10 February 1865, Beauregard was in Columbia, South Carolina, awaiting the arrival of elements of Hood's dispirited Army of Tennessee. Barrett, *Sherman's March Through the Carolinas,* 59–72; Long, *The Civil War Day by Day,* 636–37; Williams, *Beauregard,* 240–51.

115. Between 14 and 17 February 1865, elements of Wheeler's cavalry corps were engaged in several skirmishes in defense of Columbia. *OR,* 47, pt. 1:1115–33; Miller, *Wheeler's Favorites,* 28–29; Long, *The Civil War Day by Day,* 638–39.

116. Jo Francis was in Augusta on 2–12 February 1865 and visited Charles and Catharine Barnes Rowland, Sadie Francis's brother-in-law and sister, on 6 February 1865. Rowland Journals, 270.

117. On 3 February 1865, three Confederate commissioners, Alexander H. Stephens, John A. Campbell, and Robert M. T. Hunter, met with President Lincoln and William H. Seward, U.S. secretary of state, on the *River Queen* at Hampton Roads off Fort Monroe, Vir-

ginia, to discuss a peaceful end to the war. The Hampton Roads Conference ended with Lincoln demanding the Union be restored and slavery abolished. Stephens, *A Constitutional View of the War,* 2:598–619; Robert M. T. Hunter, "The Peace Commission of 1865," *Southern Historical Society Papers* 3 (April 1877):168–76; Paul J. Zingg, "John Archibald Campbell and the Hampton Roads Conference Quixotic Diplomacy, 1865," *Alabama Historical Quarterly* 36 (Spring 1974):21, 25–27, 29–32.

118. After the Hampton Roads Conference failed to bring about an armistice, Davis called on the Confederate Congress and the people to continue the war effort until independence was established. Stephens, *A Constitutional View of the War,* 2:622–24.

119. Contrary to Jo Francis's statement, Alexander H. Stephens did not journey to Georgia to rally the southern people. He thought further resistance was ill advised and returned to Georgia as a private citizen. Ibid., 626.

120. Jo Francis retreated with Hagan's cavalry brigade northward from Columbia to Chesterfield, South Carolina, near the North Carolina state line. *OR,* 47, pt. 1:857–92, 1115–33; Barrett, *Sherman's March Through the Carolinas,* 52–54, 58–60, 80–89, 96–97, 102, 106, 110; Glatthaar, *The March to the Sea and Beyond,* 142–46.

121. Wheeler's cavalry corps, like Sherman's Union army, foraged the countryside to sustain their troops. Barrett, *Sherman's March Through the Carolinas,* 58; Glatthaar, *The March to the Sea and Beyond,* 120.

122. The heavy January rains and the bitter cold of February 1865 made the retreat to Chesterfield, South Carolina, arduous and painful for the men in Wheeler's cavalry corps. *OR,* 47, pt. 1:857–92, 1115–33; Barrett, *Sherman's March Through the Carolinas,* 50–52, 54, 99–100.

123. Jesse Ingram enlisted as a private in Company D, 51st Alabama, at Oxford, Alabama, on 7 August 1862. His service records indicate that he was detailed as a blacksmith with Captain H. J. Coleman, assistant quartermaster. *CSR/Alabama,* 446:665, 447:1474, 445:257; Miller, *Wheeler's Favorites,* 167.

124. The continuous rainfall on 23–25 February 1865 intensified the bitter cold weather and discomfort felt by Union and Confederate soldiers. *OR,* 47, pt. 1:857–92, 1115–33; Barrett, *Sherman's March Through the Carolinas,* 52, 54, 99–100.

125. Elizabeth McKinne Francis was born in Athens, Georgia, on 23 February 1865. Francis-Martin Genealogy Collection; Rowland Journals, 281.

126. Carrie Woodward was the twenty-three-year-old daughter of Edward L. and Malinda Jane Francis Woodward. She was Susan Francis's first cousin, her teacher, and associate principal. *Jacksonville Republican,* 20 June 1861; *Eighth Census/Alabama,* 2:287.

127. Mary D. Caldwell was the principal of the Jacksonville Female Academy. *Jacksonville Republican,* 20 June 1861.

128. Benjamin Jefferson Hill (1825–80), a merchant and state senator from McMinnville, Tennessee, commanded a Confederate cavalry brigade in the closing months of the war in Mississippi and Alabama. *CSR/Tennessee,* 262:934; Ezra J. Warner, *Generals in Gray: Lives of the Confederate Generals,* 135–36.

129. John Yates was listed in the 1860 census as a thirty-nine-year-old farmer living in the Cove Creek community northwest of Jacksonville. *Eighth Census/Alabama,* 2:599.

130. Confederate Brigade History Files.

131. Pettus's Alabama brigade included the 20th Alabama, 23rd Alabama, 30th Alabama, 31st Alabama, and 46th Alabama. The 23rd, 31st, and 46th were consolidated on 9 April 1865 as the 23rd Alabama, and the 30th Alabama was consolidated with the 20th Alabama on 19 April 1865 under Colonel James M. Dedman as the 20th Alabama. DuBose, "The Thirti-

eth Alabama Regiment," 83; Kelly, "A History of the Thirtieth Alabama Volunteers," 167; J. D. Arnold to T. M. Owen, Jacksonville, Ala., 4 February 1911, 30th Alabama Infantry Regiment, Confederate Regimental History Files, ADAH.

132. Despite a general scattering of men following Johnston's surrender on 26 April 1865, a remnant of Pettus's brigade continued to Union Point, Georgia, where they broke into smaller groups and Pettus and his staff took their final leave. DuBose, "The Thirtieth Alabama Regiment," 83; J. D. Arnold to T. M. Owen, Jacksonville, Ala., 4 February 1911, 30th Alabama Infantry Regiment, Confederate Regimental History Files.

133. Pettus resumed his law practice in Selma and had a successful postwar political career. He was elected to the U.S. Senate in 1896 and served until his death on 27 July 1907. Current, *Encyclopedia of the Confederacy,* 3:1203; Owen, *History of Alabama,* 4:1351–52.

Epilogue

1. *Jacksonville Republican,* 20 January 1866.

2. *1866 Alabama State Census, Calhoun County,* Schedule number 3, p. 70.

3. *CSR/Alabama,* 158:789.

4. Ibid., 445:443.

5. *CSR/General & Staff,* 98.

6. Ibid.

7. Ibid., 52; *Jacksonville Republican,* 18 November 1865; *Ninth Census/Alabama,* 3:517; Francis-Martin Family Papers; Francis-Martin Genealogy Collection.

8. *1866 Alabama State Census, Calhoun County,* 3:75; Calhoun County Tax Assessment, 1866:7, 1867:38, 52, 55, 74, 1868:83, 86, 98; *Anniston Evening Star and Daily Hot Blast,* 14 August 1920; Francis-Martin Family Papers; Francis-Martin Genealogy Collection.

9. *1866 Alabama State Census, Calhoun County,* 3:75, *Ninth Census/Alabama,* 3:678; *Population Schedules of the Tenth Census of the U.S., 1880,* vol. 3, *Alabama,* 600; *Anniston Evening Star and Daily Hot Blast,* 29 March 1926; Francis-Martin Family Papers; Francis-Martin Genealogy Collection.

10. When J. L. Mattison reported the death of Jim Francis to the *Confederate Veteran* magazine in 1895, he also noted that "Joe H. Francis is now in business in New York City, where he has lived since 1869." "Death of Capt. James C. Francis" 45; Francis-Martin Family Papers.

11. "Death of Capt. James C. Francis"; Francis-Martin Family Papers; Francis-Martin Genealogy Collection.

12. *1866 Alabama State Census, Calhoun County,* 3:27; *Ninth Census/Alabama,* 3:517; Francis-Martin Family Papers; Francis-Martin Genealogy Collection.

13. Emma Francis's obituary notes that she was living with her sister Mrs. Susan Francis Martin at the "Martin residence on North Main street" in Jacksonville and that she became ill while visiting her bother Hop Francis at Ohatchie. *Tenth Census/Alabama,* 3:510; *Anniston Star and Daily Hot Blast,* 21 February 1895, 9 January 1918; Francis-Martin Family Papers.

14. Susan Francis Martin died following a short illness at her home in Jacksonville on Monday, 6 November 1939, and was buried in the Jacksonville Cemetery near the other members of Dr. James C. Francis's family. *Anniston Evening Star,* 6 November 1939; Francis-Martin Family Papers; Francis-Martin Genealogy Collection.

Bibliography

Manuscript Sources

Confederate Regimental History Files, Alabama Department of Archives and History, Montgomery.

Adams, R. H. Account of Wheeler's Raids. 51st Ala. Cavalry Files.

———. "Diary No. 2—R. H. Adams, Co. H, 51st Cav."

Arnold, James D. Account of James D. Arnold, Pvt. Co. B. 30th Ala. Inf. Regt.

Brewer, George E. "The Thirtieth Alabama Regiment."

Confederate Alabama Militia by Companies & Counties (1860–1865).

DuBose, John Witherspoon. "The Thirtieth Alabama Regiment."

Finch, J. H. "Last Words of Lieut. J. H. Finch." Co. B, 30th Ala. Inf. Regt.

Francis, Miller W. "Report of Sick and Wounded" [July 1861–March 1862]. 6th Ala. Inf. Regt.

Howell, William P. "History of the 25th Alabama Infantry Regiment."

Kelly, Samuel Camp. Letters of Samuel Camp Kelly. 30th Ala. Inf. Regt.

Muster Rolls of the Calhoun Guards, September 13, 1860, February 23, 1861.

Muster Roll of Company B, 30th Ala. Volunteers Regiment (P. A.). March 29, 1862.

Muster Roll of Company G, 10th Alabama Infantry Regiment, C.S.A.

Whatley, George C. Whatley Letters. 10th Ala. Inf. Regt.

Calhoun County Courthouse, Anniston, Alabama.

Marriage Records, 1850–1865.

Tax Assessment, 1866, 1867, 1868.

Francis-Martin Family Papers. Alabama Department of Archives and History, Montgomery.

Francis-Martin Genealogy Collection. Clara Jackson Martin, Birmingham, Alabama.

National Archives. National Archives and Records Service, Washington, D.C.

Compiled Service Records of Confederate General and Staff Officers, and Non-Regimental Enlisted Men.

Compiled Service Records of Confederate Soldiers Who Served in Organizations from the State of Alabama.

Compiled Service Records of Confederate Soldiers Who Served in Organizations from the State of Tennessee.

Unfiled Papers and Slips Belonging in Confederate Compiled Service Records.

Rowland, Catherine B. (Whitehead). Journals of Catherine Barnes Whitehead Rowland. Vol. 1, October 29, 1863–March 17, 1865. Typescript. Francis-Martin Genealogy Collection.

U.S. Bureau of the Census

Population Schedule of the Eighth Census of the U.S. 1860.

Population Schedule of the Ninth Census of the U.S. 1870.

Population Schedule of the Seventh Census of the U.S. 1850.

Population Schedules of the Tenth Census of the U.S. 1880.

Printed Primary Sources

Alison, Joseph Dill. "War Diary of Dr. Joseph Dill Alison." *Alabama Historical Quarterly* 9 (Fall 1947):385–98.

Atlas to Accompany the Official Records of the Union and Confederate Armies. Washington, D.C.: Government Printing Office, 1891–95.

Brown, John C. "Lookout Mountain: Report of Brigadier-General J. C. Brown, Headquarters Brown's Brigade, November 30, 1863." *Southern Historical Society Papers* 12 (April 1884):182–83.

Coles, Robert T. *From Huntsville to Appomattox: R. T. Coles's History of the 4th Regiment, Alabama Volunteer Infantry, C.S.A., Army of Northern Virginia.* Edited by Jeffrey D. Stocker. Knoxville: University of Tennessee Press, 1996.

McClelen, Bailey George. *I Saw the Elephant: The Civil War Experiences of Bailey George McClelen, Company D, 10th Alabama Infantry Regiment.* Edited by Norman E. Rourke. Shippensburg, Pa.: Bard Street Press, 1995.

Mattison, J. L. "Death of Capt. James C. Francis." *Confederate Veteran* 3 (February 1895):45.

Moore, Glover. *A Calhoun County, Alabama, Boy in the 1860's.* Edited by Glover Moore, Jr. Jackson: University Press of Mississippi, 1978.

Northrup, Lucius Bellinger. "Resources of the Confederacy in February, 1865: Report of Commissary General Northrup." *Southern Historical Society Papers* 2 (August 1876): 85–105.

Stevenson, Carter L. "Report of Major-General C. L. Stevenson from the Beginning of the Dalton-Atlanta Campaign to May 30, 1864." *Southern Historical Society Papers* 3 (May–June 1877):225–29.

War of the Rebellion: A Compilation of the Official Records of the Union and Confederate Armies. 128 vols. in 70. Washington, D.C.: Government Printing Office, 1880–1901.

War of the Rebellion: Official Records of the Union and Confederate States Navies. 30 vols. Washington, D.C.: Government Printing Office, 1898.

Watkins, Sam. *"Company Aytch" or A Side Show of the Big Show and Other Sketches.* Edited by M. Thomas Inge. 1882; reprint, New York: New American Library, 1999.

Secondary Sources

Barrett, John G. *Sherman's March Through the Carolinas.* Chapel Hill: University of North Carolina Press, 1956.

Bearss, Edwin Cole. *The Campaign for Vicksburg.* 3 vols. Dayton, Ohio: Morningside House, Inc., 1985–86.

Bergeron, Arthur W. *Confederate Mobile.* Jackson: University Press of Mississippi, 1991.

Beringer, Richard E., et al. *Why the South Lost the Civil War.* Athens: University of Georgia Press, 1986.

Black, Robert C., III. *The Railroads of the Confederacy.* Chapel Hill: University of North Carolina Press, 1952.

Boatner, Mark Mayo, III. *The Civil War Dictionary.* New York: D. McKay, 1959.

Brewer, Willis. *Alabama: Her History, Resources, War Record, and Public Men from 1540 to 1872.* Montgomery, Ala.: Barrett & Brown, 1872.

Brooks, Stewart M. *Civil War Medicine.* Springfield, Ill.: C. C. Thomas, 1966.

Carter, Samuel, III. *The Final Fortress: The Campaign for Vicksburg, 1862–1863.* New York: St. Martin's Press, 1980.

Castel, Albert. *Decision in the West: The Atlanta Campaign of 1864.* Lawrence: University Press of Kansas, 1992.

Connelly, Thomas Lawrence. *Army of the Heartland: The Army of Tennessee, 1861–1862.* Baton Rouge: Louisiana State University Press, 1967.

———. *Autumn of Glory: The Army of Tennessee, 1862–1865.* Baton Rouge: Louisiana State University Press, 1971.

———. *Discovering the Appalachians.* Harrisburg, Pa.: Stackpole Books, 1968.

Cozzens, Peter. *No Better Place to Die: The Battle of Stones River.* Urbana: University of Illinois Press, 1990.

Crawford, Lee Forney. *Forney Forever.* Birmingham, Ala.: Commercial Printing Company, 1967.

Cromie, Alice Hamilton. *A Tour Guide to the Civil War.* 2nd ed. New York: E. P. Dutton, 1975.

Cunningham, Horace H. *Doctors in Gray: The Confederate Medical Service.* Baton Rouge: Louisiana State University Press, 1958.

Current, Richard N., ed. *Encyclopedia of the Confederacy.* 4 vols. New York: Simon & Schuster, 1993.

Daugette, Annie Forney. "The Life of Major General John H. Forney." *Alabama Historical Quarterly* 9 (Fall 1947):361–83.

Davis, William C. *Rebels & Yankees: The Fighting Men of the Civil War.* New York: Gallery Books, 1989.

———, ed. *The Confederate General.* 6 vols. Harrisburg, Pa.: National Historical Society, 1991.

Esposito, Vincent J., ed. *The West Point Atlas of American Wars.* 2 vols. 1959; rev., New York: Henry Holt and Co., 1995.

Evans, Clement A., ed. *Confederate Military History: A Library of Confederate States History.* 19 vols. Extended ed. 1899; reprint, Wilmington, N.C.: Broadfoot Publishing Co., 1987–89.

Fitts, Alston, III. *Selma: Queen City of the Black Belt.* Selma, Ala.: Clairmont Press, 1989.

Gates, Paul W. *Agriculture and the Civil War.* New York: Alfred A. Knopf, 1965.

Glatthaar, Joseph T. *The March to the Sea and Beyond: Sherman's Troops in the Savannah and Carolinas Campaigns.* New York: New York University Press, 1985.

Goff, Richard D. *Confederate Supply.* Durham, N.C.: Duke University Press, 1969.

Griffith, Lucille. "Mrs. Juliet Opie Hopkins and Alabama Military Hospitals." *Alabama Review* 6 (April 1953):99–120.

Groce, W. Todd. *Mountain Rebels: East Tennessee Confederates and the Civil War, 1860–1870.* Knoxville, University of Tennessee Press, 1999.

Gunn, Ralph White. *24th Virginia Infantry.* Lynchburg, Va.: H. E. Howard, 1987.

Hassler, William Woods. *Colonel John Pelham: Lee's Boy Artillerist.* Chapel Hill: University of North Carolina Press, 1960.

Henderson, Lillian. *Roster of the Confederate Soldiers of Georgia, 1861–1865.* 6 vols. Hapeville, Ga.: Longino & Porter, Inc., 1960.

Hudson, James G. "A Story of Company D, 4th Alabama Infantry Regiment, C.S.A." Edited by Alma H. Pate. *Alabama Historical Quarterly* 23 (Spring 1961):139–79.

Jones, Charles T. "Five Confederates; The Sons of Bolling Hall in the Civil War." *Alabama Historical Quarterly* 25 (Summer, Fall, Winter 1963):133–221.

Jones, Kenneth W. "The Fourth Alabama Infantry: First Blood." *Alabama Historical Quarterly* 36 (Spring 1974):35–53.

Kelly, William Milner. "A History of the Thirtieth Alabama Volunteers (Infantry) Confederate States Army." *Alabama Historical Quarterly* 9 (Spring 1947):115–89.

Krick, Robert K. *Lee's Colonels: A Biographical Register of the Field Officers of the Army of Northern Virginia.* Dayton, Ohio: Morningside House Inc., 1979.

Long, E. B. *The Civil War Day by Day: An Almanac 1861–1865.* Garden City, N.Y.: Doubleday, 1971.

Martin, Samuel J. *Kill-Cavalry: The Life of Union General Hugh Judson Kilpatrick.* Mechanicsburg, Pa.: Stackpole Books, 2000.

Massey, Mary Elizabeth. *Ersatz in the Confederacy: Shortages and Substitutions on the Southern Homefront.* Columbia: University of South Carolina Press, 1952.

McDonald, William Lindsey. *Beginnings . . . of the University of North Alabama: The Story of Florence Wesleyan University.* Birmingham: Birmingham Printing & Publishing Co., 1991.

McDonough, James Lee. *Chattanooga: A Death Grip on the Confederacy.* Knoxville: University of Tennessee Press, 1984.

———. *Stones River: Bloody Winter in Tennessee.* Knoxville: University of Tennessee Press, 1980.

McMillan, Malcolm C. *The Disintegration of a Confederate State: Three Governors and Alabama's Home Front, 1861–1865.* Macon, Ga.: Mercer University Press, 1986.

———, ed. *The Alabama Confederate Reader.* Tuscaloosa: University of Alabama Press, 1963.

Miller, Rex. *Wheeler's Favorites: A Regimental History of the 51st Alabama Cavalry Regiment.* Depew, N.Y.: Patrex Press, 1991.

Owen, Thomas McAdory. *History of Alabama and Dictionary of Alabama Biography.* 4 vols. Chicago: S. J. Clarke Publishing Company, 1921.

Parks, Joseph H. *General Edmund Kirby Smith, C.S.A.* Baton Rouge: Louisiana State University Press, 1954.

Remington, W. Craig, and Thomas J. Kallsen, eds. *Historical Atlas of Alabama: Historical Locations.* 2 vols. Tuscaloosa: University of Alabama, Department of Geography, 1997.

Rogers, William Warren, et al. *Alabama: The History of a Deep South State.* Tuscaloosa: University of Alabama Press, 1994.

Rollins, Richard, ed. *Black Southerners in Gray: Essays on Afro-Americans in Confederate Armies.* Redondo Beach, Calif.: Rank and File Publications, 1994.

Schroeder-Lein, Glenna R. *Confederate Hospitals on the Move: Samuel H. Stout and the Army of Tennessee.* Columbia: University of South Carolina Press, 1994.

Schwab, John Christopher. *The Confederate States of America, 1861–1865: A Financial and*

Industrial History of the South During the Civil War. 1901; reprint, New York: Burt Franklin, 1968.

Steiner, Paul E. *Disease in the Civil War: Natural Biological Warfare in 1861–1865.* Springfield. Ill.: C. C. Thomas, 1968.

Stephens, Alexander H. *A Constitutional View of the War.* 2 vols. Philadelphia: S. A. George, 1868, 1870.

Stern, Philip Van Doren, ed. *Soldier Life in the Union and Confederate Armies.* Bloomington: Indiana University Press, 1961.

Sutherland, Daniel E. *The Expansion of Everyday Life, 1860–1876.* New York: Harper & Row, Publishers, 1989.

Symonds, Craig L. *Joseph E. Johnston: A Civil War Biography.* New York: Norton, 1992.

Tennesseans in the Civil War: A Military History of Confederate and Union Units with Available Rosters of Personnel. 2 vols. Nashville: Civil War Centennial Commission, 1964.

Tennessee: A Guide to the State. New York: Hastings House, 1949.

Thomas, Emory M. *The Confederate Nation, 1861–1865.* New York: Harper & Row Publishers, 1979.

Wakelyn, Jon L. *Biographical Dictionary of the Confederacy.* Westport, Conn.: Greenwood Press, 1976.

Warner, Ezra J. *Generals in Gray: Lives of the Confederate Generals.* Baton Rouge: Louisiana State University Press, 1959.

Wiley, Bell I. *The Life of Johnny Reb: The Common Soldier of the Confederacy.* Indianapolis: Bobbs-Merrill, 1943.

Williams, T. Harry. *P.G.T. Beauregard, Napoleon in Gray.* Baton Rouge: Louisiana State University Press, 1954.

Woodhead, Henry, ed. *Echoes of Glory: Illustrated Atlas of the Civil War.* Alexandria, Va.: Time-Life Books, 1991.

Wyeth, John A. *That Devil Forrest: Life of General Nathan Bedford Forrest.* 1899; reprint, New York: Harper & Brothers Publishers, 1959.

Index